10.22.86

# Christian Apologetics

## NORMAN GEISLER

BAKER BOOK HOUSE
Grand Rapids, Michigan

To my beloved mentor
who both taught
and inspired me
in the apologetic task,
**DR. EVAN WELSH**

# *Preface*

This work on Christian apologetics is in three parts. Part One surveys various tests for truth in order to lay the groundwork for testing the truth of various world views. Part Two applies the test for truth to the various world views and concludes that theism is the only adequate world view. Part Three works within the context of a theistic world view to verify the unique claims of historical Christianity as to the deity of Christ and the authority of the Bible.

The basic movement in this historic apologetic takes its roots from the apostles in the New Testament, was developed by Augustine, and comes to fruition in later Christians like Aquinas. It is in essence the approach used by the old Princetonian theologians like Warfield and Hodge in the tradition of Calvin and it has been more popularly represented in recent times in the writings of C. S. Lewis.

The heart of this apologetic approach is that the Christian is interested in defending the truths that Christ is the Son of God and the Bible is the Word of God. However, prior to establishing these two pillars on which the uniqueness of Christianity is built, one must establish the existence of God. For it makes no sense to speak about an *act* of God (i.e., a miracle) confirming that Christ is the *Son* of God and that the Bible is the *Word* of God unless of course there is a *God* who can have a Son and who can speak a Word. Theism, then, is a logical prerequisite to Christianity. What is more, an adequate test for truth is a methodological prerequisite to establishing theism. For unless the Christian apologist has a test by which he can show other systems to be false and theism to be true, then there is no way to adjudicate the conflicting claims of various religions and world views. In view of this important problem we unapologetically commit Part One to the prior question of truth tests before an attempt is made to defend theism (Part Two) and the uniqueness of Christianity (Part Three).

# Contents

## PART ONE
### Methodology

1 Agnosticism ........................................... 13
2 Rationalism ........................................... 29
3 Fideism .............................................. 47
4 Experientialism ....................................... 65
5 Evidentialism ......................................... 83
6 Pragmatism ........................................... 101
7 Combinationalism ...................................... 117
8 Formulating Adequate Tests for Truth ................. 133

## PART TWO
### Theistic Apologetics

9 Deism ................................................ 151
10 Pantheism ............................................ 173
11 Panentheism .......................................... 193
12 Atheism .............................................. 215
13 Theism ............................................... 237

## PART THREE
### Christian Apologetics

14 Naturalism and the Supernatural ...................... 263
15 Objectivism and History ............................. 285
16 The Historical Reliability of the New Testament ...... 305
17 The Deity and Authority of Jesus Christ .............. 329
18 The Inspiration and Authority of the Bible ........... 353

Bibliography ............................................. 379
Index .................................................... 391

# Part
# ONE

## *Methodology*

Agnosticism
Rationalism
Fideism
Experientialism
Evidentialism
Pragmatism
Combinationalism
Formulating Adequate Tests
  for Truth

# Chapter

# 1 | *Agnosticism*

There are various approaches or methods to the question of God, some positive and some negative. Perhaps the most widely held in the latter category is agnosticism. There are two basic kinds of agnostics: those who claim that the existence and nature of God are not known, and those who hold God to be unknowable. Since the first type does not eliminate all religious knowledge, attention here will center on the last one.

The term *agnosticism* was coined by T. H. Huxley. It means literally no-knowledge, the opposite of a gnostic.[1] However, over a hundred years before Huxley the writings of David Hume and Immanuel Kant laid down the philosophical basis of agnosticism. Much of modern philosophy takes for granted the general validity of the types of arguments they set forth.

## The Basic Arguments of Agnosticism

Even Immanuel Kant was a rationalist until he was "awakened from his dogmatic slumbers" by reading David Hume.

### The Skepticism of David Hume

Technically Hume's views are skeptical but they serve well the agnostic aim. Hume set forth the basis of his position in the concluding lines of his famous *Enquiry Concerning Human Understanding*.

If we take in our hands any volume; of divinity or school metaphysics,

---

1. See T. H. Huxley, "Agnosticism and Christianity" (1889), in his *Collected Essays* (London: 1894), vol. V.

for instance; let us ask, *Does it contain any abstract reasoning concerning quantity or number?* No. *Does it contain any experimental reasoning concerning matter of fact and existence?* No. Commit it then to the flames: for it can contain nothing but sophistry and illusion.[2]

That is, any statement that is neither purely a relation of ideas (definitional or mathematical) on the one hand or a matter of fact (empirical or factual) on the other hand is meaningless. Of course all statements about God fall outside these categories, and hence knowledge of God becomes impossible.

*Only Two Kinds of Propositions.* At the basis of Hume's conclusion that all meaningful propositions are reducible to two is a radical empiricism that may be summarized as follows. All of our knowledge or ideas is derived either through sensation or by the reflection on ideas (derived from sensation) in the mind. There is nothing in the mind that was not first in the senses. Furthermore, all sensations are experienced as "entirely loose and separate." Causal connections are made by the mind only after one has observed a constant conjunction of things in experience. All one really experiences is a series of unconnected and separate sensations. Indeed, there is no direct knowledge even of one's "self," for all we know of ourselves is a disconnected bundle of sense impressions. It does make sense of course to speak of connections among ideas, even necessary connections. But these are connections made only in the mind a priori or independent of experience. A posteriori (i.e., from experience) there are no known and certainly no necessary connections. In fact, all matters of experience imply a possible contrary state of affairs. For anything we experience in one way could be otherwise.

*Causality Is Based on Custom.* Many who believe in God are willing to admit that they have no direct knowledge of God but claim nonetheless to have access to the existence and nature of God via his effects or the things he has made or said. Hume's epistemology (theory of knowledge), if true, would seem to eliminate this possibility as well. For, according to Hume "all reasoning concerning matters of fact seems to be founded on the relation of *cause and effect.* By means of that relation alone can we go beyond the evidence of our memory and senses."[3] And knowledge of the relation of cause and effect is not a priori but arises entirely from experience. And the idea of a causal relation appears in the mind only after there has been an observation of constant conjunction in experience. That is, only when we observe death to occur *after* holding another's head under the water for five

---

2. London, 1748; modern edition by C. W. Hendel (New York: 1955).
3. *Enquiry,* sec. IV, pt. 2.

minutes do we assume a causal connection. Once one event is observed
to happen *after* another repeatedly, we begin to form the idea that one
event happens *because* of the other. In brief, the idea of causality is
based on custom.

Customary conjunction of events leads one to believe in or posit
a connection between them. Of course this connection cannot be *known*
but is simply *believed* because of the repetition of the conjunctions.
There is always the possibility of the post hoc fallacy—namely, that
things happen after other events (even regularly) but are not really
caused by them. For example, the sun rises regularly *after* the rooster
crows but certainly not *because* the rooster crows. One can never
know causal connections. And without a knowledge of the Cause of
this world, for example, one is left in agnosticism about such a supposed
God.

*Knowledge of God by Analogy Is Highly Problematic.* Even if one
were to grant that every event has a cause, nevertheless he cannot build
any knowledge of God upon this fact because the analogy is weak at
best. In his famous *Dialogues Concerning Natural Religion*[4] Hume contends that the cause of the universe may be (1) *different* from human
intelligence since human inventions differ from those of nature; (2) *finite,*
since the effect is finite and one only need infer a cause adequate for
the effect; (3) *imperfect,* since there are imperfections in nature;
(4) *multiple,* for the creation of the world looks more like a long-
range trial and error product of many cooperating deities; (5) *male and
female,* since this is how humans generate; and (6) *anthropomorphic,*
with hands, nose, eyes, and so forth, such as his creatures have. Since
no theist will admit that analogy leads to these anthropomorphic deities,
it leaves us in skepticism about the nature of any supposed Cause of
the world.

## The Agnosticism of Immanuel Kant

The writings of Hume had a profound influence on the thinking of
Kant. Before reading them Kant held a form of rationalism in the
tradition of Leibniz. Leibniz and Wolfe following him believed reality
was rationally knowable and that theism was demonstrable. They followed a long line of Western thinkers from Plato through Augustine,
Anselm, and Aquinas who held that there were proofs for the existence
of God. It was the pen of Kant that put an abrupt end to most of this
thinking in the philosophical world.

*The Impossibility of Knowing Reality.* Kant granted to the rational
tradition of Leibniz that there was a rational, a priori dimension to
knowledge, namely, the *form* of all knowledge is independent of ex-

4. London, 1779; recent edition by Norman Kemp Smith (New York: 1972).

perience. On the other hand, Kant granted Hume and the empiricists their basic contention that the *content* of all knowledge came via the senses. The *"stuff"* of knowledge is provided by the senses but the *structure* of knowledge is attained eventually in the mind. This creative synthesis solved the problem of rationalism and empiricism. However, the unhappy result of this synthesis is agnosticism, for if one cannot know anything until *after* it is structured by the a priori forms of sensation (time and space) and the categories of understanding (such as unity and causality), then there is no way to get outside one's own being and know what it really was *before* he so formed it. That is, one can know what something is *to-him* but never what it is *in-itself.* Only appearance can be known, but not reality. In Kant's words, we know the *phenomena* but not the *noumena.* There is a great impassable gulf between the real world and our knowledge of it; we must remain agnostic about reality. We know only *that* it is there but can never know *what* it is.[5]

*The Antinomies of Human Reason.* There is another argument for Kant's agnostic conclusion. Not only is there an unbridgeable gulf between knowing and being, between the categories of our understanding and the nature of reality, but there are also the inevitable contradictions that result once we begin to trespass the boundary line. In other words, when we take the necessary forms of sensation or categories of understanding, such as the principle of causality, and apply them to reality we run headlong into unavoidable contradictions.[6]

There is, for instance, the antinomy of *time.* If we assume that the form of sensation known as time (the "whenness" with which we time bound creatures sense things) applies to reality, we must conclude the following contradictions. On the one hand, if the world had a beginning in time, then an infinity of moments must have elapsed before the world began. But this is impossible because an infinity of moments can never be completed. On the other hand, if the world did have a beginning in time, then there must have been a time before time began—which is impossible. But either the world began in time or it did not, and both positions are impossible. Hence, by applying time to reality one eventuates necessarily in contradictions. And since contradictions do not yield knowledge, reality is unknowable.

Another antinomy concerns the category of *causality.* First, not every cause can have a cause or else a series of causes would never begin to cause—which they in fact do. On the other hand, if every-

---

5. See *The Critique of Pure Reason,* trans. Norman Kemp Smith (New York: St. Martin's Press, 1965), especially p. 173 f.
6. Kant, *Pure Reason,* p. 393 f.

thing has a cause, then there cannot be a beginning cause and the causal series must stretch back infinitely. But it is impossible that the series be both infinite and also have a beginning. Such is the impossible paradox resulting from the application of the category of causality to reality.

There is also the antinomy of *contingency*. We must posit that not everything is contingent; otherwise there would be no basis or condition for contingency. On the contrary, everything must be contingent for necessity applies only to thought and not to things, since any state of affairs could be otherwise. But again reality cannot be both contingent and necessary. The way to avoid such contradiction is to acknowledge that reason cannot know reality, viz., by agnosticism.

These arguments do not exhaust the agnostic's arsenal, but they do lie at the heart of the contention that God cannot be known. However, even some who are unwilling to admit to the validity of these arguments opt for a more subtle form of agnosticism. Such is the case with the school of thought to which we turn our attention next, logical positivism.

## The "Acognosticism" of A. J. Ayer

Following up on Hume's distinction between definitional and empirical statements, Ayer offered the principle of empirical verifiability. This affirmed that in order for statements to be meaningful they must be either analytic (Hume's "relation of ideas") or synthetic (Hume's "matter of fact")—that is, definitional or empirical.[7] The former are devoid of content and say nothing about the world; the latter have content but tell us nothing about any alleged reality beyond the empirical world. Furthermore, the latter are only probable in nature and are never philosophically certain. They are useful in empirical and practical matters but not at all informative about reality in any metaphysical sense.

*All God-Talk Is Nonsense or Empty.* The result of Ayer's logical positivism is as devastating to theism as is traditional agnosticism. God is unknowable and inexpressible. In fact, it is even meaningless to use the term *God.* Hence, even traditional agnosticism is untenable, since the agnostic assumes that it is meaningful to ask the question whether God exists. For Ayer, however, the word *God* or any transcendent equivalent, has no meaning. Hence, it is impossible to be an agnostic. For the term *God* is neither analytic nor synthetic; that is, it is neither offered by theists as an empty, contentless definition corresponding to nothing in reality nor is it a term filled with empirical content, since "God" is

---

7. A. J. Ayer, *Language, Truth and Logic* (New York: Dover Publications, Inc., 1946; first published 1936).

allegedly a supraempirical being. Hence, it is literally nonsense to talk about God.

It is true that Ayer later revised his principle of verifiability.[8] But even in this form (that admitted the possibility that some empirical experiences are certain, such as those of a single sensory experience, and that there is a third kind of statement, viz., some analytic or definitional statements that are not purely arbitrary such as his own principle of verifiability) he did not thereby allow for the meaningfulness of God-talk. This third class would be neither true nor false nor factual but meaningfully definitional. However Ayer believed that "it is unlikely that any metaphysician would yield to a claim of this kind," even though he acknowledged that for "an effective elimination of metaphysics it needs to be supported by detailed analyses of particular metaphysical arguments."[9] In short, even a revised principle of empirical verifiability would make it impossible to utter meaningfully true statements about a transempirical reality such as God. There is no cognitive knowledge of God; we must remain "a-cog-nostic."

*"God" Is Inexpressible or Mystical.* Following a tip from Wittgenstein's *Tractatus,* Ayer held that while God might be *experienced,* such an experience could never be meaningfully *expressed.* Wittgenstein believed that *"how* things are in the world is a matter of complete indifference for what is higher. God does not reveal himself *in* the world." For "there are indeed, things that cannot be put in words. . . . They are what is mystical," and "what we cannot speak about we must consign to silence."[10] If God could express himself in our words it would indeed be "a book to explode all books," but such is impossible. Hence, there not only is no propositional revelation, but there are no cognitively meaningful statements that can be made about any alleged or real transcendent being. Hence, whether one takes the more strict logical positivist's principle of verifiability or even the broader Wittgensteinian linguistic limitations, God-talk is metaphysically meaningless.

To be sure, as Wittgenstein taught, language games are possible, even religious language games. God-talk can and does occur, but it is not metaphysical; it tells us nothing about the existence and nature of a being beyond this world. About this we must, because of the very necessary limitations of language, remain silent. In summary, for religious noncognitivists Ayer and Wittgenstein, metaphysical acognosticism is the net result of language analysis.

It makes little difference to the Christian or theist whether he can-

8. See "Introduction" to rev. ed., p. 10 f.
9. Ayer, p. 16.
10. *Tractatus Logico-Philosophicus,* 6:44, 6432, 6522 (London: 1922; trans. D. F. Pears and B. F. McGuinness [London: 1961]).

not *know* God (as in Kant) or whether he cannot *speak* of God (as in Ayer). Both traditional agnosticism and contemporary acognosticism leave us in the same dilemma philosophically: there are no bases for making true statements about God.

*The Unfalsifiability of Religious Beliefs.* The other side of the principle of verifiability is that of falsifiability. Taking his cue from John Wisdom's parable of the invisible gardener, Antony Flew posed a challenge to believers as follows: "What would have to have occurred to constitute for you a disproof of the love of, or of the existence of, God?"[11] For one cannot allow anything to count for his belief in God unless he is willing to allow something to count against it. Whatever is meaningful is also fasifiable. There is no difference between an invisible, undetectable gardener and no gardener at all. Likewise, a God who does not make a verifiable or falsifiable difference is no God at all. Unless the believer can indicate how the world would be different if there were no God at all, he cannot use conditions in the world as evidence that there is a God. In short, unless the theist can answer the challenge head-on, then it would appear that he must have what R. M. Hare called a "blik."[12] That is to say, he has an unfalsifiable belief in God despite all facts or states of affairs. It matters little whether the believer calls his "blik" a parable, a myth, or whatever; the fact remains that he is an acognostic believer with no meaningful or verifiable knowledge of God, and this is little or no improvement on Kant's traditional agnosticism.

## An Evaluation of Agnostic Arguments

As was indicated earlier, there are two forms of agnosticism: the weak form simply holds that God is unknown, that is, that we *do not* know God. This of course leaves the door open that one may know God and indeed that some do know God. As such this kind of agnosticism forms no threat to Christian theism. The second or strong form of agnosticism is mutually exclusive with Christianity. It claims that God is unknowable, that is, that God *cannot* be known. Even here one must make an important distinction before embarking on a critique. There is unlimited and limited agnosticism about God. The former claims that God and all reality is completely unknowable. The latter claims only that God is partially unknowable because of the limitations of man's finitude and sinfulness. We will take it that the latter form of agnosticism is both possible and desirable. Paul wrote, "For now we see in a mirror dimly. . . . Now I know in part" (I Cor. 13:12).

---

11. "Theology and Falsification," in *New Essays in Philosophical Theology*, ed. Antony Flew and Alasdair MacIntyre (London: SCM Press, Ltd.: 1955), p. 99.
12. Flew and MacIntyre, p. 100.

This leaves us with three basic alternatives with respect to knowledge about God. First, we can know nothing about God; he is unknowable. Second, we can know everything about God; he is completely and exhaustively knowable. Third, we can know something about God but not everything; he is partially knowable. The first position we will call agnosticism; the second, dogmatism; and the last, realism. Now it is evident that the dogmatic position is untenable. One would have to be God in order to know God exhaustively. Finite man can have only a finite knowledge of the infinite, not an infinite knowledge. Few if any informed believers have seriously held this kind of dogmatism. However, theists sometimes argue against agnosticism as though *partial* agnosticism is wrong too. They argue that agnosticism is wrong simply because one cannot *know* something is unknowable about reality without thereby implying a knowledge about that something. But this is faulty reasoning. There is no contradiction in saying, "I know enough about reality to affirm that there are some things about reality that I cannot know." For example, we can know enough about observation and reporting techniques to say that it is impossible for us to know the exact population of the world at a given instant (unknowability in *practice*). Likewise, one may know enough about the nature of finitude to say that it is impossible for men to know exhaustively an infinite being (who could not be exhaustibly knowable in *principle* for finite man as we know man). In the following critique we will be concerned only with the *complete* agnostic who rules out in theory and practice all knowledge of God. This kind of complete agnosticism is self-defeating.

## Agnosticism Is Self-Defeating

Complete agnosticism is self-defeating; it reduces to the self-destructing assertion that "one knows enough about reality in order to affirm that nothing can be known about reality." This statement provides within itself all that is necessary to falsify itself. For if one knows *something* about reality, then he surely cannot affirm in the same breath that *all* of reality is unknowable. And of course if one knows nothing whatsoever about reality, then he has no basis whatsoever for making a statement about reality. It will not suffice to say that his knowledge about reality is purely and completely negative, that is, a knowledge of what reality is not. For every negative presupposes a positive; one cannot meaningfully affirm that something is *not*-that if he is totally devoid of a knowledge of the "that." It follows that total agnosticism is self-defeating because it assumes some knowledge about reality in order to deny any knowledge of reality.

Some have attempted to avoid the logic of the above critique by putting their skepticism in the form of a question: "What do I know about reality?" However, this does not avoid the dilemma but merely delays it. This question can and ought to be asked by both agnostic and Christian. But it is the *answer* that separates the agnostic from the realist. "I can know something about God" differs significantly from "I can know nothing about God." Once the answer is given in the latter form a self-defeating assertion is made.

Neither will it help to take the mutist alternative of saying nothing. For thoughts can be as self-stultifying as assertions. The mutist cannot even think he knows absolutely nothing about reality unless in that very thought he implies that he does know something about reality.

Of course someone may be willing to grant that knowledge about finite reality may be possible but not willing to allow any knowledge about an alleged infinite reality, such as the God of Christian theism. If so, two things should be noted. First, the position is no longer complete agnosticism, for it holds that something can be known about reality. This leaves the door open to discuss whether or not this reality is finite or infinite, personal or impersonal. Second, the latter discussion takes us beyond the question of agnosticism to the debate between finite godism and theism (which will be discussed later). Before we take up some of the specific arguments of agnostics it will be helpful to further illustrate how agnosticism involves a self-defeating assertion.

*Reply to Kant's Agnosticism.* Kant's argument that the categories of thought (such as unity and causality) do not apply to reality is unsuccessful, for unless the categories of reality corresponded to those of the mind no statements could be made about reality, including that very statement Kant made. That is to say, unless the real world were intelligible no statement about it would apply. A preformation of the mind to reality is necessary whether one is going to say something positive about it or something negative. We cannot even *think* of reality that it is unthinkable. Now if someone should press the argument that the agnostic need not be making any statement at all about reality but simply defining the necessary limits of what we can know, it can be shown that even this is a self-defeating attempt; for to say that one cannot know any more than the limits of the phenomena or appearance is to draw an unsurpassable line for those limits. But one cannot draw such firm limits without surpassing them. It is not possible to contend that appearance ends here and reality begins there unless one can see at least some distance on the other side. In other words, how can one know the difference between appearance and reality unless he already knows both so as to make the comparison?

Another self-defeating dimension is implied within Kant's admission that he knows *that* the noumena is there but not *what* it is. Is it possible to know that something is without knowing something about what it is? Can pure that-ness be known? Does not all knowledge imply some knowledge of characteristics? Even a strange creature one had never seen before could not be observed to exist unless it had some recognizable characteristics as size, color, or movement. Even something invisible must leave some effect or trace in order to be observed. One need not know the origin or function of a brand-new he-knows-not-what. However, he must observe something of what it is or he could not know that it is. It is not possible to affirm *that* something is without simultaneously declaring something about *what* it is. Even to describe it as the "in-itself" or the "real" is to say something. Furthermore, Kant acknowledged it to be the unknowable "source" of the appearance we are receiving. All of this is informative about the real: namely, it is the real, in-itself source of impressions we have. Even this is something less than complete agnosticism.

*Reply to Hume's Skepticism.* There are several levels on which we may reply to Hume. First, the overall skeptical attempt to suspend all judgment about reality is self-defeating, since it implies a judgment about reality. How else could one know that suspending all judgment about reality was the wisest course, unless he knew indeed that reality was unknowable? Skepticism implies agnosticism and, as was shown above, agnosticism implies some knowledge about reality. Unlimited skepticism which commends the suspension of *all* judgments about reality implies a most sweeping judgment about the knowability of reality. Why discourage all truth attempts, unless one knows in advance that they are futile? And how can one be in possession of this advance information unless he already knows something about reality?

Second, Hume's contention that all meaningful statements are either a relation of ideas or else about matters of fact is itself neither of these. Hence, on its own grounds it would be meaningless. It could not be purely a relation of ideas, for in that case it would not be informative about reality as it purports to be. And clearly it is not purely a matter-of-fact statement since it claims to cover more than empirical matters. In short, Hume's distinction is the basis for Ayer's empirical verifiability principle, and the verifiability principle is itself not empirically verifiable.

Third, Hume's radical empirical atomism that all events are "entirely loose and separate" and that even the self is only a bundle of sense impressions is unfeasible. If everything were unconnected there would be no way of even making that particular statement, since some unity and connection are implied in the affirmation that everything is disconnected. Further, to affirm "*I* am nothing but the impressions about myself" is self-defeating, for there is always the assumed unity of the "I (self)" making the assertion. But one cannot assume a unified self in order to deny the same.

*Reply to Ayer's Acognosticism.* As has already been noted, the principle of empirical verifiability as set forth by Ayer is self-defeating. For it is neither purely definitional nor strictly factual. Hence, on its own grounds it would fall into the third category of non-sense statements. Ayer recognized this problem and engaged in recovery operations by way of a third category for which he claimed no truth value but only a useful function. Verifiability, he contended, is analytic and definitional but not arbitrary or true. It is meta-cognitive, that is, beyond verification as true or false but simply useful as a guide to meaning. This is a classic but ill-fated move for two reasons. First, it no longer eliminates the possibility of making metaphysical statements. Rather, it admits that one cannot *legislate* meaning but must *look* at meaning of alleged metaphysical statements. But if it is possible that some meaningful statements can be made about reality, then we are not left with complete agnosticism and acognosticism. Second, can cognitively restrictive meta-cognitive statements be made without self-stultification? It seems not, for to restrict the area of what is meaningful is to limit the area of what could be true, since only the meaningful can be true. Hence, the attempt to limit meaning to the definitional or to the verifiable is to make a truth claim that must itself be subject to some test. If it cannot be tested, then it becomes an unfalsifiable view, a "blik" of its own.

*Reply to Wittgensteinian Mysticism.* Ludwig Wittgenstein engages in a self-stultifying acognosticism. He attempts to define the limits of language in such a way as to show that it is impossible to speak cognitively about God. God is literally inexpressible. And that whereof one cannot speak, he should not attempt to speak thereof. But Wittgenstein can be no more successful in drawing the lines of linguistic limitation than Kant was in delimiting the realm of phenomena or appearance; for how can one know that God is inexpressible without thereby revealing something expressible about God? The very attempt to deny all expressions about God is an expression about God. One cannot draw the limits of language and thought unless he has transcended those very limits he would draw. It is self-defeating to express the contention that the inexpressible cannot be expressed. In like manner even to think the thought that the unthinkable cannot be thought is self-destructive. Language (thought) and reality cannot be mutually exclusive, for every attempt to completely separate them implies some interaction or commerce between them. One cannot use the scaffold of language and thought about the limits of reality only to say the scaffold cannot be so used. If the ladder was used to get on top of the house, one cannot thereupon deny the ability of the ladder to get one there.

*Reply to Flew's Falsifiability.* Two things must be said about Flew's principle of falsifiability. First, in the narrow sense of empirical falsifiability it is too restrictive. Not everything need be *empirically* falsifiable. Indeed that very principle is not itself empirically falsifiable. But in the broader sense of testable or arguable, surely the principle is alive and helpful. For unless there are criteria for truth and falsity, then no truth claims can be supported. Everything, including opposing views, could be true. But in this case nothing can be maintained to be true (as versus what is false), for no such distinction can be made.

Second, not everything that is verifiable need be falsifiable in the same manner. As John Hick pointed out, there is an asymmetrical relation between verifiability and falsifiability. One can verify his own immortality, for example, if he consciously observes his own funeral. But one cannot falsify his immortality, for if he does not survive death then he is not there to disprove his own immortality. Nor could another person falsify one's immortality unless he were omniscient or God. For it is always possible that my existence could be somehow beyond his limited knowledge. But if it is necessary to posit an omniscient mind or God, then it would be eminently self-defeating to use falsification to disprove God. So we may conclude that every truth claim must be testable or arguable but not all truth claims need be falsifiable or disconfirmable. A total state of nonexistence of anything would be unfalsifiable, for example, since there would be no one and no way to falsify it. On the other hand, the existence of something is testable by experience or inference.

## Reply to Some Specific Agnostic Claims

Hume denied both the traditional use of causality and analogy as a means of knowing the theistic God. Causality is based on custom and analogy would lead to either a finite manlike god or to a totally different God than the alleged analogue. Let us examine each of these in turn.

*Causality Is Not Unjustifiable.* First, Hume never denied the principle of causality. He admitted it would be absurd to maintain that things arise without a cause.[13] What he did attempt to deny is that there is any philosophical way of *establishing* the principle of causality. If the causal principle is not a mere analytic relation of ideas but is a belief based on customary conjunction of matter-of-fact events, then there is no necessity in it and one cannot use it with philosophical justification.

---

13. See David Hume, "A Letter from a Gentleman to His Friend in Edinburgh," ed. Ernest C. Mossner and John V. Price (Edinburgh: University Press, 1967).

But we have already seen that dividing all contentful statements into these two classes is self-defeating. Hence, it is possible that the causal principle is both contentful and necessary. In point of fact, the very denial of causal necessity implies some kind of causal necessity in the denial. For unless there is a necessary ground (or cause) for the denial, then the denial does not necessarily stand. And if there is a necessary ground or cause for the denial, then the denial is self-defeating; for in that event it is using a necessary causal connection to deny that there are necessary causal connections.

Some have attempted to avoid the logic of the above objection by limiting necessity to the reality of logic and propositions but denying that necessity applies to reality. But this will not succeed because in order for this statement to accomplish what it intends to do, namely, to exclude necessity from the realm of reality, it must itself be a necessary statement about reality. That is, it must in effect be claiming that it is necessarily true about reality that no necessary statements can be made about reality. It must make a necessary statement about reality to the effect that necessary statements cannot be made of the real. This is clearly self-canceling, for it actually does what it claims cannot be done.

*Analogy Is Not Unfoundable.* Likewise, there is no way Hume can deny all similarity between the world and God, for this would imply that the creation must be totally dissimilar from the Creator. It would mean that effects must be entirely different from their cause. In actuality this statement too is self-destructive; for unless there were some knowledge of the cause there would be no basis for denying all similarity with its effect. Comparison, even a negative one, implies some positive knowledge of the terms being compared. Hence, either there is no basis for the affirmation that God must be totally dissimilar or else there can be some knowledge of God in terms of our experience, in which case God is not necessarily totally dissimilar to what we know in our experience.

One should be cautioned here about overdrawing the conclusion of these arguments. Once it has been shown that total agnosticism is self-defeating, it does not *ipso facto* follow that God exists or that one has knowledge of God. These arguments show only that if there is a God, one cannot maintain that he *cannot* be known. From this it follows only that God *can* be known, not that we *do* know anything about God. The disproof of agnosticism is not thereby the proof of realism or theism. In other words, agnosticism only destroys itself and makes it *possible* to build Christian theism. The positive case for Christian knowledge of God must be built later.

*An Answer to Kant's Antinomies.* In each of Kant's alleged antinomies there is a fallacy. One does not end in contradictions when he begins to speak about reality in terms of the necessary conditions of human thought. For instance, we need not speak of the world beginning *in* time, as though time were already there and there was a time before time. We may speak of the world as the beginning *of* time. That is, time is a concomitant of a created world in process—in which case there would be no time before time. All that is prior to time is eternity.

It is likewise a mistake to view everything as needing a cause, for in this case there would be an infinity of causes and even God would need a cause. Only limited, changing, contingent things need causes. Once one arrives at an unlimited, unchanging, necessary being there no longer is a need for a cause. The finite must be caused, but the infinite being would be uncaused.

Finally, the so-called antinomy of contingency fails as well, for everything cannot be contingent. There must indeed be a ground for contingency that is beyond the contingent, namely, the necessary. And, as was previously noted, it is self-defeating to claim that necessity applies only to thought and propositions but not to being or reality; for that claim itself necessarily entails an affirmation about reality. Thought and reality cannot be radically bifurcated without being irrevocably united; there is no way to affirm their separation unless they are in fact joined. This is not to say that the rational is the real, but it is to affirm that the real is rationally knowable.

## Summary and Conclusion

There are two kinds of agnosticism: limited and unlimited. The former is no threat to Christianity but is compatible with its claim of finite knowledge of an infinite God. Unlimited agnosticism, however, is self-destructive; for it implies knowledge about reality in order to deny the possibility of any knowledge of reality. Both skepticism and noncognitivisms (acognosticism) are reducible to agnosticism. For unless it is impossible to know the real, it is unnecessary to disclaim the possibility of all cognitive knowledge of it or to dissuade men from making any judgments about it. Skepticism and acognosticism imply agnosticism.

Finally, unlimited agnosticism is a subtle form of dogmatism. In completely disclaiming the possibility of all knowledge of the real, it stands at the opposite pole from the position that would claim all knowledge about reality. Each is equally dogmatic. Both are *"must"* positions regarding knowledge as opposed to the position that we *may* or *do* know something about reality. And there is simply no way short of omniscience that one can make such sweeping and categorical statements about reality, whether they are positive or negative. Agnosticism is negative dogmatism, and every negative presupposes a positive. Hence, total agnosticism is not only self-defeating but it is self-deifying. Only an omniscient mind could be totally agnostic, and finite men confessedly do not possess omniscience. Hence, the door remains open for some knowledge of reality. Reality is not unknowable.

## SELECT READINGS FOR CHAPTER ONE

**Exposition of Agnosticism**

Hume, David. *An Enquiry Concerning Human Understanding.*
Huxley, T. H. *Collected Essays,* vol. V.
Kant, Immanuel. *Critique of Pure Reason.*
Stephen, Leslie. *An Agnostic's Apology.*

**Evaluation of Agnosticism**

Collins, James. *God in Modern Philosophy,* chaps. IV and VI.
Flint, Robert. *Agnosticism.*
Garrigou-Lagrange, Reginald. *God: His Existence and His Nature.*
Hackett, Stuart. *The Resurrection of Theism,* pt. I.
Ward, James. *Naturalism and Agnosticism.*

# Chapter 2 Rationalism

The seeds of rationalism have been firmly implanted in the Western world since at least the time of Plato. In the Middle Ages the cause was advanced by thinkers like Avicenna and scholastics like Duns Scotus. But the movement flowered in the modern triumvirate of Descartes, Spinoza, and Leibniz. Rationalism is characterized by its stress on the innate or a priori ability of human reason to know truth. Basically, rationalists hold that what is knowable or demonstrable by human reason is true.

## An Exposition of Rationalism

Rationalism can be most easily understood by contrast with empiricism. The former stresses the *mind* in the knowing process and the latter lays emphasis on the *senses*. In the ancient world these emphases were found respectively in Plato and Aristotle. In modern times Descartes, Spinoza, and Leibniz are the chief exponents of rationalism; whereas Locke, Berkeley, and Hume are the prime examples of empiricism.

Along with its stress on the mind, rationalism holds to an a priori aspect to human knowledge, that is, something independent of sense experience. By contrast empiricists stress the a posteriori, or what comes through empirical experience. In like manner rationalists argue for innate ideas or principles, whereas empiricists believe that the mind is a *tabula rasa* or blank slate on which sense experience writes its impressions.

It is not uncommon for empiricism to lead to skepticism or materialism, as in Hume and Hobbes. But rationalists tend to argue for the existence of God. Characteristic of a rationalist's approach to God is the ontological argument from the idea of a perfect or necessary Being. However, empiricists who are theists tend to support their belief in God with the cosmological argument from the world to a cause beyond the world.

Perhaps the best way to understand rationalism is to see how it unfolded in its three major representatives in the modern world. Each has his distinctiveness but all exemplify the movement generally.

### René Descartes (1596-1650)

Amid a period of increasing skepticism and doubt, Descartes felt called to bring certainty into philosophy. Since in Descartes' day mathematics and particularly geometry held out most promise in this direction, Descartes applied the mathematical method to human reasoning. The result was what may be called a geometric epistemology. In order to arrive at demonstrable conclusions one must have unquestioned premises or axioms and from these he must deduce logically irrefutable conclusions. But where is one to find these archimedean axioms in the flux of doubt? Descartes' answer to this is both fascinating and illustrative of a classic rationalistic move. Doubt is a negative form of thought. And the more we doubt, the more certain we are of one thing, namely, that we are doubting. Complete doubt would bring complete certainty that one was thinking. I doubt; therefore, I am thinking. But if one is thinking, he must be a thinking thing. Thus he moves from the *dubito* to the *cogito* to *sum,* from "I doubt" to "I think" to "I am." The indubitable starting point or axiom is that one is both a doubting and a thinking being.[1]

The mind then is a thinking thing and this cannot be doubted. But what of the body? According to Descartes the body is an extended thing, and this can be doubted. The senses deceive us and we could be merely dreaming about our body and the physical world. Indeed a malevolent demon may be deceiving me about the world. Just how Descartes overcomes this sensory doubt is an instructive lesson in a classic rationalistic move. Since the only thing of which he is certain is the existence of his own mind, Descartes moves next to prove the existence of God. Then, on the grounds that God would not deceive us, Descartes attempts to demonstrate the existence of an external world of bodies.

Descartes offers two proofs for God and both are rationalistic. His a posteriori proof begins in doubt and thought.[2] I doubt. But if I doubt,

---

1. See Descartes, *Meditations on the First Philosophy,* I.
2. Descartes, II.

I am imperfect; for a lack in knowledge is an imperfection. But if I know what is imperfect, I must have knowledge of the perfect; otherwise I would not know it is not-perfect. However, knowledge of the perfect cannot arise from an imperfect mind, since there cannot be an imperfect source or basis of what is perfect. Therefore, there must be a perfect Mind (God) who is the origin of the idea of perfection I have. The rationalistic character of this argument is not difficult to detect. The proof begins in the mind, then proceeds by a rational deduction to the conclusion that a perfect Mind exists.

The second proof Descartes offers is an a priori ontological argument in the tradition of Anselm. It may be summarized as follows.[3] Whatever is necessary to the essence of a thing cannot be absent from that thing. For example, a triangle must have three sides. Devoid of three sides it would not be a triangle. Now existence or being is necessary to the nature of a necessary Being. Without existence it would not be by nature a necessary existent. It follows then that a necessary Being must necessarily exist. For if it did not exist it would not be by nature a necessary Being. God's existence is logically necessary to affirm. Descartes' other statement of this argument reveals the same rationalistic character. The idea of an absolutely perfect Being cannot be devoid of any perfection. If it were, the idea would not be of what is absolutely perfect. But existence is a necessary element in the idea of an absolutely perfect Being. Anything lacking existence is lacking in perfection. Hence, an absolutely perfect Being must exist. For if it did not exist, the idea we have would not be of an absolutely perfect Being.

Not only is this second proof undertaken strictly in the realm of the mind, but it illustrates the innate, a priori stress on conceptual necessity in the reasoning process. God's existence is conceptually or rationally inescapable.

Beneath the above argument lies a geometrical method of truth. Whatever is a clear and distinct idea (such as the indubitable ones) is true. (These are known intuitively; everything else is deducible from them.) Sensations and unclear ideas are not true. Errors arise not in the mind but in the will. Errors result when we *judge* to be true what the mind does not clearly *know* to be true. The corrective for error is found in four rules of valid thinking. First, the rule of *certainty* states that only indubitably clear and distinct ideas should be accepted as true. Second, the rule of *division* affirms that problems must be reduced first to their simplest parts. Third, the rule of *order* declares that we must proceed in our reasoning from the simplest to the most complex. Finally, the rule of *enumeration* demands that we check and

---

3. Descartes, III.

recheck each step of the argument to make sure no mistake has been made.[4] By following this method Descartes was assured that error could be overcome and certainty could be attained in our knowledge of God.

## Benedict Spinoza (1632-1677)

Spinoza was a younger contemporary of Descartes. Unlike Descartes his rationalistic method brought him to pantheistic conclusions rather than to Christian theism. Spinoza's method, however, was even more rigidly geometric than Descartes'. He begins his work by setting forth eight definitions, seven axioms, and thirty-six propositions. Everything else is geometrically deduced from these.

The starting point of Spinoza is also different. Rather than beginning in methodological doubt in order to anchor the *indubitable idea,* Spinoza begins with the absolutely *perfect idea* of an absolutely perfect Being. He rejects both hearsay and conventional signs as guides to truth, along with the undisciplined experience of empiricists. These are unreliable in that they never attain the true nature or essence of things. Even scientific inferences approach the essence of things only indirectly. For an essential knowledge of things we must exercise direct rational insight into the very essence of reality. In this way the mind can be united with the whole of nature and be healed of the injury of error. The most suitable method for engaging in this pursuit is by meditating on the absolutely perfect Idea of God. To begin anywhere short of the perfect Idea is to end in imperfection.[5]

For Spinoza error has four causes: the partial nature of our minds, which provide only fragmentary expressions of ideas; our imagination, which is affected by the physical senses and confuses us; our reasoning, which is often too abstract and general; and, above all, the failure to begin with the perfect Idea of God. The geometric method is the remedy for error because it aids the weak mind, it is impersonal, and it yields conclusions that are proven (Q.E.D.). Furthermore, the more we feed on the perfect Idea, the more perfect we become. And the inner growth that results helps one distinguish clear ideas from confused sensations.

When Spinoza's method is applied to God it yields for him the following results. First, in accordance with the traditional movement of the ontological proof, he argues that God must be conceived as a Being in and of himself, existing necessarily and independently.[6] Anything less than this is inadequate and less than perfect. The first form of his argument runs as follows. A necessary Being must necessarily

---

4. Descartes, *Discourse on Method,* pt. II.
5. Spinoza, *Ethics,* pt. I, Proposition xi.
6. Spinoza.

exist unless there is a cause adequate to explain why it does not exist, for everything must have a cause either for its existence or for its nonexistence. But there clearly is no cause adequate to explain why a necessary Being does not exist. But since nothing either inside or outside a necessary Being could possibly annul it, there is no cause adequate to explain God's nonexistence. Hence, God must necessarily exist.

Spinoza's second argument for God begins with the affirmation that something necessarily exists.[7] This he holds to be rationally inescapable, for even when one attempts to deny that anything exists he must affirm his own existence in so doing. But this existence must be either infinite or finite. And since everything must have a cause, there must be an adequate cause as to why this existence is not infinite. But in view of the fact that no finite existence can hinder it being infinite, it follows that this existence must be infinite.

The rationalistic method of Spinoza does not end in theism but in pantheism; for the infinite substance must be one, since it is impossible to have many infinite beings and finites are no more than many modes or moments of an infinite substance. All thoughts and attributes flow from the unity of this one substance with necessity just as 180° flows necessarily from the nature of a triangle. And the effects (creation) are just as infinite as the cause (Creator). Indeed, the world with all its degrees of perfection (and corresponding imperfection) is both a necessary outflow from God and the best world possible. Viewing the world fragmentarily or segmentally leads to the misconception of evil. The world must be viewed as a whole, and the whole is both good and God in his multitudinous manifestations.

### Gottfried Leibniz (1646-1716)

The last and perhaps most influential of the rationalistic theists was Leibniz. His particular brand of rationalism, as developed by Christian Wolff, has been the modern world's chief example of rational theism. It is to the Leibniz-Wolffian theism that Kant reacted, and it has been subject to constant criticism since his day.

Unlike Descartes, Leibniz' approach is not exclusively a rational one. He does not begin simply by an a priori analysis of ideas but with an examination of scientific findings from experience. He views the world as a grouping of simple natures (monads)[8] in a calculus of combination possessing overall harmony by way of God. However, Leibniz' rationalism becomes apparent as he proceeds to argue for the existence of God by way of the principle of sufficient reason. The basis of Descartes' rationalism was a clear or *indubitable* idea; Spinoza's

7. Spinoza.
8. See Leibniz, *Monadology,* pp. 1-9.

was the *perfect* Idea; but Leibniz bases his thoughts on God around the *sufficient* idea or reason.

There are several innate principles in the human mind that are not derived from the senses. First, the principle of sufficient reason says that nothing is without a reason; that is, everything has a reason or cause. This is the ground of all true propositions and it is known to be true analytically. One cannot deny it without using it. That is, he must have a sufficient reason for even denying the principle of sufficient reason, in which case he affirms it in the process of denying it. Second, there is the law of contradiction or identity which affirms that something must be itself and cannot be other than itself. While sufficient reason regulates all truth, contradiction and identity determine or establish necessary truths. That is, identity is the sufficient reason for all necessary truths. Third, the principle of perfection or the principle of the best holds for all contingent truths, namely, since God is most perfect and wise he is morally (though not logically) obligated to create the best of all possible worlds. Finally, there are the principles of order including continuity and reaction. In brief they hold that the best world has no "gaps" but is a plenum (fulness) of different substances (monads). Breaks would violate the harmony of science. There is ultimate (mathematical) intelligibility in the universe. It is with the aid of these and other rational principles that Leibniz constructs his rationalistic theism.

The Leibnizian argument for the existence of God amply illustrates his rationalistic methodology in both his ontological and cosmological proofs for God's existence. First, Leibniz argued (as had Anselm and Descartes) that if it is possible for an absolutely perfect Being to exist then it is necessary for it to exist.[9] For by definition of its very nature an absolutely perfect Being cannot lack anything. So if it cannot lack anything it surely cannot lack existence. And it is indeed possible or noncontradictory for God to possess absolutely all possible perfections, since perfections are irreducibly simple and therefore compatible qualities. That is, since there is no area of "overlap" with simple characteristics then there can be no conflict among them; they can all exist harmoniously in God. It must be concluded then that an absolutely perfect Being must exist; the very possibility of an absolutely perfect Being ensures its necessity. Reason demands God.

Leibniz' cosmological type argument is likewise rationalistic.[10] By experience we know that the entire observed universe is changing. But whatever changes lacks within itself the reason for its own existence.

9. Leibniz, pp. 40-45. Cf. *Discourse on Metaphysics,* xxiii.
10. *Monadology,* pp. 36-39.

And yet there is a sufficient reason for everything either in itself or beyond itself. But since the world has not the sufficient reason for itself in itself in that it changes, there must be beyond the world a sufficient reason or cause for its existence. Further, there cannot be an infinite regress of sufficient reasons, for the failure to reach an explanation is not an explanation. But the principle of sufficient reason demands that there be an explanation. Therefore, it is rationally necessary to conclude that there is a First Cause of the world which is its own sufficient reason for existing.

Several distinctively rationalistic aspects about this argument should be noted. First, although it *begins* with sense experience the conclusion is *based* on an analytical a priori principle of reason. Second, the principle of sufficent reason at the heart of the argument is held to be analytically true independent of experience. Third, "cause" is understood in terms of "reason" and "explanation" not distinctly as an ontological "ground" or "basis." Fourth, notice also the difference between Leibniz' principle of sufficient reason and, say, Aquinas' principle of existential causality. The latter says that only finite, changing, or contingent beings need a cause. The former says *everything* needs a reason. Further, Leibniz uses "cause" and "reason" somewhat interchangeably, whereas Aquinas considered a cause to be an ontological ground but not a rational explanation. Finally, by logical reduction Leibniz' principle of sufficient reason leads to a Self-caused God, since everything must have a reason or cause including God. Hence, God must be his own cause. Aquinas' principle of the cause of existence leads to an uncaused Cause. For if only finite things and so forth need causes, an infinite being (God) would not need a cause but would be uncaused. The Leibnizian principle is distinctively rationalistic by comparison with the thomistic one. And it is noteworthy to observe that the fate of the cosmological argument in the modern world in the hands of Kant and followers has been largely identified with the Leibnizian rationalistic argument.

## Stuart Hackett: Theistic Rationalism

Modern and contemporary Christian thought has not been without its strong strains of rationalism. A good bit of thomism has had strong rationalistic leanings since at least the time of Leibniz. Perhaps the best example of a contemporary evangelical is the work by Stuart Hackett, *The Resurrection of Theism.*[11] Hackett entitles his view "rational empiricism," but it might with equal justice be called "empirical ration-

---

11. Professor Hackett has since modified the claim that these arguments are rationally inescapable to something more like actual undeniability (see Chapter Eight).

alism" since he claims rational certainty for knowledge about God's existence and nature derived from sense experience.

*The Rejection of Kant's Agnosticism.* Hackett agrees with Kant that the *content* of all knowledge comes via the senses and that the *form* of knowledge is finalized by the a priori categories of the mind. He disagrees, however, with Kant's agnostic conclusions. Kant was wrong in rejecting the preformation of the mind to reality. There must be a correspondence between the categories of the mind and reality, he argues, because the position which denies this "is self-contradictory and reduces to skepticism." For the assertion "that the categories yield no knowledge of things-in-themselves would be an unintelligible proposition if it were not false; since it assumes the very knowledge of noumenal reality which it denies." It follows, then, that "the denial of the synthetic a priori is either self-contradictory or meaningless." That is, contrary to empiricism which affirms that all contentful knowledge is based on sensation and cannot be known with certitude, it is logically necessary to maintain that the categories of the mind (such as unity and causality) are informative about reality. In fact, "every attempt to derive the categories from the data of experience presupposes their use in the attempted derivation." One cannot deny that there are universal and necessary truths, for "this proposition itself . . . is either true or false. If the proposition is false, it is refuted at once. Suppose then it is true," Hackett continues, "in this case, since it asserts, or better denies, the predicate universally and necessarily, it is, by its own criterion, false—which is self-contradictory."[12] And since by logical necessity the opposite of the false must be true, it is logically necessary to conclude that the innate categories of the mind do inform man about the noumenal or real world.

*Rational Proof for God's Existence.* Having laid the ground for theism in his rational realism, Hackett turns his attention to proving the existence of God. It is impossible to deny the existence of everything because the one making the denial "at least exists to effect the denial, which is therefore self-contradictory." Now what exists is either an effect or not. If not, then we have already arrived at an absolutely necessary Being. But if it is an effect, "its character and being must therefore, by definition, be determined by antecedent and contemporaneous existences external to itself. . . . But an infinite number of successive causes and effects . . . is rationally inconceivable." It follows then that "whether a given entity is an effect or not, we rationally conclude the existence of an absolutely necessary being."[13]

---

12. Stuart Hackett, *The Resurrection of Theism,* pp. 54, 60, 62, 65.
13. Hackett, pp. 194-95.

This argument is elaborated and defended with a great deal of rational sophistication, after which Hackett summarizes the important things about it. "In the first place, it rests upon that very a priori structure of rationality with which the mind approaches the experience and without which intelligible experience itself does not exist." And "in the second place, the argument has likewise an a posteriori or existential premise; for it reasons to the existence of an absolutely necessary being from the granted reality of some particular entity of experience." Finally, "the sum of the whole matter is this: that rationality and experience have together established the existence of an absolutely infinite being that transcends the world of experience and is its only sufficient explanation."[14] In brief, it is rationally inescapable to conclude God's existence, because it is logically necessary to conclude both that our minds correspond to reality and that there must be in reality an absolutely necessary Being (God).

## Gordon Clark: Revelational Rationalism

There is yet another kind of evangelical rationalism. It claims no rationally inescapable arguments. Indeed, it disavows all such. "As a recourse for Christian theism," writes Clark, "the cosmological argument is worse than useless. In fact Christians can be pleased at its failure, for if it were valid, it would prove a conclusion inconsistent with Christianity."[15] Hume and Kant put theistic rationalism to rest over one hundred fifty years ago.

*The Need for Presuppositions.* The failure of all philosophical attempts to establish truth either secular or religious points up the need for a Christian presupposition. "The various systems all fail on the two points at which failure is fatal. First, they do not furnish a systematic, consistent set of universal principles." Second, "they give no guidance in making concrete decisions of everyday living. . . . Failing thus both theoretically and practically, the failure is complete."[16]

From this Clark draws two conclusions: "The first is that no construction in philosophy is possible without some sort of presupposition or *a priori* equipment." The second conclusion is "that the secular philosophers who use presuppositions have not selected those which can solve their problem." To this Clark adds "a third conclusion, or at least an hypothesis for consideration. It is that revelation should be accepted as our axiom, seeing that other presuppositions have failed."[17]

---

14. Hackett, pp. 202-3.
15. Gordon Clark, *Religion, Reason, and Revelation,* p. 41.
16. Ronald Nash, *Philosophy of Gordon Clark,* p. 54.
17. Clark, pp. 57-59.

*Testing the Christian Presupposition.* Clark admits that the fact that "revelation should be accepted without proofs or reasons, undeduced from something admittedly true, seems odd when first proposed." Nevertheless, he feels "it will not seem so odd . . . when the nature of axioms is kept in mind." For "axioms, whatever they may be and in whatever subject they are used, are never deduced from more original principles. They are always tested in another way." Every philosopher makes a voluntary choice of his axioms. "Axioms, because they are axioms, cannot be deduced from or proved by previous theorems." What we must ask with respect to the axiom of the propositional revelation of Scripture is: "Does revelation make knowledge possible? Does revelation establish values and ethical norms? Does revelation give a theory of politics? And are all these results consistent with one another?" In short, "we can judge the acceptability of an axiom by its success in producing a system." Logical consistency is the essence of truth, and logical contradiction is the core of falsity.[18]

*The Status and Defense of the Law of Noncontradiction.* According to Clark, "the denial of the law of contradiction, or even the failure to establish it as a universal truth, was the downfall of secular philosophy." Even the intelligibility of the Scriptures presupposes logic. But this does not mean that logic should be conceived as a prior or separate axiom from Scripture. For logic is embedded in Scripture and Scripture is the logically consistent thoughts of God expressed in verbal form. In fact, John's prologue should be translated, "In the beginning was Logic, and Logic was with God, and Logic was God." This should not sound offensive to the Christian because the Word is the expression or thought of God. Therefore, "the law of contradiction is not to be taken as an axiom prior to or independent of God. The law is God thinking." In this sense, "if one should say that logic is dependent on God's thinking, it is dependent only in the sense that it is the characteristic of God's thinking." It is not subsequent temporally "for God is eternal and there was never a time when God existed without thinking logically." Hence, logic is to be considered as an activity of God's mind.[19]

Clark believed "it is strange that anyone who thinks he is a Christian should deprecate logic. . . . The law of contradiction cannot be sinful" simply because man's mind is fallen. "Quite the contrary, it is our violations of the law of contradiction that are sinful." He asks, "Can such pious stupidity really mean that syllogism which is valid for us is invalid for God? If two plus two is four in our arithmetic, does God

---

18. Clark, pp. 59-60.
19. Clark, pp. 64, 67, 68.

have a different arithmetic in which two and two make three or perhaps five?" Nonsense. "To avoid this irrationalism, which of course is a denial of the divine image, we must insist that truth is the same for God and man." For "if we know anything at all, what we must know must be identical with what God knows. . . . It is absolutely essential therefore to insist that there is an area of coincidence between God's mind and our mind."[20]

*The Relation of Scripture and Logic.* Clark concludes that "since secular philosophy had failed to solve its problems, the alternative hypothesis of revelation, verbal communication, the Bible was proposed." In this we may anticipate the relation of logic to the Scripture. "First of all, Scripture, the written words of the Bible, is the mind of God. What is said in Scripture is God's thought." For "the Bible consists of thoughts, not paper; and the thoughts are the thoughts of the omniscient, infallible God. . . ." and, "as might be expected, if God has spoken, he has spoken logically. The Scripture therefore should and does exhibit logical organization." Further, "this exhibition of the logic embedded in Scripture explains why Scripture rather than the law of contradiction is selected as the axiom." For "this *sine qua non* is not sufficient to produce knowledge. Therefore the law of contradiction as such and by itself is not made the axiom of this argument." Even God is not the axiom for " 'God' as an axiom, apart from Scripture, is just a name. We must specify which God." Spinoza began with the axiom of a pantheistic God. Other axioms that define God in other ways are possible. "Therefore the Scripture is offered here as the axiom. This gives definiteness and content, without which axioms are useless. Thus it is that God, Scripture, and logic are tied together."[21]

All non-Christian world views are ultimately self-contradictory. For example, skepticism refutes itself because it is internally self-contradictory. If skepticism is true, it is false. This "method of procedure stresses coherence or self-consistency, and the implication of each position must be traced out to the end. A *reductio ad absurdum* would be the test." And if there seem to be two systems fairly coherent, then one must choose between them with regard to "the widest possible consistency." Of course, "no philosopher is perfect and no system can give man omniscience. But if one system can provide plausible solutions to many problems while another leaves too many questions unanswered, if one system tends less to skepticism and gives more meaning to life," or "if one world view is consistent while others are self-contradictory, who can deny us, since we must choose, the right to choose the more

---

20. Clark, pp. 76, 77.
21. Clark, pp. 71, 72.

promising first principle?" And this principle is for Clark the axiom of propositional relation in Scripture. In short, the Bible is God's thoughts expressed verbally, and God thinks logically and consistently. For logic is a characteristic of God's thinking. Hence, the system that is ultimately consistent is ultimately true. But since only an omniscient mind can know this system is ultimately consistent, finite minds must choose the one that seems most coherent. Such, for Clark, is the system of Biblical Christianity.[22]

## Some Basic Tenets of Rationalism

Our concern here is not with a complete list and critique of rationalistic premises but simply with an evaluation of essential rationalistic methodology as it bears on establishing the truth or falsity of theism. In line with this purpose we may single out several central tenets of rationalistic epistemology.

*Reality Is Rationally (i.e., Mathematically) Analyzable.* One of the central assumptions of modern rationalism, as of its Pythagorean and Platonic predecessors, is the belief in the union or communion of the mathematical and the metaphysical. That is to say, reality is analyzable by mathematical methods. The real is rational and the heart of rationality is mathematical identity.

*There Are Innate Ideas or Principles.* Certain truths are innate to the mind and known independently of experience. The precise number and nature of these may vary from rationalist to rationalist, but all would agree that the basic laws of logic, such as the law of noncontradiction, are known innately. Men are born with an a priori aspect of knowing that enables them to come to explicit knowledge of truth. Without innate ideas or principles there would be no knowledge at all and certainly no demonstrations or proofs. The mind is not a *tabula rasa;* sense experience is parallel to or the occasion of intellectual knowledge but is not the cause or basis of it. Truth is based in the ideas or principles innate to the mind and not in the changing flux of sense experience.

*Truth Is Derived by Deduction from Self-evident Principles.* Another characteristic of modern rationalism is the use of geometric deductions based on intuitively known self-evident truths. The starting point is some apodictic axiom known innately by direct rational intuition. For Descartes it is the intuition of self-evidently clear and distinct ideas. For Spinoza it is insight into the perfect Idea of God and the axioms implied in that. Leibniz held to intuitive first principles such as sufficient reason and identity. From these axioms one can proceed by logical mathematical deductions to necessary conclusions.

---

22. Gordon Clark, *Christian View of Men and Things,* pp. 30, 34.

*The Claim for Rational Certainty in Arguments for God.* Common to modern rationalists is the claim of rational inescapability. God is known to exist not by scientific probability but by mathematical certainty. Spinoza did not blush to write Q.E.D., indicating that the proof was completed and the demonstration made. Neither Descartes nor Spinoza was embarrassed to claim rational certainty for their arguments. God exists, they insisted, as necessarily as 180 degrees flows from the nature of a triangle. Leibniz too considered his argument as certain as the laws of thought.

*The Rationally Inescapable Is the Real.* Beneath the foregoing tenet of rationalism is an all-important proposition usually implied by the proponents and often missed by the opponents of rationalism, namely, the rationally inescapable is the real. That is, whatever is logically inescapable in the realm of thought about reality (or, God) is necessarily true. The ontological argument is the classic case in point. In each case the hidden premise is that whatever is logically necessary is actually so. For if it is logically necessary to think of God as a necessary Existent, then it is actually true that he does necessarily exist.

Rationalists are sometimes unfairly criticized for holding that the rational is the real. This is not so. The rational is only the *possibly* real, but the rationally inescapable is the *actually* real. Mermaids are possible realities, since there is no contradiction in the concept or thought of them. But God is an actual reality because it would be a contradiction to deny his existence for a rationalist.

## An Evaluation of Rationalism as a Method of Knowing God

There are some obvious problems with rationalism as a method of establishing truth, but there are some significant emphases that should not be overlooked. We will first center our attention on these positive features.

### Valuable Strains in Rationalistic Thought

1. One of the more basic contributions of rationalism is its stress on the inescapability of the basic laws of thought. Unless the law of noncontradiction holds, then there is not even the most minimal possibility of meaning nor any hope for establishing truth. As a negative test for truth at least, the principle of noncontradiction is absolutely essential. Without this law, truth cannot be distinguished from falsity; all is equally true and false, which is to say nothing can be true.

2. The second contribution is sometimes overlooked by overzealous empiricists, namely, there must be an a priori dimension to knowledge. These need not be innate ideas but there must be at least some natural

inclinations of the mind toward truth or toward the first principles of knowledge. If not, nothing could ever be known. But something is knowable; agnosticism is self-defeating (see Chapter One). Without some categories or at least capacities of the mind to know reality, the very possibility of truth would be nil. Even *if* all knowledge came *through* the senses it could not be known as true *by* the senses. There may be nothing in the mind that was not first in the senses, *except the mind itself.* And the mind must possess some innate or natural abilities of its own to engage in the pursuit of truth. This a priori contribution of rationalism is essential to any realistic epistemology.

3. Along with the first two contributions we must list another, namely, the rationalistic stress on the intelligibility and knowability of reality. Agnosticism is self-destructive; reality is not paradoxical and unknowable. There is a correspondence or adequation between the mind and being. The real is rational, even though the rational is not always real. There is no way of denying that thought relates to reality without, in that very thought, applying thought to reality. The rationalists rightly preserve the truth that reality is intelligible.

## The Inadequacy of Rationalistic Methodology

Despite the significant and abiding contributions of some of its emphases, rationalism as a methodology for establishing truths about reality or the truths of theism is inadequate for several reasons.

1. First, it is based on an invalid move from thought to reality, from the possible to the actual. Just because something is thinkable does not make it actual. The thinkable describes only the realm of the possible and not necessarily that of the actual. What is not contradictory could possibly be true; what is contradictory could not possibly be true. That is, there could be centaurs (possible beings); there are humans (possible and actual beings); but there cannot be square circles (impossible beings). One may not legitimately move from the possible to the actual, from thought to reality.

At this point the rationalist might agree but insist that he is not moving merely from the logically possible to the actually real but from the logically necessary to the ontologically inescapable. If he so insists, two observations are pertinent. First, it is not logically necessary for a human being to exist. It is always at least logically possible for whatever contingent being that exists also not to exist. One's own existence may be actually *undeniable,* but this is something quite different from saying it is logically *necessary.* Logic does not determine existence; rather, it is reality that governs the nature of thought. Second, if the rationalist insists that at least in one case (viz., the argument for God) there is rational necessity that leads us to reality, then we must point out the fallacy in the hidden premise in the ontological argument, namely, the contention that the rationally inescapable is the real. This leads to the next point.

2. Contrary to the central claim of traditional rationalism, the rationally inescapable is not the real. First of all, this claim *assumes* but does not prove—certainly not with rational inescapability—that something is real.[23] There is no purely logical justification for that claim. The arguments offered by rationalists reduce not to logical necessity but to actual.undeniability. For example, if one attempts to deny that anything exists, he thereby affirms his own existence. But this does not at all imply that he exists with logical necessity. One's own nonexistence is logically possible and the affirmation of one's existence is actually unavoidable. But in no case is it logically necessary that one exist. Hence, the rationalist confuses actual undeniability with rational inescapability. There is no purely logically compelling reason for reality. No strictly rational proof is available for the existence of anything. It is a mistaken effort to contend that reality can be rationally proven.

The invalidity of the ontological argument is illustrative of the point being made here. Certainly, a triangle must be conceived as having three sides and, *if* a triangle exists, it must exist with three sides. But it is not logically necessary that any triangle exists anywhere. In like manner, it is logically necessary to predicate existence of a necessary Existent and, *if* such a Being exists, it must necessarily exist. But it is not logically necessary for a necessary Being to exist any more than it is for a triangle to exist. Of course, *if* something exists, then the ontological argument takes on new strength; for if something exists it is possible that something necessarily exists. But the point here is that there is no purely logical way to eliminate the "if." I know undeniably but not with logical necessity that I exist. And this is precisely the point at which the proponents of the ontological argument covertly borrow the fact of an undeniable existence in order to strengthen their argument. They know that it is undeniable that something exists (viz., one's self). And once it is thereby granted that something is real, they can move more easily toward proving that it is logically necessary that something exists. But even here their argument is misdirected. For God cannot be a *logically* necessary Being. If there is a God he would be an *actually* necessary Being, but it is confusing categories to make conceptual or rational necessity constituative of the reality of God. Further, the ontological argument as such does not even prove that anything exists necessarily but only undeniably that some-

23. See my article, "The Missing Premise in the Ontological Argument," *Religious Studies* IX, No. 3 (Sept. 1973).

thing exists. It remains to be shown that this something is a necessary Being. And the ontological argument provides no rationally inescapable way of demonstrating that that which is, undeniably exists or entails a necessary Being.

One attempt to fill in the gap in logical necessity left by the ontological argument might be an appeal to a premise from the cosmological argument by arguing that there must be a sufficient reason for whatever exists (à la Leibniz). This would lead us ultimately to a necessary ground for whatever contingent beings exist. But even here there is a fatal flaw in the rationalist's argument. For the principle of sufficient reason cannot be proved with logical necessity. For it is possible to deny the principle of sufficient reason without involving a contradiction. For example, one can affirm that *some* things do not have a sufficient reason; and the world is one of them. Now whereas it would be contradictory to affirm that *nothing* has a sufficient reason including this very statement, nevertheless it is not contradictory to affirm that *something*(s) does not have sufficient reason. In point of fact, many theists (as Aquinas) claim precisely this about God: he has no sufficient reason or cause but is an *un*caused cause. In any event, there is no purely rational contradiction in denying the principle of sufficient reason of one's self or of the world. And if it is logically possible that some things do not need a sufficient reason, then it is not logically necessary that God exists. Hence, even Leibniz' cosmological proof imports a premise that lacks rational inescapability. Rationalism thus fails in its attempt at rationally apodictic certainty. It is logically possible that there is no God.

3. Growing out of the previous criticism is one final criticism of rationalism: it fails to demonstrate that its first principles are rationally necessary. As Aristotle said long before, first principles cannot be proved. Or, as Wittgenstein has noted, all justification must come to an end. If indeed, as Descartes claimed, there is a rational *intuition* of the basic axioms of thought from which all other deductive demonstrations proceed, then it is evident that there can be no demonstration of the basic axioms. But herein lies the problem. Not only did the rationalists offer no demonstration of their axioms, but they differed in their conception of them and even drew differing conclusions from them. It must be remembered that Spinoza "logically" deduced pantheism from his axioms, while Descartes and Leibniz "logically" deduced differing theisms from theirs. But the central point remains that rationalism cannot be completely rationalistic. All its rational processes begin with ideas or principles to which its proponents are committed without a logically necessary basis.

The point of this criticism can be focused by showing the circularity of a rationalistic attempt to prove the validity of the principle of contradiction. One cannot legitimately argue that the law of noncontradiction is valid because it is *contradictory* to deny it. For in that case he is using the law of noncontradiction as the basis of his proof of the law, which begs the whole question. Likewise, one cannot meaningfully affirm that it is irrational to deny the first principles of rationalism. But if it is not necessarily contrary to reason to deny that rationalism is true, it is not rationally necessary to hold that rationalism is true. Herein lies the dilemma of rationalism: there is no strictly rational way to establish itself. There is both logical and historical evidence to support the thesis that rationalism is based in intuitivism and leads to either mysticism or, by way of reaction, to fideism.

4. Even the weaker form of Christian rationalism represented by Gordon Clark is insufficient as a test for truth. For as Clark admits, one would have to be omniscient in order to apply with certainty the logical consistency test for truth. Some systems seem equally consistent with their own presuppositions. And there is no way on purely rationalistic grounds to challenge those presuppositions. Clark, then, must choose between fideism and some other form of confirmation. Logic alone is at best a negative test for truth. That is, it is a test for falsity by way of internal inconsistency. Spinoza's pantheism is as consistent with his axioms as Descartes' theism is with his axioms. But since many opposing views may be internally noncontradictory and consistent with their own presuppositions, then logic alone is an insufficient test for truth.

## Summary and Conclusion

The heart of rationalism is the thesis that the rationally inescapable is the real. Rationalistic theism holds that the existence of God can be demonstrated with logical necessity. We have seen that this is wrong for at least three reasons. First, logic is only a negative test for truth. It can eliminate what is false but cannot in and of itself establish what must be true. Logic can only demonstrate what is possibly real but not what is actually real. Second, there are no rationally inescapable arguments for the existence of God because it is always logically possible that nothing ever existed including God. Of course, it is actually undeniable that something exists (e.g., my own existence is undeniable). But even here there is no logical necessity that I exist. My nonexistence is logically possible, as is that of the whole world and God. And if there is no logically necessary basis for either my existence or that of anything else, then it is not logically necessary to conceive the existence of anything including God. Finally, there is no rationally inescapable way of establishing the first principles of reasoning. They are intuitive but nondemonstrated givens. Rationalism is without a necessary rational basis of its own. Hence, the existence of God cannot be demonstrated with logical necessity. If Christian theism is to be established as true, then some other test of truth must be found.

## SELECT READINGS FOR CHAPTER TWO

**Exposition of Rationalism**

Clark, Gordon. *A Christian View of Men and Things.*
Descartes, René. *Meditations.*
Hackett, Stuart. *The Resurrection of Theism.*
Leibniz, Gottfried. *Discourses on Metaphysics.*
Spinoza, Benedict. *Ethics.*

**Evaluation of Rationalism**

Gurr, Edwin. *The Principle of Sufficient Reason in Some Scholastic Systems: 1750-1900.*
Hume, David. *An Enquiry Concerning Human Understanding.*
Montague, W. P. *The Ways of Knowing,* pt. I, chap. IV.
Nash, Ronald. *The Philosophy of Gordon Clark.*

# Chapter

# 3 | *Fideism*

In view of the fact that empiricism led to skepticism in Hume (see Chapter One) and that rationalism cannot rationally demonstrate its first principles, fideism becomes a more viable option in religious epistemology. Perhaps, there is indeed no rational or evidential way to establish Christian theism. Does truth in religion, then, rest solely on faith and not on a reasoning process? To this question fideists give an affirmative answer. And in this way philosophical skepticism or agnosticism and religious fideism are comfortably compatible positions.

## An Exposition of Some Major Fideistic Views

The stress on the operation of faith in the truth of a religious system has been with Christianity since at least the time of Tertullian (d. A.D. 230). "I believe because it is absurd," he cried. "What indeed has Athens to do with Jerusalem? What concord is there between the Academy and the Church?"[1] Perhaps the best modern example of a fideistic position is found in Blaise Pascal.

### The Fideism of Blaise Pascal (1623-1662)

By comparison with some others, Pascal's fideism was moderate. He lived in a France drunk with the wine of Cartesian rationalism and increasingly drifting to deism. Pascal sensed an accelerated tendency to reject God's revelation in favor of human reason. In view of this his fideism was intended as an existential shock treatment to his complacent contemporaries.

---

1. Tertullian, *The Prescription Against Heretics,* 7.

*The Critique of Rationalism.* Pascal desired to destroy faith in reason so that he could restore "faith in faith." Reason to him is the geometric or mathematical mind, the mind of science. However, the first principles of science cannot be demonstrated. Further, the Biblical doctrine of original sin informs us that man is sinful and God is hidden (No. 445).[2] Hence, human corruption stands in the way of Descartes' theistic proofs. Furthermore, reason is really dependent on the heart for its very basis and function. The heart is the intuitive center of man which views all things synoptically as opposed to partially. By contrast with reason, it is both more sensitive and more comprehensive. Even knowledge of first principles is intuitive "and reason must trust these intuitions of the heart, and must base on them every argument" (No. 282). Pascal's conclusion to the analysis of man's reason is skepticism and humility. Man is a "thinking reed" incapable of both total ignorance and absolute knowledge. "Know then, proud man, what a paradox you are to yourself. Humble yourself, weak reason; be silent, foolish nature.... Hear God" (No. 434).

*The Way to Truth Through Faith.* For Pascal, "the heart has its reasons which reason knows nothing of" (No. 277). The heart is the absolute bedrock of all knowledge. It knows intuitively and holistically, not discursively or abstractly. Hence, "it is the heart which experiences God, and not the reason" (No. 278). Reason must submit to the heart, for "submission is the use of reason in which consists true Christianity" (No. 269). It is not that Christianity is opposed to reason per se. "On the contrary, the mind must be open to proofs, must be confirmed by custom, and offer itself in humbleness to *inspiration, which alone can produce a true and saving effect"* (No. 245, emphasis added).

Reason alone will never find God. For "it is the heart which experiences God, and not the reason. This, then, is faith: God felt by the heart, not by the reason" and this "faith is a gift of God; do not believe that we said it was a gift of reasoning" (Nos. 278, 279). It is therefore futile for man to attempt to reason his way to God. Faith, for Pascal, is generated by humility, submission, and inspiration. Man must submit to the authority of God revealed in the Scriptures and the Fathers. God must take the initiative, for "those to whom God has imparted religion by intuition are very fortunate, and justly convinced. But to those who do not have it, we can give it only by reasoning, waiting for God to give them insight, without which faith it is only human, and useless for salvation" (No. 282).

---

2.   Unless otherwise noted, quotations of Pascal are taken from his *Pensées,* Brunschvicg edition.

For Pascal, "faith is different from proof; the one is human, the other is the gift of God. It is this faith that God himself puts into the human heart, of which the proof is often the instrument; but this faith is in the heart, and makes us not say *scio* [I know], but *credo* [I believe]" (No. 248). A proof at best may be the instrument by which God places faith in one's heart. But what are these proofs? What are the tests for the truth of Christianity? A true religion is one that cures human pride and sin. In this regard Christ alone is the proof of Christianity, "for in Jesus Christ, we prove God, and teach morality and doctrine" (No. 547). And "it is not only impossible but useless to know God without Jesus Christ" (No. 549). Pascal does appeal to the miraculous history of Christianity, its high morality, its perpetuity and spread as evidence of its truthfulness (No. 482). However, none of these is absolutely convincing proof because "there is enough light for those who only desire to see, and enough obscurity for those who have a contrary disposition" (No. 144). The decision to accept or reject must be made by faith.

*The Great Wager.* Pascal's famous Wager is perhaps the best example of his test for truth in operation.[3] He begins by asking, "Who then will condemn Christians for being unable to give rational grounds for their belief, professing as they do a religion for which they cannot give rational grounds?" For "if they did prove it they would not be keeping their word. It is by being without proof that they show they are not without sense." Pascal then proceeds to pose the alternatives: "Either God is or he is not. But to which view shall we be inclined? Reason cannot decide this question. Infinite chaos separates. . . . Reason cannot make you choose either, reason cannot prove either wrong. Nonetheless, one must choose. Which will you choose then?" he asks. "Let us weigh up the gain and the loss involved in calling heads that God exists. Let us assess the two cases; if you win you win everything, if you lose you lose nothing. Do not hesitate then; wager that he does exist." There is eternal life and happiness to gain if God exists and nothing at all to lose if there is no God. So," asks Pascal, "what have you to lose?" Wager on God.

From the standpoint of reason, faith in God is a bet in which the purely rational odds are about even (No. 144), but in which the existential dice are highly loaded in favor of faith. There are no purely rational tests for religious truth. Even "contradiction is a poor indication of truth. Many things that are certain are contradicted. Many that are false pass without contradiction." Hence, "contradiction is no more an indication of falsehood than lack of it is an indication of truth"

---

3. Pascal, "Wager" in *Pensées,* trans. A. J. Krailsheimer (Penguin Books, 1966).

(No. 177 [384]).[4] Truth is tested in the heart not the mind, and the criteria are existential rather than rational.

### The Fideism of Sören Kierkegaard (1813-1855)

Few pens have pierced the rationalist's conscience as that of Kierkegaard. As Pascal disquieted the Cartesian rationalism, Kierkegaard declared war on Hegelian idealism. Hegel was interested in true *propositions* known logically (i.e., dialectically), but Kierkegaard was concerned with truth in *persons* who are known only paradoxically. Reality is not found in the objective world of universal reason but in the subjective realm of individual choice.

*Life's Three Stages.* One of the easiest ways to capture the spirit of Kierkegaard's thought is in his elaboration of the three stages of life: the aesthetic, the ethical, and the religious. Each stage is separated by despair and is spanned by a leap of faith. When one passes to a higher level, the lower level is dethroned but not destroyed. The contrast between the aesthetic life and the ethical life is the difference between feeling and deciding; it is a move from a self-centered to a law-centered life.[5] In the ethical stage one comes from a life without choosing to the point of choosing life, from being a spectator to a participator, from deliberation to decision. It is no longer a life of the intellect but one of the will. Nor is it a life determined by immediate interests but one controlled by ultimate concern—that is, a shift of man's center of interest from the present moment to lifetime duty.

The ethical life is a decided advance over the aesthetic but it is by no means final.[6] The religious transcends the ethical as God transcends his law. In the ethical stage one chooses life but in the religious he chooses God. The ethical concentrates only on a lifetime duty; whereas the religious focuses on eternity. The ethical·man has utmost respect for the moral law, but the religious man gives an ultimate response to the moral law Giver. In moving to the religious center of gravity one leaves the realm of the objective and propositional for the subjective and personal; he moves from the essential to the existential.

The manner in which the religious transcends the ethical is beautifully dramatized by Kierkegaard in his use of the story of Abraham.[7] The moral law said, "Thou shalt not kill," but God said to Abraham, "Take your son, your only son Isaac, whom you love . . . and offer him there upon one of the mountains of which I shall tell you" (Gen. 22:2). In this teleological suspension of the ethical Abraham's faith transcended

---

4. Pascal, "Wager."
5. Sören Kierkegaard, *Either/Or.*
6. See Kierkegaard, *Fear and Trembling.*
7. Kierkegaard, *Fear and Trembling.*

his reason, his existential decision superseded his ethical obligation. Herein is the paradox, namely, that "the individual is higher than the universal." "Faith is precisely this paradox, that the individual as the particular is higher than the universal, is justified over against it, is not subordinate but superior. . . ." So this "is and remains to all eternity a paradox inaccessible to thought." By this act of religious faith Abraham "overstepped the ethical entirely and possessed a higher *telos* [end] outside of it, in relation to which he suspended the former."[8]

*The Nature of Religious Truth.* Like the ethical, the rational is not discarded by Kierkegaard but it is disenfranchised. Religion does not relinquish reason entirely but it relegates it to a lower level. Objective scientific and philosophical truth has its place but by it a man can never reach God. This point is strongly emphasized in Kierkegaard's later distinction between Religion A and Religion B.[9] The former is natural religion but the latter is supernatural. The first is religiosity but the last is Christianity. A man with Religion A is still operating in the realm of the rational; whereas Religion B is paradoxical. The former involves an immanent concept of God but the latter is a transcendent or "totally other" God. Religion A originates in man's general need for God but Religion B rests on the believer's specific need for Christ.

Religious or existential truth in the highest sense, then, can be characterized as follows: it is *personal* and not impersonal; it is not something one has but what he *is;* it is not what one knows but what he *lives.* Objective truth is something we grip but religious truth is something that *grips us.* It is *appropriated* and not merely acknowledged. It is discovered by *commitment* and not by any alleged correspondence to the world. In a word, truth is *subjectivity.* Kierkegaard wrote, "It is subjectivity that Christianity is concerned with, and it is only in subjectivity that its truth exists, if it exists at all; objectively Christianity has absolutely no existence."[10] This point is clearly illustrated in Kierkegaard's conception of the relation of Christianity with history. If the first century contemporaries of Christ "had left nothing behind them but these words: 'We have believed that in such and such a year the God appeared among us in the humble figure of a servant, that he lived and taught in our community, and finally died,' it would be more than enough."[11] In brief, one cannot derive the eternal from the historical nor the spiritual from the rational.

---

8. Kierkegaard, *Fear and Trembling,* pp. 80, 66, 69.
9. Kierkegaard, *Concluding Unscientific Postscripts,* sec. II, p. 483 f.
10. Kierkegaard, *Postscripts,* p. 116.
11. Kierkegaard, *Philosophical Fragments,* p. 130.

*The Nature of Faith and Its Relation to Reason.* For Kierkegaard, faith is man's highest passion. Faith is not assent to objective propositions; rather, it is a subjective submission to a person, to God through Christ. It is a solitary act of an individual confronted with God. By faith man's spirit is actualized. Faith is prompted by paradox and is directed toward a person. It is an act of the will exercised without the aid of reason or objective guides. Reason plays only a negative and dialectical role in relation to faith; it enables us to understand that Christian truth is paradoxical. Man's basic problem is not ignorance of God's revelation but offense at its intrusion into his life. Original sin hinder's man's ability to know truth. He cannot know the truth without being in the truth, and he cannot be in the truth without God placing him in it. The difference between human reason and God's revelation is illustrated by Kierkegaard in the contrast between Socrates and Christ.[12] Socratic wisdom brought forth truth from within by a backward recollection; whereas God's revelation brings truth from without by a forward expectation. Human truth is immanent and comes from the wise man, but God's truth is transcendent and is mediated through the God-Man. The truths of human reason are rational but those of divine revelation are paradoxical. God's truth is neither analytic nor synthetic but antithetic and, hence, it can only be accepted by a leap of faith.

God is the center of the meaningful but real paradox of our faith. He is the Unknown limit to knowing that magnetically draws reason but which causes a passionate collision with man. Human reason can neither penetrate nor avoid God. The supreme paradox of all is the attempt to discover something thought cannot think. God is unknown in himself and even unknown in Christ; his presence is indicated only by signs or pointers. The paradoxical revelation of the Unknown is not knowable by reason. Man's response must be by a leap of faith which is given (though not forced on us) by God. Faith in God is neither rationally nor empirically grounded; so the existence of God is neither rationally certain nor empirically evident. The empirical evidence for Christ tells us only that an unusual, humble man lived and died; and rationally man cannot even comprehend God let alone prove him. We cannot imagine what God is like nor what he is unlike. The most we can do is to project familiar qualities in the direction of the Transcendent that always fall short of him.

The existence of God cannot be proved from nature, for nature assumes God for believers and leads unbelievers to doubt God. The very attempt to prove God is folly, "for if God does not exist it would of course be impossible to prove it; and if he does exist it would be

12. Kierkegaard, *Fragments,* chap. 2.

folly to attempt it. For at the very outset, in beginning my proof, I will have presupposed it, not as doubtful but as certain ... since otherwise I would not begin, readily understanding that the whole would be impossible if he did not exist."[13] What is more, even if we could prove God's *being* (in himself) it would be irrelevant to us; it is God's *existence* or relatedness to us that alone has religious significance. God is presented to man for an existential choice, not for rational reflection. "For to prove the existence of one who is present is the most shameless affront, since it is an attempt to make him ridiculous.... The existence of a king, or his presence, is commonly acknowledged by an appropriate expression of subjection and submission...."[14] Thus it is that one proves God's existence by worship not by proofs.

Kierkegaard is not claiming that there is an ultimate irrationality in God but rather a suprarationality which upholds finite rationality by transcending it and holding it in place. The real absurdity is in man's situation: he must act in response to God as though he were certain without any reason for doing so. And God is an absolute paradox to man not simply because of the inability of the human mind but because of the depravity of the human heart. Man's task is not to comprehend God intellectually but to submit to God existentially. The paradox is not centered in the theoretical but volitional; it is not so much metaphysical as axiological. In short, God is both a folly to our finite minds and an offense to our sinful will.

*The Test for Truth.* As can readily be seen, there are no objective historical or rational tests for religious truth. Truth is *subjective* and personal, and the acid test is one's submission to and abiding in truth. The surest test of the truth of Christianity is *suffering.* Suffering is the infinite dissatisfaction one realizes as he approaches nearer to God. Another earmark of living in the truth is *solitude.* Faith is essentially a private relation to God; loneliness is the clear mark of that solitude. Finally, truth is realized in the *suprahistorical,* that is, when one becomes contemporary with the eternal Christ. Christ is not a past individual but a person present in the now of Christian experience.

In summary, fideism is not equivalent to irrationalism for Kierkegaard but it is an antirationalism. God cannot be known intellectually by reason but only existentially by faith. Truth is not testable objectively by logical criteria but only subjectively by a personal commitment. Faith, not reason, is the door to truth.

## The Fideism of Karl Barth

*The Early Barth.* Karl Barth dropped a bombshell on the theological

13. Kierkegaard, *Fragments,* p. 49.
14. Kierkegaard, *Postscripts,* p. 485.

world with the publication of his *Commentary on Romans* (1919).[15] In it he took a highly Kierkegaardian view of God and revelation. God is "wholly other" and revelation strikes the world with judgment from God, not knowledge of him. Nothing in the world can be identified with God's revelation, not the flesh of Christ nor the Bible. The Bible is only the crater left by the meteorite of God's Word. Even Christ in his humanity stands fallen and under the condemnation of God. Revelation reveals man's lostness but it tells us nothing positive about God.

*Barth's Shift from Radical Existentialism.* In 1920 Barth republished his *Commentary on Romans* in which he shifts from an extreme Kierkegaardian emphasis to a more moderate position under the influence of Heppe's *Reformed Theology.* And by 1931, in his work on Anselm,[16] Barth acknowledges that God can be known by revelation. The ontological argument makes no sense as a rational proof but it is an affirmation of faith: "I believe in order to understand." Once one knows God by revelation, the ontological argument takes on meaning. We do understand God analogously by faith.

*The Later Barth.* Barth began his *Dogmatics*[17] in 1927 but restated them in a nonexistential way a few years later. There is knowledge of God for man because revelation is the action of the triune God. The Father is revealed through the Son (the objective reality) and through the Holy Spirit (subjective reality). And the Bible is the record or witness to this revelation.

The Word of God takes several forms for Barth. *Christ* is the primary and personal form; God is revealed in and through the person of Christ. The *Bible* is the secondary form of God's revelation in that it is a verbal witness to Christ. The Bible is God's Word in the sense that he speaks through it. It is a sacrament which gives us indirect access to God. We do not know the Bible is God's Word by any objective evidence. It is a self-attesting truth. We can no more stand outside God's revelation than we can get outside our own experience. We must put the Bible to the test and allow it to speak to us.[18]

Our knowledge of God is not univocal; this kind of knowledge is possible in mathematics and chemistry but not in theology. On the other hand, neither is our knowledge of God through the Word of God purely equivocal, since we do know God indirectly through his self-revelation. The only remaining alternative is an analogous knowl-

---

15. Karl Barth, *The Epistle to the Romans,* trans. from the 6th ed. by Edwyn C. Hoskyns (London: Oxford University Press, 1933 [first German edition published 1918]).
16. Barth, *Anselm.*
17. Barth, *Church Dogmatics.*
18. Barth, *Church Dogmatics.*

edge of God.[19] This analogy is not of course the thomistic analogy of being which Barth rejects because it makes God in man's image, thereby attaining God through human efforts. Rather, it is an analogy of faith which is mediated through the Bible and given by God's grace.

*Barth's "No" to Natural Theology.* Despite Barth's repudiation and modification of his earlier and more extreme Kierkegaardian existentialism, he remained strongly fideistic in his apologetic. There is a general or natural revelation but nothing can be built on it.[20] In fact, Barth reserves some of his strongest words for an attack on natural theology. For to him "natural theology does not even exist as an entity capable . . . not even for the sake of being rejected. If one occupies himself with real theology one can pass by so called natural theology only as one would pass by an abyss into which he is to step if one does not want to fall."[21]

Barth's attitude to natural theology is summarized in the one-word title of his book to Emil Brunner, *Nein (No).* Not only is natural theology impossible but there is not even in man an active capacity to receive God's revelation. To attribute to man the ability to receive God's revelation is a denial of sovereign grace and is inconsistent with the effects of sin on man's mind. Man has a responsibility before God's revelation but certainly no natural capacity for receiving it. And to assert, as Brunner does, a "general grace" is not to take seriously the Reformation principle of *Sola Scriptura* and to ally oneself with the Roman Catholics.[22]

Even Brunner's distinction between the material image of God in man (which is completely fallen) and the formal image or capacity to know God which remains intact is completely rejected by Barth. The image of God in man is completely destroyed by sin. There is not even a *reparatio* or capacity for repair. "The concept of a 'capacity' of man for God has therefore to be dropped. If, nevertheless, there is an encounter and communion between God and man," continues Barth, "then God himself must have created for it conditions which are not the least supplied (not even 'somehow' not even 'to some extent!') by the existence of the formal factor."[23] It is the Holy Spirit who miraculously creates the "contact point" with man.

Barth sets forth his view most positively in his response to Brunner's contention that Calvin admitted the validity of a general or

19. Barth, *Church Dogmatics.*
20. Barth, *Nein.*
21. Barth, *Nein,* p. 75.
22. Barth, *Nein,* pp. 79-85.
23. Barth, *Nein,* p. 89.

natural revelation. First, Barth contends that Calvin did not accept any second or "double" knowledge of God for fallen man besides or in addition to the Scriptures. Second, Calvin admitted only the possibility in principle—not in fact—of a knowledge of God via creation. That is, there is a subjective or hypothetical possibility but not an objective or actual possibility of knowing God by natural reason. Third, man's "capacity" is for idolatry but not for the true deity. Rather than a "contact" point it is a "repulsion" of God. Fourth, Calvin always used the principle of possible knowledge of God only to demonstrate man's responsibility. "The fact that God is revealed in all his works is God's scriptural testimony to us against the ignorance of man. . . . It points out that man's inability to know him is his guilt."[24] Finally, for Calvin, true knowledge of God in Christ includes a real knowledge of the true God in creation. But it does not, says Barth, bring forth a second relatively independent knowledge of God through nature.

## The Revelational Fideism of Cornelius Van Til

Fideism is not limited to nonevangelicals. Cornelius Van Til speaks from a strong Reformed, Biblical perspective theologically and yet in an absolute revelational presuppositionalism apologetically. As we shall see, this position may be viewed as methodological fideism.[25]

*The Absolute Presuppositional Starting Point.* Van Til admits, "I start more frankly from the Bible as the source from which as an absolute authoritative revelation I take my whole interpretation of life." Furthermore, he writes, "I take what the Bible says about God and his relation to the universe as unquestionably true on its own authority." If this should appear to beg the whole question, we must remember that Van Til confessed that "to admit one's own presuppositions and to point out the presuppositions of others is therefore to maintain that all reasoning is, in the nature of the case, *circular reasoning.*" For, he continues, "the starting point, the method, and the conclusions are always involved in one another."[26] Presuppositions cannot be avoided; non-Christians have them as well as Christians, but they are diametrically opposed. "But the Christian, as did Tertullian, must contest the very principles of his opponent's position. The only 'proof' of the Christian position is that unless its truth is presupposed there is no possibility of 'proving' anything at all."[27]

*All Facts Are Theistic and Christian.* Apart from the Christian

---

24. Barth, *Nein*, p. 108.
25. Van Til's apologetic may be viewed as a transcendental argument. See the chapter by Knudsen in *Jerusalem and Athens,* ed. E. R. Geehan.
26. Van Til, *Defense of the Faith,* p. 118.
27. Van Til, "My Credo," C, 5, in *Jerusalem and Athens,* p. 258.

world view nothing really makes sense. For "without the presupposition of the God of Christianity we cannot even interpret one fact correctly. Facts without God would be brute facts. They would have no intelligible relation to one another." Later he adds, "We maintain that there can be no facts but Christian-theistic facts. We ... find again and again that if we seek to interpret any fact on a non-Christian hypothesis it turns out to be a brute fact, and brute facts are unintelligible." The reason for this is that no fact stands alone. "We maintain," writes Van Til, "that unless God has caused the existence of the universe, there would be no possibility of scientific thought. Facts would be utterly unrelated."[28] Non-Christian scientists do, however, discover truths because they "are never able and therefore never do employ their own methods consistently."[29] They cannot avoid God's truth entirely because they live in God's world.

*There Is No Really Common Ground with Non-Christians.* The only "common ground" with unbelievers is that they too are creatures in God's image and live in God's world. But there are no common notions or methods; non-Christians approach the world differently from Christians and they view it differently.[30] We have a common world with unbelievers but no common world view. The contact point with unbelievers is the *imago Dei.* But even here the "point of contact" is the "point of conflict." For "if there is no head-on collision with the systems of the natural man there will be no point of contact with the sense of deity in the natural man."[31] Conflict is inevitable because of human depravity and sin.

*The Effects of Sin on Human Reason.* Unbelievers not only *ought* to know there is a God but they *do* know it. There are "no atheistic men because no man can deny the revelational activity of the true God within him."[32] However, despite the fact unbelievers cannot deny God, they repress the knowledge of God. It is for this reason that no methods are really neutral. Depraved, sinful man is always in autonomous control over the methods he uses. Even the basic laws of logic cannot be used apart from God's revelation to discover truth. For "neither can [we], as finite beings, by means of *logic* as such, say what reality *must* be or *cannot* be." For in this case "man must be autonomous, 'logic' must be legislative as to the field of 'possibility' and possibility must be above God." This is why all traditional apologetics

28. Van Til, *Defense,* pp. 11, 69, 86.
29. Van Til, *Defense,* p. 120.
30. Van Til, "My Credo."
31. Van Til, *Defense,* p. 116.
32. Van Til, *Common Grace,* p. 55.

are doomed to failure, for to argue from facts to God is impossible and "on any but the Christian theistic basis there is no possible connection of logic with the facts at all."[33] By the nature of the case, then, all theistic arguments for God's existence must fail.

*The Role of Rational and Historical Evidence in Van Til's Apologetics.* Does the inability of autonomous human reason to arrive at God by "facts" and "logic" mean that Van Til has no use for reason and evidence? By no means! Historical apologetics are wrong if used to prove the existence of God or the truth of Christianity. For apart from presupposing these truths, historical "facts (such as the resurrection) make absolutely no sense at all. Nevertheless," writes Van Til, "I would engage in historical apologetics. . . . But I would not talk endlessly about facts and more facts without ever challenging the non-believer's philosophy of fact. A really fruitful approach," he adds, "argues that every fact *is* and *must be* such as proves the truth of the Christian theistic position."[34] In short, once one presupposes the truth of Christian theism then and then alone do history and historical facts (such as the resurrection) make sense.

Likewise, rational and theistic apologetics have a valid place within the framework of one's absolute presupposition of the ontological Trinity of the Bible. Indeed, Van Til believes that we must presuppose the absolute certainty of God's existence vis-à-vis the mere probable force theists give to their arguments. So there is in this sense an "absolute certain proof for the existence of God and the truth of Christian theism. Therefore," writes Van Til, "I do not reject 'the theistic proofs' but merely insist on formulating them in such a way as not to compromise the doctrines of Scripture."[35] Of course therein is the fideistic hitch in his whole approach, for it would appear that the Bible is *assumed* to be true by an act of faith in its self-vindicating authority in an admittedly circular reasoning process. If that is the case, the "proofs" of God and historical "facts" of Christianity would have absolutely no meaning or validity outside the fideistic acceptance of the presupposition that Christianity is true.

## Summary of Some Central Fideistic Premises

A number of tenets are generally common to fideism in relation to Christian apologetics. The emphasis varies from one writer to another, but the central contentions are very similar. Fideists characteristically claim or stress that:

1. Faith alone is the way to God. There is little disagreement among

33. Van Til, *Defense*, pp. 264-65.
34. Van Til, *Defense*, pp. 263, 258.
35. Van Til, *Defense*, pp. 120, 256.

fideists on this point; the only way to the truth about God is through faith. God cannot be attained by human reason. Indeed, human reason often hinders, if not obscures, the knowledge of God.

2. Truth is not found in the purely rational or objective realm, if it is there at all. Certainly religious truth does not have an objective basis or character. Truth is subjective and personal, not objective or propositional.

3. Evidence and reason do not point definitively in the direction of God. On the contrary, one is left by reason in a state of equipollence or even paradox. And certainly there are no valid proofs for the existence of God.

4. The tests for truth are existential, not rational. Truth is tested personally in one's life by submitting to God, and so forth, but not by human reason. Even such a time-honored principle as that of non-contradiction, if used as a positive test for religious truth, is a rationalistic hangover. Some fideists would even reject noncontradiction as a negative test for truth, namely, as a guide to what is false.

5. Not only God's revelation but his grace is the source of all truth. Truth comes from the top down. If man could know God by natural reason, God's grace would be negated and human works would be established as a means of knowing God.

## An Evaluation of Fideism

Like other positions, fideism is not devoid of significant contributions to our understanding of Christian truth and life. But as a methodology for establishing the truth of a theistic or Christian world view, fideism is completely inadequate. First, let us outline some of the positive features.

### The Positive Contributions of Fideism

1. The antirationalistic emphasis of fideism has significant value. Man can neither rationally comprehend nor logically demonstrate the existence of the transcendent God of Christian theism. God is beyond reason's futile attempt to grasp him completely and with logical necessity. Especially is this true of the geometric and deductive rationalisms of Descartes, Spinoza, and Leibniz. The mathematical model is insufficient; God is more than the Great Mathematician. God's nature cannot be understood in purely mathematical terms nor can his existence be demonstrated with mathematical certainty.

2. Further, fideists are right that neither evidence nor reason is the basis for one's commitment to God. A believer does not love God *because of* the objective evidence any more than a husband loves his wife *on the grounds* that he possesses objective evidence about her nature

and existence. One's faith in God is based on who God is and not on the alleged evidence about his nature and existence. The basis for belief in God must be God himself. To deny this is to replace God with evidence about God. It is to replace God as the object of one's faith with human reasoning about God. This leads to a related point.

3. Objective evidence alone does not induce a religious response. Apologetics as such does not and cannot produce faith in Christianity. Whatever preliminary, instrumental or confirmatory role Christian evidence may have, only the response of the believer to the work of the Holy Spirit can result in a personal appropriation of Christ. Rational arguments cannot coerce faith in God, and historical evidence cannot produce a commitment to Christ. Faith operates in the subjective and personal dimension that goes beyond purely rational processes. Objective evidence at best is only a tool through which God can operate, but faith is never the product of historical facts alone.

4. Another contribution of fideism is the understanding that faith is more than intellectual, it is volitional. Fideism has rightly stressed that faith in God is not mere intellectual assent; it is a heart commitment. Faith is more than rational, it is volitional. When one believes *in* God, it involves a commitment of his whole person and not merely an acknowledgment of the truth of certain statements *about* God. The mind can know something is objective without the will responding positively or the heart trusting in it.

5. In addition, the fideistic stress on the personal dimension of truth is an important contribution to our understanding. For religious truth is ultimately truth about a Person (God); it is truth that must be appropriated by a person (the believer) in a personal way, namely, by a personal commitment. Whatever propositions about God one can utter and however accurately they may depict God, there are no substitutes for God himself. In the final analysis religious propositions are about a Person. The subject and object of religious statements are personal; religious truth is deeply personal in nature. In short, fideism is a welcomed corrective to the abstract and deadening influences of religious rationalism.

6. An overlooked contribution of Van Til's view is his insistence that no scientific or historical "facts" make any sense outside of a metaphysical framework. Non-Christians too have stressed this point.[36] All facts are "interprafacts." Without an overall context and relationship there is no structure for meaning and truth. Even the resurrection of Christ makes no sense in a naturalistic world view; it is simply an

36. See Paul Feyerabend, ed., *Mind, Matter, And Method:* University of Minnesota Press, 1966.

unusual event at best in anything but a theistic universe. Unless there is a God, miracles are not even possible. Hence, one can never use a miracle as such to prove God's existence, since the very fact of a miracle (as an act of God) presupposes that God already exists. How can one know there is an act of God unless there is already presupposed a God who can act? The same events and "facts" do have different meanings within different world views. Van Til is correct: there is no Christian truth unless this is a theistic world.

7.  Another emphasis that should be acknowledged by evangelical Christians is the insistence by the above fideists that man's sinful condition affects his response to God. Men ought to love and serve the true God but they do not, and their choice does indeed influence their whole way of thinking about reality. In actual practice, the non-Christian operates on different presuppositions and comes to different conclusions. His basic "faith" or beliefs are different since he refuses to obey God. Nonbelievers cannot avoid having presuppositions about the world; there must be something to think *with* in order for one to think *about* the world. Some framework is necessary if one is to have thoughts about reality, even for those who allegedly refuse to think about it. In short, world views are unavoidable, and different world views are based on differing presuppositions. And man's sinfulness does indeed influence the world view he formulates.

## A Critique of the Fideistic Test for Truth

In spite of the many important insights fideists offer into the nature of religious truth, their method and test for truth are decidedly inadequate. There are several reasons this is so.

1.  First of all, fideists confuse epistemology and ontology. That is, they fail to distinguish the order of *knowing* and the order of *being*. The Christian fideist may very well be right about the *fact* that there is a God, but this begs the question unless he can tell *how* he knows this is the case. God may indeed have revealed himself to us through the Bible, but how do we know that the Bible is the Word of God? Other books with contrary teachings also claim to be the Word of God (e.g., the Koran). Assuming the truth of Christianity, a Christian fideist is right in *what* he believes about God but wrong in the *reason* for that belief. Certainly if there is a God and all truth comes from him, it follows that even the very criteria of determining truth from error will be God-given. But God is what is to be proven, and we cannot begin by assuming his existence as a fact. If we do not have any tests for truth with which we can begin, we can never make truth claims nor can we even know something is true. We can simply believe without justification what we want to believe. But in this case so can any idiotic,

insane, or contrary view be simply believed. And how is one to say who if anyone has the truth? Without an epistemological way of knowing the truth, no ontological truth claims can be pressed.

2. Fideism also fails to clearly distinguish belief *in* and belief *that* there is a God. The fideist shares some important insights on belief *in* God. Such a belief must be personal and existential and not purely abstract and intellectual. On the other hand, is it possible to have an intelligible or credible belief *in* God unless one has some way first to believe *that* there is a God? Can one, for example, place his trust *in* his wife unless he first has some warrant for believing *that* she is his wife? Would it not be the greatest folly at day's end to rush into the arms of the waiting wife at the front door if that is the wrong door and another's wife? One must have some evidence *that* he is taking the right path and embracing the true object of his love before he makes the existential commitment. Likewise, before one makes a leap of faith *in* God he must have some reason to believe *that* it is the true God to which he is committed. Another overlooked distinction follows from this.

3. Fideists do not differentiate clearly the difference between the *basis* of belief in God and the support or *warrant* for that belief. This distinction has been clearly drawn by some major theists. Thomas Aquinas, for example, held that faith rests solely on the testimony and authority of God. Evidence may be used to support, confirm, or even accompany this belief; but it must never be the basis for believing.[37] The fideists properly stress the basis for belief, namely, God or his revelation; but they seem to neglect entirely the warrant or support for exercising this belief. In short, evidence bears directly on belief *that* there is a God but not directly on belief *in* God. "Belief *that*" is an intellectual matter and there are rational arguments for it. But "belief *in*" is an existential concern that has no such objective tests for truth. Fideism is right on the latter but almost completely overlooks the need for criteria or test for the truth that there is a God, or that the Bible is the Word of God, and so on.

4. In line with the foregoing criticism, fideism often neglects and sometimes virtually negates the need for the propositional in its zeal to stress the personal. There is no reason, in contrast to Kierkegaard and Barth, that God's revelation cannot be *both* personal and propositional. The Bible claims to be a propositional revelation, that is, a revelation in and through words.[38] Indeed, it is difficult to understand any meaningful sense of the words *know* or *understand* as applied to the person

---

37. Thomas Aquinas, *On Truth*, XIV, 8 and XIV, 1, ad 2. Cf. *Summa Theologica*, II-II, 2, 10.
38. See my *From God to Us*, chap. 2.

of God unless they have some cognitive content that is expressible in words or propositions. Surely the object of religious faith is a Person (God), but there is no way to rule out of hand that propositions can be uttered about that person.[39] Revelations do not have to be impersonal just because they are written, as anyone can testify who has carried on a romance by mail! As a matter of fact, the complete fideistic attempt to deny that God is verbally expressible entails necessarily some verbal expressions about God. As such, fideism—like agnosticism and rationalism before it—is self-defeating.

5. Fideists fail to understand the implications of the difference between the unavoidability of and the justifiability of presuppositions. We may grant that presuppositions are unavoidable; men cannot think without epistemological and even ontological assumptions. However, the crucial question is not whether we can *avoid* using presuppositions but whether we can *justify* those we use. There are all kinds of differing presuppositions available. We may presuppose that this is a naturalistic world, or a pantheistic one, or a theistic one, and so on. But which presupposition should be chosen and with what warrant? In one sense all men are fideists—that is, all have basic things they believe about reality which they have no purely factual nor demonstrably rational grounds for holding. However, the important questions about these differing beliefs are these: Are they arguable? Is there any way to adjudicate their conflicting truth claims? Can some beliefs be eliminated as false and others be established as true? If so, by what method or test for truth? Fideists do not face these questions squarely; or if they do, they tend to provide nonfideistic answers, such as to believe otherwise is contrary to one's experience, to reason, to his hope for the future, or it brings undesired results. But to answer this way is to return to rationalism or to move on to experientialism or pragmatism as tests for truth. This is no longer methodological fideism.

6. Fideism faces a final dilemma. Either it makes a truth-claim or it does not. If fideism is not making a claim to be true, then it is not a position in philosophy but simply a study in psychology. For where there is no truth claim, one has not entered the arena of truth. On the other hand, if fideism makes a truth-claim then it must have a truth-test. For not all truth claims can be true, at least not contrary ones. And if one is to be able to sort out the true from the false, there must be a test for truth. Hence, either a fideist offers a justification for his belief or else he does not. If he does not, then as an unjustified belief it has no rightful claim to knowledge (since human knowledge is justified belief). On the other hand, if the fideist offers a justifica-

---

39. See my *Christ, The Key to Interpreting the Bible,* chap. 6.

tion for his belief—as indeed the whole argument for fideism would seem to be—then he is no longer a fideist, since he has an argument or justification for holding his belief in fideism. In short, either fideism is not a rightful claimant to truth or else it is self-defeating. But in neither case can it be established to be true.

## Summary and Conclusion

There are many significant insights provided by fideism into the total picture of religious knowing, such as the stress on the personal, subjective, and existential dimensions of religious truth and life. However, as a test for truth of a world view (such as Christian theism), fideism is entirely inadequate because it really offers no test. Contrary beliefs can be "experienced" or claimed to be true by fideists. But unless there is some rational or objective way to adjudicate these conflicting claims, the truth question cannot be settled. At the bare minimum, fideists must allow the principle of noncontradiction to be a negative test for truth; else there would be no way to distinguish the true from the false. As has already been shown (in Chapter One), there is no way to deny the validity of the law of noncontradiction without employing it in the very denial. This too is a self-destructive movement in total fideism. Fideists must either justify their beliefs (which destroys fideism) or else it disqualifies its claim to truth.

## SELECT READINGS FOR CHAPTER THREE

**Exposition of Fideism**

Barth, Karl. *Nein.*
————. *Church Dogmatics,* vol. I.
Kierkegaard, Sören. *Fear and Trembling.*
————. *Philosophical Fragments.*
Pascal, Blaise. *Pensées.*

**Evaluation of Fideism**

Bartley, William. *Retreat to Commitment.*
Collins, James. *God in Modern Philosophy,* chap. X.
Diamond, Malcolm. *The Logic of God.*
Geehan, E. R., ed., *Jerusalem and Athens.*
Sauvage, G. M. "Fideism" in *Catholic Encyclopedia,* vol. V (1909).

# Chapter

# 4 | *Experientialism*

As was observed in the previous chapter, fideism often involves an implicit appeal to experience as the test for the truth of its belief. Pascal appealed to the heart's experience of God, and Kierkegaard and Barth to a personal encounter with God through Christ. Both psychologically and logically fideism reduces to experientialism. But technically speaking the difference between fideism and experientialism is that the former neither claims nor offers any test for truth, whereas experientialism offers experience as the final court of appeal. The experience may be special or general, private or available generally, but it is the self-attesting character of experience which verifies the truth-attached claim.

The experiential "proof" for religious beliefs is characteristic of both Christian mysticism and pietism. It is offered with both intellectual sophistication and held with everyday naiveté. The purpose of this chapter will be to show that, despite its essential contributions to religion, experientialism is an inadequate test for the truth of Christian belief.

## An Exposition of Some Major Forms of Experientialism

Not every experientially based religious position uses experience as a test for truth. There is an important difference between the *source* of one's beliefs and the *warrant* for holding them. Some of the following positions tend to use experience for both; others have primarily a grounding in experience. Both types are included because of the appeal of experientialism to what is sometimes used only as a source for truth in one view but offered as a warrant for truth in another view.

## Plotinus: Mystical Experience as the Test for Religious Truth

It can be accurately claimed that Western philosophy is a series of footnotes on Plotinus. His influence extends far beyond those who recognize it. It is not only Christian mysticism but hegelianism, existentialism, and pragmatism that find roots in Plotinus. His description of the ultimate, ineffable, intuitive experience of God has formed most of Western mystical thought and bears a parallel resemblance to Eastern mysticism.

*A Brief Sketch of Plotinian Pantheistic Mysticism.* In Plotinus (d. A.D. 270.) platonism flowers into neo-platonism and the rational comes to fruition in the mystical. The Greeks' quest for being ends in the One beyond all being, and knowledge is fulfilled in noncognitive intuition. For the rational quest for unity leads to the One beyond rational duality. The ultimate experience is an indescribable experience of the ineffable Source of all being which is experienced only by mystical union.

"God" for Plotinus is the One beyond all knowing and being. God has neither knowledge, being, nor personality; God consists only of absolute unity. But this unity unfolds into Mind *(Nous)* as necessarily as a flower from its seed, and this Mind unfolds into Soul other minds and souls (VI, 8, 9 and V, 1, 8).[1] There is a whole hierarchy of beings from best (Mind) to least, which is Matter (II, 4, 11). The more being something has, the greater is its unity right on up to Mind, which is a basic unity of knower and known. The only absolute unity with no duality of even knower and known is the unknown and the Unknower (the One). The less being things have, the less their unity until we reach at last the most multiple of all, Matter. Matter is the point at which if being became more multiple it would become absolute non-being (II, 4, 12). Indeed Matter is relative non-being, for it is the mere capacity for being with no being of its own. In like manner, the more unity something has, the greater good it is. And the less unity, the more evil a thing is. Hence, Nous is the best and Matter is the worst of all things (I, 8, 7). The One is the Source of all good and being but It has neither Itself. For "he had no need of being, who brought it to be" (VI, 8, 19). Likewise, what need for good is there in the Source of all good? And surely there is no duality in the Source of all duality, any more than there is multiplicity in the center from which the many radii emerge.

God transcends not only all good and all being but also all knowing.

---

1. Unless otherwise noted, quotations are from Plotinus' *Enneads,* MacKenna translation.

For only being can be known; the mind cannot know what is not (V, 6, 6). How then can one even speak of "God" or the "One" if It is entirely beyond intelligibility? And how can he experience God if he does not even know he is having the experience? The answer to the first question is that we name God only negatively and from the emanations of God. Even the "name, The One, contains really no more than the negation of plurality," and "if we are led to think positively of The One, name and thing, there would be more truth in silence" (V, 5, 6). For "The One is in truth beyond all statement" (V, 3, 13). The statements we do make about It are simply about things that come from It. God causes goodness, being, and knowledge. Hence we call God Good and Being, but It does not have either goodness, being, or knowledge. That is "The One is all things and no one of them; the source of all things is not all things; and yet it is all things in a transcendent sense" (V, 2, 1). In reality, "it eludes our knowledge, so that the nearer approach to it is through its offspring" (VI, 9, 5). In short, although we cannot speak *It,* we are able to speak *about* It in terms of what comes *from* It (V, 3, 14). In and of Itself the One is absolutely unknowable and unspeakable. And "if we nevertheless speak of it and write about it, we do so only to give direction, to stimulate toward that vision beyond discourse" (VI, 9, 4). In short, all such language is essentially negative, that is, of what God is not. Any positive ascriptions are at best pointers or indicators without descriptive content and are based on what God produces but does not possess (VI, 7, 15).

*God Is Experienced Only by Mystical Intuition or Union.* If God cannot be described, how can one even know that he is experiencing God? The answer for Plotinus involves rejecting the question. God cannot be *known* for he is literally the Unknowable; God can only be *felt* or intuited by mystical union. Of course, man bound by his sense and body to material multiplicity is a long way from home. He is "busy about many things" (I, 3, 4). Seeing that our soul is "befouled by its housing, made fragmentary by corporeal extension," Plotinus urges man to turn inward and upward to the true Source of all unity. "Let us flee then to the beloved Fatherland," he wrote (I, 6, 8). This is accomplished by asceticism (purification from the multiple things of the sense world) (I, 3, 6). The first unity realized as one moves from the external to the internal, from the sensible to the intellectual is unity with the *Nous.* Our mind merges with Mind; our thoughts find their ultimate basis in Thought (V, 3, 4). Mind, however, involves a basic duality of knower and known; hence, ultimate unity must move on to yet loftier heights.

Since "the Supreme is not known intellectually" (VI, 7, 35), one desiring to experience "what transcends the Intellectual attains by putting away all that is of the intellect" (V, 5, 6). For awareness of the One "comes to us neither by science nor by pure thought . . . but by a presence which is superior to science. . . . We must therefore arise above science [philosophy] and never withdraw from unity" (VI, 9, 4, Katz trans.). In order to know the Supreme, one must be "merged with the Supreme, sunken into it, one with it: centre coincides with centre" (VI, 9, 10). Just as one must "become godlike and each [one] beautiful who cares to see God and Beauty," so he must become one with the One if he is to experience the One (I, 6, 9). The mind puts away all multiplicity, including that involved in thought, so that "alone it may receive the Alone" (VI, 7, 34). In this exalted mystical union "no longer is there thing seen and light to show it . . . ; this is the very radiance that brought both Intellect and Intellectual object into being . . ." (VI, 7, 36). In point of fact, "only by a leap [from the intellectual] can we reach to this One which is to be pure of all else . . ." (V, 5, 4). And the man who experiences this mystical union does so by "coalescence, unification; but in seeking thus to know the Unity it is prevented by that very unification from recognizing that it has found." For once the union is attained "it cannot distinguish itself from the object of this intuition" (VI, 9, 3).

*The Self-Attesting Nature of the Mystical Experience.* This ineffable experience of God cannot be compelled but simply prepared for. "We must not run after it, but fit ourselves for the vision and then wait tranquilly for its appearance, as the eye waits on the rising of the sun, which in its own time appears above the horizon . . ." (V, 5, 8). But "if one does not succeed in enjoying this spectacle, . . . if one does not rise in a purified state but retains within oneself something that separates one from the One, if one is not yet unified enough . . . , one has no one to blame but oneself and should try to become pure by detaching oneself from everything" (VI, 9, 4, Katz trans.). In short, the experience is both unknowable and inexpressible. It is a self-attesting awareness of the Transcendent in which one is absolutely alone with the Alone, one with the One. The experience is its own "proof." There is neither reason nor evidence applicable to it. Either one has had it or he has not. Those who have, need no other "proof"; and those who have not will never be so convinced until they have experienced it themselves (VI, 7, 34 and VI, 9, 4).

## Schleiermacher's Experience of Absolute Dependence

Unlike Plotinus, Friedrich Schleiermacher (1768-1834) built religion on a general experience rather than a special mystical experience. The feeling of absolute dependence was for Schleiermacher something possessed by all men, even by those who did not identify it with religion. Although Schleiermacher did not test the truth of religious statements or expressions simply on the religious experience behind them, his analysis of religious experience is classic. As such Schleiermacher's grounding of religion in experience is the groundwork for much later pietistic appeal to the experience itself as "proof" of the truth of religion.

*Experience Is the Basis of All Religion.* According to Schleiermacher, men reject religion as a general idea arbitrarily conceived, but to do so is to look only at the shell and reject the kernel. In view of this, Schleiermacher exhorts his contemporaries to "turn from everything usually reckoned religion, and fix your regard on the inward emotions and dispositions. . . ."[2] Dogma is only the echo of religion; true religion is an immediate feeling of the Infinite and Eternal. And since religion is an inner sense of the Absolute, we cannot understand it by an examination of the outward manifestations of religion but only by a study of ourselves. The contrast between inner state and outward statements of religion will help focus his meaning. True religion is related to doctrine the way the original sound is related to an echo. Religion is based in experience and creeds are only expressions of that experience. One is the feeling and the other a form; religious experience is the "stuff" and religious language and ritual the structure of religion. The experience of God is the primary reality and religious thought is but a later reflection on that reality.[3]

Another contrast is helpful in understanding Schleiermacher's concept of religious experience. Ethics is a way of *living,* science is a way of *thinking,* but religion is a way of *feeling.* It is not just any way of feeling but it is the feeling of being utterly dependent on the All. Again, ethics is a way of *acting,* science is a way of *knowing,* whereas religion is a way of *being or sensing* one's dependence. Religion does not influence specific ethical actions. However, it does influence the way a man behaves in the sense that a sum total of actions flows from the inner unity religion brings to one's life. So "while a man does nothing from religion, he should do everything with religion."[4] In like manner religion influences science not directly but indirectly, for piety removes the presumption to knowledge which is ignorance. Finally, the ethical life is one of *self-control* but the religious life is one of *self-surrender.* Thus ethics operates in the *practical* realm, science in the *intellectual,* but religion in the *intuitional* realm.

---

2. Friedrich Schleiermacher, *On Religion: Speeches to Its Cultural Despisers,* trans. John Oman (New York: Harper Torchbooks, 1958 [first published 1799]), p. 18.
3. Schleiermacher, pp. 1-18.
4. Schleiermacher, p. 59.

*The Nature of Religious Intuition.* According to Schleiermacher, the way to understand religion is by an examination of the intuition at the very root of it. For once we begin even to think about this intuition we are already separated from it. The moment of religious experience is so fleeting that it perishes the very moment it appears. Religion can be experienced but not expressed as such.

The essence of religion is a feeling of piety that results from the operation of God on the soul by means of the world. This feeling is universal, but the ideas by which men express this feeling are foreign to the religious experience itself. For no description is equal to the intuition being described. This is why religion cannot be learned by rote. The religious feeling cannot be taught; it must be caught. Schleiermacher is careful to point out, however, that "what we feel and are conscious of in religious emotion is not the nature of things, but their operation on us." Religious feeling does not reach reality or things-in-themselves (Kant's noumenal realm). We sense only the ceaseless operations of the multitudinous forms of the infinite upon us. And religion does not consist in submitting to any one of the endless variety of these forms individually or in isolation but only to the Whole of which they are part. "The sum total of religion is to feel that in the highest unity, all that moves us is one; to feel that aught single and particular is only possible by means of this unity; to feel, that is to say, that our being and living is a being and living in and through God."[5] However, the religious feeling is not to be confused with the feeling of the majesty and greatness of the material boundlessness of the universe. The latter is only an "arithmetic amazement" that is both finite and calculable. Such is only a feeling of personal incapacity; it is a religious feeling in kind but not in extent. On the other hand, neither is mysticism the essence of religious intuition. All truly religious people have mystical traits, but the mystic is turned inward and does not know how to go beyond this.

Schleiermacher summarizes the nature of religious life as follows: "The whole religious life consists of two elements, that man surrender himself to the Universe and allow himself to be influenced by the side that is turned toward him in one part," and second "that he transplant this contact which is one definite feeling, within, and take it up into the inner unity of his life and being. . . . The religious life is nothing else than the constant renewal of this proceeding."[6]

*Commonality and Universality of Religious Intuition.* The basic religious experience is the same for all men but religious systems fashion

---

5. Schleiermacher, pp. 49-50.
6. Schleiermacher, p. 58.

themselves in endless variety even down to individual personalities. This multiplicity is necessary for the complete manifestation of religion; there is no universal religion common to all any more than there is only one way to be related to God. However, nothing is possible for the individual except through the unity of the Whole. Further, since religion is not constituted by ideas, the concepts of true and false do not apply to it. All religions are "good" and "true" in an infinite variety of forms. We need not attempt to bring all these feelings and beliefs together. Rather, it is sufficient to open up an experience of the original Unity of all things for those who have not had it. In this respect religion is the capacity for many-sidedness not found elsewhere. Science, morality, and philosophy are limited and narrow; but religion is the sworn enemy of narrow-mindedness and one-sidedness.[7]

The aim of religion is the love of the World-Spirit, and this World-Spirit is received through the love of humanity. This longing love is the essence of religion. So in order to discover the best in religion we must enter what we love the most. Humanity must be sought in each individual for each is a revelation of the Infinite. But each must be contemplated as part of the Whole, for in the face of the Whole each individual ego must vanish in humility. We have an intuition of the Whole only in fellowship with others who have been freed from dependence on their own being by dependence on the All. Yet since each man is a compendium of humanity, he can love himself with a pure and blameless love as one in whom he has discovered the Infinite.[8]

The religious intuition is not different in kind from other feelings. Rather, it is the sum of all higher feelings. It is a feeling not found easily in nature but more easily found in ourselves and transferred to nature. The universe reveals itself in our inner life and in this way the corporeal is comprehensible through the spiritual. This inner feeling of the universe makes us whole and unified. Dogmas are formed as a result of reflecting on this feeling but they are merely general expressions of definite feelings. Dogmas are not necessary for religious life and aid little in the communication of it. In order to be religious one need only be conscious of this feeling—not just any feeling but a feeling wherein one's whole being is related to the Whole. God is essential to religion via his presence in our feeling of dependence. But this is not to be confused with the idea of God which is merely a reflection on this feeling. Depending on one's personal needs, there is a tendency to conceptualize God in one way or another. Those who are content with mysterious obscurity tend to think of God pantheistically; those

---

7. Schleiermacher, pp. 53-56.
8. Schleiermacher, pp. 65-74.

who seek definiteness in thought generally view God theistically. Both are based on the same basic religious intuition, which is the important thing. Irreligion is not to have God in the consciousness; it does not consist in whether one views God personally or impersonally. Hence, theism is not the beginning or end of religion nor is personal immortality necessarily involved. "Immortality" should be understood experientially, namely, in the sense of enjoying life by giving up to the Infinite. It is a pious longing to be one with the Infinite and Eternal in the midst of our finitude and temporality.[9]

Every man has an inborn capacity for religion which infallibly develops unless it is crushed by culture. The World-Spirit is revealed to every man at least once. Certain points in life like birth and death provide openings to the Infinite and are surrounded by It. However, the Infinite may be discovered from all levels of consciousness: from the ego (as in Eastern mysticism), from the outer world (as in Egyptian polytheism), or from our sense of art (as in the Greeks). Again, the important thing is not the direction of approach so much as it is the basic intuition of the Divine or awareness of the All one experiences through it. "Have you not often felt this holy longing?" asked Schleiermacher. "Become conscious of the call of your deepest nature and follow it, I conjure you."[10]

To summarize, there is at the level of consciousness a sense of being related to the Whole, an awareness of one's identity with the All. The individual stands utterly dependent on "God" for his existence; it is a felt relation of absolute dependence. No thinking or acting on man's part can change the fundamental sense of his own contingency. The core of religion is in the intuition of this deep-seated feeling of finitude. No description of it can replace it nor can rational process produce it. And yet it is an experience natural to all men if culture has not crushed it. Truth and falsity do not apply to this feeling because they are conceptual and it is experiential. The feeling can be verified by its appearance in one's own consciousness. No other "proof" is possible, for it can only be caught but not taught as such.

### Rudolf Otto: The Experience of the Numinous

Rudolf Otto (1869-1937) continued the analysis of religious experience after Schleiermacher. The central difference in their starting points was noted by Otto. Schleiermacher had begun with the feeling of dependence and moved from there to "God." For Otto the "Holy" is taken as the primary datum and a feeling of dependence results from

---

9. Schleiermacher, pp. 87-101.
10. Schleiermacher, p. 92.

this. The latter works from the top down, we may say; and the former works from the bottom up.

*The Characteristics of a Religious Experience.* According to Otto, all religious experience involves an awareness of the "Holy" or the "Numen."[11] A religious experience, then is a numinous experience. The divine as such can be felt but not thought. However, it is essential to religion to have both the mystical and rational aspects. The rational is essential to but not exhaustive of God. The "Holy" is a necessary a priori category for the understanding of the suprarational aspects of religion.

There are five characteristics of a religious experience. Essentially it is an experience of the *mysterium tremendum.* The first three characteristics are associated with its terribleness and the last two with its mysteriousness. First, a religious experience is one of *Awefulness.* It involves a sense of awe or religious dread. Second, there is in a religious experience an awareness of *Overpoweringness,* that is, of the unapproachable majesty of the Divine. Third, there is an awareness of *Energy* or *Urgency,* which is expressed in emotion or force. These three characteristics together comprise the *tremendum.* Fourth, the religious man is conscious of the *Wholly Other.* It is beyond intelligibility and causes blank wonder in the beholder. Fifth, just as the Wholly Other repels, so there is an attractive element in the Holy, namely, that of *Fascination.* This element allures or captivates the religious person.[12]

Otto is convinced that the experience of the Holy is neither derived from nor reducible to other feelings. It differs in kind from other experiences. It may on occasion be excited by other feelings, particularly by an aesthetic experience which is closely associated with the religious; for the sense of the sublime is sometimes closely related to the sense of the Supreme.

*The Schematization of Religious Experience.* The aesthetic may be used to schematize the religious the way nonrational sex instincts surface and are concretized in one's personal feeling. The rational schematization of religious experience is by no means unimportant to Otto. On the contrary, he believed it to be the most important part of salvation history. For by a penetration of the nonrational and the rational, our concepts of God are deepened, not blurred. So the "Holy" is a complex a priori category with both rational and nonrational elements in it. And the connection between them is felt as self-evident. Hence, all men have the form or capacity for religion, just as all men *can*

11. Rudolf Otto, *The Idea of the Holy,* trans. John W. Harvey (London: Oxford University Press, 1967 [first published 1917]), chap. 2.
12. Otto, chaps. 3-6.

sing, even though some do not. The concept of the Holy did not evolve; its first appearance was unique. Its earliest manifestations were crude (e.g., magic, manna) but were elevated when it became manifest in higher feeling and thought. The Holy is occasioned by sensation but springs from the depth of the soul.[13]

The *tremendum* is schematized by the "Wrath of God" and the *mysterium* is schematized by the "Grace of God." This rationalization of the nonrational dimensions of the *Numen* guards against both rationalism and mysticality. Rationalism is ruled out since the source and depth of religion spring from experience of the nonrational. Mysticality is eliminated because schematization or rationalizing the *Numen* is essential to understanding and expressing the religious experience. A balance between the rational and the mystical elements is the measure of the value of a religion. And on this ground Otto concluded that Christianity was the most valuable religion. For Christ was more than a prophet; he was one in whom the Spirit dwelt in all his plenitude (mystical aspect) and yet who was the most perfect object of religious experience (objective, rational aspect).

*The Communication of Religious Feelings.* The Holy not only cannot be thought but it cannot be taught as such, for the rational has no meaning without the inner spirit. The *tremendum* element is communicated best by imaginative sympathy, gestures, attitudes, holy situations, living fellowship, and personal contact. Basically, it must be caught and not taught. Likewise, the *mysterium* is revealed directly via miracles and quasi-intelligible religious language and indirectly by way of the sublime (e.g., in architecture). Darkness summons the mystical, silence calls forth a spontaneous response, and emptiness evokes otherness. But there is no purely cognitive or creedal way to produce a religious experience. All men have the capacity for religious awareness of the Holy, but the experience cannot be evoked by purely rational means. The religious experience stands on its own. It can be expressed but not exhausted. One can sense but not systematize the Holy. He can feel it but never really completely formulate it. Conceptualization of this consciousness is not possible. Schemata can be made of it and rationalization about it, but these are like Kant's categories—they are not truly descriptive of it. They cannot be, for the Holy is and remains Wholly Other. It can be felt but not thought in anything but purely negative concepts. The mystery of the Holy can be experienced but not really expressed.[14]

*God and the Inexpressible.* Many mystics both before and after

---

13. Otto, chap. 7.
14. Otto, chap. 9.

Otto have emphasized the inexpressibility of God. Mystical emphases from Pseudo-Dionysius to Meister Eckhart and on to Thomas à Kempis and modern pietism have stressed the ineffability of God. A more recent statement of this point will suffice. Thomas McPherson wrote: There are some things that just cannot be said. . . . We ought not to try to express the inexpressible. The things that theologians try to say (or some of them) belong to the class of things that just cannot be said. The way out of the worry is retreat into silence."[15]

McPherson claimed a similarity of his view to that of Ludwig Wittgenstein who wrote much the same in the last line of the *Tractatus:* "whereof one cannot speak, thereof one must be silent."[16] Both men believe that God is actually inexpressible because he is mystical. That is to say, "the feeling of the world as a limited whole is the mystical feeling," but then we cannot ask *why* the world is this way. According to Wittgenstein, *"how* the world is" can be meaningfully asked but not the fact *that* the world is. To ask, Why is there a world anyway? is to ask the unaskable question. One can feel his creatureliness or the limitedness of the world, but he cannot ask why it is this way. It is mystical and inexpressible and, therefore, unaskable.

From this analysis McPherson concludes from Wittgenstein that skepticism about religious experience is senseless. For, as the latter put it, "doubt can only exist where there is a question; a question only where there is an answer, and this only where something *can* be *said."* Since God's existence is unsayable, it is likewise undoubtable. From this McPherson suggests we conclude that positivistic philosophy "can be interpreted as a return to the truth about religion." For "Otto travels the same road as Wittgenstein. Are we to call Otto an enemy of religion? Why not call Wittgenstein its friend?" For "by showing, in their own way, the absurdity of what theologians try to utter, positivists have helped to suggest that religion belongs to the sphere of the unutterable. . . . Positivists may be the enemies of theology, but the friends of religion."[17] For both Otto and Wittgenstein, religious experience is inexpressible.

## Summary of Some Important Tenets of Experientialism

Experientialists differ as to the nature of religious experience but there are some common strains of emphasis throughout their stress on

15. Thomas McPherson, "Religion as the Inexpressible" in *New Essays in Philosophical Theology* (London: SCM Press Ltd., 1963), ed. Antony Flew and Alasdair MacIntyre, pp. 132-33.

16. Ludwig Wittgenstein, *Tractatus Logico-Philosophicus* (London, 1922), trans. D. F. Pears and B. F. McGuinness, 1961.

17. McPherson, "Religion as the Inexpressible," pp. 139-41.

experience. Not all of these elements will be true of each particular man discussed above. Together, however, they will aid in characterizing the experiential test for truth.

1. First and foremost there is the experientialist's insistence that the *sine qua non* of all religious truth is religious experience. Truth does not rest in formal abstractions from or about experience; truth is primarily experienced and only secondarily expressed. Without a primary awareness of God no one can claim to have the truth about God.

2. Second, experience is the final court of appeal for religious truth. There is no more ultimate standard for deciding truth than experience. Appeal to ideas, principles, or propositions fails unless they are filled with and based on the "stuff" of experience. One cannot determine the truth of an experience by a statement or expression about it; on the contrary, the validity of any statement is based on the experience behind it.

3. Third, a religious experience is ultimately self-verifying. There is no outside source by which a religious experience can be validated as real or genuine; the experience of God (the Holy, etc.) is self-sufficient. The authenticity of religious experience rests not in any external evidential or rational justification—these are secondary spin-offs at best—but in the very nature of the religious experience as such.

4. Finally, there is often a contention by experientialists that God, or Ultimate Reality, and so forth, is actually indescribable. Words cannot capture religious consciousness; God can be evoked but not really expressed. The Divine is literally inexpressible. God can be felt but not really thought.

## An Evaluation of Experientialism as a Test for Truth

There is an apparent plausibility about experientialism vis-à-vis rationalism that immediately commends itself to many minds. From this we may unpack several positive features of experientialism before attempting to penetrate its methodological inadequacies.

### Some Positive Features of Experientialism

Experientialism stands as a polar opposite to formalism in religion. Propositional and creedal truths are, as such, existentially inept and inadequate. Experience is necessary to religion, and within this context several valuable insights of experientialism emerge.

1. First and most importantly, experience is the "stuff" out of which all religious truth must be built. Without a basic source or root in experience there is no meaningful religious expression. Apart from our consciousness of God there would be no valid conceptualizations about him. For all affirmations about the Divine presuppose some prior

awareness of him. The real content of religion is, and must be, grounded in experience, whatever form the construction of that content may take.

2. A second contribution follows from the former, namely, in the broad sense experience must be the final court of appeal. This follows for a very simple reason: nothing is broader than experience. Even reasoning is an intellectual "experience." There are primary experiences such as consciousness of God and secondary experiences such as one's conceptualizations and cogitations about God. But all is experience— that is, all involves a consciousness or awareness of something or some- one, or at least by someone.

3. Furthermore, primary experience is the ground for secondary experience.[18] That is to say, consciousness of something is more basic than one's concept about it. For affirmation grows out of awareness and expressions grow out of experience—not the reverse. In this sense primary experience of God is the final court of appeal as to the genu- ineness of one's experience of God. Unless God were so experienced, there would be no valid basis for speaking of the reality or truth of that experience.

## Some Crucial Difficulties with Experientialism

Despite the important contributions just mentioned, experientialism as a test for the truth of a world view is decidedly insufficient for several reasons.

1. First, it is a confusion of categories to speak of a *true* experience. Experience in the primary sense is neither true nor false. Experience is something one *has,* and truth is something one *expresses* about ex- perience. That is, experience is a *condition* of persons but truth is a characteristic of *propositions* or expressions persons make. Hence, no experience as such is true; one simply has the experience or the aware- ness. But once one begins to make affirmations about that awareness or experience, then these statements are subject to the test of truth or falsity.

2. Second, an experience cannot be used to support or prove the truth of that experience. For to use experience to prove the truth claimed about that experience is to beg the whole question. At best the only truth established by an experience is the truth that the person has had that experience, and this is private to the individual having that experience. The *basis* of truth rests in the experience but not the *support* of that truth. Truth finds its *source* in primary experience but not its *substantiation.* The *whence* of religious truth is rooted in re-

---

18. For further elaboration of religious experience see my *Philosophy of Religion* (Grand Rapids: Zondervan Publishing House, 1974), chaps. 1-4.

ligious experience but the *warrant* for claiming truth for this is something else.

3. Third, no experience *as such* is self-interpreting. Experiences as such do not come with truth labels on them, at least none that have not been placed there by the meaning-context in which the experience occurred. Even when experiences do come with interpretations, the same experience is capable of different interpretations depending on the overall framework one applies to the experience. The experience of being short-changed at the food market takes on quite a different meaning if it is intentional rather than accidental. Or, to use a Biblical example, the same phenomenon was interpreted three different ways in John 12:28, 29. Some took it as the voice of God, others as an angel speaking, and some as thunder. *That* there was some common phenomenon need not be questioned, but *what* it meant differed in accordance with the overall perspective taken by the perceivers. So the event itself was not self-interpreting; meaning is given to an event by the context in which one sees it. Since a world view is an overall interpretation of *all* facts and experiences, there is no valid way to use any particular experience within that overall interpretive framework to establish the overall framework or world view. Following from this is another criticism.

4. Fourth, experiences are capable of different interpretations. Different systems account for different experiences in different ways. The experience the theist calls "conversion" may be explained by the naturalistic psychologist as a subliminal explosion caused by repression followed by frustration with one's way of life.[19] Likewise the naturalistic scientist may explain the event a Christian calls miraculous healing as an anomaly or unusual natural event for which there is no known explanation. Each major world view is able to account, on its own grounds, for all the data of experience. The pantheist is able to account for evil as a "persistent illusion" or for pain as an "error of moral mind," and so on. He does not need to deny that someone feels or experiences pain, but merely points out that there is no ultimate reality to such sensible experiences. Now if conflicting world views such as theism, pantheism, and naturalism can explain all of the facts and experiences in the world, then no one of these views can have its truth claim justified by experience in face of the others. All the views have a basis in experience and a way of explaining it. And it will not suffice to plead special case for some particular experiences over others since they can all make the same plea. On what basis would one decide which experience is "key" or "special"? There is no way within ex-

19. See William James, *Varieties of Religious Experience* (New York: A Mentor Book, 1958 [first published 1902]), chaps. 9, 10.

perience to mediate this dispute without arguing in a circle, and any appeal outside experience defeats the whole experiential test for truth. But if opposing world views have equal access to experience and no way within primary experience alone to differentiate and distinguish some experiences as "special" or "key," then one is forced to go beyond pure experience to reasoning or interpretation of experience in order to support his truth claims about that experience. But once one goes beyond primary experience as a test for truth, then he no longer, strictly speaking, has an experiential test for truth.

Of course there is always the overall and broad sense in which everything including reasoning is an experience, but this is not helpful in solving the dilemma. For one can always ask the warrant for choosing one interpretation given by reason rather than another. What warrant is there for viewing the primary experience through pantheistic eyes rather than theistic ones? This cannot be justifiably answered by a circular appeal right back to the primary experience, since several conflicting world views can make the same move. And if the appeal is made to something beyond the primary experience such as reason or interpretation, then we may immediately ask again for the justification for one interpretation over another.

5. Another criticism emerges from the former, namely, in the final analysis one cannot even talk meaningfully about experience unless he is employing cognitive categories that are at least formally independent of that experience. Experience *as such* has no meaning. It is pure "stuff" with no structure; it is content without form. And consciousness of something without conceptualization or predication of it is cognitively meaningless. No experience is even meaningful unless it is describable. But therein is the problem for the experientialist, for he would like to believe that a religious experience at least is self-interpreting, that it comes with its own structure. However, this is highly problematic. For those who have made the most careful analysis of religious experience use quite different ways to describe it: "ultimate commitment," "feeling of absolute dependence," a "numinous experience," an "existential encounter," and so on. Those who have attempted to determine any common content to all of these descriptions seem to arrive at only purely formal and interchangeable definitions. Indeed, to be consistent to experientialism, we must admit that all the *content* of these concepts comes from experience. But since it is precisely how to define or form this content of experience that is in question, it would beg the question to argue that the meaning of "absolute dependence" is based on experience. As we have already seen, experience as such has no truth or meaning apart from the framework or interpretation given it. So experientialism is in the dilemma of not being able to understand

the experience without the interpretation and not being able to have an interpretation unless it is derived from the experience. And there is no purely experiential way out of the dilemma.

6. At this point a word should be said of the mystical way out. Is it self-defeating for experientialists to speak of the experience without being able to describe it but only to evoke it? How would one know that it was "it" being evoked, and how can he know the "it" without knowing something about *what* it is in distinction from what it is not? Like Kant's noumenal realm, one cannot know pure that-ness without knowing something of what it is. Likewise, one cannot speak of the unspeakable or describe the indescribable and express the inexpressible without engaging in a self-defeating activity. McPherson candidly admits the problem but does not offer a successful solution when he writes, "Otto, then, uses language in order to explain what cannot be said in language" for he "is writing about the non-rational in a supremely rational way."[20] But like Wittgenstein, McPherson wishes us to believe that this allegedly descriptive language is not really descriptive but only evocative. It is a kind of descriptive ladder by which we get to the point where we recognize that God is not really descriptive at all. In response, it should be observed that if the descriptive ladder is able to get one to the religious "roof," then it is self-defeating to thereupon kick the ladder down and deny that the ladder is able to do what the ladder did indeed do. For if the ladder enables us to arrive at God as opposed to the devil or at good as versus evil, then our mystical or religious experience cannot be totally devoid of cognitive content. If it were, then we could not even make meaningful denials of it. In short, the very affirmation "no cognitively meaningful statements can be made about God" is either itself a totally meaningless statement (and therefore cannot be true) or else it is wholly self-defeating, since it just made a meaningful assertion about God to the effect that no meaningful statements about God can be made.

## Summary and Conclusion

Experientialism claims that all truth is determined by experience and that there is a recognizable and self-attesting religious experience. As a *source* and basis of truth the experientialist's claim may be correct, but as a *test* or warrant for the truth of that claim he is decidedly wrong. For no experience is self-interpreting and there are conflicting truth claims built on experience with no purely experiential way to adjudicate between them. Experience is merely a condition of persons; whereas truth is a characteristic of propositions. And one must have

---

20. McPherson, "Religion as the Inexpressible," p. 136.

some justification as to why he interpreted the raw data of the experience itself one way over the other. Further, the retreat to mystical and inexpressible experience is inadequate because it is both self-defeating to meaningfully describe the indescribable and impossible to recognize or distinguish it from anything else unless it is describable. In brief, no religious experience as such is either understandable or justifiable apart from some truth framework independent or separate from the experience itself. Experientialism is either meaningless, self-defeating, or begs the issue.

## SELECT READINGS FOR CHAPTER FOUR

**Exposition of Experientialism**

Bonaventura, Saint. *The Mind's Road to God.*
James, William. *Varieties of Religious Experience.*
Otto, Rudolf. *The Idea of the Holy.*
Plotinus. *Enneads.*
Schleiermacher, Friedrich. *On Religion.*

**Evaluation of Experientialism**

Ayer, A. J. *Language, Truth and Logic.*
Feuerbach, Ludwig. *The Essence of Christianity.*
Flew, Antony, ed. *New Essays in Philosophical Theology.*
Freud, Sigmund. *The Future of an Illusion.*
Sargant, William. *The Battle for the Mind.*
Yandell, Keith. "Experience and Truth in Religion," chap. IV in *Basic Issues in the Philosophy of Religion.*

# Chapter

# 5 | *Evidentialism*

Christianity is a historical religion and it has been common for Christian apologists to appeal to the historical evidence of the life, death, and resurrection of Jesus Christ as a verification of its claim to be true. However, the appeal to evidence is by no means limited to the past or historical evidence. Other apologists appeal to the present evidence in the natural world. And some contemporary Christian thinkers have made appeal to future or eschatological evidence for the verification of Christianity. It is the purpose of this chapter to assess evidentialism as a test for the truth of Christianity.

## An Exposition of Evidentialism as a Test for Truth

Perhaps the most common appeal to evidence by Christian apologists is to the past. The great facts of Christian history including the incarnation, crucifixion, and resurrection of Christ are seemingly irresistible focal points of Christian apologetics. Two examples will suffice.

### The Appeal to Past Evidence: Historical Approach of C. H. Dodd

*The Historical Nature of Christianity.* Dodd is in agreement with those who react against a pure "historicism" or quest for the bare facts of the historical Jesus. The history of Christianity, he feels, is written "from faith to faith." Nevertheless, when all this is admitted it still "belongs to the specific character of Christianity that it is an historical religion." While "some religions can be indifferent to historical fact, and move entirely on the plane of timeless truth, Christianity cannot." For "it rests upon the affirmation that a series of events happened, in which God revealed Himself in action, for the salvation of men." The Gospels of the New Testament profess to tell us what happened. They do not set out to gratify our curiosity about past events "but they do set out to nurture our faith upon the testimony to such events."[1]

As a historical religion Christianity is to be contrasted with both mysticism and nature-religion. The former concerns itself wholly with man's inner life and rejects the world of nature, and the latter recognizes the external world as in some sense a medium of divinity. And while Christianity neither repudiates God's revelation in nature nor his work within the spirit of man, it stresses that "the eternal God is revealed in history." There is no claim, however, that "the truth about God can be discovered by treating history as a uniform field of observation (like the 'nature' studied in sciences), in which it is possible to collect *data* from all parts of the field, and to arrive by induction at a conclusion."[2]

*The Meaning of History: Fact and Interpretation.* "History" is used in two senses: a series of events *or* the record of this series which in the wider sense have not merely a private but a public interest. Hence, history cannot be a mere "diary" or "chronicle" without context and interpretation. For even here the selection and context of what is recorded provides some meaning to the events recorded. A "historical 'event' is an occurrence *plus* the interest and meaning which the occurrence possessed for the person involved in it, and by which the record is determined." Hence, when we speak of God revealed in history we do not mean the bare occurrences but also the rich and concrete meaning of these events.[3]

Further, "since events in the full sense of the term are relative to the feelings and judgments of the human mind, the intensity of their significance varies, just as in the individual life certain crucial experiences have more than everyday significance." Therefore, we can "understand that an historical religion attaches itself not to the whole temporal series indifferently, nor yet to any casual event, but to a particular series of events in which a unique intensity of significance resides." So then "this selection of a particular series is not incongruous with the nature of history itself." For "the particular, even the unique, is a category entirely appropriate to the understanding of history." And since "one particular event exceeds another in significance, there may well be an event which is uniquely significant, and this event may give a unique character to the whole series to which it belongs." According

---

1. C. H. Dodd, *History and the Gospel* (Hodder and Stoughton, 1938), pp. 11-12.
2. Dodd, pp. 15, 18.
3. Dodd, pp. 19-21.

to Dodd, "this is in fact the assertion which Christianity makes." For "it takes the series of events recorded or reflected in the Bible, from the call of Abraham to the emergence of the Church, and declares that in this series the ultimate reality of all history . . . is finally revealed, because the series is itself controlled by the supreme event of all—the life, death and resurrection of Jesus Christ." And, adds Dodd, "this valuation of the series is not imposed upon it from without, but is an integral part of the history itself."[4]

*The Central Facts of Sacred History.* By means of Form Criticism Dodd constructs what he admits is a limited number of facts about Jesus of Nazareth. Nonetheless, the essential elements recovered from the documents "inevitably include both fact and interpretation" about the central facts of Christianity. These include an overall sketch of Jesus' life, his teaching, as well as his death and resurrection (although Dodd is not sure it involved a physical resuscitation of a corpse). But "the Resurrection remains an event within history, though we may not be able to state precisely what happened." So Christianity is not a "massive pyramid balanced upon the apex of some trivial occurrence . . ." but rather it is a "significant occurrence *plus* the meaning inherent in it. . . ." In view of this there is no mere incidental connection of historical events. For "the connection of events ceases to be 'accidental' if the tradition as we can recover it from the New Testament represents in substance a true memory of the facts, with the meaning which they really bore as an episode in history." For "either the interpretation through which the facts are presented was imposed upon them mistakenly . . . or the interpretation was imposed by the facts themselves, as they were experienced in an historical situation . . . and in that case we do know in the main what the facts were." Dodd believes that this "conclusion may not be demonstrable but it is not unreasonable."[5]

*The Relation of Sacred and Secular History.* History itself is, according to Dodd, "the whole succession of events in time, in which the spontaneity of the human spirit interacts with outward occurrences." Part of this succession of events is recorded in the Scriptures. And "part of this record is a source of evidence for secular history, dovetailing into the records of Egypt, Assyria, Babylon, Persia, Greece and Rome." However, "the events recorded are presented in the Bible as a history of the dealings of God with men, interpreted by the eschatological event of the coming of Christ, His death and Resurrection." That is, Biblical history is *Heilsgeschichte* or sacred and redemptive history. But "it is important to bear in mind that the same events enter into sacred and

---

4. Dodd, p. 22.
5. Dodd, pp. 72, 75-77.

secular history; the events are the same, but they form two distinguishable series." The "empirical series which is secular history extends over all recorded time, to our own day, and is still unfinished." This series is "linked together by succession of time, and by the operation of efficient causes, whether these causes be physical or psychological." But "the attempt to find a general pattern and universal meaning in this succession meets admittedly with no more than doubtful success." The basic reason for this is that "it is impossible in the empirical series to work backwards to a real beginning, or forward to a real end." Using any process without a beginning or end—just a sheer process—makes it difficult to predict an absolute meaning or value. For "any period or event which we may choose as a standard of judgement—our own period for instance—is only part of the process." Likewise, any ideas in our minds we may wish to use as criteria are "in part at least, a product of our particular historical condition."[6]

*The Redemptive Meaning of History.* Dodd believes that this uncertainty about the meaning of history in general may be the reason many turn to mysticism or to nature instead of history as the basis of their religious views. The Christian, however, affirms that there is another series into which historical events may fall, namely, sacred history. Of this redemptive series the Biblical history forms the inner core. "But the Bible always assumes that the meaning of this inner core is the ultimate meaning of all history, since God is the Maker and Ruler of all mankind, who created all things for Himself, and redeemed the world to Himself." In this case, "the whole of history is in the last resort sacred history, or *Heilsgeschichte*." And the "principle of the universality of the divine meaning in history is symbolically expressed in Christian theology by placing the history of the Old and New Testaments within a mythical scheme which includes a real beginning and a real end."[7]

The "Creation and Last Judgement are symbolical of the truth that all history is teleological, working out one universal divine purpose." Hence, "the story of Creation is not to be taken as a literal, scientific statement that the time series had a beginning—an idea as inconceivable as its opposite, that time had no beginning." Neither should "the story of the Fall . . . be taken as a literal, historical statement that there was a moment when man began to set himself against the will of God." Both Creation and Fall are "a symbolic summing-up of everything in secular or empirical history which is preparatory to the process of redemption and revelation." These stories affirm "that in man and

---

6. Dodd, pp. 114-15.
7. Dodd, p. 117.

his world there is implanted a divine purpose, opposed by a recalcitrant will. This is universally true . . . of the entire human race at all points in the temporal process." And "the myth of a Last Judgement is a symbolical statement of the final resolution of the great conflict. Serious difficulties are raised if we attempt to treat it as a literal and quasi-historical statement that the succession of events in time will one day cease—once again an idea as inconceivable to us as its opposite." Nor is the myth to be taken as "a prediction that before man dies out of this earth, or before the earth itself perishes in some astronomical catastrophe, the good will finally and manifestly triumph over the evil in human history." Rather "this triumph is something actually attained, not in some coming Day of the Lord, near or distant, but in the concrete historical event of the death and resurrection of Jesus Christ." Thus Christianity is a "realized eschatology," symbolizing by the Last Judgement "the relation of *all* history to the purpose of God. For the essential feature of the Last Judgement is its universality." It includes "the quick and the dead," that is, "all generations of mankind." It means in essence "that *all* history is comprehended in that achievement of the divine purpose of which the coming of Christ, His death and resurrection, is the intra-historical expression."[8]

In summation, history "as a process of redemption and revelation, has a beginning and an end, both in God. The beginning is not an event in time; the end is not an event in time. The beginning is God's purpose; the end is the fulfillment of His purpose. Between these lies the sacred history which culminates in the death and resurrection of Christ." And it is "the task of the Church to bring all historical movements into the context of the death and resurrection of Jesus Christ, in order that they may be judged by the divine meaning revealed in that event." And this "divine judgement is not a bare sentence, or expression of opinion. It is historical action in the Cross and the Resurrection." Thus "full meaning is not reserved for the last term in a temporal series, which supersedes and abolishes all previous stages in the process." For "every situation is capable of being lifted up into the order of 'sacred' history." So "in any given situation there are factors at work belonging to the empirical order . . . but the ultimately constitutive factor is neither nature nor the spirit of man, but the Kingdom of God." In it "the temporal order, which is the 'body' of the human spirit on earth, is 'raised in glory' in the eternal order. That is the ultimate destination of the historical process."[9]

*The Apologetic Implications of History.* According to Dodd, cer-

8. Dodd, pp. 115-17.
9. Dodd, pp. 118, 125.

tain facts about the life of Christ are historically determinable. These facts are both public and historically verifiable by historical methodology. Central to these is that Jesus of Nazareth died and rose from the dead. These facts come with the interpretation of Jesus' contemporaries but this interpretation is not arbitrary; it grows out of the facts themselves. For some facts are more significant than others and these sacred facts stand out as the most significant in history. And by means of these key sacred facts we can give meaning to all of history, that is, to secular history which otherwise has no apparent meaning growing out of its series of events as such. Thus Christian facts are historically discoverable, and on the basis of these facts one can determine the truth about all of human history and destiny. That is, historical evidence—the cross and resurrection—is the basis and test for truth for one's life and view of the universe. Evidence from the *past,* from history, is the basis and test for truth in both the present and the future. Dodd's view is an example of historical evidentialism.

Others have made a far stronger claim for the evidential value of history than Dodd. John W. Montgomery, for example, appeals to what he believes is the historically demonstrable fact of the resurrection as the verification of Jesus' claim to be God and thereby of Christ's attestation of the divine authority and inerrancy of Scripture.[10] From the earliest Christian times Christian apologists have made recourse to historical justification of their beliefs in the miraculous events of the first century. For many apologists it is these historical events that provide the crucial test for Christian truth.

### The Appeal to Present Evidence in Nature

Evidence is by no means limited to the past, to history. Apologists often appeal to evidence available in the present. Since the appeal to what we may call internal evidence of experience has already been discussed (see Chapter Four), we will center our attention here on what may be called external evidence, on nature or the external world.

*Paley's Watchmaker.* Perhaps the most common appeal to nature as evidence of God is some form of the Teleological Argument. Although the argument has been around since before the time of Plato, one of the more popular modern forms of it was set forth by William Paley (1743-1805). Paley insisted that if one found a watch in an empty field he would naturally and correctly conclude that it had a watchmaker. Likewise, if one studies the more complex design found in the natural world, he cannot but conclude that there is a world Designer behind it. For a watch indicates that it was put together for an in-

---

10. See chap. 16 for a presentation of historical apologetics.

telligent purpose (viz., to keep time) by virtue of its intricate series of parts from spring to glass cover. And in like manner the natural world has far greater and more subtle adaptations of means to an end. It follows then that if a watch needs a watchmaker, the natural world demands an even greater Designer (viz., God).[11]

John Stuart Mill (1806-1873) saw an important weakness in Paley's argument. The argument is built on the assumption that similarity in effect implies similarity in cause. But in this kind of analogy the argument is weaker when the dissimilarity is greater. And there is a significant dissimilarity that weakens Paley's argument, for watches imply watchmakers only because we know by previous experience that watches are things made by watchmakers. In like manner one would not know that dung was something left by an animal unless he had previously observed animals deposit dung. Mill did feel, however, that a more plausible argument from nature could be stated based on his inductive method of agreement. For example, there is an amazing concurrence of many diverse elements in the human eye. It is not probable that random selection brought these together. The inductive method of agreement would point to a common cause of the eye in some purposing Designer.[12]

*Taylor's Teleological Evolution.* Even before Paley, David Hume had proposed a criticism of Paley's type of argument that many feel is decisive. The apparent "design" may be nothing more than a "happy accident," Hume argued. Given enough time it is possible that chance reshuffling would produce any given combination of elements including the human eye, the human anatomy, and the whole of the so-called order of nature.[13] With the rise of Darwinism, a hypothesis to provide the *modus operandi* of chance, an alternate explanation to design became more plausible to many modern minds. As Bertrand Russell later pointed out: the adaptation of means to end in the world is either a result of intelligent preplanning or else a consequence of evolution. But since it can be accounted for on strictly evolutionary bases, there is no need to posit an intelligent Designer.[14]

It is to this type of argument that A. E. Taylor directs his form of the teleological proof for God. Taylor contends that nature reveals an *anticipatory* design that chance evolution cannot account for. For example the body's need for oxygen is anticipated by the membranes that provide it. Some insects deposit their eggs where the developing

---

11. See William Paley, *Natural Theology*, pp. 1-8.
12. John Stuart Mill, *Three Essays on Religion*, pp. 167-75.
13. David Hume, *Dialogues Concerning Natural Religion*, pt. VIII.
14. Bertrand Russell, *Why I Am Not a Christian*, pp. 9-11.

young will have food available in anticipation of their need to eat, and so on throughout nature. Neither can nature's advanced planning be accounted for by physical laws alone, since there are innumerable ways electrons *could* run, but they *do* invariably move in accordance with an advanced planning that preserves the organisms, whether they are healthy or unhealthy (e.g., antibodies). In fact, mind or intelligence is the only known condition that can overcome the improbabilities against the developmental preservation of life. Without advanced planning in nature, life would not survive. In short, the order evident in natural development of life is evidence of God.[15]

Some purely naturalistic evolutionists have attempted to overcome Taylor's type of argument by an appeal to natural selection. Julian Huxley, admitting that the mathematical odds against evolution are staggering (one chance in 1,000 to the millionth power, i.e., one followed by three million zeros), argued nonetheless "it has happened, thanks to the working of natural selection and the properties of living substance which make natural selection inevitable."[16] Another broader attempt to make the mathematical odds appear less formidable is to consider the world in which life has developed a mere "oasis of design" surrounded by a vast desert of chance. That is, in comparison with the immensity of the universe it is not nearly so unlikely, but even probable, that a "happy accident" such as the succession of favorable conditions for the advancement of life would occur in this small pocket of the universe (and perhaps even in others).

*Tennant's Objections to Chance.* F. R. Tennant has done more to keep alive the evidence for God from the order of nature than almost any modern theist. He admits the conceivability of the "oasis of design in a desert of chance" thesis but denies its plausibility. He argues that mere possibilities within the unknown world can never be used to refute the probabilities in the known world. And the world as we know it shows marked evidence of adaptation to ends. For example, there is an adaptation of thought to thing or mind to the world which makes the external world thinkable. Internally, there is the adaptation of the parts of organic beings. Nature is adapted to man's aesthetic needs, the world is adapted to human moral goals, and the world process is adapted to a culmination in man with his rational and moral status. And in view of the strong probability of design in the known world we have no reason to believe that the evidence for design in the known world is a lie to the unknown world. Indeed, the second law of thermodynamics (entropy) makes completely random development unlikely.

---

15. A. E. Taylor, *Does God Exist?*, chap. 4.
16. Julian Huxley, *Evolution in Action*, pp. 45-46.

For if the world is tending to disorder, unless there is behind it an ordering power it would be more and more—if not completely—chaotic by now. Nor, argues Tennant, does a mere chance reshuffling of matter by mechanical means account for the origin of mind and personality. In short, the odds against a chance explanation of the world are extremely great. The preadaptive order of the world we now have is good evidence for a Designer (i.e., God).[17]

*Bishop Butler's Analogy of Nature.* Sometime before Paley, the classic work of Bishop Butler on the *Analogy of Religion* (1736) presented an important defense of an evidential apologetic based on the natural order. Even the skeptic Hume considered it the best defense of Christianity he had ever read. Butler considered his highest obligation to Christianity that of "examining most seriously into its evidence, supposing its credibility; and of embracing it, upon supposition of its truth." Butler's method was both empirical and inductive. He made constant appeal to the canons of reason to which he believed the wise man must grant assent. Of course, it is foolhardy to demand absolute proof for anything. Rather, "probability is the very guide of life."[18] The reasonable man will without absolute knowledge guide his life by the trends observable in experience. That is, by analogies drawn from nature one can argue for the probability of the truth of Christianity and live accordingly.

By analogy with nature we can know that God governs the world and that there is a future life. Butler's argument for immortality is illustrative of his approach. Nature reveals to us that many creatures live in different states of perfection (e.g., worms become flies). Indeed, the doctrine that we shall live on after this life in another state has many analogies in nature. Further, there is a natural momentum in things that fits beautifully with the persistence of man's personality after death. There is no more reason to believe that death ends all than that inactivity in sleep implies that one will not awaken to consciousness after sleeping. And just as one carries his powers of personality through the changes of childhood, adulthood, and old age, there is by analogy no reason to believe that he cannot carry them through death.[19]

Some have criticized Butler's analogy or probability argument from nature on the grounds that the improbable sometimes happens. A hunch sometimes pays off. Why then should one always act on the basis of the most probable? Butler's rejoiner is that probability is the *guide* of

---

17. F. R. Tennant, *Philosophical Theology*, vol. 2, pp. 78-120.
18. Bishop Butler, *Analogy of Religion*, pp. 197, 69.
19. Butler, pt. One, chaps. 1 and 2.

life. It is usually cold in Alaska so the prudent man will take his over-coat. If he does not, he will spend more days shivering than not. A man cannot guide his life entirely by hunches without eventually running into serious difficulty. Although probable knowledge is not absolute, it is sufficient. In fact, it is all we have. The wise man, then, will base his beliefs on the most probable conclusion to which the evidence of nature points. For Butler, that means the wise man will believe in Christianity, despite the fact he lacks any compelling proofs of its truth.

### Appeal to Future Evidence: John Hick's Eschatological Verification

The appeal to evidence as a means of verifying the truth of Christianity has been made to the past (history) as well as to present experience either internally (as in mysticism) or externally (in nature). But some have also appealed to the future as a source of evidence for the possible truth of Christianity. Such was the suggestion of John Hick in his eschatological verification.[20]

The minimum demand of linguistical empiricism is that one specify some conditions under which one could know if his religious assertions were true. That is, religious assertions need not be actually verified to be meaningful but they must at least be somewhere, somehow, some-time verifiable in order to be meaningful or true. Hick responds to this challenge by suggesting that it is meaningful to believe in God since this can be verified upon death, if one has an experience of meeting God in a future life.

Hick begins his argument by disavowing a necessary symmetrical relation between verification and falsification. For instance, one's immortality can be verified if one day he observes his own funeral. But he cannot falsify his nonimmortality if he does not survive death to do so. Hence, it may be that belief in God is not falsifiable by anything in this world or beyond it. But God's existence is verifiable in principle if we can state the conditions in the next life under which one would recognize that he had met God. And, of course, belief in God would be verified in actual practice if one actually had this experience of meeting God one day. Hick admits that "the alleged future experience of this state cannot, of course, be appealed to as evidence for theism as a present interpretation of our experience; but it does suffice to render the choice between theism and atheism real and not a merely empty or verbal choice."[21]

According to Hick there are "two possible developments of our experience such that, if they occurred in conjunction with one another

---

20. John Hick, ed., *The Existence of God,* pp. 253-73.
21. Hick, pp. 257, 261.

(whether in this life or in another life to come), they would assure us beyond rational doubt of the reality of God, as conceived in the Christian faith." These are *"first,* an experience of the fulfillment of God's purpose for ourselves, and this has been disclosed in the Christian revelation; in conjunction, *second,* with an experience of communion with God as he has revealed himself in the person of Christ." Hick wards off anticipated criticism as to how one would know God when he met him by appeal to the incarnation of Christ, claiming with Barth that "Jesus Christ is the knowability of God." Further, the purpose of life for the Christian is final self-fulfillment and happiness in eternal life. This too would be readily recognized when experienced, says Hick. And the skeptic cannot press any falsification charge on the basis that thousands of years have passed and such a blessed state has not yet arrived. For "no final falsification is possible of the claim that this fulfillment will occur—unless, of course, the prediction contains a specific time clause which, in Christian teaching, it does not."[22]

Hick concludes with the reminder that his purpose is not to seek to establish that fact or truth of a given religion "but rather to establish that there are such things as religious facts. . . ." In particular he wishes to show "that the existence or non-existence of the God of the New Testament is a matter of fact, and claims as such an eventual experiential verification." In brief, even though the eschatological method cannot establish Christian theism now, nevertheless, one day it can be verified in the eschaton. Meanwhile, it is at least possible to *believe* the truth of Christianity.[23]

## Some Characteristic Tenets of Evidentialism

The above analysis indicates some marked differences among evidential attempts to establish the truth of a world view. Some appeal to past or historical events (as Dodd); some appeal to present religious experience (following Schleiermacher); others appeal to the evidence for God in the external world of nature (as Paley or Butler). And still others (like Hick) call on the evidence of experiencing God in the future for a verification of religious claims. Despite this diversity, there is a characteristic commonality in the evidential appeal that bears exposition and evaluation.

1. First, evidentialism is empirically or experientially based. It calls one to the basic facts or events of the world or at least to some of them. Truth must be based in facts, not in ideas or theories, or else it is not grounded at all. Truth is based in facts or events.

---

22. Hick, pp. 269, 271.
23. Hick, p. 273.

2. Second, evidentialists state or imply a distinction between fact and interpretation. The facts are both separate and distinguishable from the interpretation men place on these facts. It is possible to relate and structure many, if not all, facts in differing ways. But the interpretation does not constitute the facts. Facts stand by themselves apart from frameworks that may be given to them from differing points of view.

3. Third, the evidentialists believe that not all facts can be interpreted in entirely different ways. They contend that meaning grows out of the facts. Somehow, the facts finally "speak for themselves." To be sure, facts need interpretation but the interpretation cannot be arbitrarily imposed from without; rather, it arises from the facts themselves in a natural way.

4. Fourth, evidentialists often appeal to some special or unique facts as being definitive in determining truth. For some it may be past miraculous events, for others it may be a present mystical experience, and for still others it may be a final blessed state. Christians most often appeal to the fact of the incarnation, to the crucial events of the life of Jesus, as definitive for truth.

5. Fifth, many evidentialists place strong emphasis on the objective and public nature of facts. In this respect they regard private and subjective experience as nonevidential. Truth must be observable and general or it is unsubstantiatable.

## An Evaluation of Evidentialism as a Test for Truth

Evidentialism provides some notable insights into the relation of truth and human events. Among these are several of general interest to the task of an apologist.

### Positive Contributions of Evidentialism

Evidentialists are to be commended for anchoring truth to facts or events. In this regard several positive contributions can be noted.

1. First, evidentialists make a significant point when they stress the objective and public nature of evidence. Completely private and purely subjective events or experiences are not really evidence at all. The subjective and personal may very well be a significant *source* of truth, but it definitely cannot be a deciding *test* for truth. If truth is to be tested, it must be available to others. In point of fact, it is highly questionable, if not completely impossible, even to express or communicate a private "truth." If language or the medium of expression is always common to a group, then it is impossible for an individual to understand a truth solitary to himself. Publicity or objectivity is essential to verifiability. Truth may be subjectively realized but it must be objectively grounded.

2. Second, truth is factually based, as evidentialists point out. Facts are not based in theories but theories in facts. Experience is the basis for expressions about it. Events are fundamental to interpretation; the viewpoint does not constitute the factualness of the events. Evidentialism rightly places the horse before the cart. For the actual is not based in and constituted by the theoretical. Rather, the interpretive framework provided by the latter simply gives a certain structure or significance to the facts which stand independently in and of themselves.

3. Third, *given* a certain context of facts or events, there is no reasonable basis for saying that meaning is entirely arbitrary to the facts. Such facts cannot be interpreted capriciously. Some meaning is essential to certain series of events in a given context. Given the context of hateful intentions, stabbing another twelve times in the heart must be reasonably viewed as murder, and so on. And no fact should be interpreted out of its intended context, for the meaning and the fact of an event are concomitantly related. That is, facts are not known to us as bare facts but as interpreted by the context from which or through which they are viewed. In this sense, no facts can be justifiably isolated or arbitrarily interpreted apart from their proper context. For example, given the context of a theistic world, not every series of unusual happenings can be justifiably understood as chance events. Some could very well be miracles.

## Some Negative Criticisms of Evidentialism as a Test for Truth

Although evidentialism provides some significant contributions to the apologist's task, nevertheless, as a test for the truth of a world view it is entirely inadequate. For evidence gains its meaning only by its immediate and overall context; and evidence as such cannot, without begging the question, be used to establish the overall context by which it obtains its very meaning as evidence.

1. First, facts and events have ultimate meaning only within and by virtue of the context of the world view in which they are conceived. Hence, it is a vicious circle to argue that a given fact (say, the resuscitation of Christ's body) is evidence of a certain truth claim (say, Christ's claim to be God), *unless it can be established that the event comes in the context of a theistic universe.*[24] For it makes no sense to claim to be the Son of *God* and to evidence it by an act of *God* (miracle) unless there is a God who can have a Son and who can act in a special way in the natural world. But in this case the mere fact of the resurrection cannot be used to establish the truth that there is a God. For the resurrection cannot even be a miracle unless there already is a God.

---

24. See chap. 15.

Many overzealous and hasty Christian apologists rush hastily into their historical and evidential apologetics without first properly doing their theistic homework.

2. Second, contrary to evidentialism, meaning is not inherent in nor does it arise naturally out of bare facts or events. Nothing happens in a vacuum; meaning always demands a context.[25] And since the facts are admittedly distinct from the interpretation, it is always possible that in another context or framework of meaning the said facts would not be evidence for Christianity at all. For example, in the context of a naturalistic world the resuscitation of Jesus' corpse would not be a miracle but merely an unusual natural event for which there is no *known* scientific explanation but which, by virtue of its occurrence, both demands and prods scientists to find a natural explanation. Meaning, then, does not really grow out of the event by itself; meaning is given to the event from a certain perspective. The earthquake that an Old Testament theist believed was divinely instigated to swallow Korah (Num. 16:31 ff.) would undoubtedly be explained by a naturalist as geological pressures within the crust of the earth. What the New Testament claims was the "voice of God" in John 12 was admittedly interpreted by someone standing nearby as "thunder." No bare fact possesses inherent meaning; every fact is an "interprafact" by virtue of a necessary combination of both its bare facticity and the meaning given to it in a given context by a specific perspective or world view.

3. Third, there is no way from pure facts themselves to single out some facts as having special, crucial, or ultimate significance. "Singling out," "selecting," "comparing," and the like are processes of the mind based on principles or perspectives one brings to the facts and not characteristics inherent in raw data. Events simply occur in a series; only one's perspective or view of those events can determine which one is to be honored over another with special significance. Not even unusual or odd events as such have inherently more significance than usual or common ones. For if that were so, anomalies would be more important than scientific laws and more human significance would be attributed to freaks than normal people. In fact, in the context of a random universe, even series of odd events bear no more significance than unloaded dice that roll the same numbers on several successive throws. Of course, in the context of a designed or theistic universe a series of unusual events, such as the point by point correspondence of the life of Christ with a significant number of predictions made hundreds of years in advance, would be an entirely different matter. For

---

25. See Karl Popper, *The Poverty of Historicism* (London: Roulledge and Kegan Paul, 1957).

if there is a God who can make a series of predictions of unusual events that come to pass as foretold, surely it is *not* unreasonable to consider them miraculous. But to return to the point, whether or not there is a God is precisely the point at issue. And it is invalid to appeal to "theistic evidence," that is, to allegedly miraculous events as a proof that this is a theistic world. That begs the whole question. *If* this is a theistic universe, of course certain odd series of events can be given special significance. However, the significance does not reside in the events as such but is attributed to them by virtue of the important overall context in which they occur, namely, the theistic context. But if this is a random natural world rather than a theistic world, neither the life of Christ nor any other unusual series of events has any more special religious significance than an odd series of combinations on a Las Vegas gambling table.

The real problem for the Christian apologist is to find some way apart from the mere facts themselves to establish the justifiability of interpreting facts in a theistic way. No appeal to the mere events or facts themselves will aid in determining which of the alternative interpretations should be placed on the facts. Viewpoints and world views come from without and not from within the facts. Hence, facts or events as such cannot establish theism. The selection, relation, and relative weight given the facts is not inherent to the facts themselves. Even Dodd reveals this when he appeals to the paradigm importance of the Christian mythological or symbolical structure in order to interpret the events of the secular world. But the question as to the warrant for choosing one myth or symbol over another remains unsettled by mere facts or events.

4. Fourth, a word must be said about the appeal to so-called order of nature as evidence of God. First of all, this kind of argument makes sense only within the context of design such as was supposed in the theistic or deistic days of Paley and Butler. Since Christianity (with its emphasis on order and regularity) spawned modern science, it is understandable that men speaking out of a scientific context would tend logically to conclude that there is a God. However, this is a large but vicious circle. For if the supposition and application of a Christian world view gave birth to its child, science, it is not strange that the offspring should naturally pay homage to its parent. Put another way, "order" and "design" are read into, not out of, nature. Indeed, the very word *nature* is loaded with theistic or, perhaps, deistic connotations. There is no natural order in a pantheistic world, and in a random world it begs the question to speak of the *order* of nature. Of course, design implies a Designer and order entails an Orderer. But on what

basis does one have the right to label events as "ordered" or "designed," unless he is already presupposing a theistic view?

5. Finally, a word is in order about eschatological verification. Simply put, at best it is only a test for meaning (i.e., for the possibility of truth) but not a test for truth itself. At least it is not a current test for truth. Even if in the long run it may serve to confirm a theist's claim, nonetheless for the present it offers (and Hick admits this) no hope for deciding which world view is probably true vis-à-vis the others. In other words, it is not really a present test for truth at all. For the present we are left to simple fideism or to find some other test for truth. And what rational man would want to leave the *total* determination of his lifetime—even eternal—decision on the simple hope that the end will vindicate him! If the future fails him, it may be too late. The wise man will seek a firmer ground *now* on such ultimately important questions.

## Summary and Conclusion

Evidentialism, like experientialism, offers some significant contributions to our understanding of the role of events and facts to religious truth. Truth must be objective and public; it needs a basis in fact. Interpretation is distinguishable from the facts being interpreted. And in a given context not just any interpretation can be given to any fact. However, there is no way for facts themselves to determine in which context or by which framework they are to be viewed. No meaning is inherently and inseparably attached to a given set of facts. And there is no ultimate meaning or truth attributable to facts unless it is from the overall perspective of a world view. But no fact, event, or series thereof within an overall framework which derives all of its meaning from the framework can be determinative of the framework which bestows that meaning on it. For no fact or set of facts can of and by themselves, apart from any meaning or interpretation given to them, establish which of the alternative viewpoints should be taken on the fact(s).

## SELECT READINGS FOR CHAPTER FIVE

**Exposition of Evidentialism**

Burrill, Donald. *The Cosmological Argument,* pt. II, "The Teleological Argument."

Butler, Bishop. *Analogy of Religion.*

Dodd, C. H. *History and the Gospel.*

Montgomery, John W. *History and Christianity.*

## Evaluation of Evidentialism

Clark, Gordon. *Historiography,* especially chap. 6.
Hick, John. *The Existence of God,* pt. III.
Popper, Karl. *The Poverty of Historicism.*
Van Til, Cornelius. *The Defense of the Faith,* especially chaps. 8 and 10.

# Chapter

# 6 | *Pragmatism*

The failure of theoretical and even purely factual tests for truth lends support to a pragmatic test. Pragmatists contend that one cannot *think* or even *feel* truth, but he can discover it by attempting to *live* it. Truth is not what is *consistent* or what is empirically *adequate* but what is experientially *workable*. Did not even Jesus say that "by their fruits you shall know them"? Although Christian apologists of the pragmatic variety have not been abundant, they are by no means nonexistent. Indeed, sophisticated philosophical systems have been built on a pragmatic theory of meaning and/or truth.

## An Examination of Pragmatic Approaches to Meaning and Truth

Kant used the word *pragmatic* to mean a "contingent belief, which yet forms the ground for the actual employment of means to certain actions. . . ."[1] But the thought of developing Kant's use of "pragmatic" into a theory of meaning or test for truth was not German but American in origin.

### Charles Sanders Peirce (1839-1914): Pragmatic Theory of Meaning

Properly speaking, Peirce did not offer pragmatism as a test for truth but as a theory of meaning. He was not concerned as such with verification of a theory but with clarification of thought.

*The Four Methods of Belief.* After dismissing Francis Bacon's approach to science as cavalier and Descartes' starting point in doubt

---

1.  Immanuel Kant, *Critique of Pure Reason,* A 824, B 852.

as difficult if not impossible to attain, Peirce suggests that beliefs may be fixed in a much better way. First, our problem would be greatly simplified if instead of speaking of "truth" one would/could attain belief unassailable by doubt, namely, a state of confidence. The process of attaining this he calls "The Fixation of Belief." Peirce declares that there are only four methods of stabilizing one's beliefs: (1) The method of *tenacity* is evident when "a man may go through life, systematically keeping out of view all that might cause a change in his opinions. . . ." Despite the satisfaction and peace of mind this method may bring to the individual, it "will be unable to hold its ground in practice. The social impulse is against it. The man who adopts it will find that other men think differently from him. . . ." It would work only for a hermit but is ineffective for a community. (2) The method of *authority* backing one's belief by social convention, by creating a priesthood or aristocracy to pontificate. Although Peirce granted this method "immeasurable mental and moral superiority to the method of tenacity," he considered it unfeasible. For "no institution can undertake to regulate opinions upon every subject." Some minor freedoms must be allowed, and these will always be the breeding grounds for major dissent. (3) The *a priori* method of fixing beliefs is one which is "agreeable to reason." This method "is far more intellectual and respectable from the point of view of reason than either of the others which we have noticed," wrote Peirce. However, "its failure has been the most manifest. It makes of inquiry something similar to the development of taste." For the unshakable views of today are tomorrow out of fashion. (4) Only the method of *science* is sufficient for fixing beliefs. The fundamental thesis of this is that "there are real things, whose . . . realities affect our senses according to regular laws . . . yet, by taking advantage of the laws of perception, we can ascertain how things really are." Furthermore, "any man, if he has sufficient experience and reason enough about it, will be led to the one true conclusion."[2]

The evidence Peirce offers for this is fourfold: First, even if investigation cannot prove this thesis, "no doubts of the method . . . necessarily arise from its practice, as is the case with all the others." Second, "nobody . . . can really doubt that there are realities, for, if he did, doubt would not be a source of dissatisfaction." For doubt always results from the repugnance of two propositions that presuppose the reality of "some one thing to which a proposition should conform." Third, "everybody uses the scientific method about a great many things, and only ceases to use it when he does not know how to apply it." Fourth,

---

2. C. S. Peirce, "The Fixation of Belief" V, collected in *Charles Sanders Peirce: The Essential Writings,* ed. Edward C. Moore, p. 133.

"experience of the method has not led us to doubt it, but, on the contrary, scientific investigation has had the most wonderful triumphs in
the way of settling opinion." Hence, "this is the only one of the four
methods which presents any distinction of a right and wrong way. If
I adopt the method of tenacity, and shut myself out from all influences,
whatever I think necessary to doing this, is necessary according to that
method." Likewise, "with the method of authority . . . the only test
*on that method* is what the state thinks; so it cannot pursue the method
wrongly. So with the *a priori* method. The very essence of it is to think
as one is inclined to think." And on this ground, of course, one can
never be wrong. "But with the scientific method the case is different,"
concludes Peirce. For "the test of whether I am truly following the
method is not an immediate appeal to my feelings and purposes, but,
on the contrary, itself involves the application of the method." In this
way the person who confesses that there is such a thing as truth as
versus falsity simply says this: "that if acted on it will carry us to the
point we aim at and not astray. . . ."[3]

*The Pragmatic Clarification of Ideas.* From the principles set forth
in the foregoing scientific or pragmatic method Peirce believes he has
reached "a clearness of thought of a far higher grade than the 'dis-
tinctness' of the logicians." For "the essence of belief is the establishment of a habit, and different beliefs are distinguished by the different
modes of action to which they give rise." If beliefs do not differ in
this practical way, then "no mere differences in the manner of consciousness of them can make them different beliefs, any more than
playing a tune in different keys is playing different tunes." In short, the
final rule for attaining "clearness of apprehension is as follows: Consider what effects, which might conceivably have practical bearings, we
conceive the object of our conception to have. Then, our conception
of these effects is the whole of our conception of the object." Or, in
other words, the meaning of anything is to be found in its practical
results. The final differential is a pragmatic one. A mere difference
in mode of conception is not a clear and distinct difference. But a
practical difference in experienced results is a clearly distinct difference.[4]

The components of a belief, then, are three: first, it is something
of which we are aware. Second, it satisfies the irritation caused by
doubt. And finally, it involves the establishment in our nature of a
rule of action or a *habit*. Thus Peirce wrote elsewhere, "Belief is not
a momentary mode of consciousness; it is a habit of mind essentially
enduring for some time, and mostly (at least) unconscious."[5] So the

---

3. Peirce, V.
4. Peirce, "How to Make our Ideas Clear" II, col. and ed. Moore.

essence of belief is the establishment of a habit; and different beliefs are distinguished by different modes of action to which they give rise.

*The Concept of God Clarified.* Peirce held that any normal man would come naturally to act as if there were a God. This would simply be the pragmatic clarification of an implicit belief that he possessed. It would be an overt action that demonstratively clarified that covert belief.[6] In another place Peirce said, "So, then, the question being whether I believe in the reality of God, I answer, Yes. I further opine that pretty nearly everybody more or less believes this, including many of the scientific men of my generation who are accustomed to think that belief is entirely unfounded." And "if a pragmaticist is asked what he means by the word 'God,' he can only say that just as long acquaintance with a man of great character may deeply influence one's whole manner of conduct, so that a glance at his portrait may make a difference, . . . then that analogue of a mind—for it is impossible to say that *any* human attribute is *literally* applicable—is what he means by "God." However, our knowledge of God is more than purely negative "because the discoveries of science, their enabling us to *predict* what will be the course of nature, is proof conclusive that, though we cannot think any thought of God's, we can catch a fragment of His Thought, as it were [in nature]."[7]

As to whether there really is such a being as God, "the only guide to the answer to this question lies in the power of the passion of love which more or less overmasters every agnostic scientist and everybody who seriously and deeply considers the universe." Peirce quickly adds, "But whatever there may be of argument in all this is as nothing, the merest nothing in comparison to its force as an appeal to ones' own instinct, which is to argument what substance is to shadow, what bedrock is to the built foundation of a cathedral." The idea of God comes, then, from direct experience. "As to God, open your eyes—and your heart, which is also a perceptive organ—and you see him." Of course delusions are possible. "I may think a thing is black, and on close examination it may turn out to be bottle-green. But I cannot think a thing is black if there is no such thing to be seen as black." Likewise, one cannot be totally deceived as to the reality of God, however wrong he may be about his precise nature.[8]

5. Peirce, "What Pragmatism Is," col. and ed. Moore.
6. C. S. Peirce, "A Neglected Argument for the Reality of God," *Hibbert Journal,* 1908.
7. "Concept of God" in *Philosophical Writings of Peirce,* chap. 28, ed. Justus Buchler (New York: Dover Publications, Inc., 1955).
8. Buchler.

## William James: The Pragmatic Test for Truth

James's first major venture into religious writing was one of descriptive psychology. His description is classic, and it sets the stage for his pragmatism.

*A Description of Religious Experience.* Upon examining religion on the experiential level he concluded there are two types: the "once-born" and the "twice-born." The former is optimistic in outlook and the latter is pessimistic. The one maximizes good and the other evil. The first type is healthy-minded and the second is sick-souled. For the once-born are born with a sense of harmony but the twice-born have inner discord naturally. For the former, happiness is the evidence of God; but for the latter, unhappiness manifests man's need for the Divine. In the case of once-born men there is a continuity with God. At worst man is only maladjusted and is naturally curable. But in the case of the twice-born there is discontinuity with God based on a sense of man's essential evil which calls for supernatural help. According to James, the Latins tend to be once-born type and the Germanic peoples tend to be twice-born type. In terms of conceptualization, the first group tend to be pantheistic and the last group theistic. Emerson and Whitman illustrate the former while Luther and Bunyan are examples of the latter.[9]

James described the characteristics of two types of conversion: gradual and sudden. Both are characterized by (1) a change in the habitual center of personal energy (i.e., self-surrender), (2) the undermining and replacement of one life system by another. This change generally occurs in adolescence but it takes about 1/5 the time in conversion. The symptoms of this experience are a sense of incompleteness followed by anxiety about the hereafter that leads to a sense of happy relief upon conversion. The sudden conversions are characterized by (1) a period of subconscious incubation from sublimation, followed by (2) an uprush from the subconscious called automation. (3) The larger the subconscious storehouse of sublimation, the more likely there will be a sudden conversion as opposed to a gradual one. (4) But there are no psychologically discernible differences between a natural conversion and an alleged "supernatural one" as described by Jonathan Edwards in his famous *Religious Affections.* James does not deny the working of God in conversion but leaves the door open through the subconscious as the route of divine activity.[10]

The common core of all religious experience, according to James, involves both the subjective and the objective. The subjective or emo-

---

9. William James, *Varieties of Religious Experience,* Lectures 4-8.
10. James, Lectures 9-10.

tional side involves: (1) a feeling that the visible world draws its chief significance from the wider spiritual universe, (2) a sense that union or harmonious relation with the higher universe is our true end, and (3) a feeling that prayer or inner communion with the spirit of this higher universe produces effects within the phenomenal world. The effects of these three beliefs provide (4) a new zest for life manifest in lyrical enchantment or an appeal to earnestness and heroism and (5) an assurance of safety and a temper of peace in oneself and of love toward others.

On the objective or intellectual side of the religious experience are two factors: (1) a sense that something has gone wrong about us the way we are naturally, and (2) a belief that we are saved from this wrongness by making proper connection with higher powers. This is the minimal cognitive content in all religious experience.[11]

James held that there were two sides of the religious experience: the "hither" and the "thither." The "hither" side may be identified with the subconscious continuation of our conscious self. That is, what one means by "God" is, on the psychologically describable side, said to be found in the area of one's individual subconsciousness. What the "thither" or "higher" side may be is not subject to direct scientific investigation. It is a matter of "over-belief." However, James believes that one can posit a hypothesis about this "more" or "God" that can be practically tested.[12]

*The Will to Believe.* Even before James put together his classical analysis of religious experience (1902), he had already written on how to justify a religious belief in his famous essay, *The Will to Believe* (1896). He argued that one's will to believe can be based on very personal and practical bases. A hypothesis, wrote James, is "anything that may be proposed to our belief." As such it may be either living or dead. "A live hypothesis is one which appeals as a real possibility to him to whom it is proposed." And "the maximum of liveness in a hypothesis means willingness to act irrevocably." Further James writes, "Let us call the decision between two hypotheses an *option*." Options may be "first, *living* or *dead;* secondly, *forced* or *avoidable;* thirdly, *momentous* or *trivial.* And for our purposes we may call an option a *genuine* option when it is of the forced, living, and momentous kind." A live option is one in which each alternative "makes some appeal, however small, to your belief." A forced option is one "based on a complete disjunction, with no possibility of not choosing. . . ." Finally, a momentous option is a unique opportunity as versus a trivial one where

11. James, Lecture 20.
12. James, Lecture 20.

"the stakes are insignificant, or when the decision is reversible." Science abounds with trivial options. Needless to say, religion for James is a genuine option, that is, one that is forced, living, and momentous.[13]

James believed that "our passional and volitional nature lay at the root of all our convictions." Free will is not a "fifth wheel to the coach." Even as scientists "we want to have truth; we want to believe that our experiments and studies and discussions must put us in a continually better and better position towards it." And "as a rule we disbelieve all facts and theories for which we have no use." Hence, James concludes that *our passional nature not only lawfully may, but must, decide an option between propositions, whenever it is a genuine option that cannot be decided on intellectual grounds.* For "to say, under such circumstances, 'Do not decide, but leave the question open,' is itself a passional decision—just like deciding yes or no—and is attended with the same risk of losing the truth." James believed there was no way to settle the religious question on purely intellectual grounds. "Objective evidence and certitude are doubtless very fine ideals to play with," he continues, "but where on this moonlit and dream-visited planet are they found?" Indeed, "no concrete test of what is really true has ever been agreed upon." "For what a contradictory array of opinions have objective evidence and absolute certitude been claimed"![14]

Of course, "whenever the option between losing truth and gaining it is not momentous, we can throw the chance of *gaining truth* away, and at any rate save ourselves from any chance of *believing falsehood,* by not making up our minds at all till objective evidence has come." In scientific matters it is almost always the case that such skepticism in the absence of evidence is called for. However, religious and *"moral questions* immediately present themselves as questions whose solution cannot wait for a sensible proof." Of course, "the question of having moral beliefs at all or not having them is decided by our will." For "if your heart does not *want* a world of moral reality, your head will assuredly never make you believe in one." Moral skepticism can be no more refuted or proved by logic than can intellectual skepticism. And the religious skeptic says, *"Better risk loss of truth than chance of error."* When in the presence of a religious option he always believes that "fear of its being error is wiser and better than to yield to our hope that it may be true."[15]

James, however, responded to the skeptic by saying, "I do not wish, by putting your extinguisher upon my nature . . . to forfeit my sole chance

13. See "The Will to Believe" in *Essays in Pragmatism,* ed. Alburey Castell (New York: Hafner Publishing Co., 1968), pp. 88-89.
14. Castell, pp. 90-98.
15. Castell, pp. 101-6.

in life of getting upon the winning side. . . ." For religion is a genuine option that says "the best things are the more eternal things . . ." and "we are better off even now if we believe her first affirmation to be true." This means that religion is both a living option (to all who are tempted to believe it) and it is a momentous option in view of the unique opportunity for betterment it offers. Likewise, religion is a forced option because "we cannot escape the issue by remaining skeptical and waiting for more light, because although we do avoid error in that way *if religion be untrue,* we lose the good, *if it be true,* just as certainly as if we positively chose to disbelieve." Hence, "we have the right to believe at our own risk any hypothesis that is live enough to tempt our will." And "any rule of thinking which would absolutely prevent me from acknowledging certain kinds of truth if those kinds of truth were really there, would be an irrational rule." For "there are, then, cases where a fact cannot come at all unless a preliminary faith exists in its coming. And where faith in a fact can help create the fact, that would be an insane logic which should say that faith running ahead of scientific evidence is the 'lowest kind of immorality' into which the thinking being can fall." But "since belief is measured by action, he who forbids us to believe religion to be true, necessarily also forbids us to act as we should if we did believe it to be true. The whole defense of religious faith hinges upon action."[16] Thus James believed that faith in God did make a difference from one who believed only a naturalistic hypothesis. And some years later in his classic on religious experience James offered the evidence for his belief that religion does make a difference.

*The Value and Fruit of Religion in One's Life.* Religion is not to be judged by its source or root but by its result or fruit. Both the inner and outer characteristics of "saintliness" are superior. Internally, the religious man gains (1) a satisfying feeling of being in a wider (Ideal) life than this world's selfish interests, (2) a sense of friendly continuity between oneself and this Ideal Power, (3) an immense sense of freedom and elation as our confining self melts down, and (4) a shifting of our emotional center toward love and harmony with the other. Externally, religion manifests itself in (1) asceticism where self-surrender becomes self-sacrifice, (2) strength of soul by enlargement to new reaches of patience and fortitude, (3) purity or a spiritual sensitizing that results from a shift of our emotional center, and (4) charity where the same shift brings increased tenderness to our fellow creatures.[17] In summary James wrote, "In a general way, then, and

16. Castell, pp. 105-8.
17. James, Lectures 11-15.

'on the whole,'. . . our testing of religion by practical common sense and the empirical method, leave it in possession of its towering place in history." For "economically, the saintly group of qualities is indispensable to the world's welfare. The great saints are immediate successes; the smaller ones are at least heralds and harbingers, and they may be leavens also, of a better mundane order. Let us be saints, then, if we can. . . ."[18]

*The Pragmatic Test for Truth.* James's pragmatism is implicit in *Varieties of Religious Experience* (1902) when he said that "over-beliefs" cannot be scientifically proved but that the pragmatic and experiential grounds of religious belief are so plausible that "scientific logic will find no plausible pretext for vetoing your impulse to welcome it as true." This "thoroughly pragmatic view of religion," says James, "has usually been taken as a matter of course by common men" but "I believe the pragmatic way of taking religion to be the deeper way."[19]

Several years later James explicated his pragmatic method very clearly in his work on *Pragmatism* (1907). "True ideas," he wrote, "are those that we can assimilate, validate, corroborate and verify. False ideas are those that we can not." Ideas are not intrinsically true or false. Rather, "truth happens to an idea." Ideas are made true by events. On the common sense level truth is "a leading that is worth while." To borrow a banking analogy, "truth lives on a credit system." Ideas pass along until someone wants to "cash in" on them. Truth, then, is the "cash-value" of an idea. "We trade on each other's truth. But beliefs verified concretely by *somebody* are the posts of the whole superstructure." Verification then may be direct or indirect but eventually "all true processes must lead to the face of directly verifying sensible experiences *somewhere,* which *somebody's* ideas have copied." The true, to put it very briefly, "is only the expedient in the way of our thinking, just as the 'right' is only the expedient in the way of our behaving."[20] Pragmatism's "only test of probable truth is what works best in the way of leading us, what fits every part of life best. . . . If theological ideas should do this, if the notion of God, in particular, should prove to do it, how could pragmatism possibly deny God's existence?"[21]

The pragmatic method yielded for James a pluralistic rather than a monistic universe, one which was melioristic rather than either opti-

18. James, p. 280 (Mentor Paperback).
19. James, pp. 385, 390, 391.
20. See William James, *Pragmatism and Other Essays* (New York: Washington Square Press, Inc., 1963), pp. 89, 90, 92, 95, 96.
21. James, *Pragmatism,* "What Pragmatism Means," p. 38.

mistic of inevitable salvation or pessimistically resigned to ultimate doom. But traditional theism is ruled out for a "pragmatic or melioristic type of theism" which involves a superhuman but finite God. In the final analysis, however, "pragmatism has to postpone dogmatic answer, for we do not yet know certainly which type of religion is going to work best in the long run."[22]

## Pragmatic Element in Evangelical Apologetics

Pragmatic elements have been present in orthodox apologetics from the very beginning. Jesus' statement, "by their fruits you shall know them," has long been taken to be a pragmatic test for the truth about a religious teaching. Even Thomas Aquinas spoke of believing "what another says because it seems fitting or useful to do so. Thus, too, we are moved to believe what God says because we are promised eternal life as a reward if we believe."[23] The emphasis among Christians that "the proof of the pudding is in the eating" is found extensively on the popular level.

Few contemporary Christians, however, have given more thoughtful and philosophical backing to a kind of pragmatic test for truth than has Francis Schaeffer. In a chapter entitled "How Do We Know It Is True?" Schaeffer outlines his test for truth as follows: "The theory must be non-contradictory and must give an answer to the phenomenon in question" and, second, "we must be able to live consistently with our theory." Schaeffer admits that a non-Christian view such as materialism may fit the first criterion "but it will not fit the second, for man simply cannot live as though he were a machine." The Christian view of the universe, however, "can be lived with, both in life and in scholarly pursuits." And "it should be added in conclusion that the Christian, after he is a Christian, has years of experimental evidence to add to all the above reasons. . . ." Thus crucial to the falsity of the non-Christian view is its unlivability while the truth of Christianity is confirmed by its livability and experiential verification.[24]

Schaeffer illustrates his point by what may be thought of as a kind of broad experiential teleological argument.[25] He notes that no one can really live a chance philosophy of pure materialism. Jackson Pollock, who dipped paint on his canvas by chance, after exhausting his method, com-

---

22. James, *Pragmatism,* "Pragmatism and Religion," pp. 129, 125, 131, 132.

23. Thomas Aquinas, *Summa Theologica,* XIV, i, reply.

24. Francis Schaeffer, *The God Who Is There,* pp. 109-11. Schaeffer, of course, has *more* than a mere pragmatic test for truth. He has in some places what appears to be a transcendental argument or one based on actual undeniability (see *He Is There and He Is Not Silent,* chap. 1).

25. Thomas Morris, *Francis Schaeffer's Apologetics: A Critique* (Chicago: Moody Press, 1976), chap. 1.

mitted suicide. On the other hand, the American musician John Cage, who flipped coins to determine notes, took up hunting mushrooms as a hobby. He confessed, "I became aware that if I approached mushrooms in the spirit of my chance operations, I would die shortly. So I decided that I would not approach them in this way!" Pollock is dead because he tried in vain to live his chance philosophy. Cage lived on because he was inconsistent with his random view of the universe. Both proved that disteleology is unlivable. Therefore, one must believe, if he is to live consistently, that this is a designed and personal universe (viz., a theistic one). Of course Schaeffer gives much more elaboration and sophistication to his position, but the broad pragmatic emphasis is there nonetheless. Only the Christian view is consistent and livable, and all non-Christian views are in the final analysis unlivable. Experience confirms this to be true.[26]

## Some Common Characteristics of the Pragmatic Test for Truth

Pragmatists, like rationalists or empiricists, differ in the outcome or result of their test for truth. Some are theists while others are not. But whatever the difference in conclusion, there is a central agreement on the nature of the pragmatic test itself. These common tenets may be briefly summarized now.

1. First and foremost is the belief that the testing ground of a theory of truth is human experience. Is the position livable? Does it work in the lives of men for whom it is proposed? What is its cash value in human experience? There is a difference as to the source and nature of the *theory* of truth among pragmatists—some get it from sense experience and others from divine revelation—but the *test* is the same, namely, what are the fruits of this theory in the lives of persons? As a test for truth, then, pragmatism is decidedly experiential.

2. Pragmatism, as proposed by William James, is characterized by other things like *futurity*. That is, it is not present and individual experience that will decide the truth of a hypothesis but general, continual, and long-run experience. Over the long haul our experiences will determine the truth of a religious hypothesis. Truth may have tentative confirmation in the present, but it is subject to revision and disconfirmation by our experiences in the distant future. The next point follows directly from this.

3. Pragmatism disavows absolute results of its test. All conclusions about truth are less than absolute and final. Knowledge is always progressive if not processive. Some views may be more widely confirmed than others, but none are really universally and finally settled.

---

26. Schaeffer, pp. 73-74.

There are many other things that characterize philosophical pragmatism, such as its distaste for or denial of essential truth, its progressivism, and its instrumentalism; but the foregoing are at the heart of its test for truth. And this latter point is our only concern here.

# An Evaluation of the Pragmatic Test for Truth

There is undoubtedly a pragmatic strain in all men. Both the need for and appeal of results in human operations add to the attractiveness of the pragmatic theory. Emerging from this are several commendable features of the pragmatic emphasis.

## Positive Contributions of Pragmatism

The offers of pragmatism are a refreshing contrast to those of rationalism. It brings one back from the ivory tower of the abstract possibilities to the concrete realities of life. In this regard we may note several important contributions to the truth question.

1. Pragmatism provides a balance in the reaction against the purely formal and rationalistic approach. It stresses the practical vis-à-vis the purely theoretical. It is not content with seeking causes but also is concerned with producing effects in lives. It does not judge an idea solely on its root but considers also its fruit. Pragmatism rightly stresses that contemplation is not always sufficient; action is sometimes necessary. It points out that truth does not abide merely in the abstract but that it has concrete dimensions and applications.

2. Truth, at least religious truth, is finally confirmed in personal experience. Any theory that offers itself as a world and *life* view must be applicable to life. Human experience is the proving ground where many beautiful theories have been ruined by brutal gangs of facts. If a view is actually unlivable, how can it be considered a true perspective on life? Certainly religious truth, with its life-transforming claim, must be applicable to life or else it must be disqualified as a claimant of truth.

3. Pragmatists also provide a helpful reminder of the tentative or probable nature of much of our knowledge. Perhaps no truth about reality can be known with rational inescapability. And certainly many truths about the world of our experiences are held on less than absolute grounds. Finite man must be content with the limits of his finitude. Even if there are absolute truths, he does not have an absolute grasp on them. And even if there is an Infinite Being, limited humans have far less than an infinite understanding of him. Pragmatists serve a corrective role to dogmatists and a reminder to the Christian that "now we see through a glass darkly" (I Cor. 13:12).

4. Finally, pragmatists, like existentialists, remind us again of the role of the personal and volitional in truth. The process of understanding and applying truth to one's life is more than purely rational. There must be a will to believe. The horse can be led to the water but cannot be made to drink—not at least by purely rational arguments. Even if one could prove rationally *that* God exists, it does not follow that one must believe *in* God. A young man may know *that* there are many wonderful young ladies who would make excellent wives but at the same time he may not desire to place his marital trust *in* any of them. Faith is essential to religious experience. Without an ultimate commitment to the Ultimate, to borrow Tillich's terms, there will be no ultimate or religious satisfaction.

## Some Criticisms of the Pragmatic Theory of Truth

Despite the many obviously commendable features of pragmatism, as a *test* for the truth of a world view it is clearly insufficient. When it is tried in the methodological scales it is found wanting. Many men have undertaken to criticize pragmatism from many perspectives. We summarize here only those observations that apply to pragmatism as a test for truth.

1. First, the results or consequences of an action do not establish what is true but simply what happened to *work*. But success is not truth and failure is not necessarily falsity. Even when given or desired results are attained, one can still ask of the view or action, "Was it true?" The truth question is not settled but is still open after the results are reached. Pragmatism shows only what works (and one would expect truth to work) but it does not prove that what worked is true.

2. Second, truth may be unrelated to results. The results may have been accidental, in which case there would be no more relation to truth than accidentally discovering a million dollars proves one is the rightful owner of it. And even if the results are not accidental but follow regularly from a given belief or action, it does not prove that that belief is true. Unlawful entry by picking a lock will work regularly, but that result does not demonstrate that this was either a right way to enter or that entry was the right result. But it worked. Further, sometimes truth may not bring the desired results (e.g., being honest on one's income tax may be economically painful). And sometimes the desired result may not be true (e.g., desired economic gain by oppressing the poor). Neither the desired nor desirable is necessarily the truthful.

3. Third, truth is more than the expedient. As Josiah Royce once put it, one wonders whether James would be satisfied to put a witness on the stand in court and have him swear to tell "the expedient, the whole expedient, and nothing but the expedient, so help him future

experience."[27] At the heart of this criticism is the contention that we do mean more by truth than what works. The meaning of truth cannot be limited to the functional and practical. And if it were, we would have to determine whether it means what is meaningful for the individual or for the race. If the former, solipsism would follow; that is, truth would be entirely relative to the individual, to what is expedient for him at that moment. And if truth is what is meaningful to most men in the long run, then other problems emerge to which we now turn.

4. Fourth, James admits that it is impossible for us to know the long-run consequences. Further, he admits that pantheism has seemingly worked well for vast masses of men for centuries of time. And were he alive today he would witness even more Westerners adopting pantheistic views. Does this confirm its truth or merely the fact that more people are trying it and finding that it works for them? Maybe, as fads go, there will be a great reversal in the long run. What then? How is one to know *now* which view is true? Must one rely solely on the will to believe? On purely pragmatic grounds there appears to be no other alternative for a finite person who cannot divine the distant future.

5. Fifth, a passional and volitional basis alone for deciding truth is insufficient. It is subject to the same critiques leveled against fideism (see Chapter 3). Faith is certainly necessary for belief *in* God; but one must have some evidence or reason to believe *that* there is a God before he can meaningfully believe in him. But if the pragmatist is unable to decide the momentous religious issue of whether there is a God on intellectual grounds, then he must rely on purely passional bases. And in this case there is really no objective or public test for truth at all. A purely personal and private test for truth cannot meet even the minimal standards for truth criteria, for it is neither available to others nor can it really exclude other views. In short, at this point, pragmatism reduces to fideism.

6. Sixth, on purely pragmatic grounds opposing world views may work equally well. James admitted that pantheism has worked for millions of men for hundreds of years. If what some pantheist desires is the cessation of all craving, then attaining Nirvana (i.e., the extinguishing of all craving) will not only work well but it would work better than heaven as Christians conceive of it (i.e., as a continual fulfilling of all desires forever). Heaven would be a perpetual frustration to one who does not want to experience desire and fulfillment any more. Likewise, Nirvana would not be a fulfillment of Christian desire but a cessation of even the ability to desire. So, on a purely pragmatic ground,

---

27. Quoted by Joseph L. Blau in "Introduction" to *Pragmatism and Other Essays*, p. XIV.

one would have to say that Nirvana works best for pantheists and heaven for Christians. But they are opposing world views; both cannot be true at the same time and in the same sense.[28] Hence, the only alternative for adjudication of these conflicting truth claims is to contend that one view (or both) has the *wrong* goal. But on a purely pragmatic basis there is no way to affirm this, since truth and rightness are known only from attaining desired consequences. And we have already seen that the consequences are best for each view in accord with its own goals but not in accord with those of the other. The pragmatic test for truth cannot rescue us from total relativism in this regard.

## Summary and Conclusion

There is a difference between a pragmatic *theory* of truth and a pragmatic *test* for truth. Christian apologists disavow the former but often employ the latter as part, if not all, of their test for the truth of Christianity. There are indeed some important insights provided by pragmatists that are not foreign to Biblical Christianity. Truth must work in one's life; faith in God is essential; by their fruits you shall know them; and so on. All of these are good. Of course all truth must work, but not everything that works is necessarily true. However, it is both an ill-advised and fatal apologetic move to employ pragmatism as a total test for truth or as the test of a total world view because it reduces to relativism, fideism, or experientialism—all of which are inadequate to establish the truth of Christianity vis-à-vis other world views. Many differing views work for many different people. But results are often unrelated to truth. Further, who can know what the long-run consequences or results of belief will be? How can a person believe *in* God on a purely passional basis when he has no evidence to support a belief *that* God is there? The Christian apologist believes that truth will work in the short run and in the long run, but he cannot hold that what works is true. For many false and evil things have worked for many people for many years. And no finite can see the distant future. Hence, pragmatism fails as a sufficient test for truth in the present.

## SELECT READINGS FOR CHAPTER SIX

**Exposition of Pragmatism**

Dewey, John. *Reconstruction in Philosophy.*
James, William. *Pragmatism.*

---

28. Alan Watts' more recent attempt to build a two-level parallel between pantheism and Christianity will not work. See Watts, *The Supreme Identity* (New York: Vintage Books, 1972), pp. 12, 13, 45, 52, 53. As Watts later saw, both systems must lay claim to truth; but as contrary views, both cannot be true (*Beyond Theology*, pp. VI, VII).

————. *The Meaning of Truth.*

————. *The Will to Believe.*

Peirce, Charles Sanders. *Charles Sanders Peirce: The Essential Writings.*

## Evaluation of Pragmatism

Ayer, A. J. *The Origins of Pragmatism.*

Blanchard, Brand. *The Nature of Thought,* bk. II, chap. 10.

Driscoll, John T. *Pragmatism and the Problem of the Idea.*

Hackett, Stuart. *The Resurrection of Theism,* pt. I, chap. 4.

# *Chapter*

# 7 | *Combinationalism*

The failure of the traditional tests for the truth of a world view such as experientialism, rationalism, evidentialism, and pragmatism shifts hope for an adequate methodology to the combinational approach. There are many approaches, varying according to the number of factors included in the test. However, each view incorporates some presupposed model or framework by which the whole of experience can be understood. And the means of testing the model often includes consistency, coherence, factual adequacy and/or existential relevance. An examination of several important examples will indicate just how combinationalists employ their tests.

## An Exposition of Several Major Presuppositional Methodologies

Combinationalists come from various epistemological backgrounds. And although there is no necessary logical connection between their test for truth and their supposed source of truth, nonetheless there is sometimes a carry-over from one to the other. For instance, Ian Ramsey's empirical background carries over into his emphasis on empirical fit as a test for truth. The important thing, however, is the fact that whatever the epistemological source of truth, each combinationalist feels that a combination of tests for truth is necessary to establish the truth of a world view.

### The Test of Religious Models: Ian Ramsey and Frederick Ferré

As was evident in the analysis of evidentialism (see Chapter 5), experience or facts alone are not self-interpreting; a framework of interpretation is necessary for meaning. Bare facts bear no meaning. Only when they are placed in a meaningful framework or model do they convey more than mere facticity. C. H. Dodd acknowledged that history, for example, was fact *plus* meaning. And for him it was the Christian myth or model that provided the framework to make meaning of history.

*The Qualified Disclosure Models of Ian Ramsey.* Ramsey approaches the problem from an empirical rather than from a historical direction. First, he seeks to clarify what a religious experience is. It is a discernment-commitment situation. A discernment situation is an ordinary empirical experience that suddenly "comes alive" when the "ice breaks" or the "light dawns." For example, "eye meets eye" when a judge suddenly recognizes that the one he is sentencing is his long-lost lover! A commitment situation is one that calls for a response, a total response. It is like Kant's "duty for duty's sake" or a patriot's "my country, right or wrong." There are some partial commitments to the whole of the universe (as mathematics), and there are some total commitments to part of the universe (as a hobby). But a religious response of commitment is a total commitment to the whole universe.[1] It is, as Paul Tillich said, an ultimate commitment to the Ultimate. Hence a religious experience is an empirically grounded disclosure experience in which the "more" or "beyond" disclosed therein calls for a complete commitment. It is a disclosure-commitment situation.[2]

Various models and qualifiers can be used to evoke religious disclosure. By "model" Ramsey means a disclosure model, not a picture model. For religious models do not describe God but merely evoke religious insight. For instance, "When we speak of God as supreme love we are not making an assertion in descriptive psychology. . . ." Rather we are simply modifying the model "love" by the qualifier "supreme" so as to evoke religious insight and commitment. And by use of models and qualifiers one can build up "family resemblances." And from the tangential meeting of these many religious models one can build a religious macromodel, that is, the concept of "God." So the word *God* serves as an integrator term for religious experience similar to the way in which the word I serves as an integrator word for all our self-awareness.[3] Not all God concepts or macrometaphors need be the same. Indeed, models can be qualified endlessly, providing new insights and evoking further responses. But models do help us to be reliably articulate in theology.

---

1. Ian Ramsey, *Religious Language*, pp. 20-55, and *Models and Mystery*, passim.
2. Ramsey, *Models and Mystery*, p. 20, and *Religious Language*, pp. 104, 99.
3. Ramsey, *Prospect for Metaphysics*, pp. 153-64, 174.

Furthermore, the adequacy of one's God models can be tested by what Ramsey calls its "empirical fit." That is, (1) "in all cases the models must chime in with the phenomena; they must arise in a moment of insight of disclosure," and (2) "a model in theology does not stand or fall with the possibility of verifiable deductions. It is rather judged by its stability over the widest possible range of phenomena, by its ability to incorporate the most diverse phenomena not inconsistently." This God model "works more like the fitting of a boot or a shoe than the 'yes' or 'no' of a roll call." In short, the truth of religious language is empirically anchored and experientially tested. "There must be something about the universe and man's experience in it which, for example, matches the behavior of a loving father. . . ."[4] That is, even though there is no strict verification of religious truth there is an experiential confirmation. And the wider the range of experience that can be consistently incorporated into the model of God, the better is the model. Each additional disclosure consistently incorporated makes the model fit more perfectly, in a manner similar to the way a polygon fits more perfectly into a circle the more sides that are added to it. In sum, the truth of the Christian theistic model is judged by its *empirical fit* over the entire range of human experience.

*Frederick Ferré: Metaphysical Models.* Contrary to many contemporary religious language analysts, Ferré claims that religious language cannot be purely noncognitive. He believes that there are models which can provide cognitivity and truth to religious language. He defines a model as that "which provides epistemological vividness or immediacy to a theory by offering as an interpretation . . . something that both fits the logical form of the theory and is well-known. . . ." Models are to be judged by their type, scope, and status. The type is the degree of concreteness, that is, its ability to be "built" of "picture." Scope is a model's degree of inclusiveness, that is, how much reality it purports to represent. And the status of a model indicates how much importance is attributed to it, such as its dispensability or indispensability.[5]

Religious models are characterized by four factors: (1) In contrast to scientific models, religious models do not achieve separation between reality and the observer. (2) Scientific models are only more or less helpful, but religious models cannot be separated from the truth question. (3) Religious models draw upon a different set of facts than do scientific models. In theism the facts are composed of characteristics like personality, will, purpose, and love. And in Christianity, the facts

---

4. Ramsey, *Models and Mystery,* p. 16.
5. Frederick Ferré, *Basic Modern Philosophy of Religion,* pp. 373 f., and "Mapping the Logic of Models in Science and Theology" in *The Christian Scholar,* XLVI (Spring 1963), pp. 13 f.

center in the "creative, self-giving, personal love of Jesus Christ. . . ." (4) In theology, theories (which tie models with other cognitive areas) change occasionally but high level models are quite resistant to change.[6]

The high level religious model may serve as a metaphysical model, that is, to represent the "ultimate character" of the universe. The theistic model is built on imagery taken from Scripture. And Christians justify the ascription of truth to the theistic model by building an all-inclusive system around this model and incorporating data from all other areas of knowledge into its synthesis.

Technically speaking, one cannot test the truth of a theistic model itself but only the truth of the synthesis that results from applying the theistic model to the whole range of human experience. There are really three levels of the total account of things (1) the proverbial metaphysical model or symbol taken from the imagery of Scripture, (2) the set of propositions that attempt to express this symbol in a cognitive way, and (3) the whole range of functions cognitive and noncognitive that make up the religious language game. Since the third cannot be evaluated directly and the first is precognitive, only the second can be tested for truth. These propositions on the second level do two things: they explicate the primary model and give structure to the totality of the third level.[7]

Ferré offers five tests for the truth of the theistic model: (1) *consistency* or the freedom from contradictions among and with the key statements, (2) *coherence* or external consistency extending in a unified way to all bodies of knowledge, (3) *applicability* or relatability to individual experience, (4) *adequacy* or applicability to all domains of feeling and perception, (5) *effectiveness* or usableness as an instrument to cope with the total environment of human experience.[8] Elsewhere Ferré summarized these tests under three headings: consistency, coherence, and adequacy. In short, a metaphysical synthesis is valid only if it is able "to put all experience into a pattern that is *whole,* that is *pervasive,* and that is *adequate.*"[9]

The application of these tests to the theistic model yields the following results for Ferré:[10] (1) Christianity has been *effective* in the past but there is doubt about its effectiveness in the future. (2) There is little doubt about the *applicability* of love and reverence but these are only minimal tests. (3) Christianity meets fairly well the very complex

6. Frederick Ferré, *Language, Logic and God*, pp. 164, 36.

7. Kent Bendall and Frederick Ferré, *Exploring the Logic of Faith*, pp. 165-66.

8. Bendall and Ferré, pp. 166 f.

9. "Science and the Death of God," in *Science and Religion*, ed. Ian Barbour (New York: Harper and Row, 1968), p. 147.

10. Bendall and Ferré, *Exploring the Logic of Faith*, pp. 153 f., 172 f.

test of *adequacy*. (4) No definite contradictions have been demonstrated in Christianity but neither have the proposed solutions to lesser problems gained universal *acceptance*. (5) There is a striking internal coherence in Christianity, but external *consistency* with other bodies of knowledge is not as obvious. Almost surely Scripture contains some empirical statements which are false, says Ferré, such as its claim that the sun stood still for Joshua. All in all one's conclusion must be tentative; but since commitment is integral to any way of life, we must make our leap of faith based on what seems to be the most adequate religious system arising out of one's religious models.

## The Test for a Propositional Scriptural Model: Edward J. Carnell

One of the most creative combinationalists among evangelical apologists was Edward Carnell. Firmly believing in the divine authority of Scripture, Carnell began with the Christian theistic model of the triune God propositionally revealed in sacred Scripture. From this presuppositional starting point he proceeded to test the truth of the Christian system by a combination of methods which he at first labeled "systematic consistency."

*The Rejection of Other Tests for Truth.* Carnell reviews and discards other tests for truth. (1) *Instincts* "cannot be a test for truth, since they cannot distinguish between what is legitimately natural to the species and what is acquired. Only the mind can do that." (2) *Custom* is an inadequate test for truth because "customs can be good or bad, true or false. Something beyond and outside of custom, therefore, must test the validity of customs themselves." (3) Likewise *tradition,* which is a more normative body of customs handed down by a group from early times, is insufficient. For "there are in existence so many traditions, so conflicting in essentials, that only in a madhouse could all be justified." (4) *Consensus gentium,* or the consent of the nations, fails as a test for truth for all men once believed the world was the center of the universe. "A proposition must be true to be worthy of the belief of all, but it does not follow that what is believed by all is true." (5) Neither is *feeling* sufficient, for "without reason to guide it, feeling is irresponsible. . . ." (6) *Sense perception* is rejected by Carnell for at best it is "a source for truth, not its definition or test. Our senses often deceive us." (7) Neither can *intuition* test truth "since intuitions cannot detect false intuitions (and there are many). . . ." (8) The *correspondence* of an idea to reality cannot be a test for truth for "if reality is extra-ideational, then how can we compare our idea of the mind with it? How can the piano be brought into the mind to see if our idea is like it?" (9) *Pragmatism* is likewise inadequate, for on a purely pragmatic ground there is no way to distinguish between materialism's and theism's opposing views of the highest ultimate (whether matter or spirit). Furthermore, a pragmatist has no right on his theory to expect his theory to be verified by future experience, since he has no basis on which to believe in the regularity of the world. In conclusion, Carnell argues that deductive proofs are inadequate because "reality cannot be connected by formal logic alone. . . . Logical truth cannot pass into material truth until the facts of life are introduced into the picture." And inductive proofs are invalid tests for truth, for "here one cannot rise above probability" for "a premise is demonstrated only when it is the necessary implication of a self-evident premise of when its contradiction is shown to be false.[11]

*Systematic Consistency Is an Adequate Test for Truth.* Since all we find in history is probability and all we find in logic is formal validity, we cannot have complete truth until we unite them. "Truth is the properly constructed meaning of *all* experience. Perfect coherence always involves two elements: the law of contradiction to give formal validity, and concrete facts of history to give material validity." For "without formal validity we have no universality and necessity in truth, and without material validity we have no relevance to the world in which we live." Systematic consistency as Carnell conceives of it involves two elements: (1) first, there is "horizontal self-consistency" so that "all of the major assumptions of the position be so related together that they placate the rules of formal logic, chief of which is the law of contradiction." (2) Second, there must be a "vertical fitting of the facts." This means then that "coherence involves an interpretation of the real concrete facts of human history—rocks, bones, and plants." Carnell sees "facts" as including both "external experience," that is, history and "internal experience," namely, man's rational and moral experience.[12] (3) In another work Carnell develops this last point into what he calls a "third method of knowing." Not all knowledge is by acquaintance or inference. Some knowledge comes by "moral self-acceptance."[13] This he describes as "personal rectitude, knowledge by moral self-acceptance, and moral responsibility." Since Carnell admittedly derives this third way from Sören Kierkegaard, we may call it the test of existential relevance. Summarizing then, there are three tests for truth in Carnell: consistency, coherence, and existential relevance. Or, since the second category is subdivided into internal and external, there are actually four tests for truth: logical consistency, internal personal coherence, external empirical adequacy, and existential relevance.

---

11. Edward J. Carnell, *Introduction to Christian Apologetics,* pp. 48-53, 105.
12. Carnell, pp. 105-12.
13. Carnell, *Christian Commitment,* pp. 22, 29.

At this point there is a marked similarity between Ferré and Carnell on tests for truth. However, once the tests are applied by Carnell, his conclusions clearly differ from those of Ferré.

*Testing Christianity by Systematic Consistency.* Carnell claims that systematic consistency "as a proof for any world view that is worth talking about, cannot rise above rational probability." The first reason that Christianity cannot rise above probability is that "it is founded on historical facts, which by their very nature, cannot be demonstrated with geometric certainty." The second reason why "Christianity cannot formally demonstrate its truth is that it is based upon moral values." And "value is a point of personal interest and appreciation beyond which there is no further ground of appeal." Just "as you can lead a horse to the water but you cannot make him drink, so you can lead a man to Christ but you cannot make him trust in Him." However, one can gain moral assurance which "grows out of a conviction that a proposition is coherent, not that it may be geometrically demonstrated." And by moral assurance Carnell means that "apprehended strength of evidence which causes us to be convinced of the truth of a given meaning-pattern, and to act upon its strength."[14]

With this understanding of the probability of proof and moral certainty in mind, Carnell proceeds to apply his tests to Christianity. He begins with a systematic analysis of starting points. For "the Christian believes that starting points control both the method and conclusion. Philosophy is like a railway without switches—once a man is committed to a given direction, he is determined in his outcome." Carnell sees three possible starting points: (1) a *temporal* starting point or natural conditioning that one receives from adolescence to adulthood. This he rejects because "it is common to all men and therefore cancels out." (2) A *logical* starting point or coordinating ultimate which gives being and meaning to our experience is also rejected, for "all logical ultimates must be tested," since there are radical differences between Thales' Water, Plato's Good, and the Christian's Trinity. (3) A *synoptic* starting point is necessary for it is "the answer to the question, 'How do you prove the logical starting point?' "[15]

Carnell views three possible synoptic starting points: (1) *Internal ineffable* experience or that "which brings an immediate assurance to the soul of the reality that is overwhelming and ineffable, as the mystic experience of being swallowed up in God." "We must pass over this," says Carnell, "for reasons stated earlier. Truth is systematic consistency and must be expressed in communicable propositions. But this is im-

---

14. Carnell, *Introduction to Christian Apologetics,* pp. 113-17.
15. Carnell, *Introduction,* pp. 123-25.

possible in mysticism." (2) Likewise *external effable* experience is rejected. For sense, whether of Aristotle or Aquinas, must be rejected "because of its inability to provide immutable truth. Truth, like water, rises no higher than its source." Agreeing with Hume's skeptical empiricism, Carnell argues that despite Aquinas' five futile attempts to prove God, "if truth is to be universal and necessary, it cannot be derived from an analysis of sense perception, for from flux only flux can come." (3) This leaves us with *internal effable* experience as a starting point, that is, with "universal and necessary principles, which are independent of sense perception." For in order to test the truth of a system we must have resident in the soul some unchanging principles that are capable of being expressed in words.[16]

The only alternative to empiricism, then, is a kind of "Christian rationalism" like Augustine's teaching that "the mind by natural endowment from the Creator, enjoys immediate apprehension of those standards which make our search for the true, the good, and the beautiful meaningful." For "to speak meaningfully of the true, the good, and the beautiful, . . . we must have criteria; but criteria that are universal and necessary must be found other than in the flux of sense perception." Otherwise, "how do we know that a thing must be coherent to be true, if the soul, by nature, is not in possession of the conviction?" And "how is it that we are able confidently to say that what is good today will be good tomorrow, unless we lodge our theory of the good in something outside the process of history?" In brief, "how can we know what the character of all reality is, so as to act wisely, unless God tells us?" "Revelation, then, is a condition *sine qua non* for our soul's well-being." As the psalmist rightly said, "Man can see light only in the Light; that all truth is the reflection into the soul of the truth that is in God." This revelation can be either "natural" or "special," but "the data which special revelation supplies is needed to supplement that data which natural revelation displays." For the intellect of man "is incompetent to complete a philosophy of life without special revelation from God. Because of our sinful hearts, which vitiate the evidence of nature, a more sure voice is needed to lead us into a theory of reality which is horizontally self-consistent and which vertically fits the facts."[17]

Within natural revelation Carnell includes the knowledge of himself and the knowledge of God. For in "knowing what truth is, we know what God is, *for God is truth*. God is perfect consistency." But Carnell hastens to say, "This argument for God does not constitute a demon-

---

16. Carnell, *Introduction*, pp. 125, 126, 139.
17. Carnell, *Introduction*, pp. 152-57.

stration; rather it is an analysis. . . . Proof for God is parallel to proof for logic; logic must be used to prove logic." With regard to the latter Carnell believes the laws of logic to be innate, for "if we have not innate knowledge of the rules for right thinking, right thinking cannot start; but right thinking *can* start; therefore, the rules are innate." For "apart from the God Who has revealed Himself in Scripture, we could not *meaningfully* say that murder will be wrong tomorrow; but we *can* so speak; therefore, God, the Author of our moral nature, exists." There is even a knowledge of God through nature. For "to be sure, the world *is* regular; it is conducive to our happiness; and it is harmonious; but it will do little good so to speak until we first possess those standards in relation to which such statements are significant." But again we are reminded by Carnell, "This is not a formal demonstration of God's existence; it is simply proof by coherence." That is, there is no other way to make sense out of our experience *except by this presupposition*. But general revelation, however helpful in these regards, is insufficient to give us knowledge of salvation. As Calvin said, general revelation "ought not only excite us to the worship of God, but likewise to awaken and arouse us to the hope of a future life. . . . But, notwithstanding the clear representations given by God in the mirror of his works . . . such is our stupidity, that, always inattentive to these obvious testimonies, we derive no advantage from them." We must then make recourse to special revelation.[18]

The appeal to special revelation, that is, to the "full and whole sixty-six canonical books, which make up the Bible," is—like any other hypothesis—"verified when it results in an implicative system which is horizontally self-consistent and which vertically fits the facts." But Carnell stresses one point: "When we leave natural for special revelation, we are not bifurcating epistemology; the Christian operates under *one* major premise—the existence of the God Who has revealed Himself in Scripture." And, he continues, "we are not exchanging reason for faith . . . ; rather we are seeking to strengthen the faith which we already have, for faith is a resting of the soul in the sufficiency of the evidence." The Bible is needed to give us more evidence. For "truth is systematically constructed meaning, and if the Bible fulfills this standard, it is just as true as Lambert's law of transmission. Any hypothesis is verified when it smoothly interprets life."[19]

Carnell defends both the fact and necessity of special revelation. On the first point he contends that "no cogent philosophical argument can be introduced to preclude the possibility of revelation." For "one

18. Carnell, *Introduction*, pp. 159-72.
19. Carnell, *Introduction*, p. 175.

can know whether God has revealed Himself or not only after examining all the facts of reality, for any one fact overlooked may be the very revelation itself. . . . To track God down, therefore, one must at least be everywhere at the same time, which is to say, he must be God Himself." In essence, "if a man says there is no God, he simply makes himself God, and thus revelation is made actual. If he says there is a God, the only way he can know this is by God's having revealed Himself, for the Almighty is powerful enough not to give any clues of His existence if He so elects; and again revelation is actual." And "if we have succeeded in showing that generic revelation is possible, the same argument holds for special revelation." For "the fundamental reason why we need a special revelation is to answer the question, What must I do to be saved? Happiness is our first interest, but this happiness cannot be ours until we know just how God is going to dispose of us at the end of history." If Carnell is asked which revelation one should accept, he replies: "Accept that revelation which, when examined, yields a system of thought which is horizontally self-consistent and which vertically fits the facts of history." And in view of all the facts, "the Christian does not arbitrarily accept the Bible as the word of God; he feels he cannot be restrained from so making that hypothesis, for to elect any other position would be to fly in the face of the facts. . . ."[20]

## Some Essential Tenets of Combinationalism

The starting points of combinationalists often differ. Some begin in empirical experience (as Ramsey) while others start with the revelation in Scripture as known through innate rational and moral principles (as Carnell). But the *test* for the truth of their system is essentially the same, namely, a combination of consistency, factual adequacy, and moral or religious relevance. From these similarities emerge several common emphases in combinational methodologies.

1. First, combinationalists agree that no one test for truth (such as logical consistency or empirical adequacy) is an adequate test for truth. At the minimum, both facticity and rationality are necessary, and existential or religious relevance is often included as well. Truth tests must be horizontal (logical) as well as vertical (factual). Combinationalism attempts to be comprehensive.

2. Second, combinationalists are usually presuppositional in their starting point. Starting points are all-important and are not self-justifying. One ends on the track on which he begins. Starting points are not neutral or natural; or, if they are, they must at least be justified. Certainly there are no apodictic starting points either in pure reason or

---

20. Carnell, *Introduction,* pp. 175-78, 190.

in unstructured sense experience. Formal logic is empty and sense experience alone needs structure or meaning.

3. Experience is not self-interpreting. A model or an interpretive framework is necessary for meaning. Without presupposing a world view there can be no meaning or truth. The very possibility of speaking meaningfully depends on an ordered structure within which the discourse can take place.

4. Truth is modeled after a scientific hypothesis. That is, the hypothesis proposed must be tested by consistency and its ability to fit the facts of experience. If it lacks either consistency or factual adequacy, it is falsified.

## An Evaluation of Combinationalism

### Positive Contributions of Combinationalism

There are a number of noteworthy dimensions in the combinationalistic test for truth. Before undertaking a negative critique it will be profitable to point out some of the contributions made by combinationalists.

1. First, the recognition of the need for an interpretive framework or metaphysical model is an important insight. Facts do not speak for themselves. Truth does not reside in facts as such. Only fact plus meaning can be the basis for truth. And the meaning does not arise naturally out of facts. Rather, meaning is something attributed to facts from the outside. It is necessary to presuppose a world view or framework within which a fact can have meaning. Otherwise, one is left with bare, meaningless facticity. Facts and experience may be the basis for meaning, but the data alone cannot provide what meaning should be given to it. Unless the "stuff" of experience is structured by a meaning-model, then it is not possible to speak of the meaningfulness or truth of that system of interpretation. One must indeed presuppose a metaphysical model of the universe before it is even possible to make ultimate truth claims.

2. Second, combinationalists move in the right direction by the attempt to be comprehensive in the test for the truth of a world and life view, that is, with what in German is called a Weltanschauung. Merely one dimension of the truth question is not enough. World view truths must cover all that is in the world. To single out either the rational element or the empirical element alone in order to test the truth of a world view that includes rational, empirical, and even existential elements is decidedly narrow and inadequate. Both Ferré and Carnell saw clearly the need to test the truth of the entire Christian system. Both saw at least three basic elements in this test: the rational, the em-

pirical, and the existential. Ramsey speaks of at least two, consistency and empirical fit, and implies the religious relevance in the nature of the disclosure model. Combining the various aspects of reality in the truth question does, indeed, seem to be a valid insight. For even though truth itself may be formally limited to the propositional statements, nonetheless the realities and dimensions discussed in a Weltanschauung are not limited to propositions or statements. Feelings, attitudes, virtues, and interpersonal relations—to name a few—are all part and parcel of a complete world view and must be accounted for when one is assessing the truth of the overall system. Value and livability cannot be bifurcated from truth, even though they may not be a complete or even adequate test for truth in themselves.

3. Finally, combinationalism does serve as an adequate test for truth within certain contexts. Granted a certain perspective, there is sometimes only one systematically consistent way to interpret all the facts. Granted, for example, the context of a football game, then tackling another intentionally is not morally culpable. But grant the serious context of life, sometimes knocking another down cannot be reasonably interpreted in any other way than as a morally culpable action. Or grant the context of testimony under oath in a courtroom, then intentionally falsifying information can never be reasonably justified as "jesting." Likewise, grant that this is a theistic universe in which a miracle can be defined as an unusual, naturally uncontrollable and unrepeatable event, then it may become unreasonable to conclude that the resurrection of Christ is not a miracle. However, grant the overall context or framework of a naturalistic world, then the resuscitation of Jesus' corpse could not possibly be interpreted as a miracle, for miracles can occur only where there is a God. No acts of God are possible unless there is a God who can act. But in a purely naturalistic universe there is no God; nature is, as it were, "the whole show." Facts, then, cannot be handled with complete arbitrariness within a given universe— at least not when *all* the facts are considered. But when one is in reasonable possession of all relevant facts, then, as in a courtroom context, there can sometimes be a decision "beyond reasonable doubt" as to which interpretation best fits the stated context. Ignoring or overlooking important or relevant facts can lead to the wrong interpretation in some contexts. For instance, any reasonable person of good sense with all the facts about smashed cars, broken glass, skid marks, and bleeding people, and so on, should reasonably conclude that an accident had occurred, *provided that* what he observed was *in the context of an everyday happening* at an intersection, and not, for example, on a stage in Hollywood. In short, given a specific context, logical consistency and empirical adequacy may be a very adequate test for truth.

## Negative Criticism of Combinationalism as a Test
## for Truth of World Views

1. First, the foregoing contribution of combinationalism leads to an important criticism: *when testing world views* we cannot presuppose the truth of a given context or framework, for that is precisely what is being tested. Combinationalism cannot be a test for the context (or model) by which the very facts, to which the combinationalists appeal, are given meaning. An apologist, for example, cannot legitimately appeal to the miracle of Christ's resurrection as a proof for the existence of God. Unless there was already a God to perform that miracle (or act of God), the resurrection could not be a miraculous confirmation of God's existence. Acts of God presuppose a God who can act. And to presuppose a God who can act in order to prove by one of his acts that he exists is viciously circular reasoning. On the other hand, *grant* that God already exists, then the resurrection may very well be a miraculous way of confirming that Jesus of Nazareth is the Son of God. But this is precisely what cannot be granted by nontheists, for it is the whole theistic world view that is in question, and the opponent cannot grant the entire issue under question. Facts make sense only in granted contexts. Theism is an overall context or model of meaning for the universe. Hence, no theist can rightfully appeal to a theistic interpretation of facts (such as an interpretation of a resuscitated corpse as a miraculous resurrection) as a test for the truth of the theistic way of interpreting the universe. Total world views cannot be tested from facts within the world view which gain their very meaning from the world view itself.

2. Second, combinationalism is a form of the "leaky bucket" argument. It says, in effect, that empiricism is not an adequate test for truth, existentialism is not an adequate test for truth, and rationalism is not an adequate test for truth. However, if one leaky bucket does not hold the water, then two or three leaky buckets will not do the job either. Just adding together inadequate solutions does not make an adequate solution.

Unless there is some way to correct the inadequacy of one test for truth by another, then simply adding tests will not provide an adequate test for truth. But the problem with rationalism as a test for truth is not corrected by evidentialism. Rationalism does not fail simply because it provides no factual referents for thought, but because in its strong form it provides no rationally inescapable arguments, and in the weak form it is only a test for the possibility of a system's truth. The law of noncontradiction can show only that a system is wrong if it has contradictions in its central tenets. But there may be several such systems that are internally noncontradictory. Likewise, as we have seen, there may be many world views that account for all the data of experience. Hence, once one steps inside another world view he may find that its major tenets are consistent, that it accounts for all the facts of experience as interpreted through its framework, and that it is existentially relevant to men within that life style. It is noteworthy in this regard that Ferré recognizes this very fact, admitting that other models, even nontheistic ones, may be of equal or even greater weight than the Christian model when tested by his criteria.[21] And if Western theists admit this, then surely the sophisticated Hindu or Buddhist could adequately apply a combinational test for truth and thereby avoid discarding his world view in favor of theism.

Further, the problem with factualism or experientialism is not corrected by adding an interpretive framework—not at least when there are competing models that may likewise be applied to all the facts. It merely shifts the question again to the justification of choosing one model over another. No mystical intuition of models or alleged divine revelation of them will solve the problem, for that either begs the whole question or else it opens the door for all competing views to claim divine revelation for their models (see Chapter 2). Nor will it help to claim that one model "fits" the facts better than another. For the facts take their very meaning from the "fit" given them by the interpretive model, as the next critique indicates.

3. Third, empirical fit is inadequate to test a world view because "fit" is something cut out for the facts by the overall pattern of the world view. That is, the very meaning a fact has as a fact within a system is not found in its bare facticity but by the way it is modeled or incorporated by that given world view. The following diagram illustrates that from one viewpoint the same lines may be conceived as two square legs but from another perspective they may form three round legs. In both interpretations of this figure the facts are identical; only the modeling of them differs.

A similar problem emerged in some ancient languages which did not divide letters into words but left the reader to decide from the context. For example, HEISNOWHERE, as a postmortem announcement on Jesus, could mean two entirely different things depending on how one structures the letters. No appeal to the bare facts alone can solve the problem; only a context, model, or framework from outside can do it. And when one framework works as well as another, then there is no way to adjudicate the problem by appeal to differing models that each

---

21. Bendall and Ferré, *Exploring the Logic of Faith,* pp. 153 f. Even more recently Ferré has argued for a "polymythic organicism" which allows divergent religious models to be equally adequate. See his *Shaping the Future: Resources for the Post-Modern World.*

in its own way accounts for all the facts. Or, at least differing systems may account equally well for an equal number of facts, while having difficulty with others.

The temptation to simply choose the system which best "works" or fits one's life needs has already been discussed under pragmatism (see Chapter 6). But as we saw, a pragmatic test will not suffice for it proves only what "works," not what is true. But differing systems may work equally well for different persons, at least in the short run or in this life; and no one but God can predict the long run with certainty. Yet to wait until after death for verification is too late to settle the truth question now. It would seem, then, that all roads away from the dilemma are dead-end streets. Combinationalism has no way to know whether the model fits the facts best because the facts are all prefitted by the model to give meaning to the whole from the very beginning. So it only begs the question to speak of, say, the facts of religious experience best fitting a theistic model if the facts were gathered in the first place from those having theistic religious experiences. In like manner, the fact of the resurrection of Christ is already a theistic "interprafact" and as such it will naturally fit better into a theisic scheme of things than it will into a naturalistic world view. However, if one speaks merely about the anomalous or unusual event of a resuscitated corpse in the framework of a naturalistic world view, the bare fact also fits the framework.

4. Combinationalism is at best a test only for the falsity, not the truth, of a world view. For more than one view may be both consistent and adequate. However, those that are not both consistent and adequate will be false. Hence, combinationalism would at best eliminate only false world views (or, aspects of world views). It cannot establish one world view as true over all opposing world views. This is so because more than one world view may be both consistent and adequate.

## Summary and Conclusion

Combinationalism provides some significant insights into the truth question. Models or interpretive frameworks are necessary for meaning, and meaning has both logical, factual, and perhaps even existential dimensions. However, as a test for the truth of an overall interpretive model or world view, combinationalism will not suffice. For by simply adding together inadequate tests for truth one does not get an adequate test. The second leaky bucket or the third one does not hold any more water than the first one. Furthermore, since opposing models may do the rational, factual, and existential job equally well, vindication of one truth claim over another will not emerge from the test of combinationalism. Indeed, the very claim that the facts fit better in one system than another begs the question. For the facts gain their very meaning from the system or overall model. And once the facts are "precut" to fit the pattern, then it should be no surprise to anyone that they fit better in that system. Opposing systems can account equally well for all or equal numbers of facts. Hence, combinational tests are insufficient to exclude opposing systems, in which case they are ineffective in establishing the truth of any one system over others.

## SELECT READINGS FOR CHAPTER SEVEN

### Exposition of Combinationalism

Barbour, Ian G. *Myth, Model and Paradigms.*
Carnell, Edward J. *An Introduction to Christian Apologetics.*
Ferré, Frederick. *Language, Logic and God.*
————. *Exploring the Logic of Faith.*
Ramsey, Ian. *Religious Language.*
————. *Models and Mystery.*

### Evaluation of Combinationalism

Hackett, Stuart. *The Resurrection of Theism*, pt. III, chap. 2.
Lewis, Gordon R. *Testing Christianity's Truth Claims*, chaps. 7-11.
Popper, Karl. *The Poverty of Historicism.*
Yandell, Keith. *Basic Issues in the Philosophy of Religion*, chap. IV.

# Chapter 8 | Formulating Adequate Tests For Truth

In the preceding chapters we have set forth and evaluated various tests for truth. Each in turn has proven itself inadequate in testing the truth of a world view for different reasons. But behind each insufficient test for truth has been at least one common element: the inability to establish one system and eliminate all competing systems that claim truth. Time has now come to attempt an adequate alternative. There will be two levels to this proposal: first, the basis for testing the truth of an *overall world view* such as theism or pantheism; second, the means of testing for the truth of competing truth claims *within a world view*.

## The Test for Truth of a World View

A summary of the results to this point is necessary to understanding the direction of this proposal. It was concluded that all the other proposed tests for truth failed for the same basic reason(s). This conclusion, however, cannot be used to conclude agnosticism or skepticism since these alternatives are self-defeating.

### Self-Defeating Nature of Positions That Deny Truth Can Be Known

Skepticism recommends a suspension of judgment about truth. The skeptic claims that dilemmas, equipollence of arguments, divergence of opinion, the relativity of thought, and so forth, lead one to conclude that truth is unknowable. The wise man will simply withhold belief, we are told by the skeptic. As commendable as this view may be in many cases, it cannot be consistently applied to all truth claims. Complete skepticism is self-defeating. The very affirmation that all truth is unknowable is itself presented as a truth affirmation.[1] As a truth statement purporting that no truth statements can be made it undercuts itself. If it is not a truth statement or if it is not a universal truth statement, then it is not even in the philosophical arena. In short, the claim of the skeptic and agnostic that "truth is unknowable" is either: (1) a universal truth claim, (2) a particular truth claim, or (3) neither a universal nor particular truth claim. If it is a universal truth claim, then it undercuts itself, for it is claiming that no true statements (including its own) can be made. If it is offered only as a particular truth claim, namely, that some (many, most, etc.) truths cannot be known, then it is self-consistent. However, in this case it does not eliminate the possibility that one can know or establish the truth of some other world view. And if the question of the truth of these views is important or momentous to a person, then it would be a kind of defeatism, if not a cruelty, to dissuade him from attempting to discover what seemed so significant to his life and thought. Finally, if the skeptic claims he is making no truth claim at all with his recommendation to suspend judgment about all truth claims, then he must explain how a statement about whether truth is knowable can avoid being a truth statement. To turn the tables, why could not one be skeptical about all skeptical statements without himself being a skeptic? Or, how can the skeptic claim sanctuary in alleged meta-truth statements about what is knowable in the realm of truth?

The very claim that the premise of skepticism ("all truth is unknowable") is not a truth claim would automatically disqualify it philosophically, for philosophy is concerned with truth. To allow meta-truth or nontruth statements to dictate whether or not one can know truth is as unphilosophical as one can get. So if the skeptic maintains that his claim is a truth statement, then it is self-defeating (if universal) or unsuccessful (if limited). Otherwise it is not a truth claim—in which case it is not even philosophical, that is, it has nothing to do with truth.

The claim that skepticism is merely a nontruth proposal about the question of truth which one finds most fruitful and usable for whatever theoretical or practical reasons will not suffice. First, this proposal does not eliminate contrary positions. One may conclude that dogmatism is right for the same reasons. Second, this proposal implies a consistency or pragmatic test for the truth of skepticism and opens it to all the criticisms of these positions (see Chapters 2, 6, 7). Furthermore, especially the pragmatic test for the skeptical proposal is double-edged and it boomerangs. Skepticism may not work for most in the long run. Indeed, as Hume confessed, one of the most persistent arguments against

---

1. See chap. 1 for further discussion on this point.

skepticism is that even the skeptic can not live it completely and consistently. Hence, skepticism cannot be established pragmatically. And even if the allegedly nontruth proposal of skepticism were not defeated pragmatically, it is still self-defeating. No statement about all truth can disavow all truth implications, and the skeptical proposal is a statement about all truth. Even working presuppositions about truth must be cognitive and meaningful. And whatever is meaningful must be subject to truth or falsity via the law of noncontradiction, for apart from noncontradiction one cannot even know what the statement means. But if the skeptical proposal is subject to the truth test of noncontradiction, it cannot avoid being offered as a truth statement. In short, to disclaim the possibility of knowing any truth is indeed a truth claim of the highest and most serious kind. Truth cannot be denied unless some truth is being affirmed.

Agnosticism is likewise self-defeating.[2] In its unlimited form it claims that all knowledge about reality (i.e., truth) is impossible. But this itself is offered as a truth about reality, in which case it defeats itself. In the weaker form of limited agnosticism there is no problem but neither is there success in eliminating all knowledge about reality. Simply to affirm that one does not (or even cannot) know something about reality does not really eliminate the possibility that he can (or even does) know something about reality. But the disclaimer of *all* knowledge about reality is self-stultifying, for it is offered as a truth about reality that no truths about reality can be known. If true, this would be false. For if it is true about reality that no truth can be affirmed of reality, then neither can this alleged truth (of agnosticism) be true about reality. But if it is not a true claim about reality, then it must be false. Hence, if it were true, then it would be false. And if it is false, then it is false. So in either case total agnosticism cannot be true.

There is a more subtle form of philosophical agnosticism to which even evangelical thinkers fall victim.[3] It may be called the perspectivity of all truth. The basic premise is that even though truth is knowable, nonetheless *all truth is perspectival*. What is not always clearly seen nor fully appreciated under cover of the apparent humility in this position is that it either harbors within its bosom a radical dogmatism or else it reduces to a complete agnosticism. Either the claim is that all truth is perspectival, or else it claims that all truth except this view of truth is perspectival. If it means the former, then it is either self-defeating or special pleading. It is self-defeating to say all truth

2. See chap. 1.
3. See Arthur Holmes, *Faith Seeks Understanding*, pp. 46 f.

is perspectival including this one nonperspectival statement about all truth. In this case one is making a nonperspectival statement to the effect that all truth including itself is perspectival. On the other hand, if one claims special status for that one statement to the effect that all other statements are perspectival except his, then he is special pleading. Why cannot any other opposing position claim the same for itself? Why cannot a nonperspectivalist claim that the perspectivity view is itself only a limited perspective on reality? In which case a broader perspective might eliminate the need to say that all truth is limited by perspective. Indeed, the central issue of the perspectivity view misses the very nature of a total world view. There are limited perspectives within an overall view, but the *overall* view itself is no longer a claim about limited perspectives. Hence, if perspectivity is offered as a world view, then it is either self-defeating or else it is in the same category as other world views. For if the perspectivity view is an overall perspective on everything that is—which is what "world view" means—the so-called perspectivity view, like any other view, is no longer a limited perspective. One may have a limited *basis* for justifying that he is taking this nonperspectival view of everything that is; nevertheless, the *perspective* he is taking in the view is not one among many limited stances but is the overall view that he considers to be the only true and ultimate way to look at all things. That is precisely what a metaphysical position is, namely, the claim to possess the one true way to look at all of reality. Hence, the apparent humility of the perspectivity people is a confusion of the limited basis for taking a metaphysical position and the unlimited or all-encompassing perspective demanded by the very nature of the world view taken. A finite person's basis will always be limited, but his view can be all-encompassing. One's grasp of metaphysical truth is conditioned by his finitude; but the truth itself, if it is metaphysical, is unconditional.

## The Inadequacy of Alternative Tests for Truth

Six alternative tests for truth were examined in the preceding chapters: rationalism, fideism, experientialism, evidentialism, combinationalism, and pragmatism. Each was weighed in the balances and found wanting for different reasons. The one insufficiency common to all these tests for truth is that none of them could definitively establish one world view over another. Whatever applicability they may have *within* a world view, none was sufficient to decide or adjudicate *between* or among world views.

*Rationalism Is Insufficient.*[4] Rationalism in the strong form of logic-

---

4. See chap. 2 for further elaboration of this point.

ally inescapable arguments proves nothing, since there is no way to logically prove the very laws of thought which are used to prove things. All rational justification must come to an end in first principles. These first principles cannot be rationally proven, for if logic is used as the basis for proving logic, then one is simply arguing in a circle. Further, even granting the validity of the laws of thought, they cannot be validly used to demonstrate any reality by logical necessity. It is always *logically* possible that nothing ever existed, including myself, the world, and God. Reality is not based on logical necessity. Nonexistence of everything is a *conceivable* state of affairs. And to say that the nonexistence of everything is an unaffirmable premise because someone must exist to have the conception or to make the affirmation only diverts the issue. For in this case one is defending the existence of something by its undeniability and not by its logical necessity. There is no logical necessity which demands that the conceiver or affirmer exist in the first place.

In the weak form of rationalism, that is, noncontradictoriness, it is also insufficient; for many competing world views may be internally consistent. The law of noncontradiction as such is only a test for falsity, not a test for truth. That is, a view is wrong if it is contradictory to itself, but it is not automatically true if it is noncontradictory or consistent with itself. There is no way by logic alone to prove that all views except one are contradictory, thus forcing one to adopt as true the only remaining view. Every major world view is or can be consistent with its own basic axioms or presuppositions. Spinoza deduced pantheism logically from his axioms and Descartes deduced theism logically from his axioms. But how are we on the basis of reason alone to choose between the two competing sets of axioms? Other rationalists accept revelation as their basic axiom. But how do we know which alleged revelation to accept? Even revelational rationalists admit that one would have to be omniscient in order to definitively and finally apply the consistency test for truth, for he would have to know all the facts and relationships about all the truth systems in question in order to know which of them is ultimately consistent and which are ultimately contradictory. But since this is impossible in practice, the rational test for truth via noncontradictoriness is inadequate to establish the truth of one view over another.

*Fideism Is Insufficient.*[5] As was seen earlier, fideism is not really a *test* for truth at all, it is simply a claim for truth. It reduces to the claim "this is true because I believe it to be true." But contrary beliefs are possible. Hence simply believing a position is an inadequate basis for contending it is true vis-à-vis other views. Any appeal to some

---

5. This point is discussed in more detail in chap. 3.

ground for belief other than the belief itself is, strictly speaking, not fideism. For instance, if someone believes Christianity to be true rather than Islam because it is more consistent or livable, then he has imported a rational or pragmatic test for truth to support his belief. In this case he is fideistic in his *claim* but rational or pragmatic in his *test* for truth. But we are only discussing fideism as an inadequate test for truth. In fact, the frequent recourse of fideists to other means of justifying their beliefs tends to verify its inadequacy as a test for truth. Beliefs alone are not self-justifying; they are only claims that call for confirmation outside themselves. *Credo ad absurdum* may be admirable to some but it is justifiable to no one.

*Experientialism Is Inadequate.*[6] As a test for truth, experientialism does not eliminate the possibility of other views being true. Experience is not self-justifying; it is not even self-interpreting. Experience is what persons have, while truth is what is affirmed about these experiences. Truth is propositional; it is an expression about experience. Whether or not the expression about experience is adequate cannot be determined by the experience alone; for the experience apart from the expression is like content without form, or "stuff" without structure. Events and experience can be structured and expressed in different ways. The most adequate or true structure or model cannot be determined by the experience itself, any more than Jello can by itself determine which mold should form it into which shape. Differing models or world views refer to the same core of human experience as the basis of their opposing metaphysical views. Hence, theism cannot be established over pantheism on experience alone since both theists and pantheists have the same human conditions beneath their opposing systems. In a word, whatever is common to many cannot be used as uniquely supportive of only one.

The appeal to special experiences (mystical or whatever) will not aid any one world view's claim over another because all can claim to have special experiences. Furthermore, if the experience is truly unique to one view and unavailable to another, then there is no way to use it as a truth support for one view *as opposed to* the others because it is private to that view. In other words, what is not available to them cannot be used against them. A world view has a right to face its accusers and to view the evidence of their accusations; private experience cannot be a legitimate part of a public test for truth. Any test for truth competing for the minds of men in general is a public test for truth. The tests for truth claimed by world views are definitely of this variety.

*Evidentialism Is Insufficient.*[7] It was concluded earlier that eviden-

---

6. For further information see chap. 4.
7. Chap. 5 treats this at greater length.

tialism, like experientialism, is insufficient for testing a world view because no facts are self-interpreting. All facts are interpreted by the context in which they appear and ultimately by the world view or ultimate context in which they appear. But if the facts gain their meaning and truth by the context, then they cannot be used to determine the truth of the context. This would be viciously circular. For instance, one cannot argue that the resuscitation of Jesus of Nazareth's body— granting that it did resuscitate—is an act of God (miracle) that proves Christian theism to be true. For only if this is already a theistic universe to begin with can one even interpret this event to be a miraculous resurrection or act of God. If to interpret an event as a resurrection or act of God already *presupposes* God's existence, then an event so interpreted cannot be used as a *proof* of God's existence. If the model gives the fact its meaning and truth values, then the fact cannot in turn be used to give the model its meaning and truth. Indeed, there are many models capable of handling all the facts of experience. Naturalism can handle bodily resuscitation as an unusual natural event with no *known* cause. Pantheism can explain it as a concentrated manifestation of God who is manifest in everything. In like manner other views can handle all the facts by their macro or metaphysical models. The question is not one of bare facts but of the interpretation given the facts by divergent world views or models. There is no way to use the bare facts alone in order to justify one model of them over another. Indeed, there is probably no way to know the facts apart from the model or framework through which they are understood, for the very fact known involves the relationships or context in which it is known. Facts are not islands unto themselves; they are known in relationships or gestalts. And even if pure and isolatable facticity were knowable apart from contexts, it would be useless as a test for truth, for pure facticity or a bare fact as such has no truth value. It is neutral and cannot be given context or meaning—and hence truth value—by different models. Hence, bare facts as such cannot establish the truth of a model, and facts as interpreted by a model cannot be used to establish the truth of the model which provides the justification for interpreting the facts in that particular way.

*Combinationalism Is Insufficient.*[8] The combinational test for truth is sometimes known as systematic consistency. It involves a combination of two or more of the foregoing tests for truth. Often it entails three tests: logical consistency, empirical adequacy, and experiential relevance. Whatever the form, combinationalism is insufficient as a test for the truth of a world view because it does not eliminate the possi-

---

8. A more complete analysis is given in chap. 7.

bility of other views being true. For pantheism is as consistent to its premises, as adequate in explaining all the facts, and as relevant to the experience of a Hindu as Christianity is to a Christian. If one desires the cessation of craving and frustration, then pantheism provides a systematically coherent world view. Of course, if one desires ultimate fulfillment and individual satisfaction, then Christian theism would be more systematically coherent. But there is the rub. How is one to judge which *desire* is right or which is the desire for truth? Neither view has the right to merely assume its goal to be the true one, for this merely begs the question. Neither view can eliminate the other on the basis of systematic consistency, for both have this feature in their sophisticated forms. How then is truth to be adjudicated by a purely combinational test? In the final analysis combinationalism is not a new or different test for truth; it is simply a combination of other inadequate tests for truth. If rationalism alone or evidentialism alone or experientialism alone will not suffice, then how is combining their inadequacies going to do the job? Two more leaky buckets will not in the end hold any more water than one leaky bucket. Combinationalism does not patch the hole in any one of the tests for truth by adding others. The patches are just as porous as the pail. Adding up inadequate tests for truth, without correcting the inherent inadequacies, does not equal an adequate test for truth. Indeed, combinationalism is at best only a test for falsity of some views but not a test for the truth of one world view. For more than one world view may fit all the tests of combinationalism.

*Pragmatism Is Insufficient.*[9] The pragmatic test for the truth of a world view is not capable of eliminating opposing world views either. What works for one individual might not for another. Pantheism works for the pantheist and naturalism for the naturalist in accord with their different models. On purely pragmatic grounds we might conclude that both theism and pantheism are true, since they seem to work for adherents of each world view in accordance with their aspirations. But both cannot be true because they are mutually exclusive ways of viewing ultimate reality. Hence, pragmatism does not prove which view is true but merely which view seems to work for a person with his desires or starting premises. Further, how can we know which system will work best for most men in the long run? One would have to be God in order to know enough to establish the truth of one system. At best, finite man may guess at the long-range results and "will to believe" whichever system tempts him on existential grounds. But this is no longer a pragmatic ground but a fideistic or experiential one, and as such it

---

9. Pragmatism is expounded and critiqued in chap. 6.

is subject to the criticisms of these views already given. In short, pragmatism is not capable of establishing one view as true over another.

At best pragmatism manifests the *application* but not the *justification* of a world view. It indicates whether a view about reality really works when applied to life. But workability and truth are not identical. Some things work very well but are not right (e.g., cheating). Other things do not seem to work as well in the short run, and we cannot determine the long run (e.g., honesty). Finally, the results of a belief or view may be unrelated to its rightness or truth. Winning in the lottery does not prove the winner was right for playing any more than losing proves the others were wrong for playing. Likewise, my child's disobedience to a misstated command does not make either my statement truly what I desired nor his disobedience right, even though the results were what I really desired. Pragmatism is not a sufficient test for the truth of anything, to say nothing of the test of the truth of world views.

## Setting Forth an Adequate Test for Truth

If the foregoing tests for truth were exhaustive, the epistemological consequences would be disastrous. If no test for truth is sufficient, then truth cannot be established and tested; and if truth cannot be established, then the Christian apologist is out of business. Fortunately this is not the case, for there is light at the other end of the tunnel. There is a test for truth that meets the standards of adequacy, that is, it can establish one view over against opposing views. We propose that *undeniability* is the test for the truth of a world view and *unaffirmability* is the test for the falsity of a world view.

### Unaffirmability as a Test for Falsity

First let us examine what is meant by the unaffirmability of a position. Unaffirmability does not mean that a view is *unsayable* or unstatable. Even complete nonsense can be said or stated. For example, one can state that there are square triangles even though the statement has no meaning. One can state: "the sound of the music is the color red" but this too is nonsense. The ability to state "I cannot express myself in words" is one thing, but the ability to meaningfully affirm this is another. In this case the statement is self-defeating, since it is an expression in words claiming that no expression in words can be so made. From these illustrations we wish to draw two conclusions. First, not everything sayable is meaningful; nonsense is sayable or statable. Second, some sayable things are unaffirmable. For example, one cannot affirm that he lacks the ability to affirm anything. Also one cannot affirm his own nonexistence. In both cases what he affirms is denied in the very process or act of affirmation. This leads to a further distinction, namely, that which is directly unaffirmable and that which is indirectly unaffirmable.

*The Direct Unaffirmability of Something.* Direct unaffirmability occurs when the statement itself provides the information to defeat itself. The statement "I cannot express myself in words" is an example of this.[10] The statement is itself an expression in words. One need not look further to know it is false. It directly destroys itself. The datum uttered is self-annihilating of the thought expressed by that datum. Another example is "I cannot think," for that involves thought directly in order to even think it. This kind is obvious, but it is not the only kind of an unaffirmable self-defeating statement.

*The Indirectly Unaffirmable.* The directly unaffirmable means that the very *act* of thinking or expressing something is self-defeating. The act of thinking by which one thinks that he cannot think is not meaningfully thinkable, and the very act of speaking by which one says that he cannot speak is really unspeakable in a meaningful way (it is *sayable* in a meaningless way). But what about statements like "I came to the conclusion that I know everything intuitively"? The statement itself does not provide the data for its own self-destruction. The very *act* of thinking this conclusion does not self-destruct. So it is not directly self-stultifying in the same sense as the other examples. However, there is another sense in which the statement "I came to the conclusion that I know everything intuitively" is unaffirmably self-defeating; it is *indirectly* self-defeating, for the very *process* of "coming to" that conclusion was a deductive or inferential one, and that very process is at odds with the statement that all knowledge is possessed intuitively without deduction or inference. Hence, although the *act* of expressing the statement is not inconsistent, the *process* by which the statement was derived contradicts the thought expressed in the statement.

Another example of an indirectly self-defeating assertion is agnosticism. To say "I know that one cannot know anything about reality" implies that he does. However, the statement itself does not appear to undercut itself directly. That is, there do not appear to be sufficient data in the statement to destroy what it intends to express. However, if the statement were true as proposed there would be no way for the person to make the statement. In short, there is no *basis* for making the statement unless the statement is false, for how could the agnostic make that statement about reality unless he really did know something about reality? Here then is a second kind of indirectly unaffirmable statement, namely, one for the affirmation of which there is

---

10. See chap. 1.

no *basis*. Any statement which negates the only basis on which it can make its affirmation (or denial) is indirectly self-defeating.

Our purpose here is not to make a comprehensive typology of kinds of self-defeating statements but merely to point out some varieties sufficient to illustrate the test for truth via self-destruction whether in the act, process, or basis for making the statement. The following chapters will indicate just how this will be applied in practice to various claimants of truth.

## Undeniability as a Test for Truth

What is unaffirmably self-defeating is false. And, conversely, what is undeniable is true; this would follow logically. But one might ask if there is anything in actual practice that is undeniable. And if there is, is it anything more than the purely definitional? Let us call these two kinds of undeniability existential (relating to existence or reality) and theoretical or definitional (relating to possible realities).

*Definitional Undeniability.* The affirmation "triangles must have three sides" is undeniably true. But this does not mean that there is in fact any such thing as a triangle. It means only that *if* there were a triangle it would in fact have three sides. Or, there is no other meaningful way to define a triangle than as a three-sided figure for that is what we mean by triangularity. Likewise, one might claim, as many Christians do, that *if* there is a God he must be a necessary Being. This would not necessarily imply that there is known to be a God, but that if one exists, then he could not have come into being or cease to be but must necessarily always be. In brief, there is a definitional necessity in conceiving of God. And if one were actually found to exist, then this would actually be as true of him as triangularity would be true of an actual triangle. Both would be undeniably true definitionally, even if neither God nor triangles exist actually. Many other examples could be multiplied. A few will suffice to further illustrate definitional undeniability: all wives are married, all circles are round, the whole is always more than any one part, and so on.

All of these, it may be charged, are purely mathematical or theoretical. As such they are empty tautologies, and no tautology or definitional statement tells us anything about the real world. Are there any actually undeniable statements about existence?

*Existential Undeniability.* An affirmative answer is demanded to the foregoing question. Existence, at least my existence, is actually undeniable. I must exist in order to make the denial. Nonexistents do not affirm or deny; they are not and they speak not. Whenever I attempt to deny my existence, I catch myself existing in the process of making the denial. So at least something is actually undeniable, namely, my own existence.

As was noted earlier, the rationalist makes recourse to this argument to support rationalism. But since the argument does not show logical necessity but only actual undeniability, he has left purely rational ground for existential ground when he makes this move. My nonexistence is logically possible; it is not inconceivable that I exist not. No logical necessity is grounding my existence. Even if I cannot affirm that I *do* not exist, I can nonetheless meaningfully think that I *might* not exist. Of course, I must exist in order to conceive of my nonexistence. But the "must exist" does not mean *"logically* must" but only *"actually* must." For unless I actually exist I cannot conceive of anything, for there is no "I" or "me" there at all. But this does not mean that my existence in the first place is based on logical necessity.

Whether or not one can justify the affirmation that anything exists necessarily is a question we leave for later. It will suffice here to show that the proposition "no statement that is true by definitional necessity can also be true about reality" fails. The fact that squares must be defined as four-sided figures does not mean that one cannot exist. Furthermore, the attempt to affirm that no necessary statements can be made about reality is itself a necessary statement about reality and is, on that grounds, self-defeating. To offer as a necessary truth about reality that there are no necessary truths about reality is self-destructive. If one has no necessary basis for saying that there are no necessary statements about reality, then it is possible that there are some; the possibility cannot be eliminated in advance. Existential truth cannot be legislated; it must be looked for in experience. What this search uncovers and whether it is undeniable will be discussed later. At present the door is open for the possibility of some undeniable truth about ultimate reality. All attempts to lock the door turn out to be self-defeating.

In summation, whatever is undeniable is true, whether it is definitionally undeniable or existentially undeniable. If something definitionally undeniable is also found to be actually undeniable, then whatever is definitionally necessary to attribute to it, that it must necessarily actually have. That is, if we actually find a triangle, then it must actually have three sides. And, likewise, if a God is actually found to exist, then he must actually have all the characteristics that God must necessarily be conceived to have, such as eternity, immutability, and so forth.

Of course, there is no way to show in advance that theism is actually undeniable and all nontheisms are unaffirmable. All we can say at present is that if one view is undeniable, then conversely the other opposing views must be at least untrue, if not unaffirmable. And if any view can be found to be unaffirmable, then it is, *ipso facto,* untrue. As a work on Christian apologetics, this book will show that all non-theistic world views are directly or indirectly unaffirmable and only theism is affirmable and, hence, only theism is true.[11] Further, we believe not only that theism is the only affirmable world view but that it is undeniably true.[12] In short, nontheisms are sayable but not meaningfully affirmable; they are utterable but not justifiable. Whether or not our project is successful cannot be determined here; we must wait until after it is expounded.

# The Justification of Truth Statements Within a World View

Establishing the truth of a world view is a special problem and demands a specific test for truth. We have concluded that the traditional tests for truth will not suffice because they are inadequate to judge *between* world views. More than one world view may be true on the grounds of rationalism, experientialism, evidentialism, and so forth. However, unaffirmability can falsify a world view and undeniability can verify a world view. Supposing this to be the case when judging *between* world views, we now come to the problem of determining what is true *within* a given world view. It is here that combinationalism or systematic coherence seems to be the most adequate test for truth for several reasons, not the least of which is that it is difficult to find undeniability in historical and experiential matters.

## The Reasons for Adopting Systematic Consistency

Once an overall framework has been determined, then it follows that whatever most consistently and comprehensively fits into that system is true. If that system of truth is not only a world view but a world and *life* view, then the applicability of that truth to life also becomes a crucial aspect of that truth. Several arguments support this contention.

First of all, the grounds for rejecting systematic consistency (or combinationalism) as a test *between* world views do not apply to using it as a test for truth *within* a given system or world view. The main arguments against it as a test for a world view are based on the fact that more than one system might be equally systematically consistent and that the facts within a system are given meaning by that system. But once the system and therefore the ultimate meaning of all facts within it are determined, then these facts should not be interpreted in ways contrary to the system. And once it is determined that no other sys-

---

11. See chaps. 9-12.
12. See chap. 13.

tem is true, then there is no external competing way to interpret these facts. Within a given system consistency of interpretation and comprehensive coverage of all facts are definitive. Error arises when the interpretation is either internally inconsistent or else not factually all-inclusive. For instance, if this is a theistic universe and one refuses to accept the possibility of an empirical event indicating a miracle, then he is inconsistent. In a theistic universe miracles can happen and a given event (e.g., the resurrection of Christ) might just be a miracle. It is inconsistent with the system to rule it out. Further, if this is a theistic universe and one fails to take into account *all the facts,* then he might be led to accept Judaism rather than Christianity. Suppose it is a fact that Jesus of Nazareth fulfilled Old Testament prophecy to be the Jewish Messiah. If so, only by overlooking (or negating or not counting) these facts can one who desires truth remain in Judaism rather than acknowledge the truth of Christianity. In short, *all* the facts interpreted in an internally *consistent* way are a sufficient test for truth within a given metaphysical system.

Second, once a system of truth is established, it follows logically that whatever is consistent with that system is true and whatever is not consistent with it is not true. *Systematic* consistency follows from the establishment of a *system* of truth. Or, to state it another way, once a macromodel is established for interpreting all the experiences and occurrences in the world, then the most consistent and comprehensive way the micromodels are fitted into it is the indication of truth. Systematic consistency is inadequate to test *between* divergent systems since they all may be systematically consistent within themselves. But, on the other hand, systematic consistency is eminently qualified to test for truth *within* a system; that is what the system is all about. Anything not systematically related cannot be a truth within that system. Likewise, any fact unaccounted for in a system that claims to account for *all* facts stands against the truth of that system. A world view model must be both consistent and comprehensive. Whatever best fits within its overall interpretive framework is to be taken as true, and whatever does not fit is to be taken as false.

### The Probability of the Systematic Coherence Test for Truth

It must be admitted that systematic consistency does not provide an apodictic or undeniable test for truth. No finite mind is in actual possession of *all* the facts. Nor is any finite person able to comprehend completely *all* the relationships between facts. As in almost everything else in life, probability is the guide. Whichever view *best* fits and is *most* consistent must suffice. Of course the major apologetic problems of defending Christianity are resolved when one establishes the metaphysical view within which the facts are to be interpreted. If theism can be established undeniably as the model, then pantheism, naturalism, and panentheism are thereby eliminated. This will be the aim of Part Two of this book. The remaining choices are among competing theisms, as Judaism, Islam, and Christianity. The adjudication of truth claims among these then will not be a purely philosophical enterprise. Here the probability of historical and evidential arguments will be decisive. If Christianity best explains all the known facts in the most consistent way, then it should be accepted as truth. Part Three of this book will be an attempt to argue that this is indeed the case.

## Summary and Conclusion

The first seven chapters attempted to show that skepticism and agnosticism are self-defeating and the major traditional methods are inadequate to test the truth of a world view. Another test was offered in this chapter, namely, actual undeniability. If we can establish that all nontheistic views engage in unaffirmable statements germane to those views, then we can reject them as false. If we can show that theism is the only affirmable view or that it is undeniable, then it will be established as true.

Once this is established to be a theistic universe, then whichever form of theism can be demonstrated to best explain all known facts in the most consistent way will be the true theistic view. It is the contention of this work (in Part Three) that evangelical Christian theism qualifies as the most systematically coherent theistic view on all three tests: consistency, empirical adequacy, and experiential relevance.

## SELECT READINGS FOR CHAPTER EIGHT

Ayer, A. J. *Problems of Knowledge.*

Boyle, Joseph, *et al.* "Determinis, Freedom, and Self-Referential Arguments," *Review of Metaphysics* (Sept. 1972).

Grisez, Germain. *Beyond the New Theism.*

Hall, Evert. *Philosophical Systems.*

Johnstone, Henry. *Philosophical Arguments.*

Passmore, John. *Philosophical Reasoning.*

Yandell, Keith. "Metaphysical Systems and Decision Procedures" (unpublished doctoral dissertation, Ohio State University, 1966).

# Part
# TWO

# *Theistic*
# *Apologetics*

Deism
Pantheism
Panentheism
Atheism
Theism

# Chapter

# 9 | *Deism*

There are a limited number of mutually exclusive ways to view the whole of reality. The ensuing chapters will review these different metaphysical systems. The purpose will be to show that all the major alternate world views are self-defeating and inadequate and that only theism stands the test for truth laid down in the last chapter of Part One (Chapter 8). Theism is the belief that there is a God both *beyond* and *within* the world, a Creator and Sustainer who sovereignly controls the world and supernaturally intervenes in it. Deism holds with theism that God created the world but denies his supernatural intervention in it on the grounds that the world operates by natural and self-sustaining laws of the Creator. In short, God is *beyond* the world but he is not active in the world in a supernatural way. Pantheism holds that God is *identical* with the real world. God is all and all is God. God does not transcend reality but is immanent in reality, or rather, all reality is in God. Beyond him is only illusion or nonreality. Panentheism or finite godism (or bipolar theism) contends that God is *in* all the world; the world is the "body" of God. God in his actuality is commensurate with the changing world of our experience; only God's potentiality transcends the world. In brief, God is to the world as the mind is to the body. Atheism, of course, denies that there is a God in any of the above senses either *in* or *beyond* the world. Polytheism, the belief that there are many gods beyond the world, is not a major philosophical world view and will be treated only in passing under the theistic argument that there is only one God (see Chapter 13).

# Exposition of the Deistic World View

Deism is not presently a major world view but its significance is both historic and lasting. The deistic movement arose during the seventeenth century and flourished in the eighteenth but largely died out by the nineteenth century. It represents, however, one of the major metaphysical positions about reality that conflicts with theism.

## The Roots of Deism

Insofar as deism involved a negative destructive criticism of both supernatural revelations and miracles, it sprang from the ancient pagan writers like Celsus and Porphyry. Insofar as it was hostile to Christianity it was a reaction against an overemphasis on doctrine and ritual at the expense of ethical considerations. But as a philosophical movement, deism borrowed the theistic concept of God and understood it in terms of the mechanistic model (e.g., watchmaker) of the new scientific outlook springing from Bacon and others. Many other roots of deism have been noted by historians, for example, the Renaissance, the study of comparative religions, the discovery of non-Christian tribes, the increase of human inventions, a resurgence of gnostic pride of intellect, the revival of the allegorical method of interpreting the Bible (from Origen), and the influence of ancient naturalism and skepticism from the stoics and skeptics.

Along the way there were many philosophical figures who may not technically qualify as deists but who nonetheless gave impetus to and provided arguments for the movement. Bacon's scientific approach, John Locke's empiricism, and David Hume's skepticism about miracles definitively aided the deistic cause. The specific contributions of these influences will be pinpointed in subsequent analysis. In short, the strains in philosophy that tended either to naturalism or antisupernaturalism, that stressed the scientific processes, and that glorifed the natural creation without vilifying the Creator were influential or helpful to deism.

## The Rise of Deism

There are numerous theological antecedents of deism including pelagianism, socinianism, and arianism. In these systems man's perfectibility was stressed, the Trinity denied for God's unity, and Christ's deity diminished or denied completely.

*Herbert of Cherbury (1583-1648): "The Father of English Deism."* Incongruously, deism, a movement that denies supernatural acts of God in the world, originated in England with a man who claimed that a supernatural sound convinced him that he should publish his work.

His subsequent book (1624) *De Veritate (On Truth)* signaled the beginning of deism in England.[1]

Herbert set forth five principles of religion he believed were common to all men:

"I.   That there is one Supreme God.

II.   That he ought to be worshipped.

III.   That Virtue and Piety are the chief parts of Divine Worship.

IV.   That we ought to be sorry for our sins and repent of them.

V.   That Divine goodness doth dispense rewards and punishments both in this life and after it."[2]

Herbert maintained that these five principles are innate truths that are both universal and certain and are obtained by reflection. He declared himself happier than Archimedes upon discovering these principles. Later deists expanded this list while some omitted number V or sometimes number IV, but in general these five became a kind of creed for deism.[3]

In maintaining the first article, Herbert denied that there were any atheists, although he readily admitted that many men held unworthy concepts of deity. Since most men of his day would grant the truth of principle II, Herbert did not labor the point. In connection with the third point, Herbert stressed the ethical character of natural religion vis-à-vis the sacramental and ritualistic modes of the established church. Here the deistic anticlerical emphasis was marked. The fourth principle presented Herbert an opportunity to stress the universality of salvation against the narrow ceremonial way provided in the church. The fifth and last point implied a belief in the immortality of the soul, the providence of God, and the final day of reckoning after death. Of these principles he wrote:

> Yet the five above-mentioned truths ever were, and always will be, of that divine nature, that like sunbeams, which no weight can depress, nor any wind blow out, they have darted their glorious rays into the minds of men in all parts of the earth, where they did but exercise their natural use of reason.[4]

Herbert, like other deists to follow, had a definitely negative side to his deism. But since he lived in a time that lacked religious toleration, his criticisms of the Bible were couched in attacks on heathen religious books, sacrifices, and miracles. He made it plain that special supernatural revelation is unnecessary and that the five articles are

1. See John Orr, *English Deism*, p. 61.
2. Orr, p. 62.
3. Orr, p. 63.
4. Orr, p. 67.

sufficient for universal salvation as well as for the harmony and peace of mankind. His conditions for believing that any book was inspired were worded in such a way as to lead one to believe that he felt no book would qualify as a revelation.[5]

*Thomas Hobbes (1588-1679): Deistic Materialism.* It is difficult to determine whether Hobbes was a deist, a theist, or even an atheist. Like others in that day of religious intolerance, his true views may be concealed beneath his overt claims. But despite the fact he claimed to be a Christian, he was a sensationalist in his epistemology and a materialist in his metaphysic. In his famous *Leviathan* (1668) Hobbes reduces all ideas to sensation; and since everything man imagines is finite, he contends that there is no positive knowledge of an infinite God. In this the schoolmen deceive us, argues Hobbes, for we cannot conceive God. The name of God is only invoked to induce worship, not because we can conceive him.[6]

Religion, according to Hobbes, is peculiar to man because he is the only animal who seeks the causes of things. Since anxiety follows from not knowing the cause of what man cannot control, man posits an invincible power he calls God. Those who press for causes of natural bodies arrive finally at one God. This God is not understood dogmatically; he is only named or designated for pious purposes. Men worship this invincible Power as an expression of their thanks for the gifts he gives to them. In brief, there are four natural seeds of religion. The belief in God arises (1) out of opinions about ghosts, (2) ignorance of the cause of things in the natural world, (3) the tendency of men for devotion toward what they fear, and (4) belief in conjectures made about the future based on the opinion of others.[7]

Besides these natural causes of religion Hobbes recognizes the use of religion as a political force for inducing obedience, laws, peace, charity, and social justice. Kings stand in need of religion to rule their subjects. Hence, religion is a political instrument of the king to secure the monarchy against the beastly tendencies of man in a state of nature. In this regard, Hobbes, apparently with tongue in cheek, proceeds to make an exception for revealed religion over natural religion. Supernatural religion is confirmed by miracles whereas natural religion is not. Hence, in theory at least, Christianity is superior to paganism. However, in actual practice Hobbes contends that when a supposedly revealed religion propounds contradictions, fakes miracles, permits injustice and cruelty, enjoys luxury, and reaps self-benefit, then it cannot

---

5. Orr, p. 68.
6. Hobbes, *Leviathan,* chaps. 1, 3.
7. Hobbes, chap. 12.

be believed. In fact, Hobbes goes so far as to say that miracles even weaken one's faith; for when the miracles fail so does the faith, as is evident in the life of Moses. Roman Catholicism is definitely suspect to Hobbes since it requires for salvation many things that work to its own favor.[8] In effect, therefore, what Hobbes gives with his right hand he takes away with his left. In view of this it would not seem unfair to interpret him as a nominal Christian but an actual deist or even a covert atheist. At any rate, his arguments gave support to the overall deistic cause.

*John Locke (1632-1704): Empirical Influence on Deism.* Locke was not a deist. In one respect his work is an answer to the deistic challenge of his day. However, Locke displayed some deistic affinities and—more important—laid down some empirical principles that changed the course of deism. In his *Reasonableness of Christianity* (1695) Locke affirmed his belief in the supernatural over against deism, but he agreed with the deist's unitarian view of God as opposed to the orthodox trinitarian view. Likewise, Locke denied the deity of Christ as did the deists.

More important, however, to the future of deism was Locke's empiricism. In his *Essay Concerning Human Understanding* (1690) Locke argued that all men are born a *tabula rasa,* a blank slate. There are no innate ideas, as both rationalists and deists had been saying. The proofs for this are: (1) children are born without a storehouse of ideas and learn from experience; (2) where there is no experience of something there is a corresponding lack of ideas (e.g., those born blind do not have any visual ideas); (3) where there are different experiences, there are correspondingly different ideas; (4) finally, we have ideas in our mind of things that fit only one or more of our five senses, indicating that all these ideas come via the senses.[9] Both Bishop Berkeley and David Hume also agreed with this empiricism. So strong was this movement among the practically minded English that it came to dominate the epistemological scene, influencing even the deists whose predecessors had held to innate ideas.

*Charles Blount (1654-1693): Rationalistic Antisupernaturalism.* Blount was clearly a deist. He quotes freely from ancient and modern nontheists including Porphyry, Seneca, Montaigne, Spinoza, and Hobbes. His *Religio Laici (Religion of the Laity)* suggests a heavy dependence on Herbert of Cherbury. He presents his deism in seven articles by adding two subdivisions to Herbert's five points. Revealing the influence of Locke, Blount wavers between holding these articles of faith

---

8. Hobbs, chap. 12.
9. Locke, *An Essay Concerning Human Understanding,* bk. II, chap. 1.

to be innate or acquired, saying, "I know not whether the idea of a God be innate or no, but I'm sure that it is very soon imprinted in the minds of men."[10]

Blount has a more pronounced negativism than his predecessors. His attacks on the Bible indicate the influence of both Hobbes and Spinoza. He casts serious doubt on the virgin birth of Christ and aspersions on the integrity of many Biblical characters. He speaks of the fables of the Old Testament, ridicules the story of the Fall of Adam, and satirizes the story of the Flood. Likewise, Blount criticizes the man-centered creation story in Genesis. In short, by stressing the parallel of Biblical material to pagan literature he manages to cast substantial doubt on the divine authority and authenticity of Scripture, thus denying its supernatural claim.

## The Flourishing of English Deism

Historians cite many reasons for the flowering of English deism. Undoubtedly freedom of the press (granted 1695) and the growth of Biblical criticism (via Hobbes and Spinoza) were two major factors contributing to its rapid growth. And the empiricism of Locke as well as the new scientific spirit following Bacon also contributed to the deistic movement. The first notable deist to manifest Locke's influence was John Toland.

*John Toland (1670-1722).* Toland's *Christianity Not Mysterious* (1696) is one of the most important works of the deistic movement. The first edition was published anonymously, and was burned by the Irish parliament. Toland affixed both his name and an apology to the second edition published in London (1702).

Most of Toland's work was of a negative character, but he found occasion to state some positive religious beliefs which agreed in essence with Herbert's list. He affirmed his belief in God, in the immortality of the soul, and in the doctrine of future rewards and punishment. He also implied agreement with the article that made religion essentially ethical.

Toland primarily exerted his energy in anticlerical, anti-Scriptural, and antimiraculous attacks on traditional Christianity. With regard to miracles he manifested the influence of Locke, who had defined miracles "a sensible operation, which, being above the comprehension of the spectator, and in his opinion contrary to the established course of nature, is taken by him to be divine."[11] Miracles are the main proof of revelation, but revelations attested by miracles were limited to Christ and Moses. Toland's definition of miracles is even less supernaturalistic

---

10. Orr, *English Deism*, p. 111.
11. John Locke, *Discourse of Miracles*, p. 256.

than Locke's. Miracles for Toland are events "exceeding all human Power" but which nevertheless are "produced according to the laws of nature, though above its ordinary operations."[12] In like manner, Toland rejected as part of the nature of true Christianity anything that was mysterious, that is, that went beyond human reason. Hence, it was necessary for him to charge that numerous corruptions have occurred in Christianity and the Scriptures down through the centuries. He hints that Scripture should be allegorically interpreted to avoid these problems, but it was later deists who developed this position. Toland did, however, discredit the Christian canon of Scripture in his *Amyntor* (1699), implying that there were additional books attributed to Christ, that there was no fixed and accepted number of canonical books, and that no distinction was made between apocryphal and canonical books.

Another lasting effect of Toland was that made by way of Locke's empiricism. Mystery was rejected because it has no empirical basis. All knowledge is based on ideas which come from the senses. Nothing is to be accepted as true unless there is exact correspondence between ideas and sensation. "Whatever is evidently repugnant to clear and distinct ideas, or to our common notions, is contrary to reason."[13] Anything mysterious or "beyond reason" is thereby eliminated, including the doctrine of the Trinity and the two natures of Christ involved in his deity.

In short, Toland's contributions to deism were building it on the foundation of a Lockian empiricism, criticizing the canon of Scripture, and emphasizing antisupernatural and antimystery rationalism. Successors developed these strains of deism.

*Anthony Cooper, the Earl of Shaftesbury (1671-1713).* Shaftesbury claimed to hold orthodox views, but it is believed that he hid his real views for fear of persecution. He criticized the deists and spoke of himself as a Christian, but this is understood by many to be a part of his characteristic method of satire and irony. Shortly after his death a work on the *Cure of Deism* (1736) listed Shaftesbury and Tindal as the "oracles of Deism."[14] In view of his extensive criticism of the Bible it seems likely that Shaftesbury should be classified among the deists.

Most of the basic tenets of deism laid down by Herbert are reflected by Shaftesbury in his work entitled *Characteristics.* He believed in God, a natural sense of right and wrong, the worship of God, the possibility of a future life, and the essential moral character of religion. His main contributions to deism, however, were not on the side of his

12. Orr, *English Deism,* p. 121.
13. Orr, p. 120.
14. Orr, p. 123.

positive beliefs. On the negative side, Shaftesbury's attitude manifested a hostility to supernaturalism. He expressed an unfavorable attitude toward using miracles in support of Christianity. He rejected modern miracles, accepted Biblical miracles in principle but accorded Biblical miracles very little difference from other miracles. The Bible was subjected to ridicule, especially Old Testament stories about Moses, Joshua, and Jonah. New Testament stories such as those of the birth of Christ and Pentecost were also subjected to ridicule and doubt.[15]

*Anthony Collins (1676-1729).* Deists abounded in eighteenth century England when Collins published *A Discourse of Free-Thinking* (1713) and *A Discourse on the Ground and Reason of the Christian Religion* (1724). In the former work he added a number of new arguments against Christianity as a revealed religion. He reasoned that a book that came from God would be expected to be more exact and better written than the Bible is. He capitalized on different interpretations and differing canons of Scripture among the Christian sects. He cast doubt on the reliability of the Bible by paralleling its miracles to pagan wonder stories.

Collins's other important work sought to weaken the credibility of Scripture by dwelling on the charge of pious frauds and the gullibility of early Christians. He maintained that the Old Testament text is badly corrupted. He denied that the prophecies of the Old Testament were literal. Hence they could not be used as a supernatural confirmation of Christianity. This he maintained by means of an allegorical interpretation of Scripture adopted from Origen.[16] In support of his position Collins pointed out that both Celsus and Porphyry accused the early Christians of so interpreting Scripture as to make it appear as though the Old Testament is fulfilled in the New Testament. Collins likewise cast doubt on the actions of Jesus and the New Testament apostles by suggesting that they were merely following pagan practices in claiming fulfilment of prophecy. The doctrine of the virgin birth was given special treatment in this regard.

Collins also argued against atheism. In fact he agreed with some of Herbert's five principles, dropping only the one on the immortality of the soul. Others were not mentioned at all but may be implied to some degree in his discussion. Collins's work does manifest a more intense criticism of Christianity and a tendency toward even greater skepticism. His works stirred dozens of replies by Christian apologists, including the notable rebuttal by Richard Bentley.

*William Wollaston (1659-1724).* Other deists like Bernard de Mande-

---

15. Orr, pp. 124-25.
16. Orr, p. 132.

ville (1670-1733) continued the negative attack.[17] But one of the more popular books to come from a deist was Wollaston's *Religion of Nature Delineated* (1722). By 1746 the book had gone through seven editions. Wollaston worked out a naturalistic system of ethics that included belief in God, the immortality of the soul, and rewards and punishment whereby everyone can receive his due for this life. He also argued that since not all creatures get more pleasure than pain in this life there must be another life to rectify this situation, for a just God must certainly give his creatures more pleasure than pain. In contrast with the more optimistic tone of other deists, Wollaston indicated a rather gloomy and pessimistic view of man's life on earth.

*Thomas Woolston (1669-1731).* Woolston was perhaps the most prolific and piercing of deistic writers. His attacks were vigorous and coarse. The deistic critic Leland charged him with "scurrilous buffoonery and gross raillery."[18] His attacks on the clergy were relentless, as is manifest in *The Moderator Between an Infidel and an Apostate* (1721) and his *Free Gifts to the Clergy* (1723-24). He speaks of them as being "hired" and full of "greed" in their defense of Christianity. Woolston's primary contribution to deism was his discussion of miracles in six *Discourses on Miracles* (1727-1730). In this work he charged that there were pagan parallels and even pagan origins of Biblical miracles. In the course of criticizing Christ's miracles Woolston found occasion to declare that Christ was not even a good man.

*Matthew Tindal (1656-1733).* Tindal is probably the most representative example of English deism. His major work, entitled *Christianity as Old as the Creation; or, The Gospel a Republication of the Religion of Nature,* has been called the "deistic Bible" and its author the "apostle of deism." It called forth one hundred and fifty replies including Bishop Butler's classic critique of deism, *Analogy of Religion* (1736). The central argument of Tindal's work is based in the nature of God. God is perfect, and therefore the religion he gives to mankind must be perfect and incapable of being improved. Creation alone and not the Bible fits this description. Hence, no later revelation such as the Bible can possibly improve on God's natural revelation. And since God is immutable he cannot change the religion he gave in the first place. Further, because God is impartial he would not have specially favored one people over another by a special revelation to them. From God's justice Tindal argued that God "at all times has given mankind sufficient means of knowing what he requires of them."[19] The perfection of the first revela-

---

17. Orr, p. 135.
18. John Leland, *A View of the Principal Deistical Writers . . . ,* vol. I, p. 113.
19. Orr, *English Deism,* p. 141.

tion in creation necessitates the conclusion that any later revelation can be at best a republication of this original revelation and must be identical with it in content.

Anticipating the question "Why republish the creative revelation in a book?" Tindal replied as follows. Revealed religion is given only to liberate men from the load of superstition that has been mixed with natural religion. But since the Bible is untrustworthy and full of errors, it is obvious that it would not qualify under Tindal's criteria as special revelation. In this regard the title of Tindal's book has been criticized as misleading.

The articles of natural religion given by Tindal are: (1) belief in God, (2) the worship of God, (3) doing what is for one's own good or happiness, and (4) promoting the common happiness. Elsewhere Tindal indicates his belief in a future life.[20] But with regard to belief in the Bible as a special revelation of God, Tindal left little hope. For him the gospel could not be more plain than reason, and even so it must be interpreted by reason and not vice versa. Furthermore, a written revelation depends on the uncertain meaning of words, and there is the further problem of the uncertain transmission of the Bible with the consequent corruption of the text.

Tindal's attack on miracles was based on the many parallels found in pagan stories. He quotes with apparent approval the old statement, "Miracles for fools, the reasons for wise men."[21] The Fall of man, many Old Testament stories, the doctrine of original sin, and the integrity of the Biblical prophets are all challenged by Tindal. He vigorously presented the disagreement between science and Scripture, using the former to discredit the latter. His work represents the high tide of deism and called forth Christianity's most able defenders. There were other deists after Tindal, such as Thomas Morgan (d. 1743), but none were able to reach his stature.

## The Decline of Deism (1742)

Numerous factors contributed to the demise of deism, including the apologetic defense of Christianity provided by men like Bentley, Paley, and Butler. There were also the internal conflicts within the deistic movement and the tendency of English empiricism toward skepticism. No doubt England's political preoccupation with issues of national importance and the exhaustion of the subject also added to the death of deism. But whatever the factors, the period of decline produced the most negative and skeptical forms of deism in its history.

*Peter Annet (1693-1760).* One of the strongest cases against miracles

---

20. Orr, p. 143.
21. Orr, p. 144.

was presented by Peter Annet in *The Resurrection of Jesus Considered* (1744). In this work the author attacked the trustworthiness of the records as well as the character of the evidence presented in the Biblical records of the resurrection. Miracles are not only unnecessary but the changeless character of God and the uniformity of natural law rule out miracles. He wrote, "Natural powers are fit to answer all the ends of virtue and religion; therefore supernatural powers are needless."[22] From the very moment of creation God instituted the law of nature to operate in a uniform way. And since no improvement can be made on God's creation and no change can occur in his nature, miracles are both unnecessary and actually impossible. His argument in this regard foreshadows Hume's extreme skepticism on miracles.

Annet also attacked the canon of Scripture and the lives of Biblical figures, as had other deists before him. But his most significant contribution was in the direction of the rigidifying naturalism that had developed within the logic of deism.

*Thomas Chubb (1649-1747).* Chubb had little education but possessed some natural ability which he used to present deism in laymen's language. His work, *The True Gospel of Jesus Christ Asserted* (1739), is largely repetition of what his predecessors had already said. The author believed in God, in a moral law according to which men live acceptably before God, and that repentance and reformation are the way back to God. But he acknowledged that the content of natural revelation was more scant. Most of the rest of Chubb's writings are negative. He bitterly criticized parts of the Old Testament such as the slaughter of the Canaanites and what he called "malevolent" psalms.[23] He accused the apostles of being hypocrites and spoke contemptuously of Christ and his miracles. He rejected both prophecy and miracles as proof of divine revelation. Chubb not only confessed himself to be a deist but claimed Jesus as an ally. Chubb's writing was both clever and forceful, and it was influential among the unlettered populace.

*Henry Bolingbroke (1672-1751).* Lord Bolingbroke, like the other later deists, was not original. But his brilliant mind and literary ability added to the influence of his works. While some deists were already tending to skepticism, Bolingbroke created a late splash in the English deistic movement. His use of mockery was extensive and his outlook was generally gloomy. Other than his belief in God based on reason and occasional reference to some other deistic tenets, his work is mostly negative. He doubted a future life and denied any future punishment.[24]

---

22. Orr, p. 515.
23. Orr, p. 153.
24. Orr, p. 156.

162 / THEISTIC APOLOGETICS

Bolingbroke accused the authors and transmitters of the Bible of being selfish frauds and declared the Biblical history to be untrustworthy. Based on the new scientific outlook of men like Kepler, Copernicus, Galileo, and Newton, he rejected the Biblical picture of the world. He attacked the stories of creation, the flood, and the doctrine of inspiration. Men who thought themselves inspired were called mad and irrational. Bolingbroke attacked Christianity on philosophical as well as historical grounds. He considered the patronizing of Christianity particularly distasteful. And contrary to traditional Christian belief he argued for the materiality of the soul.[25] Bolingbroke quoted widely from the church Fathers (mostly negatively) and often from skeptics and other deists.

*Conyers Middleton (1683-1750).* Middleton's contribution to deism was largely in the realm of the antisupernatural argumentation. His *Free Inquiry into the Miraculous Powers, Which Are Supposed to Have Subsisted in the Christian Church* (1749) rejects all miracles after the time of the apostles. Apostolic miracles, however, Middleton considered authentic. For these were "delivered to us by eye-witnesses, whose honest characters exclude the suspicion of fraud, and whose knowledge of the facts, which they relate, scarce admits the probability of a mistake." In much the same vein as Locke's *Third Letter on Toleration,* Middleton contrasted with great scholarship the apostolic and postapostolic miracles. He strongly maintained the incredibility of the church Fathers' witness to supposed miraculous events in much the same way that Hume and others cast doubt on all testimony to miracles. Middleton summarized his view saying, "The History of the Gospel, I hope may be true, though the History of the Church be fabulous."[26] In this sense Middleton was only a limited deist or a qualified theist.

*Henry Dodwell, Jr., (d. 1784).* In Dodwell, skepticism forced deism to a fideistic stance. In his book, *Christianity Not Founded on Argument; and the True Principle of Gospel-Evidence Assigned* (1742), Dodwell states, "I am fully persuaded, that the judging at all of religious matters is not the proper province of reason, or indeed an affair where she has any concern." Reason by its very nature cannot be the faculty of religion; faith is essential to religion. Religion requires men to think alike; whereas men differ in their thinking. Religion teaches to pray for an increase of faith; whereas reason calls for an increase in evidence. Reason calls for neutrality and withholding decision; whereas religion demands faith. Indeed most men are capable of little reasoning but all have faith readily available. The command to believe makes

25. Orr, p. 157.
26. Orr, pp. 159-60.

no time allowance for the reasoning process. The Bible itself does not teach men to reason but to believe. Not even miracles can be appealed to as reasons for belief because counterfeit miracles are possible. And even if some apostolic miracles be regarded as reason for faith, they have lost their value by increasing antiquity. In fact faith and reason are contrary in nature and effect. "The foundation of philosophy is all doubt and suspicion, as the foundation of religion is all acquiescence and belief."[27] The world failed by wisdom to know God. According to Dodwell, philosophical skepticism and religious deism go hand in hand, one complementing the other.

*David Hume (1711-1776).* Taken at face value, Hume claimed to side more with the deist Cleanthes in his famous *Dialogue Concerning Natural Religion.* Many interpret him, however, as a tongue-in-cheek skeptic. Whatever the case, Hume's anti-Bible, anti-established religion, and especially anti-miracles emphasis make it easy to see why many people of Hume's day thought him to be a deist.

Hume did make statements to the effect that he believed in God apart from any divine revelation. In the introduction to his *Dialogues* Hume wrote, "What truth is so obvious, so certain, as the *being* of a God, which the most ignorant ages have acknowledged, for which the most refined geniuses have ambitiously striven to produce new proofs and arguments?" What Hume did claim to dispute was "the *nature* of that divine being; his attributes, his decrees, his plan of providence." In the *Dialogues,* Demea is the mystic, Philo the skeptic, and Cleanthes the believer in God. Hume concludes in the last lines, "I confess that, upon a serious review of the whole, I cannot but think that Philo's principles are more probable than Demea's; but that those of Cleanthes approach still nearer to the truth." Prima facie, then, Hume would appear to be a deist. Whether this was a covert literary way of hiding his true skepticism is moot. Hume did say a few lines earlier, "To be a philosophical skeptic is, in a man of letters, the first and most essential step towards being a sound, believing Christian."[28] This sounds like fideism.

However one interprets Hume's own personal views concerning God, there are two definite ways Hume is associated with the deistic movement, especially in its period of decline. First, the deism of Hume's day had become increasingly skeptical about rational demonstrations of religious truths. Second, Hume's extremely naturalistic stand against miracles is the climax of a characteristic tendency in the deistic move-

---

27. Orr, pp. 163-64.
28. David Hume, *Dialogues Concerning Natural Religion,* Introduction and Conclusion.

ment. Hume argued strongly that the wise man should not believe in miracles because the probability for the uniformity of nature was always higher than the probability of an exception to the laws of nature. Since the wise man bases his beliefs on the highest probability, he will always believe a miracle to be highly improbable. In short, the testimony for the uniformity of nature is built on the highest probability; hence, a miraculous event must always be most highly suspect (see Chapter 14 on Naturalism).

*Immanuel Kant (1724-1804).* Kant confesses to have been awakened from his dogmatic slumbers by reading David Hume. This awakening turned him from rational theism to philosophical skepticism. Kant retained his personal piety and interest in religion but strictly on moral grounds. He believed, as the title of his deistic classic reveals, in *Religion Within the Limits of Reason Alone* (1792). By "reason" Kant means practical or moral reason, since theoretical or philosophical reason was given up in his famous *Critique of Pure Reason* (1781).

Not only did Kant reject all rational proofs for the existence of God in favor of his moral postulate, but he also rejected the need for historical evidence, especially by way of the miraculous. Miracles are superfluous to true religion. Miracles may be appropriate to man's ordinary way of thought to serve as an introduction to moral religion, but they are not strictly necessary to religion. Although a man cannot deny the theoretical possibility of a miracle occurring, it is senseless deceit on a man's part to believe that he has the gift of performing them. Kant admits that Christ's life and death may "all be nothing but miracles. . . . But it is essential that, in the use of these historical accounts, we do not make it a tenet of religion that the knowing, believing, and professing of them are themselves means whereby we can render ourselves well-pleasing to God." The account of Christ's resurrection, however, is clearly rejected by Kant. These "more secret records, added as a sequel, of his *resurrection* and *ascension,* which took place before the eyes only of his intimates, cannot be used in the interest of religion within the limits of reason alone. . . ."[29]

Kant defined miracles as "events in the world the *operating laws* of whose causes are, and must remain, absolutely unknown to us." Hence, "we have not, and can never hope to have, the slightest conception of the law according to which God then brings about such an event. . . ." In fact, "we cannot know anything at all about supernatural aid. . . ." One thing we do know about a miracle is that "if it flatly contradicts morality, it cannot, despite all appearances, be of God (for example,

---

29. Immanuel Kant, *Religion Within the Limits of Reason Alone,* pp. 79, 80, 83, 119.

were a father ordered to kill his son ...)." In contrast to Hume, for Kant it was uniform accord with the moral law rather than natural law that was the criterion by which alleged miraculous events were to be judged. Kant did accept, nonetheless, that all the species and events of the plant and animal kingdoms are "nothing but natural effects and *ought* never to be adjudged otherwise." Only the rash and immodest would venture beyond natural explanation in support of miracles.[30]

Although Kant admits the theoretical possibility of miracles he both denies their moral relevance to religion and offers this practical argument against them: Either miracles occur *daily* hidden under the guise of natural events, or else they occur *seldom,* or else they *never occur.* If they occur regularly then it could not be accounted as a miracle but simply as a natural event. On the other hand, if miracles occur only seldom, then the objective question can be transformed into a frivolous subjective question by asking, "How seldom? Once in a hundred years? Or in ancient times but never now?" But since practical reason must operate by objective principles, we must conclude that miracles must occur either daily or *never.* And since they cannot occur daily, "nothing remains but to adopt the latter maxim—for this principle remains ever a mere maxim for making judgments, not a theoretical assertion." In short, Kant admits that miracles are theoretically possible but he will live as though they never occur. Since miracles are morally unnecessary, it will be morally assumed that religion can be lived within the limits of reason alone without appeal to the supernatural. The supernatural may be there and miracles may even occur, but they are unknowable by nature and impractical—even embarrassing—for religion. Hence, it is morally best to simply eliminate the miraculous from religion. Our practical reason demands this nonsupernatural approach.[31]

*Other Deistic Influence of Note.* English deism strongly influenced later French deism and skepticism, of which Diderot and Voltaire are notable examples. In America deism flourished after it had declined in England. Thomas Jefferson, Benjamin Franklin, and Thomas Paine are classed as deists. Jefferson cut all the miraculous stories out of the Gospels and put the rest together in a form that was published posthumously. His "Bible" ends this way: "there laid they Jesus, and rolled a great stone to the door of the sepulchre, and departed."[32] Since the rest of the story is the miracle of the resurrection, Jefferson omitted it. Thomas Paine is notorious for his attack on the Bible in *The Age of Reason.* Perhaps more than anywhere else in the United States, deistic

30. Kant, pp. 81, 179, 81-82, 84.
31. Kant, pp. 83, 84.
32. *The Jefferson Bible,* ed. Douglas Lurton.

tendencies of naturalism and Biblical criticism have lived on in modernistic or liberal Protestantism. Harry Emerson Fosdick is no doubt the classic representative of this position; but other modern exponents, such as Nels Ferré, have carried on the spirit of the movement. And in many respects contemporary process theology (see Chapter 11) carries on the naturalistic deistic tradition.

Historians have listed many reasons for the decline and fall of deism. The high scholarship of its opponents, the internal problems of the deistic view, the increasing skepticism of the period, its mechanistic model of God, its lopsided criticism of Biblical characters, and even the shifting political scene have been given as reasons for the demise of deism. But before we provide a philosophical critique of deism it is necessary to outline the central tenets of the deistic world view.

## The Central Tenets of Deism

The foregoing survey of deism amply indicates the diversity within the deistic movement. There are few if any hard and fast lines of demarcation. The movement fades off on a continuum from qualified theists (e.g., Locke) to those whom some consider to be outright skeptics (e.g., Hume). In between, the grounds for holding to deism vary from rationalism to fideism. Likewise, the degree of and basis for skepticism on miracles ranges from accepting only apostolic miracles to the rejection of all miracles, from rejecting miracles in practice to rejecting all miracles in principle.

For systematic purposes we will have to ignore the historical shades and overlappings with theism and skepticism, and describe a deistic position that is mutually exclusive to both supernatural theism and to pure naturalism. In this regard, a deist will be defined as one who believes there is a God beyond the world who created the world but that the world runs by natural law without supernatural interference. Deists will differ as to why they reject miracles. Some will say God *cannot* perform them because it would be contrary either to his own nature or to the nature of natural law. Others will simply point out that God *does not* perform miracles, at least that we have no convincing evidence that he has done so. They agree that miracles are not needed to support religion; a natural basis is sufficient for a natural religion.

1. The first premise of a deistic world view is that there is a God who created the universe. In contrast to dualism, which holds that matter is eternal, the deists believe that the material universe was created by God. God alone is eternal. And in contrast with pure naturalism or atheism, a deist believes that it is necessary to posit a God as the author and architect of the universe. There is a First Cause beyond

the natural world who originated all of the natural processes. Likewise, in distinction from pantheism, a deist believes that God is not identical with the real world. All is not God and God is not all for a deist. The world is as different from God as the painting is from the painter or the watch from the watchmaker. Of course, the mind of the Maker is revealed and manifest in what is made, but there is nonetheless a real difference between Creator and creation.

2. The second major premise of deism is antisupernaturalism. Miracles do not occur. Some argue that a perfect God could not make an imperfect universe which would demand miraculous interruption and repair. This would be contrary to the nature of God. Others stress the unchanging nature of God. If miracles were unnecessary from the beginning of natural creation, then there is no reason to believe that a changeless God would change his mind about their subsequent usefulness. Other deists stress the uniformity of natural law. God set up the laws of the natural world and he cannot (or, will not) violate the law he established in the natural world. A miracle would be a violation of an inviolable law. But the inviolable cannot be violated. Hence, miracles cannot happen. In the weaker form of deistic antisupernaturalism, extreme skepticism is expressed about the actuality of any miracle occurring. Doubt arises either because of the unreliability of the witnesses, the inutility of miracles, the lack of authenticity of the documents, or the general antiquity and inaccessibility of the evidence. And even some limited supernatural theists, who admitted some miracles (usually apostolic ones), so undermined belief in other miracles that if their arguments were applied to apostolic miracles the grounds for believing in all miracles would be eliminated. Antisupernaturalism is a distinguishing characteristic of deism.

3. The third major tenet of deism is a unitarian concept of God that involves a denial of the orthodox doctrines of the Trinity and the deity of Christ. In this respect even John Locke was a deist, although he admitted the validity of apostolic miracles. This third tenet is consistent with the first premise and flows necessarily from the second. If no supernatural event occurs then assuredly Christ was not a supernatural being and definitely not Deity incarnate. And a denial of the deity of Christ involves a denial of the doctrine of the Trinity, which holds that there are more persons than one who are God by nature, one of whom is Jesus of Nazareth. Deists, then, are unitarian in the doctrine of God.

There were of course many other associated tenets of deism. Being a natural religion it scoffed at all supposed revelation as well as at established religions whose demands went beyond the natural revelation of God. And the minimal content of the natural revelation most often included a belief in a moral law, the good life in accord with this natural moral law, and a future life of rewards or punishments to follow. The three tenets of deism expounded above, however, are the major ones and will be the basis of our evaluation here.

# An Evaluation of Deism

There are some positive values that emerge from a deistic emphasis, some directly and others as by-products. Let us briefly note the more important ones here.

## Some Positive Contributions or Consequences of Deism

1. Deists emphasized natural revelation. In accord with traditional Christian theism, deists believed in a natural revelation of God to all men. From Old Testament times (Ps. 19) to the New Testament (Rom. 1:19-20), from Augustine to Aquinas to Calvin there has always been an acknowledgment among theists that God is revealed in his creation. All men know God via conscience and creation and are held responsible for this knowledge. No rational moral creature is beyond this natural revelation. Man may and does distort and suppress it, but he is nonetheless aware of it. And indeed, the natural revelation is logically prior to any supernatural revelation; for how could one know something to be a special revelation of God if he has no general context in which to place it? How could one even know that it is God giving the special revelation unless he has some prior knowledge as to who God is? The God of creation (Gen. 1:1) comes logically and actually prior to the God of supernatural revelation (Heb. 1:1, 2).

2. Another important contribution of deism is the stress on reason in matters of religious belief. Most deists were not fideists; they believed that supposed miracles and revelations should be brought before the bar of reason to separate the false from the true. In this they should not be faulted. As many orthodox theologians have rightly argued, reason must be used to judge whether indeed the Scriptures are a revelation of God. This does not mean that reason is superior to God, for God is the source of reason and of the principles of reason— such as the law of noncontradiction. And if a supposed revelation is logically contradictory, then there is no way it can be the object of a reasonable belief such as the Scriptures command Christians to have (I Peter 3:15). Deists should not be faulted, then, for using reason to judge revelation or miracles, but for misusing reason and for being unreasonable in its use.

3. Further, the deistic attitude toward miracles is not without some justification, even though it is not entirely in accord with an authentic supernaturalism. The theist can readily admit that reason should be

used to sort out the false and spurious claims to the supernatural. Even Scripture commands believers to "test the spirits" and to beware of "false prophets" (I John 4:1; Matt. 7:15). Indeed, if many miracles are found to be without justification because of lack of supporting evidence, then a true miracle is in a better position to be vindicated by its justifiable support. And if conflicting religious claims are supported by pseudomiracles, and if it is possible to support unique miracles without competitors, then such miracles would have a valid apologetic use. In short, deism's attack on spurious miracles is a helpful prelude to establishing Christian theism on authentic miracles.

4. Finally, an important by-product emerged from the strong and sustained attack on traditional Christianity. The deistic siege called forth some of the most scholarly and stout defenses of orthodox Christianity in modern times. Bishop Berkeley, Bishop Butler, and William Paley all contributed masterful works to this apologetic cause. Even skeptics like Lord Lytleton and Frank Morison were converted and became ardent defenders of Christianity. Deistic criticism gave impetus to the study of archaeology which yielded not only the conversion of such notable men as Sir William Ramsay, but hundreds of thousands of archaeological confirmations of the Biblical world view. For all of this the bitter and sustained attack of deism on Biblical Christianity is to be indirectly thanked.

## A Negative Critique of the Deistic World View

As a world view deism suffers some insurmountable internal and even external difficulties. Let us now summarize the most significant problems.

1. First of all, the deists' understanding of God is incompatible with their stand against miracles. Since God performed the miracle of creation *ex nihilo* (from nothing), it follows from the very nature and power of this kind of God that other lesser miracles are possible. Walking on water is little problem for a God who created water to begin with. To make a human being through a female ovum (virgin birth) is not difficult for a God who made a world from nothing. And multiplying loaves is surely not a greater feat than creating matter in the first place. In short, it is self-defeating to admit the miracle of creation and to deny that other miracles are possible.

2. Second, the deistic concept of God is built on an invalid mechanistic model rather than on a personal model. God is not a mere Master machine-maker. On this model it is no wonder deists conclude that a "perfect" creation would be one that does not demand personal attention and miraculous intercommunication. For the more perfect the mechanic the more perfect the machine, and the most perfect mechanic could

create the most perfect machine that should need no subsequent "tune-ups." However, if God is personal, as even the deistic concept of God would admit, then there is no reason why a "perfect" universe for a personal God would not be one which involves personal attention. Miraculous commerce between the personal Creator and the persons created would not only be possible, it would seem to be most probable. If the desire to have personal communication between the supernatural and the natural realm flows from God as personal, then not to perform miracles of personal communication (viz., revelation) would show God to be something less than perfectly personal. It is inconsistent to disallow a personal communication from the supernatural realm to the natural realm once one has admitted God is personal.

3. A God concerned enough to create men in the beginning should be concerned enough to intervene on their behalf, men who have fallen into grave difficulties. "You have made your own bed, lie in it" is something less than the attitude a good Creator ought to have. If he had enough love and concern for man to create him, then it would seem to be most compatible with such a nature to believe that God would miraculously intervene to help him if he were in need. And surely a God strong enough to create the world is strong enough to help it. The laws of creation are not inviolable; they are created and contingent. And what is created and contingent can be laid aside if need be for the moral good of man. Hence, the nature of God, even as conceived by deists, would be compatible with miraculous intervention into the natural world when the situation calls for it.

4. The deistic arguments intended to eliminate the basis for belief in a supernatural revelation apply equally as well to elimination of the deistic belief in creation. The deist has no more right to believe that God created the world from nothing than the supernaturalist does that God has performed miracles. If the Bible cannot be trusted to teach one doctrine then there is no grounds for believing the other one is true. Both creation and revelation are miracles, and a miracle as such cannot be discovered by purely scientific or natural means. One cannot *prove* by reason the doctrine of *ex nihilo* creation, the attempts by some theists notwithstanding. That the originating Cause of the universe produced this world out of nothing is a supernatural act, and supernatural acts are not scientifically observable or demonstrable. One can see certain observable *results* of a supernatural act (e.g., a human body that results from a virgin birth) but one cannot observe the *modus operandi* by which the miracle occurred. Hence, the deist defeats his own case against revelation when he accepts from revelation the doctrine of creation.

5. Further, the deistic criticism of the trustworthiness of the Biblical documents and writers is definitely lacking. Archaeological confirmation

of the authenticity of Scripture has been overwhelming since the hey-day of deism. Over twenty-five thousand finds have confirmed the picture of the Biblical world presented in Scripture. The integrity of the eyewitnesses and writers of the documents of the New Testament has been sufficiently established. The alleged contradictions within the Bible have been answered. No scientific errors have been proven in the Bible.[33] In short, deism has failed to cast sufficient doubt on the supernatural either in principle or in fact.

## Summary and Conclusion

A deist believes that God made the world but does not "monkey" with it. God created the natural world but never interrupts it with supernatural events. God is beyond the world but does not operate within it in a miraculous way. But despite the many helpful emphases and prods to Biblical theism, the deistic position is decidedly inade-quate. For once the miracle of creation is admitted, the possibility of other miracles follows. Indeed, the very concept of a deistic God is one that is not reducible to a purely mechanistic model that would allow for no personal intervention in the world. A personal God shows his perfection by his miraculous personal commerce with his creatures. To hold otherwise is inconsistent. And if God was concerned enough about man to create him, it would seem to follow that he would be concerned enough to intervene on his behalf. Indeed, there is ample evidence to believe that God has miraculously interposed himself in the world. Deism is defunct both historically and philosophically.

## SELECT READINGS FOR CHAPTER NINE

**Exposition of Deism**

Herbert of Cherbury. *De Veritate.*
Kant, Immanuel. *Religion Within the Limits of Reason Alone.*
Paine, Thomas. *The Age of Reason.*
Tindal, Matthew. *Christianity as Old as Creation.*
Toland, John. *Christianity Not Mysterious.*
Woolston, Thomas. *Discourses on Miracles.*

**Evaluation of Deism**

Bentley, Richard. *Remarks upon Late Discourses of Free-Thinking.*
Butler, Bishop. *Analogy in Religion.*
"Infidelity." New York, American Tract Society (no date).
LeLand, John. *A View of the Principal Deistic Writers. . . .*
Orr, John. *English Deism.*

---

33. See pt. III below, chaps. 17 and 18.

# Chapter

# 10 | *Pantheism*

Pantheism is the polar opposite of deism. The latter stresses God's distinction from the real world and the former emphasizes God's identity with it. Deism holds that God is beyond the world but not in it in a miraculous way; pantheism believes that God is in the world or, rather, God *is* the world. So deism stresses God's transcendence and pantheism his immanence in the world.

There are several kinds of pantheism. The *absolute* pantheism of Parmenides identified only one being in the universe and designated all else as non-being. There is the *emanational* pantheism of Plotinus who believed that everything flows from God the way a flower unfolds from a seed. Further, there is *developmental* pantheism wherein God is unfolded in an evolutionary or historical way. Hegel is a developmental example of the latter where God unfolds historically. Other pantheisms are *modal* such as in Spinoza where finite things are considered modes or moments in one infinite substance. Finally, there are *manifestational* or multilevel pantheisms such as are found in various forms of Hinduism. It will be instructive to look at several of these pantheistic systems.

## An Exposition of Pantheism

The metaphysical background of pantheism is monism, and Parmenides is the father of Western monism. Hence, it is philosophically foundational to begin our analysis of the pantheistic world view with Parmenides.

### Parmenidean Monism

A monist believes that reality is ultimately unified. An absolute monist believes that reality is ultimately and only one; all multiplicity lacks any reality. Being is, and non-being is not. All is One and One is All. Being is one and multiplicity is non-being and illusion.

Parmenides' logic of monism can be summarized very simply. There cannot be two realities or beings; for if this were so, one would have to differ from the other. If there were no difference then they would be one identical reality and not two. In order for there to be really different things, there must be some real difference. Everything that differs must differ either by being or by non-being, since there are no other ways to differ. However, two beings cannot differ by nothing or non-being, for to differ by nothing is not to differ at all. And if they do not differ at all then they are identical and one. On the other hand two things cannot differ by being for being is the very feature they have in common and things cannot differ by what they have in common; that is, the point of identity cannot also be the point of diversity. It follows, then, argued Parmenides, that there cannot be two beings in the universe. All things are ultimately and absolutely one. Any seeming multiplicity is but an illusion.

Parmenides' disciple, Zeno, used a *reductio ad absurdum* argument to prove his master's monistic position. If one assumes multiplicity is possible, said Zeno, he ends in irresolvable paradoxes. For instance, if a line is divisible from point A to point B, then it can be divided in half and half of half and so on infinitely. But infinite divisibility is impossible since an infinite number cannot be reached. Hence, divisibility is not possible. Therefore reality is indivisible. Likewise Zeno argued that motion is impossible since to move from A to B, one must first go halfway and half of half before that and so on infinitely. But since an infinite can never be traversed, one can never really move from one point to the next. It follows then that all is one indivisible and untransversible point of absolute identity. Or as Parmenides would have said, there is one solid, eternal indivisible ball of Being.

### Plotinian Emanational Pantheism

Early Greek monism came to final fruition in the late Greek mysticism of Plotinus who is the classic example of Western pantheism. In him Greek rationalistic monism blossoms into pantheistic mysticism. A survey of his system from the *Enneads* will exemplify an emanational type of pantheism.

Contrary to Greek thought generally, Plotinus held that ultimate reality goes beyond being to absolute unity. (1) The *One* is the absolute source of all being and multiplicity. Everything in the universe differs as to its degree of unity as it both flows from and varies from the absolute Unity (God). God must be absolutely One because all multiplicity presupposes some prior unity, but each multiple is made up of little unities. Further, the absolute Unity (God) is not self-conscious, since self-reflection involves a basic duality of knower and known; and absolute unity as such has no duality. (2) Hence, when out of the absolute necessity of its own nature the One unfolds as a seed into a flower or as center into radii, there emanates *Nous* (Mind). This first emanant is the universal Mind which makes all knowing possible. Nous is the One becoming self-conscious and forming what Plotinus calls *One-Many*. When Nous reflects backward upon its source (the One) it becomes knowingly self-conscious. Then when Nous reflects inward upon itself it produces other minds or knowing beings. (3) And when it reflects outward it gives rise to Life (or World Soul); this is called *One-and-Many* by Plotinus. From World Soul springs all other living things (souls) as species within a genus. The One, Nous, and World Soul form an emanational triadic Godhead from which all other things flow both emanationally and necessarily.[1]

(4) Beneath Mind and Soul there is Matter, which is the most multiple of all, the *Many*. Since the entire process is a necessary unfolding from unity to greater and greater multiplicity, it is necessary at last that the most multiple should be reached: this is Matter. Matter is not absolutely nothing; it is the last remnant of something before the emanations reach the brink of oblivion. Matter is the point at which no more multiplicity is possible without going into non-being. Further, since unity is absolutely good, it follows that multiplicity is evil. Matter itself has no residue of good; it has only the bare capacity for good. There is then a complete hierarchy of being and goodness from First to last, from God to evil, from Unity to multiplicity, and from the One beyond Mind to matter.[2]

This process, however, is not one-directional. God not only emanates forth but the emanants return to the Source from which they come. There is a kind of boomerang of being whereby what comes down must go up again. What flows from ultimate Unity seeks to return again to this sanctuary. But the lower and latter is always inferior to the higher and former. Hence, absolute multiplicity cannot destroy absolute unity; evil cannot defeat good and non-being cannot annihilate being.[3]

Man, the microcosm who possesses mind, soul, and matter, is the point at which the return trip is made conscious. Wandering about as he does in the foreign land of evil and multiplicity, man's higher soul becomes homesick for the Fatherland of goodness and unity. Man's

---

1. Plotinus, *Enneads,* VI, 8, 9; III, 8, 9; V, 1, 8; VI, 8, 18; VI, 7, 37; IV, 2, 2.
2. Plotinus, II, 4, 11; I, 8, 7; VI, 9, 1; I, 8, 3.
3. Plotinus, IV, 8, 4; I, 7, 7; VI, 9, 11; I, 3, 6; II, 4, 12.

higher soul is as it were on an elastic band that can be stretched only so far into the material world. Sooner or later a "snap" pulls man back toward the source from which he was originally stretched out. When a being overlooks the brink of utter oblivion, it recoils backward toward Being and the Source of Being. The final remnant of good is repelled as it stares into the naked face of evil.[4]

Mounting one's way back to unity is not easy; matter is a drag on the soul. Hence, asceticism is a necessary preliminary stage in the ascent to God. One must turn from the outward multiple world to the inner more unified world of soul. The denial of the physical is essential to the attainment of the spiritual. The move from the *external* to the *internal* is the first move toward attaining union with God.[5]

The second stage is a move from the *internal* to the *eternal,* that is, the inward to the upward. This movement is from the lower soul to the higher soul and from soul to mind which is above soul. This is accomplished by meditation. In short, one must move from the sensible to the intellectual, by which Plotinus does not mean the realm of one's individual intellect but an identification of our mind with Mind (the Nous). Knower and known must become one; herein is the highest and most unified act of knowing. However, even when one's individual mind has become one with Mind there is still a basic duality of knower and known; absolute unity has not yet been attained.[6]

For the highest and final union neither the preparatory asceticism nor the preliminary meditation will suffice; the One can be attained only by a "leap" of mystical intuition in which one becomes "one with the One" and "alone with the Alone." It is a leap beyond Being and beyond knowing. There is no consciousness but only convergence. The center of our being corresponds with the Center of all Being. In this state one has gone beyond the cognitive to the intuitional, beyond the rational to the mystical. Herein everything is absolute unity again. The prodigals have returned home and the strays are back in the fold. What emanated out has returned; everything came from God *(ex deo)* and to him all must return.[7]

Plotinus acknowledges that he has but negative knowledge of the One. He knows not what it is but that it is not-many. All positive, rational, or cognitive knowledge of absolute Unity is impossible. The best one can do is attribute to the One perfections that it produces but does not itself possess. Hence, we call what the One produces good, beauty, and being; but it does not really and intrinsically possess these characteristics

4. Plotinus, I, 6, 8; I, 2, 4; I, 8, 5; I, 8, 4.
5. Plotinus, I, 6, 3-4; I, 6, 8; VI, 9, 11; I, 3, 6.
6. Plotinus, III, 8, 10; V, 3, 4.
7. Plotinus, VI, 7, 35; V, 5, 6; VI, 9, 4; VI, 7, 34; VI, 9, 10.

that are attributed to It. We can speak about It only in terms of what comes from It, but the sequents do not really tell us anything of their Source. God is literally ineffable.[8]

In summary, Plotinus' form of pantheism is emanational in that everything flows out of God and returns to him. Ultimately All is in the One; the One is not in the All. The source of all reality is Unity, and it is the degree of unity by which something is constituted in the very nature of its being. The less unified, the less real something is. Hence, there is not in Plotinus a rigid and inflexible monism but an emanational and unfolding divine unity that cascades down the great chain of being from Unity toward greater multiplicity.

## Spinoza's Modal Pantheism

Benedict Spinoza was a rationalist in his epistemology but a pantheist in his metaphysical position. He begins axiomatically and definitionally. "By *God,* I mean a being absolutely infinite—that is, a substance consisting of infinite attributes, of which each expresses eternal and infinite essentiality." By "substance" Spinoza means "that which is in itself, and is conceived through itself." "Attribute," differing only formally not actually from "essence," means "that which the intellect perceives as constituting the essence of substance." A "mode," on the other hand, is a "modification [affection] of substance, or that which exists in, and is conceived through, something other than itself." Armed with these definitions and some basic axioms, Spinoza proceeds to deduce the existence of a pantheistic God.[9]

First, "substance is by nature prior to its modifications." Two substances whose attributes differ would have nothing in common. Two or more distinct things would have to differ either by their substance or by their attributes, since "everything which exists, exists either in itself or in something else." It follows then that "there cannot exist in the universe two or more substances having the same nature or attributes." The proof Spinoza offers for this is reminiscent of Parmenides: "If several distinct substances be granted, they must be distinguished one from the other, either by the difference of their attributes, or by the difference of their modifications." But if they differ "only by the difference of their attributes, it will be granted that there cannot be more than one with identical attributes," for they cannot differ by that in which they are identical. On the other hand, if they differ by their modifications only, "it follows that setting the modifications aside, and considering substance in itself, that is truly, there cannot be conceived one substance different from another—that is (by Prop. IV),

---

8. Plotinus, V, 5, 6; V, 3, 13; VI, 9, 4; VI, 7, 29; V, 3, 14.
9. Spinoza, *Ethics,* Part I, Definitions I, III, IV, V.

there cannot be granted several substances, but one substance only. Q. E. D." Hence, monism follows geometrically from self-evident definitions and axioms of thought.[10]

Not only is there only one substance in the universe—everything else being merely a modification of it—but that substance is infinite. Spinoza's proof of this contention is as follows: "There can only be one substance with an identical attribute, and existence follows from its nature (Prop. VII); its nature, therefore, involves existence, either as finite or infinite." But "it does not exist as finite, for (by Def. II) it would then be limited by something else of the same kind, which would also necessarily exist (Prop. VII); and there would be two sub-stances with an identical attribute, which is absurd (Prop. V). It therefore exists as infinite. Q. E. D." So there exists one and only one infinite substance, namely, God.[11]

According to Spinoza, "the more reality or being a thing has, the greater the number of its attributes." From this it follows that "there is but one substance in the universe, and . . . it is absolutely infinite. . . ." For "nothing in nature is more clear than that each and every entity must be conceived under some attribute, and that its reality or being is in proportion to the number of its attributes expressing necessity or eternity and infinity." Consequently, "it is abundantly clear, that an absolutely infinite being must necessarily be defined as consisting in infinite attributes, each of which expresses a certain eternal and infinite essence." And if God must be defined as a substance consisting of infinite attributes, he must necessarily exist. For "if this be denied, conceive, if possible, that God does not exist: then his essence does not involve existence. But this (by Prop. VII) is absurd. Therefore God necessarily exists."[12]

God then is the only substance that can exist. For "if any substance besides God were granted, it would have to be explained by some attribute of God, and thus two substances with the same attribute would exist, which (by Prop. V) is absurd; therefore, besides God no substance can be granted, or, consequently, be conceived." From this it follows "that extension and thought are either attributes of God or accidents (affections) of the attributes of God." For "whatever is, is in God, and without God nothing can be, or be conceived." This does not mean that God has a body, mind, and passions like man. This is wrong because there is no definite quantity in God; he is absolutely infinite. Yet we must draw the conclusion that "extended

10. Spinoza, Propositions, I, II, IV, V.
11. Spinoza, Proposition VIII.
12. Spinoza, Propositions X, VII.

substance is one of the infinite attributes of God." The fallacy in opposing arguments, said Spinoza, is that they all assume wrongly that extended substance is composed of parts. This is not true. God is infinitely extended and yet he has no parts. God's substance is indivisible, for "if it could be divided, the parts into which it was divided would either retain the nature of absolutely infinite substance, or they would not. If the former, we should have several substances of the same nature, which (by Prop. V) is absurd." And "if the latter, then (by Prop. VII) substance absolutely infinite could cease to exist, which (by Prop. XI) is also absurd," for nothing can divide and destroy what is by nature a necessary existence. Therefore, God must be infinitely extended and without parts.[13]

In summary, "all things . . . are in God, and all things which come to pass, come to pass solely through the laws of the infinite nature of God, and follow . . . from the necessity of his essence." For "from the necessity of the divine nature must follow an infinite number of things in infinite ways—that is, all things which can fall within the sphere of infinite intellect." This follows because "from the given definition of any thing the intellect infers several properties which already necessarily follow therefrom." And since God is necessary, "it follows that from the necessity of its nature an infinite number of things . . . must necessarily follow." Hence, "God acts solely by the laws of his own nature, and is not constrained by anyone." In this sense God is said to be "free"; that is, God "acts by the sole necessity of his nature, wherefore God is . . . the sole free cause. Q. E. D." God is not "free" in any deliberative sense, for "neither intellect nor will appertain to God's nature."[14]

Since God is necessary and since all things flow necessarily from him, it follows that "an infinite number of things . . . have necessarily flowed forth in an infinite number of ways, or always follow from the same necessity; in the same way as from the nature of a triangle it follows . . . that its three interior angles are equal to two right angles." So "all things which are, are in God. . . . God, therefore, is the indwelling and not the transient cause of all things." And since God is eternal as well as necessary, then all things flow both eternally and necessarily from God. For "all things which follow from the absolute nature of any attribute of God must always exist and be infinite." This is true of modes as well as attributes. For a mode which can only be conceived to exist through some necessary perfection of God must therefore itself exist necessarily. Otherwise, it could not even be conceived to exist.

---

13. Spinoza, Propositions XIV, XV.
14. Spinoza, Propositions XV, XVII.

From this it follows that every event and act in the finite world is determined by God. For "every individual thing, or everything which is finite and has a conditional existence, cannot exist or be conditioned to act, unless it be conditioned for existence and action by a cause other than itself. . . ." But since this causal-conditioned series cannot go on to infinity, we must arrive alas at a first conditioning cause of every other act or event in the finite world. In short, "all things which are, are in God, and so depend on God, that without him they can neither be nor be conceived." For "nothing in the universe is contingent, but all things are conditioned to exist and operate in a particular manner by the necessity of the divine nature." Whatever is, is in God. "But God cannot be called a thing contingent. For he exists necessarily, and not contingently. Further, the modes of the divine nature follow therefrom necessarily, and not contingently."[15]

In Spinoza's pantheistic universe, as well as in Plotinus', evil flows necessarily from God. For "things could not have been brought into being by God in any manner or in any order different from that which has in fact obtained." It clearly follows that "things have been brought into being by God in the highest perfection, inasmuch as they necessarily followed from a most perfect nature." For "God's will cannot be different . . . from God's perfection. Therefore neither can things be different." If one were to ask Spinoza why, if God is perfect, there are so many imperfections in nature, he would reply: "The perfection of things is to be reckoned only from their own nature and power; things are not more or less perfect, according as they delight or offend human senses." As to why God created men who could and would be controlled by anything less than reason, it was, according to Spinoza, because "matter was not lacking to him for the creation of every degree of perfection from highest to lowest; or, more strictly, because the laws of his nature are so vast, as to suffice for the production of everything conceivable by an infinite intelligence, as I have shown in Prop. XVI."[16]

In summary, God is an infinitely perfect and necessary being. Everything else is either an attribute or mode of his substance. Since God is infinite and necessary, an infinity of necessary degrees of perfection flow necessarily from his nature. Evil is necessary because with degrees of perfection come also corresponding degrees of imperfection. All is in God and flows from God. God's substance is absolutely good; it is only the infinite modal manifestations of this one substance that manifest the degrees of perfection (and imperfection). Hence, there is no

---

15. Spinoza, Propositions XVII, XVIII, XXI, XXVIII.
16. Spinoza, Propositions XXXIII, XXXII, and Appendix.

evil in the infinite oneness and necessity of God. Evil is found only in the modal manifestations which are less than ultimately real.

## Radhakrishnan's Neo-Hindu Pantheism

The Indian religious experience is rich in variety. Everything from impersonal monisms to various forms of theism is found in the Upanishads. One of the most interesting and influential forms of neo-Hinduism is that of Radhakrishnan. His pantheism is modified in the direction of a favorable appeal to those influenced by Western theism.

According to Radhakrishnan there are several statuses or levels of reality. "We have (1) the Absolute, (2) God as Creative power, (3) God immanent in this world. These are not to be regarded as separate entities. They are arranged in this order because there is a logical priority." One proceeds from and is based on the preceding. "We thus get the four poises or statuses of reality, (1) the Absolute, *Brahman,* (2) the Creative Spirit, *Isvara,* (3) the World-Spirit, *Hiranya-garbha* and (4) the World [*virāj*]."[17]

Radhakrishnan compares this to neo-platonic pantheism: "In Plotinus we have a similar scheme. (i) The One alone, the simple, the unconditioned.... (ii) The *Nous.* The Intelligible world which Plotinus calls One-Many, the world of Platonic forms or archetypes.... (iii) One and Many. The soul of the All is the third, which fashions the material universe on the model of divine thoughts, the ideas laid up within the Divine Mind.... (iv) The many alone. It is the world-body, the world of matter without form."[18] The Hindu scheme of reality, however, differs from plotinian emanationalism in that Brahman is manifest on different levels but does not emanate forth, with lower levels flowing out of higher ones. In this sense neo-Hindu pantheism is more a multi-level pantheism than emanational pantheism.

*Brahman, the Ultimate Reality.* For Radhakrishnan, *Brahman* comes from the root, *brh,* meaning "to grow, to burst forth." Brahman is the one single reality from which the world of multiplicity springs. It is the subtle and infinite essence of which everything perceived is made. As formally defined in one Upanishad, "That from which these beings are born, that in which born they live, and that into which they enter at their death is Brahman." That "on which all else depends, to which all existences aspire, *Brahman* which is sufficient to itself, aspiring to no other, without any need, is the source of all other beings...." It is the Primordial and the Supreme. "Verily, in the beginning this world was *Brahman.*"[19]

17. Sarvepali Radhakrishnan, *The Principal Upanishads,* intro., p. i.
18. Radhakrishnan, pp. 65, 66.
19. Radhakrishnan, pp. 52, 55, 56, 59.

Like Plotinus, Radhakrishnan believes *Brahman* to be indescribable. "We can only describe the Absolute in negative terms. In the words of Plotinus, 'we say what he is not, we cannot say what he is.' The Absolute is beyond the sphere of predication. It is the *sunyata* of the Buddhists."[20]

*Isvara, the Creative Spirit.* The next level of this neo-Hindu triadic manifestation of God is personal. It is like the plotinian *Nous* or the platonic *Logos.* Here there is simple duality of subject and object. It is *mahat,* the great one, or *buddhi,* the intellect. As cosmic intelligence it contains all the ideas which serve as the principle of individuation for all other things. *Isvara* is the Supreme Light, the principle of communication. He is the Supreme Lord who, like Plato's Demiurgos, is the creative Mind behind the universe. Together with *Brahman,* "we thus get the conception of an Absolute-God, *Brahman—Isvara,* where the first term indicates infinite being and possibility, and the second suggests creative freedom." As the Absolute Brahman is perfect and needs nothing. "It is free to move or not to move, to throw itself into forms or remain formless. If it still indulges its power of creativity, it is because of its free choice." In *Isvara* "the Supreme who is unmeasured and immeasurable becomes measured and defined. Immutable becomes infinite fecundity."[21]

*Hiranya-garbha, the World-Spirit.* The world is not only a creation of *Isvara* but it is a manifestation of *Hiranya-garbha.* The world is the free self-determination of God. For the power of self-expression belongs to God. *Hiranya-garbha* is the spirit that pervades and animates the universe. "The World-soul is the divine creator, the supreme lord *Isvara* at work in the universe." It is a definite possibility of the Absolute being realized in the universe. According to Radhakrishnan, the World-Soul is grounded in *Isvara;* there is no sharp distinction drawn between them in the Upanishads. In point of fact, each is a successive manifestation of the absolute. "The absolute conceived as it is in itself, independent of any creation, is called *Brahman.*" And "when it is thought of as the spirit moving everywhere in the universe, it is called *Hiranya-garbha;* when it is thought of as a personal God creating, protecting and destroying the universe, it is called *Isvara.*" *Isvara* becomes *Brahma, Vishnu,* and *Siva* when his three functions are taken separately, but "the real is not a sum of these. It is an ineffable unity in which these conceptual distinctions are made. These are fourfold to our mental view, separate only in appearance. If we identify the real with any one de-

---

20. Radhakrishnan, p. 67.
21. Radhakrishnan, pp. 63, 64.

finable state of being, however pure and perfect, we violate the unity and divide the indivisible."[22]

Virāj, *the Manifestation of the Absolute in the World.* According to Radhakrishnan, the world is not an illusion but a lower level manifestation of the Absolute.[23] By contrast with Brahman itself, the world seems almost nothing, but it is the last manifestation of reality. *"Maya* is the power of *Isvara* from which the world arises."* However, "God does not create the world but becomes it. Creation is expression. It is not a making of something out of nothing. It is not making so much as becoming." Hence, *maya* is not illusion but the creative manifestation of God in the multiple world. Of course the world of duality and multiplicity is admittedly not the absolutely real. It is only an echo of the real. "The world is neither one with *Brahman* nor wholly other than *Brahman."* The world is grounded in *Brahman.* "The many are parts of Brahman even as waves are parts of the sea. All the possibilities of the world are affirmed in the first being, God."[24]

Karma, *Rebirth and Eternal Life.* When *buddhi,* intelligence, turns itself from *jiva* (individual self, ego) toward *atman* (universal self) it develops true knowledge or intuition *(vidya).* Atman is Brahman as the universal basis of human personality. Hence, *Brahman* is known through the inner self of man. Thus one must turn from the outward and multiple to the inner world of thought and unity. "Knowledge presupposes unity or oneness of thought and being, a unity that transcends the differentiation of subject and object." Logical reasoning is incapable of comprehending God and "logical incapacity is not evidence of actual impossibility." The individual should develop the habit of introversion, of abstracting from the outside world and looking within himself. For "by a process of abstraction we get behind knowing, feeling and willing to the essential Self, the God within. We must silence our speech, mind and will. We cannot hear the voice of the spirit in us, so long as we are lost in vain talk, mental rambling and empty desires."[25]

"Until we negate the ego and get fixed in the Divine Ground we are bound to the endless procession of events called *samsara"* (cycles of rebirth). The principle which governs this world of becoming is *karma.* It is the law of retribution by which a man inherits in the next life his deserts from this life. *Karma* is not an external law imposed by God

22. Radhakrishnan, pp. 71, 66.
23. Other commentators on Hinduism, as M. Hereyanna, understands the world as *maya,* i.e., an illusory appearance of Brahman the way a rope may appear to be a snake from a distance (*The Essentials of Indian Philosophy,* pp. 158-59.). In the Sankara tradition the world *(maya)* is completely illusory or non-being.
24. Radhakrishnan, pp. 80, 82, 83.
25. Radhakrishnan, pp. 77, 96, 97, 102.

but an unfolding of the law of our being. As Radhakrishnan noted, "If there is a fundamental difference between Christianity and Hinduism, it is said that it consists in this, that while the Hindu to whatever school he belongs believes in a succession of lives, the Christian believes that 'it is appointed to men once to die, but after this the judgment.'" By meditation, however, the Hindu believer can overcome the cycle of rebirths dictated by the law of *karma* and be united to *Brahman*. For "he who knows *Brahman* becomes *Brahman*. Perfection is a state of mind, not contingent of time or place." Life eternal, or *moska,* is liberation from births and deaths, for "he who knows himself to be all can have no desire. When the Supreme is seen, the knots of the heart are cut asunder. . . . There can be no sorrow or pain or fear when there is no other."[26]

Radhakrishnan believes "the individual soul is eternal. It endures throughout the cosmic process." Nevertheless, "the individual soul is an aspect of the Transcendent in the universe and when liberated from all limitations, he acts with his centre in the Supreme."[27] And its inner peace is manifested in the joyous freedom of outer activity. Thus union with *Brahman* is a state of bliss or nirvana that is not only attainable in this life but is the guarantee that one will not have to undergo another life of pain and frustration stemming from selfish desire. For in nirvana the self attains its release from individual striving by achieving union with God.

### Summary of the Central Tenets of Pantheism

There are many kinds of pantheism. There is the *absolute* pantheism of Parmenides where all reality is one monistic whole and all multiplicity is an absolute illusion or non-being. But all other forms of pantheism provide some reality status to some things other than God, at least for a time. Spinoza's *modal* pantheism holds that everything other than the one infinite substance exists as a mode or moment in the divine essence. Plotinus' *emanational* pantheism provides that creation comes out of God in various degrees of reality depending on their distance from God and their degree of multiplicity. Hindu pantheism comes in various varieties but the position of Radhakrishnan is a kind of *manifestational* or multilevel pantheism in which the one absolute is revealed on different or descending levels of reality. Other forms of Hindu pantheism would claim that lower levels are not so much manifestations of the absolute as they are mere appearance or, in the case of some, that the world of senses is an outright illusion, an unreality. Finally, there is *developmental* pantheism in which God is unfolding himself in the historical

---

26. Radhakrishnan, pp. 114, 18.
27. Radhakrishnan, p. 127.

or evolutionary process. In the view of Hegel the development is manifest in history. History is the footprints of God in the sands of time. Or, better, history is a phenomenological theophany.

Since space will not permit detailed evaluation of the various kinds of pantheism, we will concentrate on theses which are common to most forms, noting significant points in some of the representative types discussed above.

1. A basic *intuitive epistemology* is characteristic of pantheistic approaches to God. God is understood in the highest and most significant sense not by sensible observation nor by rational inference but by mystical intuition that goes beyond the law of noncontradiction.

2. The stress of the *way of negation* in religious language is essential to pantheism. God cannot be adequately expressed in positive terms. Nothing in our experience may be appropriately affirmed of the way God is. God is beyond being and beyond rational knowing.

3. The central pantheistic conception of God is the *absolute unity* and *transcendence* of God. The supremacy and unity of God are the core of ultimate reality and the basis for everything derived from him.

4. *Creation is ex Deo, out of God.* Creation from nothing, *ex nihilo,* is meaningless. God is the source for everything; all is rooted in his being. Creation springs out of God's being either by manifestation, emanation, or some kind of unfolding.

5. Both *creation and evil flow necessarily from God.* The absolute is not personal and creation is not a free choice. It flows from God with necessity. Plotinus would say, "The good is diffusive of itself," that is, it must issue forth the way rays must radiate from the sun or radii from the center of a circle or as a seed unfolds into a flower. And whatever evils, lacks, or deficiencies are seen in the emanations or manifestations are there because they must be there.

6. In the highest and absolute sense God is *neither personal nor conscious.* The Absolute and Supreme is not a He but an It. Personality comes about at best by emanation or manifestation on a lower level.

7. The *universe is ultimately One,* not many. In absolute monism, as in Parmenides, there is no reality status to anything but absolutely one Being. In other pantheisms there is agreement that whatever lesser reality there is in multiplicity and finitude, the many is always in the One but the One is not in the many. That is, unity is the basic reality from which multiplicity flows, not the reverse. Further, whatever lesser reality is accorded to the finite and many, *ultimately* there is only one reality. Temporarily and/or manifestationally there are many modes and aspects of reality. But like radii, there is really only one central point of reality all have in common, i.e., in the only Being or One.

# An Evaluation of Pantheism

As a world and life view pantheism has had a broad and persistent influence in the world. Much of the Far Eastern world for most of its recorded history has been influenced by pantheism. Even much of the Western world has been a series of footnotes on plotinian pantheism. The appeal of pantheism has not been without both truth and value. Examples may be briefly noted.

## Positive Insights in Pantheistic Positions

Pantheism has provided much of value to its adherents and has given both insight and challenge to those who do not embrace it as a world view. Among these values we may take special note of six.

1. First, pantheism attempts to be *comprehensive* in its perspective. Pantheism is not a piecemeal philosophy. It is an all-embracing view of the sum total of reality from that perspective. In this sense it is both metaphysical and comprehensive, two commendable dimensions essential to any world view.

2. Second, pantheism has laid special emphasis on an ultimate dimension of reality that cannot be overlooked or denied, namely, *unity*. Unity and harmony are constituitive elements in any adequate world view. If this is a uni-verse, there must be some reality basis for its uni-ty.

3. Third, no adequate view of a God who is worthy of serious human interest can neglect his *immanent* presence and activity in the world. A God who is totally and completely Other lacks relatability and no doubt, at least to many, he will lack worshipability. Pantheism appropriately stresses that God is really *in* the world, at least within the depths of the human soul.

4. Fourth, pantheism acknowledges that only God is *absolute* and *necessary*. Everything else is less than ultimate and absolute in the supreme sense in which God is. No part of creation is independent or ontologically detached; all is completely dependent on God who is All in all. This insight is a valuable corrective for many materialisms as well as for deisms.

5. Fifth, pantheism invariably involves an *intuitive* epistemological emphasis which is often unappreciated by more empirically oriented minds. This stress on the direct and unmediated intimacy with the object of knowledge (especially God) is not only valuable but it is unavoidable. Indirect or inferential knowing must rest finally on direct and immediate seeing. All justification must come to an end; first principles must be known intuitively. Hence, some form of intuitive knowledge is essential to knowing God who is the ultimate principle (person) in religion.

6. Sixth, pantheists place strong and appropriate emphasis on the *via negativa*. God cannot be expressed in positive terms with limited

meaning. God is infinite and transcendent and all limitation must be negated from terms applied to him. Without the way of negation verbal idolatry results, namely, the finitizing of God. Pantheists have preserved this important dimension of religious language.

One could take note of numerous other contributions pantheistic thinkers have made to the philosophy of history (e.g., Hegel), to comparative religions and human toleration (e.g., Radhakrishnan), to the preservation of mystical and spiritual emphases, as well as to many other areas. But time has come to critically evaluate the system as a world view.

## Some Criticisms of Pantheism as a World View

Understood as a metaphysical interpretation of the universe, pantheism is decidedly lopsided and lacking. There are many reasons for this conclusion and a number of areas in which it may be illustrated.

1. The most fundamental criticism of a strictly pantheistic world view is that it is actually unaffirmable by man, for no finite individual reality exists as an entity really different from God or the absolute. In essence a strict pantheist must affirm, "God is but I am not." But this is self-defeating, since one must exist in order to affirm that he does not exist.

Of course most pantheists are not absolute monists in that they allow for some reality to finite man whether it be modal, manifestational, emanational, or whatever. In this way they hope to escape the self-destructive dilemma just mentioned. Their attempt, however, is not convincing for the following reasons. Claiming that man, as a self-conscious person, is merely a mode or aspect of God is a denial of the way man experiences himself. If we are only self-conscious modes, "why are we not conscious of being so? How did this metaphysical amnesia arise and (yet more seriously) come to pervade and dominate our whole experience?"[28] In point of fact, is it not self-defeating to claim that individual finite selves are less than real? How can any of our individual statements be true including the statement that pantheism is true? If we are being deceived about the consciousness of our own individual existence, then how does a pantheist know that he is not being deceived when he is conscious of reality as ultimately one?

2. Second, granting that there are no real finite selves or "I's," then there is no such thing as an I-Thou relationship between finite selves nor between men and God. Both fellowship and worship become impossible. All alleged I-thou or I-I relations reduce to I. Indeed there is no true changing relation at all, since there are no separate changing relata to relate. Religious experience is impossible in any meaningful

---

28. H. P. Owen, *Concepts of Deity*, p. 72.

sense of the term since all meaningful experience involves something or someone other than oneself with whom one enters the changing experience. For if when one is conscious of experiencing God it is really only an experience internal to the modes or manifestations of God, then *he* is not really having an experience; only God is having the experience.

Some pantheists hope to avoid this problem by giving man a manifestational or emanational status, at least temporarily, as a self. This is true of both Plotinus and Radhakrishnan. Their attempt, however, is unsuccessful because when all is said and done there is no reality in the finite individual that is his own. His selfhood is real only at the point at which it is one with the absolute. Logically this means that *as finite* and *as individual* it is not real, despite all attempts to say that it has some kind of lesser reality. They wrongly assume that whatever is not really ultimate is not ultimately or actually real.

Other pantheists, like Alan Watts, appeal to the Christian Trinity as a model where there is more than one person in communion, I-Thou relations, and yet only one being or essence. This move, however, will not suffice, since the persons of the Trinity are not anchored to finite and changing natures. They interrelate in accordance with the perfect and unchanging unity of one absolute and eternal nature. By contrast, finite egos bound to a space-time continuum (our "world") are an entirely different matter. In this case, plurality of persons involves also a plurality of changing essences.

3. Third, the basic metaphysical assumption of monism begs the whole question. From Parmenides to the present, monists of numerous varieties invariably assume a univocal notion of being without justification. This is apparent in Parmenides' premise that things cannot differ in what they have in common (viz., being) for *that is the very respect in which they are identical.* If one assumes that being is identically the same wherever it is found, then of course it follows that being is ultimately one. That is, if being always means *exactly the same thing* (i.e., univocity of being), then the attempt to show there is more than one being in the universe is futile. Whatever being one points to and however distant and separate it may *seem* from other beings, in the final analysis they are all identical in their being. Not only is no proof offered for this monistic assumption, but a pluralistic alternative to it is overlooked, namely, that being is analogous. If being is not entirely the same wherever it is found but is only similar, then there can be more than one being in the universe. That is, there may be different kinds of being, for example, finite and infinite. And as long as the principle of differentiation is within the very being of the finite beings, then there can be many beings. Each of these can have its own

identity different from the others, but each will have an element of similarity in that each has being. This analogous concept of being is at least a metaphysical possibility, and if it is possible then pantheism is not necessarily true. In brief, the central metaphysical premise of pantheism is the unproven assumption that being is to be understood univocally.

4. Fourth, the ship of pantheism is wrecked on the reef of evil. Pronouncing evil illusory or less than real is not only hollow to those experiencing evil, but it is philosophically inadequate as well. If evil is not real, what is the origin of the illusion? Why has it been so persistent and why does it seem so real? As it has been aptly put, why is it that when one experiences suffering, he dislikes what he fancies he feels? Or, more seriously, how can evil arise from God who is absolutely and necessarily good? Making evil a necessary part of God or of the world process that flows necessarily from God does not explain evil; in fact, to the contrary, it explains away absolute Good. It makes God both good and evil. Or, as a pantheist would prefer, it puts God beyond both good or evil. But this leads to another serious inadequacy with pantheism.

5. Fifth, there is neither ground for absolute Good nor an ultimate distinction between good and evil in a pantheistic universe. The ground of all is beyond being and knowing. It is beyond the laws of logic and distinction. Hence, ultimately and really there is no basis for distinguishing between good and evil. So, for God as God nothing is either good or evil, for he is beyond both and contains both in a transcendent way that is manifest in that which flows from him by way of mode, manifestation, or emanation.

6. Sixth, the pantheistic God is not really personal. Strictly speaking, personality is at best a lesser or lower level of God. The Judeo-Christian personal God is a second-class citizen in the heavens. The absolute as absolute and ultimate is beyond personality and consciousness. These are pure anthropomorphisms or at best lesser manifestations of the Supreme. Rather than being the most personal Being and the paradigm for all personality, the pantheistic God is an impersonal force driven by metaphysical necessity and not by volitional and loving choice. God as a loving Father freely bestowing kindness on the world of his creatures is alien to the highest level of religious reality in a pantheistic world. A personal God—if there is one—is at best a lower manifestation or appearance of the highest impersonal reality.

7. Seventh, the pantheistic God is incomplete without creation; he is dependent on the creation that flows from him for the attainment of the perfections that lie latent in his own infinite potentialities. To borrow Plotinus' illustration, God is like a seed that must unfold in

its own creation in order to blossom forth in all its potential. God must create a mirror so that by reflection on his creation he may come to know himself. For Hegel, God comes to self-realization by unfolding in the historical process; history, as it were, is necessary to develop deity.

By way of contrast, the theistic God is eternally conscious and complete and without need for anything to realize latent potentials. Indeed, the traditional theistic God is pure actuality without any potential in his being whatsoever.[29] While a pantheistic God creates out of necessity and need, the theistic God creates out of love and desire.

8. Eighth, if God is "All" or coextensive in his being with the universe, then pantheism is metaphysically indistinguishable from atheism. Both hold in common that the Whole is a collection of all the finite parts or aspects. The only difference is that the pantheist decides to attribute religious significance to the All and the atheist does not. But philosophically the Whole is identical, namely, one eternal self-contained system of reality.

What is more, statements that include everything, such as "God is All," are vulnerable to the charge that they say nothing. For to say everything of God, including opposites, is to say nothing meaningful of him. Unless some real distinction can be made between the finite and the infinite, good and evil, and so on, then nothing significant is being said. Every affirmation must imply by contrast a possible negation in order to be meaningful. Even the general statement "God is being" implies that "God is not non-being." But to affirm, as pantheism does, that "God is All and All is God" in the ultimate and absolute sense is equivocal and non-sensical because it contains within it opposites such as good and evil, being and non-being.

9. Ninth, pantheism involves a contradiction within the nature of God as infinite. For if God is infinite and yet he somehow shares his being (ex Deo) with creation, then either the finite is infinite, the contingent is necessary—which is clearly contradictory—or else the finite and contingent and many are not really finite and contingent and many. Rather, they are one, necessary, and infinite. In short, either absolute monism is clearly self-defeating (first criticism above) or else if God shares part of his infinite being with creatures, then part of it is lost and becomes less than infinite. It will not suffice for the pantheist to opt for a third alternative, namely, that when God gives being to a creature it is not God's own being that is given but a being separate from it which is created in the creature; for this position is not pantheism but theism. The choices within this overall framework, then, appear to be absolute monism, which is self-defeating; contra-

29. See Aquinas, *Summa Theologica* I, 13, 11.

dictory pantheism, which holds that God remains infinite in his being even when part of his being is given to another; or theism. Some would attempt to avoid this dilemma by opting for a panentheism, which will be discussed in the next chapter. But one thing seems certain; one must move in some other direction than pantheism for a rational and coherent world view.

10. Pantheism's stress on the unknowability or ineffability of God is self-defeating. The very assertion that God is unknowable in an intellectual way is either meaningless or self-defeating. If that assertion is one that cannot itself be understood in an intellectual way, then it is a meaningless assertion. On the other hand, if the assertion "God is unknowable in an intellectual way" is really understandable in an intellectual way, then it is self-defeating. For in this case the pantheist is offering a statement about God to the effect that such statements cannot be made about God. He is making a positive predication about God that claims that predications cannot be made about God in a positive way. Totally negative predications tell one nothing. As even Plotinus admitted, every negative predication implies some positive knowledge (*Enneads,* VI, 7, 29).

Some pantheists, like Alan Watts, frankly avoid this dilemma by admitting that their writings are not informative about God. Besides signifying that their writings are meaningless, this implies in addition that the whole communication process is fruitless. Why write? Pantheists do write and often write long books. Furthermore, it is self-defeating for the pantheist to communicate to us his view of God only to inform us that he has not done so. Despite what some pantheists *say,* what they actually *do* is use language to communicate to us a view of God which in turn they say is incommunicable.

## Summary and Conclusion

Pantheistic emphases provide numerous insights into the nature of reality including the absoluteness of God, his immanence in the world, the unity of being. Pantheism attempts to provide a comprehensive, all-embracing philosophy. In addition, many pantheists have provided valuable insights into intuitive epistemology and the need of negation in religious language in order to preserve the transcendent and infinite nature of God. On the interpersonal and social level many pantheists have stressed the need for tolerance and the desire for a spiritual unity among men. All of these, and more, are commendable contributions by proponents of the pantheistic viewpoint.

However, when we consider pantheism as a metaphysical system, there are numerous problems—some of which seem insurmountable. Most significant is the fact that pantheism is self-destructive of religious experience, of its own concept of God and of the ability even to affirm the position of pantheism without involving the existence of that which is contrary to the system, namely, the existence of a finite self making the affirmation. In addition, the inability to adequately explain the apparent reality of evil and the relegation of God to an incomplete potential for perfection dependent on manifestation or emanation for completion of his being is a shabby concept of absolute and necessary perfection compared to the God of Christian theism. Finally, pantheism is often built on an intuitive or mystical epistemology that makes self-defeating or meaningless statements about the unknowability of God. If it were true that God is actually unknowable and inexpressible by language or thought, then the pantheist could not have so expressed his view to us. The fact that pantheists in writing and speaking do express their view proves that their claim about God's unknowability is self-destructive.

## SELECT READINGS FOR CHAPTER TEN

**Exposition of Pantheism**

Hegel, G. W. F. *Phenomenology of Mind.*
Hiriyanna, M. *The Essentials of Indian Philosophy.*
Plotinus. *Enneads.*
Radhakrishnan, Sarvepali. *The Hindu View of Life.*
Spinoza, Benedict. *Ethics.*
Watts, Alan. *Behold the Spirit.*

**Evaluation of Pantheism**

Flint, Robert. *Anti-theistic Theories,* chaps. 9, 10 and apps. 39-41.
Hodge, Charles. *Systematic Theology,* vol. I.
Hunt, John. *Pantheism and Christianity.*
Owen, H. P. *Concepts of Deity,* chaps. 2 and 3.
Zaehner, Robert C. *Mysticism, Sacred and Profane.*

# Chapter

# 11 | *Panentheism*

Pan-en-theism is not to be confused with pantheism, although they have some things in common. Panentheism is the belief that God is *in* the world the way a soul or mind is in a body; pantheism is the belief that God *is* the world and the world is God. There are many names for this world view. Some call it *finite-godism* because, in contrast with traditional theism, it believes that God is not infinite in nature and power but finite or limited. Others label it dipolar or *bipolar theism* since, in contrast to traditional monopolar theism, it holds that there are two poles to God, namely, an actual temporal pole and a potential eternal pole. Because of these differences from traditional theism, some wish to call it *quasi-theism* or qualified theism. Still others, viewing its affinities with pantheism's identification of God and the world, prefer the title *panentheism*. In the contemporary world the major form of this position is represented in *process theology,* which holds that the finite, bipolar god is in a continual process of change. In this form it is sometimes called *organicism* because of its stress on the organic relationship of all factors of the world process. It is the bipolar type of panentheism with which we will be most concerned in this chapter.

## An Exposition of Panentheism

Panentheism did not begin in the modern world. The pre-Socratic philosopher Diogenes (5th century B.C.) held that God is to World as soul is to body, a root model that is still in currency among panentheists. Further, both Plato's Demiurgos and Aristotle's Unmoved Mover were finite gods that would fit into the broad category of panentheism. But the most influential forms of panentheism in the modern world emanate from Alfred North Whitehead and his successors.

## The Process Panentheism of Whitehead

There were many influences converging in the Whiteheadian view of God. The ancient philosopher Heraclitus (fl. 500 B.C.) had noted that a man "could not step twice in the same river; for other and yet other waters are ever flowing on." This process view of the world was later developed by Hegel (d. 1831) into a developmental unfolding of God in history. Herbert Spencer (d. 1903) expanded the Darwinian biological hypothesis into a Cosmic Evolutionism. Following the process evolution of Spencer, Henri Bergson developed a creative evolution (1907) involving spontaneous "leaps" produced by the *élan vital* which he later identified as God (1935).[1] This identification of God with the evolutionary world process was a significant moment in the development of process panentheism. Even before Bergson's identification, Samuel Alexander's *Space, Time and Deity* (1920) had presented one of the pioneer works on a process view of God. But despite the various contributions of these early process panentheists, the award for the first systematic presentation of bipolar theism is rightly given to Alfred North Whitehead for his classic *Process and Reality* (1929), followed by *Adventures of Ideas* (1933) and *Modes of Thought* (1938). It is to Whitehead's understanding of God that we now turn our attention.

*Process and Permanence.* For Whitehead, the world is constituted by both process and permanence. The permanent element in the temporal world is the potential element (called "eternal objects") and the process element is the actual element (called "actual entities"). "Continuity concerns what is potential; whereas actuality is incurably atomic," he wrote. For "it belongs to the nature of a 'being' that it is a potential for every 'becoming.' This is the 'principle of relativity.' " A kindred principle, the "principle of progress," states: "how an actual entity becomes constitutes what the actual entity is. . . . Its 'being' is constituted by its 'becoming.' "[2]

Process, however, cannot stand alone in a metaphysical system. Permanence must be snatched out of flux; those who disjoin the two elements find no solution to plain facts, argued Whitehead. Permanence is found on two levels: (1) In the temporal world permanence is found in the eternal objects or what he calls "forms of definiteness" which resemble platonic forms except that they are constitutively connected with the sensible world (whereas Plato's Forms were not). So, for Whitehead, "it is not 'substance' which is permanent, but 'form.' " (2) In the nontemporal or eternal realm the element of permanence is found in what is

---

1. Henri Bergson, *Creative Evolution* and *Two Sources of Morality and Religion*.
2. Whitehead, *Process and Reality,* pp. 95, 33-35.

called "the primordial nature of God," the nature of God as the orderer of all eternal objects. In the temporal world, however, actual entities and eternal objects are respectively the process and permanent sides of reality. An understanding of each of these is crucial to comprehending Whitehead's process panentheism.

a. *Actual Entities.* The most fundamental reality in Whitehead's system and the only actuality is what he calls "actual entities." They are the "final real things of which the world is made up." For "every actual occasion exhibits itself as a process; it is a becomingness." It is an "event" whose outcome is a drop or "unit of experience." So "in the becoming of an actual entity, the potential unity of many entities—actual and non-actual—acquires the real unity of the one actual entity; so that the actual entity is the real concrescence of many potentials." That is to say, "events become and perish. In their becoming they are immediate and they vanish into the past. They are gone; they have perished."[3] In short, they are becoming but never really are. Hence, the doctrine of becoming is balanced with the doctrine of perishing. But once perished, actual occasions pass only "from the immediacy of being into the not-being of immediacy." But this does not mean they are nothing, for "they remain stubborn fact."[4] What the actual entity loses subjectively by perishing it gains objectively. Forms suffer changing relations; they perpetually perish subjectively but become immortal objectively. They lose final causality, which is the internal principle of unrest in things, and acquire efficient causality.

Once an actual entity perishes and becomes objectively immortal it can act as an efficient cause for other actual entities that are in the process of "concrescence" or coming to be. For all efficient causality moves from the past to the present like tradition. Final causality, on the contrary, operates in the present. It is the "subjective aim" of the actual entity, namely, that which controls its process of becoming. In Whitehead's words, "The subjective aim is this subject determining its own self-creation." This it does by determining its own "subjectve form," that is to say, by determining *how* it will "prehend" its data.[5]

Prehension is simply the "process of 'feeling' the many data, so as to absorb them into the unity of one individual 'satisfaction.'" There are two kinds of prehension: negative and positive. Since the "principle of relativity" shows that every actual entity has a definite relationship to every other actual entity, it must be either absorbing (positively) or rejecting (negatively) them. A positive prehension is a definite inclusion of another item in the universe, and a negative prehension is a definite exclusion of items from any positive contribution to the subject's own

3. Whitehead, pp. 27, 129, 126.
4. Whitehead, *Adventures of Ideas*, pp. 304-5.
5. Whitehead, *Process and Reality*, pp. 44-45, 130, 134, 320-21.

internal constitution. If the prehension is of another actual entity it is called "physical prehension." If it is of an eternal object, it is called "conceptual prehension." For all actual entities are dipolar for Whitehead, involving both physical pole and a conceptual pole.[6]

A fundamental concept to Whitehead's understanding of actual entities is what he calls the "ontological principle." This principle declares that "every decision is referable to one or more actual entities, because in separation from actual entities there is nothing, merely nonentity." Stated otherwise, "Everything must be somewhere" or "no actual entity, then no reason," for "it is a contradiction in terms to assume that some explanatory fact can float into the actual world out of nonentity." Hence, there is nothing more fundamental than an actual entity. "There is no going behind actual entities to find anything more real. . . . God is an actual entity, and so is the most trivial puff of existence in far-off empty space."[7]

b. *Eternal Objects.* Actuality is the element of process in the temporal world but "eternal objects" provide the element of permanence. Eternal objects are like "platonic forms" that ingress into the temporal world from the realm of eternal possibility. "Thus the metaphysical status of an eternal object is that of a possibility for an actuality." They are like abstract "universals" that are understood by their concrete manifestation in the temporal world. Hence, sounds, colors, or scents are called "sense objects." As such they are "forms of definiteness" or "pure potentials" for the specific determination of facts. So "there is no character belonging to the actual apart from its exclusive determination by selected eternal objects." Since an actual entity may be definite in more than one way, it may possess more than one form of definiteness or eternal object. And despite the fact there are no novel eternal objects, nor can these eternal objects change, nonetheless there is variance from one occasion to another in respect to the difference of modes of ingression. That is, while an eternal object is just itself in whatever mode of realization it is involved, yet there may be "more than one grade of realization." The eternal objects are in themselves simple but they may be formed into complex groups and relationships called "propositions."[8]

Because eternal objects are simple they may be negatively prehended *in toto.* Because they are pure potentials, they can be prehended negatively, for "the actualities *have* to be felt [positively prehended], while the pure potentials *can* be dismissed [prehended negatively]. In their function as objects this is the great distinction between actual entities and eternal

---

6. Whitehead, pp. 66, 35, 366.
7. Whitehead, pp. 68, 73, 37, 28.
8. Whitehead, pp. 32, 367; *Science and the Modern World,* p. 150.

objects. The former is a stubborn matter of actual fact while the other never loses its nature as potential.[9]

*God and the World.* With this bit of Whiteheadian metaphysics in mind we are prepared to understand his bipolar panentheism. God too is an actual entity with two poles: an actual pole which is the world and a potential pole beyond the world. The latter is called God's "primordial nature" and the former is his "consequent nature."

a. *God's Primordial Nature.* Despite the fact that eternal objects are the forms of definiteness for actual entities, they are in themselves indefinite and unordered. They are pure potentials and as such they cannot order and relate themselves; only an actual entity can do that. But since not all eternal objects have ingressed into the temporal world, Whitehead finds it necessary to introduce a nontemporal actual entity (viz., God in his primordial nature) as the orderer of eternal objects. He wrote, "If there be a relevance of what in the temporal world is unrealized, the relevance must express a fact of togetherness in the formal constitution of a non-temporal actuality" [viz., God in his primordial nature]. That is, "by reason of the actuality of this primordial valuation or pure potentials [i.e., God], each eternal object has a definite, effective relevance to each concrescent process," for "apart from such ordering, there would be a complete disjunction of eternal objects unrealized in the world." As orderer of eternal objects, God is like a backstage director who organizes and lines up the actors, making them "relevant" for their moment of "ingression" on the stage of the temporal world. Without such ordering there would be chaos among the unrealized eternal objects and no orderly ingression into the world.[10]

The foregoing illustration should not mislead one into thinking there is a real difference between God's primordial nature and the order of eternal objects. They are in fact the same. For "viewed as primordial, he is the unlimited conceptual realization of the absolute wealth of potentiality. In this aspect, he is not *before* all creation, but *with* all creation."[11] This is why God is a finite but primordial creature who does not create eternal objects; for his nature requires them in the same sense that they require him. Without God there would be no order among eternal objects, and without eternal objects there would be no primordial nature of God.

b. *God's Consequent Nature.* Like all actual entities, the nature of God is dipolar. The conceptual pole of God is the order of eternal objects; the physical pole is the order of actual entities. The former is the permanent and nontemporal dimension of God, and the latter is the process and temporal pole of God. There are two reasons in Whitehead for

9. Whitehead, *Process and Reality,* p. 366.
10. Whitehead, pp. 48, 64, 392, 169.
11. Whitehead, pp. 521, 70, 134, 46, 392.

positing a consequent nature of God: (1) Like every other actual entity, God must be dipolar; for the physical pole is needed to complete the vision of the conceptual pole. That is, since God's primordial nature is "deficient" and "unconscious," it needs the consequent nature to realize its own subjective aim or self-creative urge. That is, it demands the concrete fulfillment of its conceptual vision. (2) God's consequent nature is necessary because of the principle of relativity which holds that every entity in the universe must be related to every other entity. Since God in his primordial nature is relative only to eternal objects, there must be another "side" to God which can be related to actual entities. "Thus," wrote Whitehead, "by reason of the relativity of all things, there is a reaction of the world on God."[12] So, as the primordial pole answers to God's relevance to eternal objects, the consequent pole manifests his relation to actual entities. Thus by virtue of both poles God is related to all items in the universe, both potential and actual.

c. *God's "Superject" Nature and Evil.* The consequent nature of God as enriched or satisfied by prehensions in the temporal world is sometimes referred to as the "superject" nature of God. It is the repository of all achieved value in the universe and is available for prehension by other actual entities. As the storehouse of all that God has accomplished in the actual world, it contains the permanent and progressive achievement of good in the universe as envisioned by God in his primordial nature. It is by virtue of God's immanence in the temporal world that the world is saved from Chaos. The world "passes into the immediacy of his own life" by "a tenderness which loses nothing that can be saved." Of course not everything can be saved. Some things simply cannot be salvaged because they do not fit into a given concrescence. Evil, then, is that which is inconsistent or incompatible with the total process by which nothing is lost but is "saved by its relation to the completed whole." Not every pigment can be used to complete the envisioned painting; many will be incorporated and others must be rejected, but the completed whole will be achieved with as little exclusion (evil) as possible for a finite God who is working with the given of this world in process.[13]

d. *God and Creativity.* Since each actual entity is separate and even causally independent from every other actual entity, there must be something which provides a "definite bond" between all actual entities and yet explains how each is distinct from the other. Whitehead calls this principle "creativity." It is his attempt to relate pluralistic subjects to each other while avoiding monism. Creativity "is that ultimate principle by which the many, which are the universe disjunctively, become the one actual occasion, which are the universe conjunctively." In fact, "every actual

12. Whitehead, pp. 527, 33, 135, 523.
13. Whitehead, pp. 169, 525, 529, 518.

entity, including God, is a creature transcended by creativity it qualifies." However, creativity is "without a character of its own in exactly the same sense in which the Aristotelian 'matter' is without character of its own." But creativity "is not an entity in the sense in which occasions or eternal objects are entities." Rather, it is more of a general metaphysical character which underlies all actual entities. Like Spinoza's infinite substance, it underlies all the individual modes that are its characteristics. Whitehead contended that "in all philosophic theory there is an ultimate which is actual in virtue of its accidents. . . . In the philosophy of organism this ultimate is termed 'creativity;' and God is its primordial, nontemporal accident." Accordingly, "no value is to be ascribed to the underlying activity [creativity] as divorced from the matter-of-fact real world."[14]

Creativity is a kind of "substance" which is real only by virtue of its "accidents." It is the potential unity which binds together the actual unity of the world. Like Plato's "receptacle" it imposes common relationship on all that happens. It can thus be termed a real potentiality or the actualization of a passive capacity of the whole world process. Creativity is the actualization of potentiality, and the process of actualization is an actual entity or occasion. Thus creativity is the real potentiality that binds together the many actualities of the universe into the form of their own novel unity. As such, "creativity is the principle of novelty" which introduces new patterns of definiteness by forming a disjunctive unity into a new oneness.[15]

e. *God and Negative Prehensions.* Creativity is not only the principle of potential unity but by way of negative prehensions it is the principle of actual separation. Negative prehension provides the "machinery" by which creativity operates. For unless some things were eliminated from a given process of concrescence, that actual entity would become everything, which would be monism. It is only by definite exclusion of other actual entities from a particular actual entity that monism is avoided. So negative prehensions are absolutely essential to pluralism. They are a "positive fact" in the coming to be of every actual entity because what is definitely excluded is at least as important as what is definitely included. As the sculptor forms a statue, what is cut away from a block of stone is as important as what remains. In this sense we may understand Whitehead when he wrote that "the negative judgment is the peak of mentality."[16]

God has no negative prehensions of eternal objects, since all potentials are included within his vision of reality. No potential is absent from the unity of God's subjective aim. It is in this way that all things are *one*

14. Whitehead, pp. 95, 66, 31, 340, 135, 47.
15. Whitehead, *Adventures of Ideas,* pp. 192, 241, 130 f.; *Process and Reality,* pp. 31-32.
16. Whitehead, *Process and Reality,* pp. 362, 72, 346, 66, 7.

potentially while remaining *many* actually; reality is potentially monistic but actually pluralistic. God in his dipolar nature corresponds to these two dimensions. He is the bipolar combination of the eternal potentials and the temporal actualities; he combines both the infinite vision and the finite realization. God has both abstract conceptualization and concrete materialization. God is both *beyond* the world in his eternal potentiality and *in* the world in his temporal actuality. The eternal and unchanging potentials of God are being actualized within the changing space-time world.

### The Process Panentheism of Charles Hartshorne

Process panentheism has taken two main courses since Whitehead: the empirical (represented by Bernard Loomer, Bernard Meland, and Henry Wieman) and the rational (championed by Charles Hartshorne, John Cobb, and Shubert Ogden). Hartshorne defends his bipolar theism by way of the ontological argument in contrast to the more empirically grounded approach of Whitehead. A comparison and contrast with Whitehead will help us to focus on the significant contribution of Hartshorne to panentheism.

*The Similar Bipolar Model.* For both Whitehead and Hartshorne,[17] God has two poles: an actual pole and a potential pole. The potential pole is the order of all that *can be,* and the actual pole is the order of all that *is.* The former is God's "mind" and the latter is his "body." The potential pole is God's conceptual vision and the actual pole is the physical realization of that vision. Since the actual world is in constant process of becoming and perishing, the actual pole of God is perishable, whereas the potential pole is imperishable. Further, the potential pole is both absolute and eternal, but the actual pole is relative and temporal. The potential pole is infinite and the actual pole is finite; God, then, is potentially infinite but actually finite. He has a pole of changeless possibility and another of changing activity. The former is called primordial nature and the latter, his consequent nature. For both Whitehead and Hartshorne, then, God is bipolar.

*The Contrast Between Bipolar and Monopolar Concepts of God.* Both Whitehead and Hartshorne would agree in contrasting their bipolar model of God to the monopolar model of classical theism. In the classical view God is *creator* of the world; for panentheism God is only the *director* of world process. For theism, God created the world out of nothing *(ex nihilo)*; for panentheism, creation is out of something eternally there at the other pole *(ex hulās)*. It follows that a theistic God is in sovereign control *over* the world, whereas the panentheistic God is working in

---

17. Hartshorne, *Man's Vision of God* and *The Logic of Perfection.*

cooperation *with* the world. In the former view God is *independent* of the world; in the latter, God is *interdependent* with the world. Further, the theistic God is unchanging in essence; the bipolar God is constantly changing with the world. With regard to perfections, the God of theism possesses all possible perfections eternally and concurrently, whereas the God of panentheism attains perfections *successively* and endlessly. In all of these ways both Whitehead and Hartshorne are in basic agreement against classical theism.

*The Methodological Differences Between Hartshorne and Whitehead.* The most basic differences between Hartshorne and Whitehead are not metaphysical but methodological. Whitehead's methodology is basically empirical by contrast with Hartshorne's highly rational approach to reality. Whereas Whitehead begins with descriptive generalizations, Hartshorne starts with analytic concepts. The former is more scientific and the latter more logical in methodology. Whitehead's starting point is hypothetical, based only on empirical necessity or adequacy; Hartshorne's point of departure is categorical, based on logical necessity. Therefore, like scientific hypotheses, Whitehead's position could be falsified by empirical inadequacy; but Hartshorne's can only be rejected by showing contradictions within it. In general, Whitehead is more a posteriori in approach and Hartshorne is more a priori. In keeping with this difference it is not surprising that Whitehead has a kind of teleological argument for God's existence but Hartshorne is a stout defender of the ontological argument.

*Hartshorne's Ontological Argument and His Dipolar God.* According to Hartshorne, all thought must refer to something beyond itself that is either possible or actual; for wherever there is meaning there must be something meant. The only thoughts which are less than possible are contradictory ones. Total illusion is impossible, since illusion necessarily presupposes a backdrop of reality. But the existence of a necessary being is at least possible—there is nothing contradictory in the concept of a being that cannot *not* be. However, with a necessary being the only way it can be is to be necessarily; a necessary being cannot have a mere possible existence. It follows, therefore, that a necessary being must necessarily exist. So all meaning implicitly affirms God in reference either to what he *has done* (God's immanence), namely, his consequent nature, or else in reference to what he *can do* (his transcendence), namely, his primordial nature. Hence, nothing either possible or actual can have meaning without reference to God. Without God as the universal ground for meaning, there is no meaning in the universe. Nothing can have objective meaning unless there is a realm that is objectively meaningful. Hence, the only way to oppose the ontological argument is to make an absolute disjunction between thought and reality. This, according to Hartshorne, is impossible. Meaning and reality must meet at some point;

this point we call "God," who is the bipolar ground for all reality both possible and actual.

*The Metaphysical Differences Between Whitehead and Hartshorne.* There are a number of modifications Hartshorne made to the White-headian concept of God. One of the more significant ones is the fact that while Whitehead considered God a single actual entity, Hartshorne views God as a society of actual entities.[18] For Hartshorne, God is a cosmic Mind resident in a Body (the world). A mind for Hartshorne is really a society of many thoughts. But since Whitehead's claim that God is an actual entity made it possible for him to claim that God is an actual entity like all others and not an exception to metaphysical principles, Hartshorne must maintain that God is modally different from the world and not univocally the same. God is a necessary being and all others are contingent. There is then an analogous relation between God and the world.

There is also a distinct difference between Whitehead and Hartshorne on how God grounds the world. For the former, the world is based on God's subjective aim, that is, God's vision for this particular world. For Hartshorne, on the other hand, the world is grounded in God as the logically necessary basis for all contingency. The former is concerned only with God as the ground for this particular world; the latter sees God as the universal and necessary ground for all possible worlds. In this respect Whitehead's God is the universal subject, but Hartshorne's God is the universal object or objective reference point for all meaning. Thus while in Whitehead only actual entities can be causes or reasons for things, in Hartshorne, God, who is a series or society of entities, is the cause of the world. In short, Whitehead's God is only concretely necessary to explain this particular world; but Hartshorne's God is universally and logically necessary to explain all possible worlds.

## John Cobb's Modifications of Bipolar Theism

Cobb belongs in the overall process panentheism of Whitehead and Hartshorne, but he offers two significant changes. First, Cobb rejects the implied disjunction between the two separate poles of God in the White-headian scheme of things. God, like man, is a unity and acts as a unity and not in just one pole as such. For instance, God's subjective aim or vision for everything is not to be limited only to his primordial nature but is to be associated as well with his consequent nature.[19]

Cobb's second modification of panentheism relates to the initial phase of God's subjective aim. He takes a less "Calvinistic" view than Whitehead who contended that the initial phase of the subjective aim is derived from

---

18. Hartshorne, *The Logic of Perfection*, pp. 64-67, 93-94.
19. John Cobb, *A Christian Natural Theology*, p. 178.

God. Not so, argues Cobb; for if every subjective aim is derived exclusively from God, we cannot avoid determinism. Hence, "the subjective aim of the new occasion must be formed by some synthesis or adaptation of these aims for which it [the actual entity] is itself finally responsible."[20]

Cobb agrees with Hartshorne against Whitehead that God is a society (or living person) and not a single actual entity for several reasons. First, if God were a single entity he could never know satisfaction (which is a culmination of a process involving many actual entities), as other persons can. Further, God's causal efficacy for the world is more like that of completed occasions than that of a single actual entity. Finally, as a society of entities we can explain how God can remember everything from the past, because he is knowing himself and he never experiences the loss of his own identity.

Like Whitehead, Cobb finds it necessary to posit "creativity" as the ground of everything including God. Creativity is "that apart from which nothing can be . . . , the actuality of every actual entity."[21]

### Shubert Ogden's Contributions to Panentheism

Whitehead came to panentheism from the field of science and math, Hartshorne approached it out of a logical context, Shubert Ogden arrived by way of Bultmannian existentialism. Ogden felt Heidegger was right that one cannot understand the world (objectively) unless he has a prior understanding of his own existence in the world (subjectively). Bultmann convinced Ogden that modern (secular) man has forced us to demythologize the Bible. The net result of demythologization is two parties: God and man. Heidegger adequately analyzed man but Hartshorne is the key to understanding God. Ogden has several reasons for choosing Hartshorne. First, Hartshorne's process theology avoids the antinomies or contradictions Ogden sees in traditional theism (see below). Second, Hartshorne proved for Ogden the necessary theocentric counterpart of Bultmann's anthropocentrism.

*Ogden's Dipolar Model of God.* God, for Ogden, has two poles: one of absoluteness and one of relatedness. Thus God is both absolute and relative.

a. *God's Relatedness.* As relative, God is related to all that is. The world, made up of many actual entities, is the body of God. God is related to the world as "I" am in my body, namely, by direct internal relations. Thus God's sphere of action is with the whole universe. In accordance with Whitehead's principle of relativity, every actual entity is related to every other actual entity by either positive or negative prehension. God is

---

20. Cobb, p. 178.
21. Cobb, pp. 204, 210.

related to all by "sympathetic participation," which synthesizes in each new occasion the whole of achieved actuality.[22]

God gives value to our lives in two ways. First, he is responsible for the concrescence of actual entities which constitute our bodies and for the structure and order of the actual world. In this way he can call forth our life's worth in the world. God alone makes life worthwhile; without him absurdity is unavoidable. Second, God gives to our lives eternal value. All actual entities return to him and become immortal as eternal objects. God makes an "imperishable difference" and in him our lives "find their ultimate justification."[23]

Since the world is God's body, his reality as an actual entity is dependent on the world. This does not mean that God is dependent for the fact *that* he is but only for *what* he is. God's nature is dependent on "what actual state of the infinite number of states possible for him is in fact actualized."[24] So God's body is contingent even though it is necessary for him to have a body which is in fact eternal.

b. *God's Absoluteness.* Ogden understands God's absoluteness by analogy, that is, by taking univocal notions and applying them to God in an eminent way.[25] Ogden distinguishes God's absoluteness from the traditional theistic sense of the word. His dipolar God is absolute in terms of his relativity, that is, by "relative absoluteness." First of all, God is absolute by his inclusion of all beings, for to experience is to experience God. Further, God is absolute in relations by virtue of his internal relatedness to every actual entity in the universe. God's perfectness lies in his continual openness to change, that is, by successive perfecting. God is not statically completed perfection, as in classical theism, but a "dynamic maximum of possibilities."[26] Also, God is absolute in knowledge in the sense that at every stage in the ongoing process everything that exists is within his sphere of relation. Finally, God is absolute in his temporality. God is the "eminently temporal one." His perfections are continually increasing because "anything we do to advance the real good either of ourselves or of one another is done quite literally to 'the glory of God,' as an imperishable contribution to his ever-growing perfection. . . ."[27]

In short, God is absolute in that his "being related to all others is itself relative to nothing but is the absolute ground of any and all real

22. Ogden, *The Reality of God,* p. 58 f.

23. Ogden, "How Does God Function in Human Life?" in *Christianity and Crises,* XXVII, 8 (May 15, 1967), pp. 106-7.

24. Ogden, *The Reality of God,* p. 10.

25. Ogden, *The Reality of God,* p. 59.

26. Ogden, "Theology and Philosophy: A New Phase in the Discussion" in *Journal of Religion* XLIV, 1 (January 1964), p. 7.

27. Ogden, *The Reality of God,* p. 59. See Hartshorne, "God as Absolute, Yet Related to All," p. 24.

relationships." His absoluteness is an absolute relatedness to all else and, hence, his perfection is a perfect relativity with all the value in the temporal world.

*Ogden's Argument for God's Existence.* For Ogden, God's existence is morally necessary. He agrees with Hartshorne that it is impossible to deny that meaning has a necessary ground. Ogden, however, seems to develop this thinking in a kind of moral argument for God's existence that may be summarized as follows:[28]

(1) All judgments imply meaning, value, and purpose in the universe.

(2) It is self-defeating to deny the possibility of making meaningful judgments.

(3) Hence, there must be meaning, value, and purpose in the universe.

(4) But meaning requires a ground; value requires a value-giver, etc.

(5) Hence, there exists a ground of meaning and giver of value, etc. (God).

There seems to be a teleological element in this argument, but Ogden rejects the traditional teleological argument on the ground that it points to a God "wholly other" than the world. For Ogden, the true view of God "is that God is nothing external to the world's order but is that order itself fully understood—analogous to the way in which the human self or person is not anything merely additional to the unified behavior of its body but is what enables us to understand and account for such unified behavior."[29]

*Ogden's Rejection of Classical Theism: The Antinomies.* Ogden sees three insoluble contradictions in the traditional notion of God as a timeless, changeless, and unrelated being. These he calls the antinomies of creation, of service, and of relationship.

a. *The Antinomy of Creation.* The classical theistic God is a necessary being and his act of creation is one with his eternal and necessary being. And yet the contingent world is supposed to flow from him in a free and nonnecessary way. This, for Ogden, leads to the "hopeless contradiction of a wholly necessary creation of a wholly contingent world."[30] In other words, if God's will is identical with his necessary essence, then creation must flow necessarily from it. This is contrary to the traditional theistic claim that creation flows from God freely and contingently. Therefore, classical theism must be corrected by Ogden's neo-classical theism by means of the doctrine of God's relative necessity. God is not

---

28. Ogden, "Love Unbounded" in *The Perkins School of Theology Journal,* XIX, 3 (Spring 1966), p. 14.

29. Ogden, "God and Philosophy: A Discussion with Antony Flew," a review of *God and Philosophy* by Antony Flew in *Journal of Religion* XXXXVIII, 2 (April 1968), p. 175.

30. Ogden, *The Reality of God,* p. 17 f.

absolutely necessary and, hence, creation of a contingent world need not be absolutely necessary.

b. *The Antinomy of Service.* There is a contradiction in classical theism, claims Ogden, between God's absolute and completed perfection on the one hand and man's service for God on the other. God is conceived by theists as "statically complete perfection" that can neither be increased nor diminished by anything else. Yet the theist is called upon inconsistently to live his life in service "for" God. But if God cannot increase in perfection, then no significant service can ever be rendered "for" him. But it is not so with the process God of panentheism; he can be significantly served, for whatever we do for him actually adds to his enrichment and the increase of his value and perfections.

c. *The Antinomy of Relationship.* This is the antinomy most often repeated by panentheists, and it involves the supposed isolation of the theistic God from the world. The God of classical theism is the changeless and independent cause of all other things: the world depends on God but God does not depend on the world. But, according to Ogden, all genuine relationships involve mutual dependence, a reciprocal give and take. From this it follows for Ogden that the world is related to God but God is not really related to the world. Theism involves a God who is in monopolar isolation from the real world. Such is not the case with the mutual interdependence of the panentheistic God of Ogden. It is for these reasons that Ogden feels impelled to reject the God of theism for the God of bipolar theism.

## A Summary of Major Tenets of Panentheism

There are significant intramural debates among panentheists as to both methodology and metaphysics. However, our concern here is to summarize the major points common to most panentheists or at least characteristic of the movement as a whole.

1. First, God is related to the world as a soul or mind is related to a body; the world is God's body. God is intimately and internally related with the time-space world. God is not identical with the world, as in pantheism; nor is God actually distinct from and independent of the world, as in theism. God is identical with the world in his body, but there is more to God than the world. God also transcends the world as a mind transcends or is more than a body.

2. Second, God has two poles: a potential pole that is beyond the world and an actual pole which is the physical world. God is absolute, eternal, and infinite in potentiality but is relative, temporal, and finite in actuality. The imperishable pole is God's primordial nature and the changing pole is his consequent nature. But God—like all actualities—is bipolar in construction.

3. Third, the world is not created *ex nihilo,* that is, out of nothing; it is formed *ex hulās,* that is, out of something eternally there at the other pole. God, then, is not a world Creator but a cosmic Director. Hence, God is not sovereign *over* the world but works rather in cooperation *with* the world. Both matter and mind are eternal. Mind does not come from matter, as in atheism; nor does matter come from mind, as in classical theism. Rather, matter is eternally directed by Mind.

4. Fourth, God and the world are interrelated and interdependent. The world depends on God for its necessary ground, and God depends on the world for his manifestation or embodiment. The world depends on God for its existence and God depends on the world for his essence. God and the world are as interrelated as mind and body in the modern scientific and organistic sense of the terms.

5. Fifth, God is continually growing in perfections due to the increase in value in the world (his body) resulting from human effort. All achieved value not only significantly enriches God but is immortalized and stored in God's consequent nature. The universe as God's body is undergoing perpetual perfection and enlargement of value.

6. Sixth, evil is an incompatibility with the given possibility of world process. Evil will not be ultimately defeated and destroyed; not all good possible is actually achievable. God will overcome all evil that it is possible to defeat with our cooperation. But God is finite and it is not possible to overcome *all* evil. Hence, there will be no final or inevitable triumph.

## An Evaluation of Panentheism as a World View

Panentheism provides some extremely valuable insights into the nature of reality, particularly as a corrective of some forms of theism and as an alternative to pantheism. First, some of the more important contributions will be noted.

### Some Positive Contributions of Panentheistic Thought

Panentheists do not lack in either the ability to see problem areas in other world views or in the attempt to construct a positive alternative to them. Some contributions in each of these areas may be noted briefly.

1. First, there is a commendably strong argumentative type of metaphysics presented by panentheists. Their arguments for God vary from ontological (Hartshorne), to teleological (Whitehead), to moral (Ogden), as do those of classical theists. And there is a sustained attempt to present a reasoned approach to reality, as opposed to the purely experiential or fideistic positions. Panentheists rightly recognize the unavoidability of doing metaphysics, and they attempt to do it in a way subject to truth tests.

2. Second, panentheism avoids the self-defeating identification of God and the world involved in pantheism (see previous chapter). God is not

identical with the world, although he is intimately related to it. God is *in* the world but panentheists reject the pantheist's view that God *is* the world. God transcends the world in a way not provided for in pantheism.

3. Third, panentheism provides some important insights into the nature of God's interaction with the world. It rightly stresses the significance of God's real relationship with the world. God is intimately and really relating and interacting with the world on a two-way street of communication. Without this facet of personal interaction any concept of God as personal is seriously lacking.

4. Fourth, following from the former contribution is the fact that in the panentheistic view of God there is an appropriate emphasis laid on the immanence of God. God is really *in* the world; he is not "Wholly other" or merely beyond the world. The world is not external and independent of God; without him there would be no world. Only by God's immanence in the world is it saved from chaos.

5. Fifth, panentheism points up the need to explain the dynamic God of Christian revelation in more than purely static essentialistic Greek categories. The God of the Judeo-Christian Scriptures is more than a static unchangeable Essence or a platonic Super-Form; he is a personal God of ceaseless creative activity. He actively sustains the creative world process. He is active in history and manifest in nature. To explain the Christian God in pure Greek categories of Being is to dress him up in the straitjacket of essentialism, rather than to see him in the light of his dynamic and changing actions and interpersonal relationships.

Many more insights can be gained through the writings of panentheists, including an explanation of novelty and creativity, the operations of a natural theology, the need for analogous God-talk, and the nature and operations of the incarnate and cosmic Christ. Space does not permit their enumeration here.

## Some Important Criticisms of Panentheism as a World View

Focus must be shifted now to the inadequacy of panentheism as a metaphysical model or world view. There are a number of reasons why panentheism fails as a world and life view.

1. First of all, it should be observed that panentheism's bipolar concept of God is inadequate. Cobb saw this and struggled to overcome it to some degree. But there is no way to overcome it without overhauling it in the direction of theism. Fundamentally, if God has both an actual pole and a potential pole, one is faced with disturbing metaphysical questions. How can God actualize his own potentialities? Potentialities cannot actualize themselves any more than empty cups can fill themselves. Capacities do not fulfill themselves; they must be activated by something outside themselves. Anything passing from potentiality to actuality, from what is

not to what is, depends on some actuality to ground it. Nothing does not produce something; possibilities to exist do not materialize on their own.

The attempt to avoid this problem by positing creativity as a ground in which God, as the primordial creature, finds it possible to actualize his own potentials will not help the panentheistic cause. It is self-destructive to the system to posit something like Whitehead's "creativity" with reality status outside the bipolar actual entities of the world. Only actual entities actually exist in the world, and beyond the world only potentialities exist, namely, eternal objects. Creativity cannot be a real ground in a Whiteheadian system; only actual entities are real causes. Should a panentheist wish to revise the Whiteheadian system by giving a reality status to something beyond God in which he is grounded, then his "God" turns out not to be God after all. For if there is a real creative ground for the bipolar "God," then it is this pure actuality beyond the bipolar potentiality-actuality that is really God. In short, panentheism needs a theistic God in order to ground its "God," which turns out after all not to be God but to be a giant creature needing a more ultimate and real cause of itself.

2. Second, not only is the bipolar God less than ultimate, he is also not really absolute and unchanging. But both absoluteness and unchangingness are necessary metaphysical conclusions. Not everything can be relative; all that is relative must be relative to something that is not relative, that is, to something that is absolute in itself. Everything cannot be to-another unless there is something that is in-itself. Likewise, change makes no sense unless there is the unchanging basis by which change is measured. If all were changing there would be no way to measure the change. But on the admitted ground that there is real change, the panentheistic metaphysic must be pushed to an unchanging ground for all change, including the change occurring in its "God."

At best the God of panentheism is only potentially absolute, for it is only his potential pole that is beyond the relative and changing world. However, a potential absolute is not actually absolute and neither will it serve as a reference point for what is actually relative and changing. Whatever has a potentiality can change, since it has the potentiality to be other than what it is. But as the first criticism above observed, whatever has a potentiality cannot actualize itself. Hence, there must be beyond every potentiality-actuality (including the panentheistic "God") a pure actuality to ground it. But whatever is pure actuality with no potentiality at all cannot change, for there must be a potential or possibility for change or else change cannot occur. Hence, this pure actuality (which is how many theists understand God) cannot change.

3. Third, the panentheistic theodicy (explanation of evil) is inadequate. It will suffice here merely to summarize some of the central

objections leveled against the panentheistic solution to evil. (1) In view of the apparent permanence of natural laws and the persistence of evil, what guarantee is there that a limited, finite god can ever achieve a better world? (2) Of what value is it to individual men that a god is allegedly being enriched by the storing of value achieved in the world? The serial appearance of maximal good over the next billions of years is of little profit to individuals now and is surely of no enduring value to those who do not survive with individual immortality but only as an eternal object. (3) Why does a god who cannot ultimately triumph over evil engage in such a wasteful project? His personal enrichment at man's expense scarcely seems to be a worthy reason. If a god is in no sense free to stop the process or is unable to see the eventual consequences, then we are led to another criticism. (4) How can anyone worship a god so impotent that he cannot even call the whole thing off? Is not such a god so paralyzed as to be perilous? (5) Further, how can the panentheistic god achieve a better world via human cooperation when most men are totally unaware of such a god or his purposes? (6) In addition, how can such a finite and limited god assure us that there is any real growth in value in the universe? The world process, as it is available to our understanding, does not manifest the alleged growth in value nor does the supposed enrichment of this god allegedly available to us appear to make increasing good in the world any easier for us. (7) Finally, does the supposed increase of value in the general process justify the countless numbers of individual evils suffered to gain it? What significance is there in suffering for the individual?

4. Fourth, the basic presuppositions of panentheism are mistaken. For one thing the whole system is built on a misapplication of an anthropomorphic bipolar model of God's relation to the world as the soul (or mind) is to the body. This is a classic error of man creating God in his own image. Further, panentheists confuse God's unchanging *attributes* with his changing *activities*. Thus what God *is* is reduced to what God *does*. There is activity but no Actor, movement but no Mover, creation but no Creator. Beginning with an anthropomorphic bipolar model of God, it is no wonder that the god of panentheism emerges finite, limited in knowledge, goodness, and power, and in possession of a physical body like the rest of us. Whatever else may be said of this whittling of God down to man's level and form, it is surely not the God presented in the Bible.

5. Fifth, the claim that the God of panentheism is the God of the Bible is unfounded. That the Bible speaks of God as engaging in temporal and changing *actions* is unquestionable. Indeed, the Bible uses many evocative metaphors of God drawn from human analogies. God is said to "repent" (Jon. 3:10), to use his "arms" (Ps. 136:12) and "eyes" (Heb. 4:13). But surely no reasonable interpretation of Scripture would take

these any more literally than the symbols which speak of God as a "rock" (Ps. 18:2), a strong "tower" (Prov. 18:10), or as having "wings" (Ps. 91:4). To understand these metaphors a consistent view of Scripture must keep sight of the fact that these images are mutually conflicting (some being mineral and others animal or human images of God). Further, they do not fit with some clear metaphysical descriptions of God as a spirit (John 4:24), as infinite (Ps. 147:5), and as unchanging (Mal. 3:6; Heb. 6:18; James 1:17).

Further, the God of the Bible is not a finite, struggling, dualistic Greek god on the order of Plato's Demiurgos who creates *ex hulās,* out of eternally preexisting matter. Rather, the God of the Bible is the supreme "I AM" (Exod. 3:14) who alone is eternal and who brings everything else into being *ex nihilo,* from nothing (Gen. 1:1; Heb. 1:2; 11:3; Col. 1:17; John 17:5; Rom. 4:17).

In addition, the God of Scripture is unlimited in knowledge and controls the course of human events (Rom. 8:29; Eph. 1:4–10; Dan. 4:25). He is infinite in power and perfections (I Kings 8:27; Ps. 71:15; 147:5; Job 42:2). What is more, the God of Christian theism is not a temporal being; he is eternal. He is the "I AM" (Exod. 3:14) who has ever been and ever will be (Ps. 90:1). It is he "alone who has immortality" (I Tim. 6:16) and who "created this world of time" (Heb. 1:2, Knox).

6. Sixth, panentheism's criticisms and qualifications of traditional theism are mistaken. That is to say, Ogden's alleged antinomies are not only ungrounded but turn out in favor of theism over panentheism. For example, the so-called antinomy of *creation* is built on the mistaken notion that a necessary Being must necessarily create. But as Aquinas pointed out over seven hundred years ago, the only thing a necessary Being must will necessarily is the necessity of his own being. Everything else is contingent and need be willed only contingently. God must be God, but God need not create. God does not have to *do* anything; he simply has to *be* God. One need not view God as less than absolutely necessary in order to secure the contingency of the creative act. God *must* will his own good, but he *may* or may not will to create any other good.

Likewise, the alleged antinomy of *service* is based on a confusion about the nature of God. While it is true that no act of the creature can add a single perfection to an already absolutely perfect theistic God, it is nonetheless also true that the believer's worship and service are eternally significant and for the glory of God. The theistic God does not *need* our service to add to his perfections; but he does *desire* it, which is even a higher motive. We cannot add to God's *attributes* by our service in the world, but we can contribute to his *activities* in the world. What service we render for God adds nothing to God's *nature,* but it does contribute significantly to his *plan* for this world. That is, it is personally pleasing and satisfying to God that we do his will; it does make a significant and eternal difference. God does care what we do and it does glorify or magnify who he is and what he wills when we serve him.

Finally, Ogden's so-called antinomy of *relationship* is likewise built on a mistaken notion. It is true that properly speaking the creature is related to the Creator, the relative to the Absolute, the changing to the Unchanging, and not the reverse. The pillar does not change its relation to the man when the man moves on the other side; it is the man who changes his relationship to the pillar. Nevertheless, the relationship of the pillar and man is different in both cases and in both cases it is a *real* relationship. An unchanging God does not need to change in order to engage in changing relationships. Furthermore, God can interact without being interdependent. God does not need man's love but he desires it, and mutual desire is sufficient for the reciprocity demanded by interpersonal relations. God's love is one-way in the sense that he does not *need* our return love, but it is two-way in the sense that he *wants* it. Not only is interpersonal reciprocity possible with a being who is unchanging love, but it is possible in a much more secure and higher sense. One can never be absolutely sure of the love of a finite being who can or may change his love and who does not have the infinite power to secure it from temporality or outside forces. Only the absolutely loving and powerful God of Christian theism can provide the highest level of real, interpersonal relationships with man.

## Summary and Conclusion

The panentheistic world view is that of a finite and (usually) bipolar god whose actual pole is identified with the changing temporal world and whose potential pole is the eternal possibilities beyond the world. This god is infinite neither in power nor perfections but is growing in the latter by the cooperation of man in the achievement of value which is thereafter stored and preserved in God. Panentheism may best be seen as a half-way house between traditional theism and pantheism. With the latter panentheism stresses the immanence of God, and with the former it attempts to preserve some meaningful sense in which God is more than the world (viz., transcendence). Panentheism is the descendent of the god of Greek philosophy. Add to the finite, dualistic world of Plato's Demiurgos the changing world process of Heraclitus and the developmental unfolding of God in the historic process (à la Hegel) and one is brought to the modern bipolar process god of Whitehead.

In attempting to avoid the extremes of some other views of God and by developing a positive metaphysics of its own, the panentheistic view has provided some important insights, such as its arguments for the existence of God, its rejection of the pantheistic identification of God and the world, and corrections in a rigid Greek essentialistic view of God. It has appropriately stressed God's immanence, provided important insights into his relational interaction with the world, and rightly rejected a static view of an inactive God for a dynamic God engaged in ceaseless creative activity.

However, as a total world view, the God of panentheism does not fill the bill. The basic dipolar concept of God as eternal potential seeking temporal actualization is self-defeating. No potential can actualize itself; and if there is some pure actuality outside the panentheistic God that actualizes it, then one must posit a theistic God of pure act in order to account for the panentheistic God. Further, a finite changing god must have a not-finite (i.e., infinite) and unchanging basis and ground for its change. The relative presupposes the absolute, for what is to-another relates ultimately to what is in-itself. There are, in addition, some serious problems with a panentheistic solution to evil. A finite god cannot guarantee the defeat of evil, holds out little prospect of a better world, and seems to be engaging in an extremely wasteful project at our expense for his own enrichment. Finally, the claim that such a god is Biblical is unfounded and the criticisms of theism are unjustified. By comparison a theistic God is more adequate both metaphysically and personally.

## SELECT READINGS FOR CHAPTER ELEVEN

**Exposition of Panentheism**

Alexander, Samuel. *Space, Time and Deity.*
Bergson, Henri. *Creative Evolution.*
Cobb, John. *A Christian Natural Theology.*
Hartshorne, Charles. *The Logic of Perfection.*
————. *A Natural Theology for Our Time.*
Ogden, Shubert. *The Reality of God and Other Essays.*
Whitehead, Alfred N. *Process and Reality.*
————. *Adventures of Ideas.*
————. *Modes of Thought.*

**Evaluation of Panentheism**

Brown, Delwin, et al. (eds). *Process Philosophy and Christian Thought.*
Cousins, Ewert. *Process Theology.*
Geisler, N. L. "Process Theology" in *Tensions in Contemporary Theology,* ed. Alan F. Johnson and Stanley N. Gundry.
Owen, H. P. *Concepts of Deity.*
Reese, William (ed.). *Process and Divinity.*
Williams, Daniel Day. *What Present-Day Theologians are Thinking.*

# Chapter

# 12 | *Atheism*

Atheists claim that there is no God. They contend that there is no God in the world (as pantheism holds) and there is no God beyond the world (as deism claims). Furthermore, there is no God who is actually both in the world and beyond the world as theism claims, nor is there any panentheistic God beyond the world who is related to the world as a mind to body. There is no God of any kind, anywhere.

Of course, atheism is not merely a negative position. Most atheists do not view themselves as antitheists but simply nontheists. As nontheists, atheists offer a positive view of their own which they may call humanism, materialism, naturalism, or positivism. Since we are primarily concerned here with the question of whether there is a God and, if so, what kind of God he is, we will consider the arguments and reasons given by selected major atheists as to why they believe there is no God. Special concern will be given as to why they believe there is no theistic God. In this context it will be necessary to discuss the negative emphasis of atheism as a world view denying the existence of God.

## An Exposition of Atheism

Atheism comes in many varieties. The term *atheism* covers a widely divergent group of thinkers. There are *traditional* atheists who believe that there never was, is, or will be a God (Jean-Paul Sartre is an example).[1] Then there is the *mythological* atheist like Nietzsche,[2] who believed that the God-myth was once alive, that is, it was a model men believed and

1. See Jean-Paul Sartre, *Being and Nothingness,* pt. Four.
2. See Friedrich Nietzsche, *Gay Science.*

lived by, but that this myth died and is no longer workable. Some years ago Thomas Altizer popularized another form of atheism which may be called *dialectical* atheism.[3] This view affirms the paradox that God was once really alive but that he died in the incarnation and crucifixion of Christ and that it has taken until modern times to realize that this is so. Finally, there is what may be called *semantical* or linguistical atheism (as in Paul Van Buren),[4] which claims that God-talk is dead, that is, that there is no cognitive meaning to religious language.

Since we are concerned here with metaphysical atheism, we will discuss primarily the forms that provide some arguments denying that there is really a God in and/or beyond the world now. Although it is a serious thing to a believer in God to deny that he can *talk* meaningfully about God, semantical atheism as such does not involve any denial that there may be a God there who can somehow be felt or experienced. This view at least leaves the door open to the fact that God exists and that he can in some way be experienced. Hence, this view is not really metaphysical atheism.

Not all atheists claim knock-down-and-drag-out arguments against God. Like theists, they claim varying degrees of certitude ranging from absolute certainty to low degrees of probability. Many of the arguments, then, are not offered as disproofs of God but merely as evidence against the existence of a God. Other arguments are considered by their proponents as definite disproofs of God. We will consider both types, attempting to put the arguments in the strongest form possible.

Another important distinction to keep in mind is that atheism makes two argumentative moves. First, it offers objections to the supposed grounds upon which others believe in God. Since these arguments do not attempt to disprove God but simply to refute the grounds upon which some men believe in God, they will be considered in the next chapter as objections to theism. Here we will consider only attempts to prove there is no God. The following summary will indicate the major kinds of arguments for atheism and the direction in which they go.

## Some Attempted Cosmological Disproofs of God

It is possible to argue from the principle of causality to atheism. This has been done in at least two related ways.

*Causality Leads to an Infinite Regress.* Some atheists argue, as Bertrand Russell did,[5] that if everything needs a cause, then so does God, in which case he would not be God. And if God does not need a cause, then neither does the world. But if the world needs no cause then there

3. Thomas Altizer, *The Gospel of Christian Atheism.*
4. Paul Van Buren, *The Secular Meaning of the Gospel.*
5. Bertrand Russell, *Why I Am Not a Christian.*

is no God. Hence, whether everything needs a cause or does not need a cause, there is no God. But if we push the principle of causality all the way and insist that *everything* needs a cause, then we launch on an infinite regress and never reach a first cause (i.e., God).

*Causality Leads to an Impossible Self-Caused Being.* Another form of cosmological disproof is presented by Jean-Paul Sartre.[6] It may be stated this way: If in accordance with the principle of causality we affirm that everything must have a cause either in itself or outside itself, then we must assume that if we arrive at a cause that no longer has need of any cause beyond itself (viz., God), then this cause must have the cause for its being within itself. That is, God must be *ens causa sui,* a self-caused being. But a self-caused being is impossible; for to cause oneself to exist, one would have to exist prior to his existing—which is impossible. We may state the argument in another way. Only what does not exist needs its existence to be caused. But to cause existence one must exist; nothing cannot cause something. Hence, to cause one's own existence he would simultaneously have to exist and not exist. Hence, the existence of God (the self-caused being) is impossible.

### An Ontological Disproof of God

One of the more ingenious contemporary attempts to disprove God comes from J. N. Findlay via a reversal of the ontological argument.[7] Findlay argued in accordance with theists that the only really adequate way to conceive of God is as an absolutely necessary and perfect Being. Anything less than this would not be God, at least not a God worthy of worship. However, contends Findlay, statements about existence cannot be necessary. He follows Kant in holding that necessity is merely a logical characteristic of propositions, but not a characteristic of reality. It would follow from this that the existence of the theistic God is impossible. For if the only way that a theistic God can exist (viz., as a necessary being) is the very way in which he cannot exist (since no statement about existence can be necessary), then it follows that God's existence is impossible. In short, if there is a God then he must necessarily exist, for to exist contingently would mean that he is not really God. But nothing can exist necessarily, since necessity does not apply to existence; necessity is simply a characteristic of propositions but never of reality. Hence, the only way God could exist—if there were one—is the very way he cannot exist. The existence of a necessary Being (God) is therefore impossible.

### Moral Disproofs of God's Existence

Most attempted disproofs of God come from the moral sphere. They

6. Sartre, *Being and Nothingness,* p. 758 f.
7. J. N. Findlay, "Can God's Existence Be Disproved?" in A. Plantinga, *The Ontological Argument,* p. 111 f.

have been stated in numerous ways by many different thinkers. We will survey some of the major attempts, centering mostly on those that purport to be disproofs of (and not simply evidence against) the existence of God. Since it is a theistic concept of God with which we are ultimately concerned, we will include some arguments which would not be definitive against a finite God but which would be telling against an infinitely good and powerful God.

*Pierre Bayle's Famous Dilemma for Theism.* In the late seventeenth century Bayle stated the classic argument from evil against a theistic God.[8] It begins with the seemingly indisputable fact that evil exists in the world. If there were an all-powerful God, he *could* destroy this evil; and if there were an all-good God he surely *would* destroy this evil. But this evil continues; it is not destroyed. Therefore, it follows, argues Bayle, that either God is: (a) impotent and cannot destroy evil, (b) malevolent and will not destroy evil, (c) both malevolent and impotent, or (d) there is no such theistic God at all. In brief, a finite God is the only kind of God possible for this dilemma. The infinitely perfect and powerful God of traditional theism is logically ruled out.

*Bertrand Russell's Moral Disproof of God.* Russell offers an argument against theism which may be formulated into a kind of disproof of God by way of the moral law.[9] Simply put, the argument goes like this: if there is a moral law as theists claim, then either it results from God's fiat or else it does not. But if it results from God's fiat, then it is arbitrary, and in this case God is not essentially good. "Good" would simply be what God arbitrarily pronounces good so that it could be otherwise. (Indeed, God could pronounce anything good including hate, cruelty, rape, and inhumanity.) On the other hand, if good does not result from God's fiat, then God is himself subject to some essential Good which is beyond himself and to which he finds himself subject. But if God is subordinate to some essential Good beyond himself, then he is not ultimate. This eternal, unchangeable, and superior Good is the most ultimate value in the universe. So, either God is not essentially God because he is arbitrary, or else he is not ultimate because he is subject to an ultimate beyond himself. However, in either case it would eliminate the theistic God of essential, eternal, and unchangeable value and worth. There could, of course, be an arbitrary theistic God; but who could worship such a being? There seems to be no theistic God worthy of ultimate respect and worship. Or, there could be a finite god like Plato's Demiurgos who is subject to some ultimate and unchanging Good beyond himself. But here again this is not the God of traditional theism. Intrinsic moral values, such as theists themselves claim, are an argument against the existence of a theistic God.

8. Pierre Bayle, *Selections from Bayle's Dictionary,* pp. 157 f.
9. Russell, *Why I Am Not a Christian.*

*Albert Camus: Theism Is Contrary to Humanitarianism.* This argument provides an interesting contemporary existential slant to the traditional moral argument against a theistic God.[10] In brief, Camus contends in his novel *The Plague* that one must either join the doctor and fight the plague of rats sent by God on the sinful city or he must join the priest and refuse to fight the plague lest he be fighting against God who sent it. But to refuse to fight the plague is antihumanitarian, for it is a refusal to help to alleviate human suffering. On the other hand, to fight the plague is to fight against God who sent it in judgment for men's sins. Therefore, it follows that if humanitarianism is right, then theism is wrong. If there is any kind of God, then he must be resisted because he is not even humanitarian. Minimally, it can be concluded that an all-good theistic God does not exist.

*The Argument from Innocent Suffering.* Contrary to some theists who contend that this is the best of all possible worlds, it seems to be an undeniable fact of life that this world could be improved. For example, not every evil is deserved; cruelty, cancer, and rape sometimes strike innocent victims. But an all-wise, all-powerful, and all-good God would not allow any innocent suffering. Even *one* injustice in the world—and surely there are many—argues against God being *all*-just.

Theists sometimes object to this argument on the grounds that it is logically possible that there are unknown reasons for all apparently innocent suffering. Atheists, however, have countered with the objection that unless a theist can supply a plausible reason for the innocent suffering, the theistic position is *practically,* if not logically, impossible.[11] That is, unless theists can supply some plausible explanation for innocent suffering, it is practically impossible that there is a God. For all practical purposes, why should someone believe in a God for whose existence one has no plausible reason? Would anyone believe that Eichmann was a morally good man on the grounds that there is a *possible* good explanation as to why he killed all those Jews? The preponderance of the evidence is against there being an all-good God, and the sheer possibility that there might be such a God is insufficient grounds to believe in him in view of the amount of innocent suffering in the world.

*The Argument from Unjustifiable Suffering.* Theists sometimes claim that some evil is a necessary condition or means of a greater good. For example, suffering is sometimes used to produce patience. But some atheists think this argument backfires into a disproof of God.[12] For if

---

10. Albert Camus, *The Plague.*

11. See Roland Puccetti, "The Loving God . . ." in *Religious Studies,* vol. 2, no. 2, p. 255 f.

12. See H. J. McCloskey, "God and Evil" in *The Philosophical Quarterly* (April 1960), reprinted in Nelson Pike, *God and Evil.*

suffering is justifiable, then it is wrong to work to eliminate it. But on humanitarian grounds we know that it is not wrong to work to eliminate suffering; it is right. Therefore, it follows that suffering is not justifiable. But if suffering is not justifiable then a theistic God does not exist, since the existence of a theistic God is incompatible with unjustifiable suffering. It must be concluded, then, that a theistic God does not exist. In other words, working against suffering is right; but if there were a theistic God using suffering as a means to a greater good, then working against suffering would be wrong, for it would be tantamount to working against God. Hence, there cannot be a theistic God who is using suffering as a means to a greater good. There is suffering that cannot be justified and, hence, there cannot be a theistic God whose existence is compatible with this unjustified suffering.

## Some Disproofs of God from the Nature of God and Creation

There are other sources of attempts to disprove the existence of God; some of them come from the nature of God or his relation to his creation or possible creations. Three of these are worthy of note.

*The Antinomy of Omnipotence.* Some atheists contend that an omnipotent God is a contradiction in terms.[13] If there were an all-powerful God then he could do absolutely anything, including making a stone so heavy that he could not lift it or creating a monster that could get out of control. But if God could make something that he could not control, then he would not be all-powerful, since there would be something that he could not overpower. Therefore, there cannot be an omnipotent God as theists claim there is.

*The Antinomy of Perfections.* Traditional theism claims that God possesses absolutely all perfections. But this seems impossible since some perfections are mutually exclusive. How can one and the same being possess both love and wrath? God cannot be both all-knowing and all-loving. If he were all-knowing then he would know with certainty what will happen in the future.[14] But if the future is certain, then when tomorrow comes men are not really free to do other than what God already knows they must do. However, an all-loving God would not coerce or force men to do anything against their will; love is never determinative or coercive. Love always permits the loved one the freedom to accept or reject the love. Hence, God cannot be both all-knowing *and* all-loving at the same time. Other perfections in an infinite God may also be contradictory. For example, how can God be both absolutely good and absolutely free? If he is free then he is free to do evil. But if he is absolutely good,

---

13. Sophisticated atheists often do not push this argument against God. See Terence Penelhum, *Religion and Rationality,* pp. 230-33.

14. See discussion in Pike, *God and Timelessness,* chap. 4.

then he cannot do evil. But he cannot be both free and not free to do evil.

*The Antinomy of Creation.* Many theists maintain that God is a necessary Being and that his will is one with his essence. But from this some nontheists argue that whatever God wills he must will necessarily.[15] On the other hand, theists also maintain that God was free not to create. But it is impossible for creation to flow both necessarily and freely from God. Either God is not necessary (which is contrary to traditional theism) or else creation is necessary (which is also contrary to the theistic view that God freely created the world). In either case the traditional theistic God cannot exist.

*The Antinomy of Time.* Many theists contend that the world had a beginning in time. The world is not eternal; only God is eternal. But if the world began in time then there must have been a time before time began.[16] It is, however, impossible to have time before time began. Hence, there cannot be a theistic God who created the world in time.

## Some Disproofs of God from the Nature of Man and Freedom

There is yet another source for atheistic arguments, namely, the nature of man or of human freedom. We may separate out three such arguments, two from Sartre and one from Feuerbach.

*Disproof of God from the Nature of Human Freedom.* If I am free then there cannot be a God.[17] Freedom implies responsibility for one's own actions. But if there is a God then I am not fully responsible for my actions. In fact, if there is a God then I cannot even be free, for my freedom would be circumscribed by his divine determination. But I am free; in fact, I am fully free. I cannot choose not to be free, for the choice not to be free is itself an act of my freedom which reveals how free I am. My freedom, then, eliminates the possibility of God. For either I am absolutely free to determine myself or else I am not free because God has determined me. But I am absolutely free to determine myself. Hence, there is no God.

*Disproof of God from the Nature of Man.* Freud had cast serious doubt on the existence of God by his argument from illusion. He contended that belief in God was based on wish fulfillment, a cosmic childhood neurosis that sought for a Father-Protector or Cosmic Comforter.[18] It would be nice if there were a God just as it would be nice if there were a pot of gold at the end of the rainbow. But the very fact that our belief

---

15. See Shubert Ogden, *Reality of God,* p. 17.

16. This kind of argument is generally found in the context of those who wish to prove that the world is eternal, as in the Latin Averroist of the thirteenth century, Siger of Brabant (in *On the Eternity of the World*).

17. See Sartre, *Being and Nothingness,* pt. Four, chap. 1.

18. Sigmund Freud, *The Future of an Illusion,* chap. 6.

in God is based on this *wish* for comfort from the tragedies of life makes it highly suspect.

Sartre carries this kind of argument all the way to atheism. Man not only wishes that there be a God but it is man's very project in life to realize God.[19] Man *needs* God in an existential way. In fact, man's whole being is a thrust toward becoming God. However, when we analyze the very nature of man's project to become God we find that it is absurd. The for-itself can never become the in-itself; the uncaused can never become the self-caused. God is *ens causa sui* (a self-caused being), and such a being is impossible. Hence, "man is an empty bubble on the sea of nothingness," a useless passion. His very project as man is hopeless and meaningless. Life is without any transcendent or objective meaning. The only meaning life has is the subjective meaning we give to it. There is no God who provides meaning for life from the outside.

*"God" Is Nothing but a Projection of Human Imagination.* Ludwig Feuerbach argued that "the nature of God is *nothing else* than an expression of the nature of feeling," for the "object of any subject is *nothing else* than the subject's own nature taken objectively." Man by nature is a being that must project or objectify. Man alone, in contrast to animals, is self-conscious. But what is it that man is conscious of in his objectifications? The answer is that religion is simply man's consciousness of himself, although he unwittingly calls it God. Feuerbach offers several forms of a basic disproof of God. First, human reason, will, and affection exist for their own sake and not as a means to something else. But, by definition, whatever exists for its own sake is God. Therefore, God is nothing but what we will in man for its own sake. In addition he argues that one can go no further than the limits of one's own nature; one cannot get outside of himself. But man can and does both feel and understand the Infinite. Hence, the infinity one feels is really the infinity of his own nature. Man is "God." In Feuerbach's words, "What he (God) is to me is to me all that he is."[20]

It is noteworthy here that Marx followed Feuerbach's basic dialectical argument for atheism. Marx wrote of man "who looked for the superman in the fantastic reality of heaven and found nothing there but the *reflexion* of himself. . . ."[21] This Hegelian-based dialectical argument of Feuerbach has enjoyed wide acceptance in Marxist thought.

## Disproof of God from the Nature of a Random Universe

David Hume had argued against a designed universe on the basis that it is *possible* the world happened by chance. Given enough time and

---

19. Sartre, *Being and Nothingness.*
20. Ludwig Feuerbach, *The Essence of Christianity,* pp. 9-12, 16.
21. Karl Marx and Friedrich Engels, *On Religion,* p. 41.

chance, any given combination can occur. The universe may be just a "happy accident" of chance reshuffling of particles in motion. If true, however, this argument would not establish the probability of atheism but simply its possibility. However, the argument may be strengthened into a *probable* disproof of God. For if matter has been in motion eternally (and given the immensity of this universe), it would be reasonable to conclude that chance occurrence of life in some tiny corner of the universe is the best explanation. Jacques Monod, contemporary French biologist, argues for chance as the only possible explanation of the evolution of man. He says, "It is today the sole conceivable hypothesis, the only one that squares with observed and tested fact. And nothing warrants the supposition—or the hope—that on this score our position is likely ever to be revised."[22] Chance, then, is not only a possible explanation of the universe, but given the immensity and the time for the origin of life, it is most probable that a "happy accident" could occur. And since it has occurred, it is reasonable to believe that it has occurred by blind chance.

## An Evaluation of Atheism

### Some Contributions of Atheism

There are two major areas in which atheists have made significant contributions toward building an adequate world view. First, they have helped to eliminate some contradictory concepts of God. Second, they have provided a corrective for some misconceptions of God and his relation to the world.

*Criticism of the Principle of Sufficient Reason Is Correct.* Atheists have been correct in pointing out that the principle of sufficient reason— that everything needs a cause or explanation—leads to an infinite regress and not to God.[23] If *everything* needs a cause then so does God and so on infinitely. If the principle is all-encompassing, then one may not special plead that God is the one exception to it. Why make God the exception; why not just start with the world as a whole and say that the universe does not need a cause? Sufficient reason does not lead to an infinite God but to an infinite regress.

*A Self-Caused Being Is Impossible.* Some theists have tried to avoid the conclusion that an infinite regress is demanded by the principle of sufficient reason by pointing out that the principle makes the qualification, "Everything needs cause *either in another or else in itself.*" On this account the world has its cause in another (viz., God), but God has his cause within himself. But atheists are correct in noting that this leads to

---

22. Jacques Monod, *Chance and Necessity,* pp. 112-13.

23. Theists too have recognized the harm done to the theistic cause via the principle of sufficient reason. See John E. Gurr, *The Principle of Sufficient Reason in Some Scholastic Systems, 1750-1900.*

224 / THEISTIC APOLOGETICS

a contradictory concept of God. If God has the cause of himself within himself, then God is a self-caused Being. But it is impossible to cause one's own existence. Causes are ontologically prior to effects, and so God would have to be prior to himself. That which needs to be caused is in a state of potential being, while that which causes is in a state of actuality. Hence, a self-caused being would be simultaneously in a state of potentiality and actuality with regard to being, which is impossible.

*Some Impossible Conceptions About God.* Atheists are correct in pointing up the fallacy of understanding omnipotence as the ability to do anything. Even God cannot do what is logically contradictory or what is actually impossible. It is logically impossible for God to make square circles and it is actually impossible for God to sin. A God who could cease being God or cease being good would not be the theistic God. There are many things impossible for a theistic God. He cannot change his nature; he cannot will contradictory things; he cannot be overpowered by a creature; he cannot achieve certain ends without certain means (e.g., he cannot be worshiped unless he creates beings who are free). Atheists are certainly correct in placing some logical restrictions on the notion of omnipotence. God can only do what is *actually possible* to do; the contradictory is not possible for even an omnipotent God.

There are numerous other criticisms of theistic conceptions that atheists have pointed up. There cannot be a time before time; God cannot be properly understood in terms of finite anthropomorphic imagery; a totally static God cannot be dynamically related to the changing world; this is not the best of all possible worlds (there are evils and injustices in it), and so on.

## Critique of Atheism as a World View

None of the above arguments or contributions of atheism really destroys theism, for most of them turn out to be helpful refinements of theism; the rest are invalid criticisms. It remains for us here to do two things: we must show the invalidity in the arguments for atheism, and we must show the impossibility or at least untenability of the atheistic position.

*The Invalidity in the Arguments for Atheism.* Each argument for atheism is invalid. It is either based on a misconception or else overlooks some possibility that would avoid atheism. We will treat each of the above arguments for atheism in the order presented.

a. Causality Need Not Lead to an Infinite Regress

The criticism "if everything needs a cause, then there must be an infinite regress" is built on a misconception of the principle of causality. Or better, it is a confusion of the principle of existential causality and the principle of sufficient reason. The latter affirms that *everything* needs a cause. This it would seem, as the atheists observe, leads to a contradiction of God being his own cause. But not all theists use this approach. Aquinas, for example, held that *only* finite, changing, dependent beings need a cause. This does not lead to a contradictory self-caused Being but to a noncontradictory un-caused Being. For if only finite beings need a cause then when one arrives at a nonfinite (i.e., infinite) being it does not need a cause. Hence, from Aquinas' principle of causality the series would legitimately stop at a *first,* Uncaused Cause of all finite beings.[24]

b. Causality Does Not Lead to an Impossible Self-Caused Being

The principle of existential causality does not lead, as does the principle of sufficient reason, to a contradictory self-caused Being. Rather, since only finite, dependent beings need a cause, it leads to an infinite and necessary Being that does not need a cause. The principle of causality, then, leads to an un-caused Being, which is not contradictory. But the principle of sufficient reason, by demanding that everything needs a cause, does lead to a contradictory self-caused being. Theists, then, must agree with atheists in rejecting arguments based on the principle of sufficient reason. But if causality is understood as Aquinas understood it, then atheists have lost their argument from causality against the existence of God.

c. The Ontological Disproof of God Is Self-Defeating

One of the premises in the alleged ontological disproof of God is that "no statements about existence are necessary." If this is true then it would apply also to that very statement itself. So either that very statement, that is, "no statements about existence are necessary," is necessarily true or else it is not. If it is necessarily true, then it is self-defeating; for in that case it is a necessary statement about existence claiming that no necessary statements about existence can be made. As such it would be self-canceling. On the other hand, if the statement is not a *necessary* statement about existence, then it is *possible* that some necessary statements about existence can be made. And this is precisely what some theists claim, namely, that "God exists" is a necessary statement about what exists. At least the atheists must examine the claim of the theist who offers such a proof. The atheist cannot rule out a priori in advance the possibility of making a necessary statement about existence without making a necessary statement about existence, which would be self-defeating. The alleged ontological disproof backfires by eliminating its own ground for asserting what it purports to be the case, namely, a proof about existence that no proofs about existence can be made. If necessary negative statements can be made about existence such as "God cannot exist," then why cannot necessary positive statements about existence be made such as "God does exist"?

---

24. See Aquinas, *Summa Theologica* I, 2, 3; I, 3, 4.

### d. Bayle's Moral Dilemma Is Invalid

The theist might object to Bayle's dilemma by challenging the argument "evil is not defeated." It assumes at least two challengeable premises: first, it assumes that nothing has been done to defeat evil up to this point. On the contrary, many Christian theists believe that evil was defeated by Christ on the cross. This is possible and one would at least have to look at the plausibility of the evidence for this claim.[25] Second, Bayle assumes that since evil has not been defeated to this point in time it will never be defeated. He offers no real proof for the implied premise that if an all-loving and all-powerful God has not defeated evil *by now* he never will defeat it. A theist may argue, on the contrary, that God *will yet* destroy evil when Christ returns.

A theist may even turn Bayle's argument around as a proof that evil will be defeated. The theist could argue as follows:[26] an all-good God would defeat evil and an all-powerful God can defeat evil. But since evil is not yet completely defeated, it follows from the nature of God that evil *will* one day be defeated. That is, the guarantee that evil will be completely destroyed is the infinitely good and powerful nature of God. A finite God cannot offer such a confident hope; only the God of theism can guarantee the defeat of evil. Hence, rather than evil eliminating the logical possibility of a theistic God, the theist can argue that only a theistic God can guarantee the destruction of evil.

### e. Moral Law Need Not Be Arbitrary or Superior to God

Russell's dilemma is a false one for theism. The theist may claim that the moral law is neither outside and superior to God nor arbitrary and unworthy of God. Rather than flowing from God's arbitrary will, the moral law may be seen as rooted in God's unchangeably good and loving nature. If morality is based ultimately on God's nature and not on arbitrary will, then the apparent dilemma is resolved. In this case there is no ultimate *beyond* God to which he is subject; he is subject only to the ultimacy of the good *within* his own nature. God cannot be less than absolutely good; his nature demands that he be absolutely good. And in this event, it cannot be said that God is arbitrary, for he cannot will contrary to his nature. God cannot decide to be unloving, nor can he desire that cruelty and injustice be performed. God's will must perform in accordance with his unchangeably good nature.[27]

### f. Theism Is Not Antihumanitarian

Camus' argument is based on a false dichotomy: it assumes a dis-

---

25. See Section III of this book for an argument for the plausibility of Christianity.
26. See my *Philosophy of Religion* for a theistic solution to the problem of evil, chaps. 14-17.
27. The voluntaristic tradition in ethics springs from Duns Scotus, but other theists (following Aquinas) argue for an ethic rooted in God's nature.

junction between fighting the plague and being a believer in God. The theist may very well hold that fighting the plague is working *for* God who is against all evil and suffering. In fact the theist may claim that the only truly effective way to counteract the plague is by belief in God.

Furthermore, Camus' argument assumes that since God sent the plague, only a humanitarian has a right to fight the plague. But the theist may argue that men have brought the plague on themselves by their rebellion against God and that the only really effective way to correct this is by surrender to God. If this were true, then fighting the plague would mean fighting against man's stubborn self-will, and this fight could very well entail the manifestation of mercy to those in need. Just because someone has made his own bed of thorns does not mean that believers should not help heal the wounds that the person gets from lying on it. The theist may claim that man has brought the plague on himself by rebelling against God, but he need not refuse to help him back to God and wholeness again. On the contrary, one could argue just the opposite. For if God lovingly warns man of the self-initiated consequences of his sin by allowing it to terminate in a disastrous dead-end street, then he would certainly encourage merciful handling that may aid a turnabout resulting in healing and Godward movement. In this way the theist could argue that only theism is truly humanitarian since only theism offers hope of saving man from his self-inflicted plague.

g. Innocent Suffering Does Not Eliminate Theism

It is mistaken for atheists to argue that there is *innocent* suffering and that therefore there cannot be a God. First of all, it is possible that *all* suffering is deserved and that it is God's mercy which saves men from more suffering which they do deserve. Second, what needs to be proved by the atheist is not that there is *innocent* suffering but that there is some *unredeemable* or *unjustifiable* suffering. The theist may argue that some "innocent" suffering is good and that this world is not the final chapter in the story of human suffering. He may contend that this is not the best of all possible *worlds,* but that it is the best of all possible *ways* to obtain the best possible world, which world is yet to come. He may argue that suffering is a necessary precondition for achieving the greatest good. And in view of the fact that the most worthwhile things in life are often achieved only through pain, there is some experiential plausibility to the theist's claim. In this way immediate evil may lead to an ultimate and greater good.

One thing is certain, the atheist cannot press his claim that evil is *ultimately* unjustifiable—which is what he must do to eliminate the existence of God via evil. For if some evil is ultimately unjust in this world, then there must be some ultimate standard of justice beyond this world. All injustice presupposes a standard of justice by which it is judged to be not-just. And an ultimate injustice demands an ultimate standard of justice. But this brings us right back to God, the ultimate standard of justice beyond the world. In short, the only way to disprove God via the problem of evil is to posit God as an ultimate moral standard of justice beyond the world. In this event, if atheism were true, it would be false; its argument turns out to be self-defeating.

It would not suffice for an atheist to contend that this moral ground is neither personal (as God) nor able to bring about ultimate justice, for the theist might plausibly argue that the standard for personal (i.e., moral) activity must be personal and that the ground for limited personal activity must be unlimited Personal Act. If so, it would follow that such an all-powerful person could achieve whatever greater good his personal moral nature demanded by way of ultimate good.

h. Working to Eliminate Suffering Does Not Disprove God

The atheist's argument that working against God's means (suffering) of attaining the end of the greatest good would eliminate theism is wrong for two reasons. First, at best the atheist's *argument* would only eliminate this solution to the problem of evil but it would not eliminate *God*. The theist may agree that God must achieve the greatest good possible. He may also agree that permitting evil is necessary to achieving the greatest good. But it does not follow from this that working against evil would eliminate God. At best this would only mean that in working against evil one is in some sense working against God. It would not prove that there is no God. But even this conclusion does not follow, for it may be that God wills only to *permit* (via human freedom) but not to *promote* suffering as a means to the greatest good. A parent may permit the pain of an operation in order to save the life of his child without really promoting pain for his child.

Here too the atheist's argument is self-defeating. From the atheist's premises one may draw a strong theistic conclusion as follows: If God must work to achieve the greatest good possible in this world and if permitting evil is the means of achieving the greatest good, then it follows that permitting evil is the best way for God to achieve the best world. For if God had done otherwise, it would have been less than his best. And if the atheist desires to back off the premise that God must do his best, then he has lost the force of his argument against God. For if God does not have to do his best, then one has no legitimate grounds for complaining that this world is not the best that God could have done. This is in many ways a good world despite the evil it contains, and this would be compatible with a God who does not have to create the best world but simply a good one. On the other hand, if God must do his best, then permitting evil in order to accomplish his best would seem to be the best way for God to operate. Some virtues (like patience and courage) are not possible without evil and the highest degree of some pleasures and virtues (like forgiveness and reconciliation) are not achievable without some evil or pain. Hence, it would be necessary for God to permit the necessary first order evils in order to achieve the second order and greater goods.

i. Inability to Do the Impossible Does Not Disprove an Omnipotent God

The fact that an omnipotent God cannot do some things does not disprove his existence; it merely shows that some activities are incompatible with omnipotence. Omnipotence does not mean the ability to do what is impossible; it entails only the ability to do what is actually possible. If it is a "limitation" on God not to be able to do evil or not to be able to go into nonexistence or not to do the contradictory, then God is severely "limited." Actually this is a misuse of the word *limited*. The only "limits" God has are the unlimited possibilities of his own nature and will. God cannot make a stone heavier than he can handle; that is impossible. For if he can create it, then he can control it. He alone holds it in existence and he alone can snuff it out of existence, and this is an effective control as one could imagine!

j. Incompatible Perfections in God Do Not Prove Atheism

It is not contradictory to hold that certain things are incompatible with an absolutely and infinitely perfect being. Imperfections, evil, and limitations cannot be affirmed of God. But rather than disprove God's existence these would establish his perfection. God cannot be a stone; he cannot have a body. An infinite body or stone is a contradiction in terms, a limited limitless. These words must be understood of God only metaphorically and not metaphysically; they may be informative of what God *does* but are not truly descriptive of what he *is*.

Perfections such as love and justice are not incompatible in God. They are different, but not everything different is incompatible. The radii of a circle are different but they are all compatible at the center. What is different, and sometimes at least seemingly incompatible in this world, is not necessarily incompatible in God. For example, there can be such a thing as just-love or loving-justice. Likewise, God can be all-knowing and all-loving, for his infinite knowledge may be exercised in allowing men the freedom to do evil without coercing them (in accordance with his love) against their will so that through it all he may achieve (by infinite power) the greatest good for all (in accordance with his justice).

Whatever can be shown to be incompatible with the established perfections of God as infinitely just, loving, and so on, does not disprove God; it merely shows that anything involving limitations or whatever is incompatible with his nature as holy-love is properly speaking not a characteristic of God. In this regard, sometimes the *activity* of God is confused with his *attributes*. Wrath, for example, is not something God *is;* it is something he *does* out of consistency with his nature, because of what creatures have freely brought on themselves. The same sun that hardens clay also melts wax. The sun maintains its same consistent impact on the elements, but the receptivity of the object it shines on will determine whether the same rays will soften or harden it. So it is with the heart of man, according to theism. God's *attributes* do not change, but his *acts* do change in accordance with the change in human attitudes toward him.

k.  Contingent Creation Does Not Eliminate a Necessary God

It is not contradictory to hold that God is necessary while holding at the same time that creation is contingent.[28] The only thing a necessary Being must will necessarily and unconditionally is the necessity of his own nature. Everything else may be willed contingently. There is no necessity in creation that demands that God will it to exist. According to theism, God was free to create or not to create. This is perfectly consistent even for an all-loving God. Love does not *demand* that God create; love may simply lead God to *desire* to create. An infinitely loving Being does not have to *do* anything; he simply has to *be* the infinitely loving God that by nature he is. Of course, no one else would know that he is loving unless he performed some loving act. But one does not have to do something in order to be something. One must exist in order to perform, but he need not perform in order to exist. In brief, God must will his own being necessarily but he need not will anything else necessarily; all else may flow freely from his love. In point of fact, the theist may argue just the opposite of this atheistic objection. The theist may contend that it is of the very nature of love to act freely and not under compulsion. Love is exercised freely or not at all. Hence, if creation flows from a loving God then it must flow freely. It is necessary to the very nature of love that it act freely.

l.  A Temporal Creation Does Not Disprove a Theistic God

It is wrong to conceive of creation *in* time. This supposes that time is already there as a continuum or reality outside God. It is more proper for theism to speak of the creation *of* time. Time is a concomitant of a created and changing world. Hence, time began when the changing process of this world was caused by God. The only thing "before" time was eternity. There were no temporal "befores" prior to time. "Befores and afters" began with time. The word *prior* or *before* can only be used in a nontemporal way in the phrase "before time began." The atheistic antinomy of time does not disprove God; at best it merely corrects a mistaken way of speaking about time and creation.

---

28. This criticism and the following one come also from panentheists. See critique at end of chap. 11.

m.  God Is Not Incompatible with Human Freedom

God's determination and human freedom are not necessarily an either/or situation; they can be a both/and situation. There are a number of ways a theist might reconcile the two. He might contend that God has determined that men be free. He may contend that God controls the world by what he knows men will freely do. Knowing what men *will* do with their freedom is not the same as ordaining what they *must* do against their freedom. The latter would seem to be incompatible with a loving God, but the former would appear to follow naturally from such a God. If love is persuasive but never coercive, then allowing men to freely determine their own destiny would seem to be the loving way to make them. Hence, a theist could argue that the love of God necessitates that if he decides to create creatures that can love him, then they must be free; it is of the very necessary nature of love that other persons be able to respond freely to it.[29] In this way both God and man would be responsible for free acts. God would be responsible ultimately because he created the free creatures. Creatures would be responsible immediately because they are not forced to choose what is morally wrong but freely choose to do so. God may cause human free acts *indirectly* by way of his knowledge of what they will freely do; men cause them *directly* by way of what they choose to do. Therefore, freedom does not eliminate God. On the contrary it involves him. The theist may argue that if man is free, then he is responsible; if he has been given freedom, then he is responsible to the One who gave him freedom. In this account God is ultimately responsible for the *fact* of freedom (which is a good thing) but not immediately responsible for the *acts* of freedom (which may be evil). Both God and men take their separate responsibilities for freedom. So rather than disproving God, ultimately freedom may be said to imply God.

n.  Man's Unfulfilled Need for God Does Not Disprove God

Sartre argued that man is a useless passion engaged in a futile project to realize God. The for-itself can never attain the in-itself by itself. This, however, by no means disproves God. It may prove that Sartre never found God. But as has been observed, if man has as great a need for God as Sartre claims, then one is cruelly unjust to give up the search as hopeless. Should all hungry and oppressed men stop striving for food and freedom? Should every thirsty wanderer in the desert conclude that there is no water anywhere?

Rather than being a disproof of God, one could argue that the deep-seated need for God is a reason for supposing that there is a God.[30] Is

29. See C. S. Lewis, *The Problem of Pain*, chap. 8; *The Great Divorce*, chap. 13; *Four Loves*, chap. 6.

30. See Geisler, *Philosophy of Religion*, chap. 4.

232 / THEISTIC APOLOGETICS

it not reasonable to assume that what men really need is really available? It is true that some hungry men will never find food and some lonely persons will never find companions, but is it reasonable to conclude from their need that neither food nor friends can be found in this world? Would it not be just as reasonable, in view of the seemingly uneradicable need for God, that man should continue his search on the assumption that God may be found? In short, Sartre's attempted disproof can be reversed into a plausible assumption that there is a God.

o.  God Cannot Be Merely a Human Projection

Feuerbach's arguments for atheism depend for their validity on a premise which is self-defeating. The only way one could know that God is *nothing but* the projection of human imagination, emotion, and so on, is if one knows *more than* these mere projections. For unless man knows more than the contents of his own consciousness there is no way to be sure that man's own consciousness is the limits of reality. The limits cannot be known unless they are transcended, and if they are transcended then they are not the limits. It cannot be known where the wall ends unless one can see beyond it. Hence, the only way Feuerbach's disproof of God would work is if the contents of reality were more than the limits of man's understanding. But if reality is more than man's understanding, then it cannot be true that reality is nothing more than the objectification of man's understanding of himself. In short, if Feuerbach's argument is true, then it is false. It is self-defeating since it entails a premise that it purports explicitly to deny.

p.  Chance Does Not Prove Atheism

There are many loopholes in the chance argument for atheism. First, it is *possible* that there is a God and that the world did not happen by chance. For if atheism can be possible and even probable by chance, then so can theism. Second, the immensity of the universe does not help the chance hypothesis; for the mere possibilities within the unknown universe cannot outweigh the probability in the known universe.[31] When all is told, it may be that the whole universe argues for design. Third, allowing more time for chance occurrence does not help the argument, since the longer the time for evolution the more likely it will be that things will be in their original random position. The longer you scramble eggs, the less *organized* they become. Chance and evolution go in both directions, and the longer the time period the more likely that things will be in the state in which they began.[32] Fourth, the odds against a chance explanation of the universe are very great. Even nonbelievers like Julian Huxley have calculated the odds against a purely chance evolution of life at 1 to 1,000

31. See F. R. Tennant, *Philosophical Theology,* reprinted in part in John Hick, *The Existence of God,* pp. 120-36.
32. See Julian Huxley, *Evolution in Action,* pp. 45-46.

to the millionth power (i.e., one followed by 3 million zeros). Others have calculated the odds at less.[33] The argument seems to have a sharp double edge at least.

In point of fact, the argument for atheism from chance is self-defeating; it presupposes design. There is no meaningful way to speak of a completely random universe. Chance makes sense only on the backdrop of design, as meaninglessness can be understood only in the overall context of meaning. Likewise, there is no way to even express the state of complete randomness without implying that there exist such characteristics of design as relatability, or even intelligibility.

*The Untenability of the Atheistic Position.* Strangely enough, atheists have provided some of the most convincing arguments against atheism. Many of their arguments boomerang into a disproof of atheism or else entail a plausible assumption that there is a God.

a. One Must Assume God in Order to Disprove God

The above analysis has shown in several ways that one must assume God in order to disprove God. For example, to disprove God via evil one must assume the equivalent of God by way of an ultimate standard of justice beyond this world. Likewise the ontological disproof of God entails making a necessary statement about existence which claims that necessary statements cannot be made about existence. The same kind of self-defeating consequence follows from any kind of absolute denial about reality. One cannot meaningfully affirm that reality has no ultimate meaning (as in God) without thereby making the claim that his statement is ultimately meaningful about reality. Most informed atheists are sophisticated enough to recognize this. But in qualifying and backing off from the universality and absoluteness of their claim they thereby dilute the strength of their argument to something far short of a proof. It would take absolute knowledge to absolutely eliminate God. But absolute knowledge can only be derived from God. Hence, to be an atheist in the absolute sense, one would have to assume God in order to disprove God.

b. Atheistic Arguments Are Reversible into Reasons for God

Even in the weaker, less universal form of the arguments for atheism, two points can be made. First, not only are many of the atheist's arguments self-defeating, but they entail premises from which one could plausibly conclude the existence of God. So rather than supporting the probability of atheism these arguments actually do the reverse. The arguments from evil, freedom, and human need all call out *for* God, rather than *against* him. Second, the argument from causality turns out to be reversible into the cosmological argument for the existence of God; for if every contingent, finite, or dependent being needs a cause, then it would seem to follow that there must be an Infinite, Necessary and Inde-

33. See Wilder Smith, *Man's Origin, Man's Destiny,* pp. 66 f.

pendent Cause of the existence of every other thing that exists. The detailed elaboration of this argument will be the subject of the next chapter.

c. Atheism Has No Adequate Explanation for Basic Metaphysical Questions

As a world view, atheism provides an insufficient explanation for several very significant questions about reality. An atheist must assume the following meaningless or untenable positions. (1) He must assume that the personal arose from the impersonal, that matter plus time and chance gave rise to mind. It seems more reasonable to hold that Mind formed matter than that matter gave rise to mind. (2) Atheism asserts that the potential gives rise to the actual, that all the world's achievements were latent in the eternal random swirling of tiny atoms. But it seems much more reasonable to believe that something actualized the potential of the universe than to believe that the potentiality actualized itself. Potentials do not actualize themselves any more than steel forms itself into skyscrapers. Potentials must be actualized by some actualizer, and the theist claims that world potentials must be actualized by some World-Actualizer (viz., God). This claim seems eminently more reasonable than the claim of atheism. (3) Atheism has no adequate answer to the question, "Why is there something rather than nothing at all?" It does not suffice to say that the world is just "there" or "given." How did it get there when it did not have to be there? Who gave it when it did not have to be given? The nonexistence of the whole—even the universe as a whole —is actually possible. If not, then it is an eternal necessary Being which is more than (i.e., transcending) all the parts and changing relationships. But this is precisely what the theists call God, namely, an eternal necessary Being that transcends all the changing parts and relationships in the universe. If, on the other hand, the universe is not necessary, then it follows that it might *not be*. In this case there is no explanation in atheism as to why the universe *is* rather than *is not*. In the final analysis atheism must hold the absurd conclusion that something comes from nothing, that is, that non-being is the ground upon which being rests. This seems highly unreasonable.

## Summary and Conclusion

Atheism provides some valuable correctives to and modifications of theism. Many of its arguments either correct misconceptions some theists have of God or of his relation to the world or else they expose contradictory theistic concepts. Atheists have been active as well in contributing to humanistic causes and earnest in scientific endeavors.

However, as a total world view atheism does not measure up. First, its arguments are invalid and often self-defeating. Second, many atheistic arguments are really reversible into reasons for believing in God. Finally, atheism provides no solution to basic metaphysical questions regarding the existence of the universe or the origin of personality and the actualization of the world process. Atheists must believe that something comes from nothing, that potentials actualize themselves, and that matter generated mind. It seems much more reasonable to believe in a God who made something where there was nothing, who actualized the potentials that could not actualize themselves, and whose Mind formed matter. The arguments to support this belief will be provided in the next chapter.

## SELECT READINGS FOR CHAPTER TWELVE

**Exposition of Atheism**

Feuerbach, Ludwig. *The Essence of Christianity.*
Freud, Sigmund. *The Future of an Illusion.*
Nielsen, Kai. *Contemporary Critiques of Religion.*
Nietzsche, Friedrich. *The Anti-Christ.*
Robinson, R. *An Atheist's Values.*
Russell, Bertrand. *Why I Am Not a Christian.*
Sartre, Jean-Paul. *Existentialism and Humanism.*
Schopenhauer, Arthur. *Complete Essays of Schopenhauer,* bk. III: Religion.

**Evaluation of Atheism**

Chalmers, Thomas. *On Natural Theology.*
Collins, James. *God in Modern Philosophy,* chap. VIII.
Flint, Robert. *Anti-theistic Theories.*
Grisez, Germain. *Beyond the New Theism.*
Lepp, Ignace. *Atheism in Our Time.*
Luijpen, W. A. *Phenomenology and Atheism.*
Robertson, J. M. *A Short History of Free Thought.*

# Chapter

# 13 | *Theism*

In Part One of this book it was concluded that the laws of logic apply to reality; reality is thinkable and one cannot meaningfully entertain the thought that reality cannot be thought. Further, it was concluded that contradiction is an adequate test for falsity of a position, as is self-stultification. Any view that contradicts itself or destroys itself in the process or act of affirming itself is self-defeating and false. We further argued that a world view, that is, a philosophical position about all that is, cannot be established as true simply on the basis of the fact that it is noncontradictory, since every major world view might be internally consistent.

In Part Two we have argued two things thus far, one explicitly and the other implicitly. First, we have argued that every major nontheistic world view may be internally noncontradictory, but that they are, none-theless, somehow self-defeating and false. Second, by implication, this would mean that theism, the only remaining noncontradictory view, would be true by the process of elimination. In this final chapter of Part Two we hope to show that there are good positive reasons for believing that theism is true on independent grounds. We will present an argument for the existence of the theistic God of the Bible on what appear to be undeniable premises.

## A Proof for the Existence of the Theistic God of the Bible

We have already conceded in the previous chapter that the traditional ontological, teleological, moral, and Leibnizian cosmological type argu-

237

ments are invalid. None of them prove that God exists. And to speak of the probability of God's existence begs the question, because probability makes sense only if it is already supposed that this is an ordered universe (which would thereby imply an Orderer, i.e., God).

We may state briefly the logic of our position. An ontological type argument moving from thought alone to reality is always invalid for it is always *logically* possible that nothing ever existed including God.[1] All other arguments moving from experience (whether internal or external) to something beyond experience imply that there must be some cause or reason for the fact(s) from which they began. The teleological argument supposes that every design must have a designer that caused it; the moral argument presupposes that every law must be caused by a lawgiver, and so on. Hence, all a posteriori arguments move from effect to cause, that is, from fact to sufficient explanation of that fact. This means that the moral, teleological, and like arguments are based on the cosmological argument.[2] Now the heart of the traditional cosmological argument is based on the principle of sufficient reason that affirms everything must have a cause either within itself or beyond itself. But as was observed in the last chapter, this principle leads either to an infinite regress of looking for a cause for *everything* including God or else it leads to a contradictory first cause that is causing itself to exist. Such is the apparent dilemma facing a theist: a priori proofs are invalid and a posteriori proofs are based on the causal principle that leads either to an infinite regress or to a contradiction.

Despite the seeming dilemma, all is not hopeless. The theist need not claim that *everything* has a cause; he need not use the Leibnizian principle of sufficient reason.[3] Rather, he can return to the thomistic principle of existential causality which claims that every finite, contingent, and changing thing has a cause. If this principle is sound and leads to an infinite, necessary, and unchanging Being, then this Being will not need a cause. God will be the Uncaused Cause of everything else that exists. Such is the direction this chapter will take in developing a proof for the existence of God.

### The Overall Logic of This Argument That God Exists[4]

First, let us outline the overall structure of this argument for theism.

(1) Some things undeniably exist (e.g., I cannot deny my own existence).

---

1. See my *Philosophy of Religion,* chap. 7, for further elaboration on this point.
2. Geisler, *Philosophy of Religion,* chaps. 6, 8.
3. For contrast of these two principles see E. Gurr, *The Principle of Sufficient Reason in Some Scholastic Systems, 1750-1900.*
4. For a similar form of this cosmological argument see my *Philosophy of Religion,* chap. 9.

(2) My nonexistence is possible.

(3) Whatever has the possibility not to exist is currently caused to exist by another.

(4) There cannot be an infinite regress of current causes of existence.

(5) Therefore, a first uncaused cause of my current existence exists.

(6) This uncaused cause must be infinite, unchanging, all-powerful, all-knowing, and all-perfect.

(7) This infinitely perfect Being is appropriately called "God."

(8) Therefore, God exists.

(9) This God who exists is identical to the God described in the Christian Scriptures.

(10) Therefore, the God described in the Bible exists.

## The Detailed Elaboration of Each Step in This Theistic Proof

With this outline in mind we will elaborate each point in detail. Since the argument cannot validly begin in the thin air of pure thought, it must establish itself firmly in the soil of undeniable existence.

*Something Exists.* It is undeniable that something exists. No one can deny his own existence without affirming it. One must exist in order to deny that he exists, which is self-defeating. But whatever is undeniable is true, and what is unaffirmable is false. Hence, it is undeniably true that I exist.

It should be noted here that this argument is not claiming that one's own existence is rationally inescapable. It is *logically possible* that I do not exist; but since I do exist, it is *actually undeniable* that I do exist. So while my existence may be contingent (i.e., it may be possible that I not exist), nevertheless, while I do exist is actually undeniable that I do exist. Hence, so long as someone exists he may begin the process of moving from the premise that something exists to the conclusion that something necessarily exists (i.e., God).

*My Nonexistence Is Possible.* Something undeniably exists. This existence must fit one of three logical categories: impossible, possible, or necessary. And reality is subject to the law of noncontradiction; reality cannot be contradictory. We will argue that since my existence is neither impossible nor necessary, it follows that it must be possible for me not to exist.

First, my existence is not impossible. I do exist and undeniably so. But what exists proves that its existence is actually possible. Only impossible things (like square circles) cannot exist. My actuality proves that it is possible for me to exist. Hence, my existence is not impossible.

Further, my existence is not necessary. A necessary existence is one that cannot *not* exist. The nonexistence of a necessary Being is impossible. If there is a necessary Being, then it must exist necessarily. There is no other way a necessary Being could exist than to exist necessarily. (1) What is more, a necessary existence would be *pure actuality* with no potentiality whatsoever. If it had any potentiality with regard to its existence, then it would be *possible* for it not to exist. But this is precisely what a necessary existence cannot do; it is not possible for a necessary existence *not* to exist. Therefore, a necessary existence would be pure actuality with no potentiality in its being whatsoever. (2) Also, a necessary existence would be *changeless*. Whatever changes must have the possibility for change. If change were impossible then it could not change. But a necessary Being has no possibility whatsoever. (3) A necessary existence would have to be a *nontemporal and nonspatial* existence. If space and time involve change of position and moment, then a necessary existence could not be either spatial or temporal in its being. Its being cannot change, and both space and time involve change. (4) Further, a necessary existence would have to be *eternal*. If it ever did not exist, then it would be a possible existence. But it has no possibility at all with regard to nonexistence. Whatever comes to be is not a necessary existence, for whatever comes to be moves from a state of potentiality to a state of actuality with regard to existence. And a necessary Being has no potentiality in its being whatsoever. Likewise, for the same reason a necessary Being could not ever cease to be. It has no possibility for nonexistence either. (5) There can be only *one* necessary existence. What is pure actuality must be one since there is no way for one thing to differ from another in its being unless there is some real potentiality for differentiation. But in a being of pure actuality there is no potential whatsoever. Hence, there is no real differentiation in it. All of it is one; there cannot be two or more, since neither would really be different from the other in its being. (6) A necessary existence would have to be *simple* and undivided. It could not be composed of different parts or elements. There is no principle of differentiation in it; all is simply one. Further, whatever is composed could be decomposed or destroyed. But it is impossible to destroy the existence of a necessary Being. If it exists at all, then it *must* be, and it cannot *not* be. Hence, a necessary existence must be simple and undivided. (7) A necessary existence would have to be *infinite* in whatever attributes it possesses. If it is knowing, then it must be all-knowing. If powerful, then it must be all-powerful. If good, then it must be all-good. The reason for this is simple enough: only what has potentiality can be limited. Limitation means that which differentiates the sphere of one thing from another. Pure actuality *is* being pure and simple; everything else only *has* being in one form or another depending on its limiting potential. Pure actuality would be unlimited by any potential in and of itself. The only limitations on pure actuality are those of possibility outside it. Even pure actuality could not know or perform the impossible. (8) Finally, a necessary Being must be an *uncaused* being. Whatever is caused passes from potentiality to actuality, for that is what causality means. But a necessary Being has no potentiality and it cannot change. Therefore, it is clear that a necessary Being cannot be caused. And since a self-caused being is impossible, it must be concluded that a necessary Being is an uncaused being.

Now from the above description of what a necessary existence would be, if there were one, it is both obvious and undeniable that I am not a necessary existence. First, I am a changing being. I change in space, time, and knowledge. I do not always live the same moment nor in the same place or relation to the world. This is an obvious fact of my experience. Further, it is an undeniable fact of experience that I change in knowledge. Even if I claim to have come to the realization that my knowledge is unchanging, I have not avoided changing in my knowledge. For anyone who "comes to realize" or know something has in fact changed in his knowledge. There was the state of realization before he believed, which was followed by the different state in which he came to believe that he is unchanging in knowledge. Hence, it is really impossible to come to know that one has unchanging knowledge. If there is anyone with unchanging knowledge, he would always have known it. But if I change in any way then I am not a necessary Being, because a necessary Being is both simple and unchanging. As simple, it has no parts and, hence, cannot be partly anything. Whatever it is, it is wholly and completely. In addition, an unchanging being could not know anything in a changing way. Things could change, but its knowledge of them could not. All it knows it would have to know always. It follows, therefore, that I am not a necessary existence. For I know in a changing way, and a necessary existence could not possibly know in a changing way.

Second, I am not alone. I use language, but no language is entirely private.[5] Language is a medium of communication shared with others. By language I speak to others. I cannot deny that I use language without using it. And I cannot deny that I use it to speak to others without speaking something to others. Not all language is emotive self-muttering. Even atheists publish books expecting others to read them. Whenever I use language with others I use it to speak to them. When I make utterances strictly by myself, I mean nothing for others; I am simply emoting and mean nothing by it. But it is impossible to deny that I mean something by language without uttering a meaningful statement, which is thereby self-defeating. All who deny there is an other for whom their statement is meant either make no meaningful statement or else really have an other in mind for whom that statement is meant. In

---

5. See Ludwig Wittgenstein, *Philosophical Investigations,* secs. 194 f.

242 / THEISTIC APOLOGETICS

short, both the fact and use of language imply others. Without others there would be no language and no meaningful statement would ever have been made. But it is undeniable that some meaningful statement has been made; otherwise that very statement would be meaningless. Hence, it follows that I am not alone; others are necessarily implied in my use of language. But more than one being cannot be necessary. There can only be one necessary Being, as was shown above. Wherever there is a multiplicity of beings, they must be limited; there cannot be many infinite beings. But where there is a limited being there must be a limiting potential. Hence, I as a limited being, among others, have both actuality (because I am) and limiting potentiality, because I am not infinite. This means that I cannot be a necessary Being. A necessary Being has no limiting potential, as was shown above. Therefore, both change and multiplicity in what exists show that what I am is not a necessary Being.

We are now in a position to put the argument together. I exist; this cannot be denied. My existence cannot be impossible since I actually exist. Nor can my existence be necessary since my existence implies both change and multiplicity, neither of which a necessary Being can have. The only remaining alternative is that my existence must be a possible existence. That is, I am but I might not be. My nonexistence is actually possible. I can come to be, and I can cease to be. I am a "may-be" but not a "must-be." Although I exist, nevertheless I have the potentiality within my very being not to exist. I could go out of existence at any moment. I am contingent as well as limited and changing.

*Whatever Has the Possibility for Nonexistence Is Currently Caused to Exist by Another.* Whatever has the possibility of nonexistence must be caused to exist by another because potentiality is not actuality. What is but could possibly not be is only a potential existence. It has existence but it also has the possibility of nonexistence. Now the very existence of this potential existent is either self-caused, caused by another, or uncaused; there are no other possibilities. But it cannot be self-caused since this is impossible. Neither can it be uncaused. For if it were uncaused, then mere possibility would be the ground of actuality. But nothing cannot produce something.[6] It must be concluded, then, that whatever has the possibility for nonexistence must be caused to exist by another. Let us now elaborate the argument.

First of all, by "causality" we mean the actualization of a potential. A "cause," then, is that which affects a transition from potentiality to

---

6. Many nontheists have difficulty in seeing how the theistic doctrine of *ex nihilo* creation can avoid contradiction. How can God "make something from nothing"? But the theist may retort, a fortiori, to the nontheist who believes that "nothing can produce something." It is *not* contradictory at all to say that an infinite power can bring into existence what did not before exist. But it *is* clearly contradictory to believe that "nothing can cause something."

actuality. Further, no being whether contingent or necessary can be self-caused. A self-caused being would have to be ontologically prior to itself. It would have to be simultaneously in a state of actuality and potentiality with regard to being, which is impossible. Potentiality is not actuality; nothing is not something. A cause of being must exist in order to cause. And what is to be caused must not exist or else its existence does not need to be caused. Hence, in order to cause one's own existence one must simultaneously exist and not exist, which is impossible.

Furthermore, a being that could possibly not exist cannot be uncaused. Its being is only possible and not necessary. It is not a must-be but only a may-be which is. But the possible is not the actual; mere possibility does not account for actuality. The impossible cannot be, the possible can be, and the necessary must be. The impossible can never come to be, the necessary can never come to be or cease to be, but the possible can come to be and cease to be. But whatever can come to be must be caused to be. For something cannot come from nothing; the mere potential for being cannot actualize itself. If it is an actualized potentiality, then it either actualized itself or else it was actualized by something outside itself. But no being can actualize its own existence. The actualization of a potentiality is what is meant by causality. Hence, to actualize one's own potential for being would mean to cause one's own being, which is impossible. However, since the existence of possible beings has actualized, it follows that there is a cause of existence outside them which actualizes their existence. In short, the actual does not come from the potential unless something outside it actualizes its potential. No potential can actualize itself. The potential for being does not account for the existence of something. Many things which could possibly exist do not exist, for example, centaurs, mermaids, and Pegasus. Why then do other things which might not exist actually exist? The only adequate explanation for why there is something rather than nothing at all is that the something that could be nothing is caused to exist by something that cannot be nothing. In brief, all contingent beings are caused by a necessary Being. Whatever is but might not be is dependent on what is but cannot *not* be.

Another way to see the need for a cause of all possible beings is to analyze the very nature or kind of existence it has. If there were a necessary Being it would be pure actuality with no potentiality in its being whatsoever. Impossible beings have neither actuality nor potentiality; they are not and cannot be. But possible beings have both potentiality and actuality in their very being. They consist of coprinciples of being. In Latin, their *ens* (being) is composed of *esse* (act of existence) and *essentia* (essence). But whatever is composed of *esse* and essence must be caused to exist by another. *Esse* cannot cause itself and essence cannot cause *esse*. *What* something is does not explain the fact *that* it is, unless it is a necessary Being whose very essence is to exist. But it is not of the essence of a possible being, such as I am, to exist. It is of my essence that I might not exist even though I do indeed exist. Hence, since it is not of my essence to exist and since it is only of the essence of a necessary Being to exist, then it follows that we must seek for the ground or cause of every possible being such as I am.[7]

There is perhaps an even easier way to see the need for a cause of every contingent or possible being. An infinite and unchanging being must be uncaused. But there can only be one such being, as was shown earlier (see p. 239ff.). Therefore, every other being must be caused by another, since to be self-caused is impossible. Since I am not a necessary Being, it must be concluded that I (and every other contingent being that exists) must be caused to exist by a cause beyond me (us).

Before leaving this point it should be stressed that all causality of existence is *current*. What is called for is not a cause for my *becoming* but for my continued *be-ing*.[8] The argument rests on conserving causality, not originating causality. The reason for this is very simple: I am right *now* a contingent being; it is not that I once was contingent when I came to be but now am not. Whatever was once contingent will always be contingent; for whatever can come to be is not a necessary Being. A necessary Being cannot come to be; it must ever be and may never not be. This means that whenever I am contingent and however long I remain contingent I will always need a cause of my existence. In fact it is misleading to speak of "existence" as though it were something one could get all at once in a package to keep for the rest of his life. What we have is not really existence but a continual moment by moment process of existing. We do not have being but continuous *be*-ing. What causes me to be when I need not be nor continue to be? This is the real metaphysical question that only theism can answer adequately. All causality of existing or be-ing is simultaneous and current. The cause of *becoming* may be before the effect, but the cause of *be-ing* must be concurrent with the effect. The cause of my here-and-now existence must be vertical and not linear. The artist is the cause of the becoming of the painting but not of its continued being. The artist dies but the painting continues to be. Likewise, the parents are the cause of the coming-to-be of the child but something else must be the cause of the child's continuing-to-be, since he continues to exist without the parents.

---

7. This argument is simply an amplification of Aquinas' argument in *De Ente* (*On Being and Essence,* chap. 4). See translation by Armand Maurer (Toronto: The Pontifical Institute of Medieval Studies, 1968).

8. Even theists sometimes miss the force and importance of this distinction. See Keith Yandell, *Basic Issues in the Philosophy of Religion* (Boston: Allen and Bacon, Inc., 1971), p. 84.

*There Cannot Be an Infinite Regress of Current Causes of Existence.*
Since all causality of existence is current and simultaneous, it can be
readily seen why an infinite regress is impossible.[9] It is not necessarily
contradictory to speak of an infinite regress of causes of becoming,
because no cause is simultaneously existing and not existing. But a chain
of causes, however short or long, wherein every cause is simultaneously
both actual and potential with regard to existence, is clearly impossible.
If there were a series of causes wherein each cause was both causing
existence and having its existence caused at the same moment, then it
would follow that they were both potential and actual simultaneously.
Furthermore, at least one (if not all) of the causes would be an impossible
self-caused being. For in every series where causality is occurring *at
least one* cause must be causing (and maybe all of them). But in an
infinite series *every* cause is being caused by another. If there were found
one cause that was causing but not being caused it would be the uncaused
cause which the infinite series seeks to avoid. Hence, the *one* (or more)
cause that is doing the causing of *every* cause must be causing itself,
since it too is being caused (as are all the other causes) by the causality
in the series. But the only causality in the series is being given to the
series by that cause itself. Hence, that one cause would be causing itself;
that is, it would be a self-caused being, which is impossible.

Another way to put the impossibility of an infinite regress of current
causes of contingent beings is to point out that either the series as a
whole is a sufficient ground for all contingent beings or it is not. If not
then there must be some being outside the series on which the series is
grounded. In this case the series would be dependent on a cause beyond
it and, hence, it would not avoid the theistic conclusion that there must
be a cause beyond the alleged series. Either the causality which is admitted
to be in the series comes from within the series or it comes from beyond
the series. If it comes from beyond the series, then the series is dependent
on a cause which is independent of the series. If the causality is within
the series, then there is simultaneous mutual self-causality going on. But
adding up an infinite number of dependent beings within a series does
not provide an adequate ground for them. If each being is a *caused*
being, as they are admitted to be by the very nature of the series, then
adding up all these *effects* does not provide a *cause* for these effects. No
amount of effects equals a cause. If the parts are contingent then the
whole is contingent. Making the series longer or even infinitely long does
not lessen the need for a grounding cause to explain it; rather, it increases
the need for a cause. If a chain with five links in it needs a peg to hang
on, then a chain with an infinite number of links would need an even

---

9. See Aquinas, *Summa Theologica*, I, 44, 1, and Duns Scotus, *Philosophical
Writings*, pp. 44 f.

stronger peg outside itself to hang on. Therefore, an infinite regress of current causes of here-and-now existence is impossible.

A point often overlooked in the question of an infinite regress is that there could not be an infinitely long series of causes of contingent beings because there *could not even be a one-link chain* between the cause of being and the being caused.[10] The very first cause of contingent being could not itself be contingent. No contingent being can cause another being to exist. What does not account for its own existence could not possibly ground the existence of another. How can what is an *effect* with regard to its own existence be a *cause* with regard to another's existence? What is in a state of *potentiality* regarding existence for itself cannot simultaneously be in a state of *actuality* for the existence of another. The only possible ground for what can pass from potentiality to actuality (viz., a contingent being) with regard to being is what cannot pass from potentiality to actuality (i.e., a necessary Being). Those things whose being is an effect cannot be causes of being. What receives its existence from another cannot be the cause of another's existence. Only what is actual can actualize; what is in a state of potentiality can be actualized but it cannot actualize. But every contingent being is in a state of potentiality regarding being. Therefore, no contingent being can cause being. Only a necessary Being can cause the existence of a contingent being. Therefore, the very first being causing the existence of a contingent being must be a necessary Being.

*Therefore, a First, Uncaused Cause of My Current Existence Exists.* This conclusion follows logically and necessarily from the above premises. If I undeniably exist and if my nonexistence is possible, then I must have a cause that actualizes my existence. For I am not nonexistent but I could be. But the cause of all contingent existence, such as I am, cannot itself be contingent. If it were contingent then it would not be the *cause* of the contingent; it too would be an *effect*. But it is the cause of the contingent, since the contingent undeniably needs a cause. Hence, the very first cause of my contingent existence is non-contingent, that is, it is a necessary Being. There cannot be any chain of such causes, surely not an infinite chain; the very first cause must be the necessary ground of all contingent existence.

This first cause of all else that exists must itself be un-caused. It cannot be self-caused (which is impossible) and it cannot be caused by another, because it is necessary and a necessary Being cannot be caused by another. Whatever is caused has the potentiality for existence, but a necessary Being is pure actuality without any potentiality. Therefore, a necessary Being cannot be caused. It is literally the not-caused cause of

---

10. Aquinas saw this in *De Ente*. He speaks only *ad hoc* to the problem of an infinite regress elsewhere in his writings in order to show it is impossible.

all that is caused. It is the not-affected effecter of all effects. It is the necessary ground of all actualized possibility. There is, then, an un-caused cause of the existence of all that is caused to exist, of which I am one undeniable example.

*This Uncaused Cause Must Be Infinite, Unchanging, All-Powerful, All-Knowing, and All-Perfect.* We have already seen that a necessary Being must be necessary, pure actuality, changeless, nonspatial, non-temporal, one, simple, infinite, and uncaused (see p. 239ff.). It remains here to see whether it must be all-powerful, all-knowing, and all-perfect.

By power we mean what can effect a change in another, that is, what can cause something else to be or not be in some way. But this is precisely what the uncaused cause is, namely, that which is causing the very being of all that exists. Further, this uncaused cause is infinite in its being. Hence, it has non-limited causal power in its very being which can effect anything that it is possible to effect. Of course, it does not have power to do what is impossible. The impossible cannot be. This unlimited cause cannot *not* be. But it has the power to make come to be whatever can come to be.

Further, this infinite cause of all that is must be all-knowing.[11] It must be knowing because knowing beings exist. I am a knowing being, and I know it. I cannot meaningfully deny that I can know without engaging in an act of knowledge. Total agnosticism is impossible. But whatever I *am,* I have been caused to be. I cause my own *becoming* (this is what freedom is), but only the necessary Being is the cause of my *be-ing.* Hence, the actual ability to know (which I possess) is caused to be by the cause of all finite beings. But a cause can communicate to its effect only what it has to communicate. If the effect actually possesses some characteristic, then this characteristic is properly attributed to its cause. The cause cannot give what it does not have to give. If my mind or ability to know is received, then there must be Mind or Knower who gave it to me. The intellectual does not arise from the nonintellectual; something cannot arise from nothing. The cause of knowing, however, is infinite. Therefore, it must know infinitely. It is also simple, eternal, and unchanging. Hence, whatever it knows—and it knows anything it is possible to know—it must know simply, eternally, and in an unchanging way.

The only thing such a Mind cannot know is what is impossible for it to know. For example, an infinite mind cannot know what it is like to be finite or changing in its knowledge or experience. Since there is no potentiality or finitude in this infinite cause, then the one way it cannot be like its effects is that it cannot be finite, potential, and so on. But

11. What follows here is the valid and supplementary role the teleological argument plays in showing what kind of cause is proven by the cosmological argument (viz., a *knowing* cause).

since what it causes has both potentiality and actuality, the infinite cause is like the effect in its actuality but not like the effect in its finitude. Therefore, whatever implies limitations in the world cannot be attributed to the cause of the world. Likewise, since the cause is pure actuality, whatever potentials it causes in other things must not be attributed to the cause which has no potentialities in its being. The cause is like the effect only in the actuality it communicates.[12] For example, hot eggs are like the hot water in which they boil, but the hardness in the eggs caused by boiling is not in the water that causes it (the water is mobile or soft). Heat communicates heat but the hot water does not communicate hardness to the egg. Hot water melts other things (e.g., wax). The hardness (or softness) is due not to the actuality communicated by the cause but to the condition or potentiality of the effect to receive causal efficacy. Likewise, not everything in the creature's knowledge can be attributed to the Creator. Some things are due to the finite and limiting potentials in which the causal power is received. It is for this reason that ignorance and other imperfections found in our knowledge cannot be attributed to the Cause of the world. Only the actual perfections communicated to the effect by its cause can be properly attributed to the cause. Man knows finitely and imperfectly but the cause of all knowledge knows infinitely and perfectly. There is a similarity in *what* is known but a great difference in the *way* it is known. In brief, if we can know some things, the Creator can know all things. With us some knowledge is possible; with him all knowledge is actual.

Finally, for the same reason that the cause of knowing must be all-knowing, the cause of goodness must be all-good.[13] Let us define good as that which is desired for its own sake. It is undeniable that some things are desired for their own sake. Persons are an end and not a means; they have intrinsic value and not merely extrinsic value. But what if an end with intrinsic value is desired for its own sake? There are two arguments that we can offer in support of this contention. First, persons do want to be desired for their own sake. Men do expect to be treated as ends, to be loved and not used. The proof of this is not how men *act* toward others nor even the way they *say* men ought to act toward others; the proof is the way they *expect* others to act toward them. In order to discover if a man really believes it is good to be just, do not look at the way he *acts* toward others; rather, look at the way he *re-acts* when others do something to him. The quickest way to convince an antinomian student that he really believes in the principle of fairness is to give him an F on

---

12. See my *Philosophy of Religion,* chap. 12.
13. What follows here is the valid and supplementary role the moral argument serves in showing that the God proven by the cosmological argument is a morally good kind of being.

his brilliant term paper *simply* because you do not like the color of the folder in which it was enclosed! The most effective way to find out if a man believes it is wrong to break promises is to break a promise made to him. Now if there is such a thing as good or that which is desired for its own sake, then it must be caused by the Creator of all that is. (It must be remembered that we are the cause of the *becoming* of good acts via our free choice, but the Creator is the cause of the *be-ing* of all good.)

Second, that there are values or goods desired for their own sake seems undeniable. For even the person denying all goods is enjoying the good of being able to express that opinion. There is an implicit good of personhood and freedom manifest in the freedom to deny that there are any such intrinsic goods. How can a person deny his value as a person without evidencing his value as a person in the act of making the denial? But the cause of good must be Good, since it cannot give what it does not have to give. All actualities actualized in the effect must preexist in the cause. But since the cause of all goodness is infinite, it follows that he must be infinitely good. For whatever the infinite cause "has," he must be in the infinity of his being. Since he is simple and has no parts he cannot be partly anything. Whatever he is, he is entirely and completely. Therefore, the infinite and necessary Cause of all good must be infinitely and necessarily good. The unchanging Cause of all changing things must be unchangingly good. The cause of personhood cannot be less than personal himself. He may be much more than is meant by finite person but he cannot be less; he may be superpersonal but he is not subpersonal.

*This Infinitely Perfect Being Is Appropriately Called "God."* By "God" we mean what is worthy of worship, that is, what has ultimate worthship. Or, in other words, "God" is the Ultimate who is deserving of an ultimate commitment.[14] "God" is that which has ultimate intrinsic value—what can be desired for his own sake as a person. Anything less than what is ultimately and intrinsically worthy of our admiration and submission is not really "God" but a false god. An ultimate commitment to what is less than ultimate is idolatry. It may be a religious commitment, but it is a commitment to an object that is less than religiously worthy or adequate.

Now if the foregoing arguments (pp. 239-249) are sound, we have good reason to believe that an ultimate value worthy of our worship or ultimate commitment does indeed exist. For what is infinitely good (and personal), and is the ground and creator of all finite goods and persons, is certainly worthy of worship. Nothing has more intrinsic value than the *ultimate ground and source of all value.* Hence, nothing is more worthy of worship than the infinitely perfect uncaused cause of all else that exists. Therefore, it is appropriate to call this infinitely perfect cause "God."

14. See Paul Tillich, *Ultimate Concern,* chap. 1.

*Therefore, God Exists.* We may conclude, then, that God exists. What in religion is known as the ultimate object of worship or commitment (viz., God) is by reason known to exist. Hence, what philosophy leads to (via the above argument) is not an abstract unmoved Mover but a real concrete Ground for our being and personal object whom we can love "with all our soul, strength, heart, and mind." The God the heart needs, the head has good reason to believe really exists.

*This God Who Exists Is Identical to the God Described in the Christian Scriptures.* The God described in the Bible is said to be eternal (Col. 1:16; Heb. 1:2), changeless (Mal. 3:6; Heb. 6:18), infinite (I Kings 8:27; Isa. 66:1), all-loving (John 3:16; I John 4:16), and all-powerful (Heb. 1:3; Matt. 19:26). But there cannot be two infinitely perfect, changeless, eternal beings. First, there can be only one infinite and necessary Being, as was shown above (p. 239f.). Second, there could not be two beings who have all possible perfections attributable to them. For in order to be two beings one would have to differ from the other; where there is no difference in being there is only one being. But there can be no difference unless one being has something the other does not. But if there is something that an infinite being can have but one lacks, then the one lacking it is not absolutely perfect. Hence, there is only one absolutely perfect being. But if there cannot be two such beings, then the God described in the Bible is identical to the God concluded from the above argument.

*Therefore, the God Described in the Bible Exists.* If there is only one God and the God described in the Bible is identical in characteristics to him, then it follows logically that the God described in the Bible exists. For there cannot be two infinitely perfect beings; there cannot be two such ultimates or absolutes, and so forth. Hence, the God portrayed in Scripture does indeed exist.

This does not mean that everything the Bible *claims* that this God said or did, he actually said or did. Whether or not what the Bible says about this God is true is another question. What we may conclude here is two things: first, the God described in the Bible does exist; second, whatever the Bible claims for this God that is not inconsistent with his nature, it is possible that he did indeed do or say.

## An Evaluation of Theism as a World View

Theism has been subject to many criticisms. They fall roughly into two classifications: first, those that attempt to disprove theism via some argument for atheism (these were discussed in the previous chapter); second, those criticisms that attempt to prove that theism is not true. The latter category may be divided into two groups: those based on a priori type arguments such as the ontological argument and those based on a posteriori type arguments such as the teleological, moral, and cosmological arguments.

## Valid Criticisms Against Theistic Arguments

Many of the criticisms against theism are valid. Of these the following may be mentioned from the writings of David Hume, Immanuel Kant, and some modern followers.[15]

*Strictly A Priori Arguments About God Are Invalid.* Nontheists have been correct in observing that there is an invalid move in every purely ontological type argument. One cannot argue from the mere concept of an absolutely perfect or necessary Being to its existence the way Anselm or Descartes did. For the rational is not the real and neither is the rationally inescapable the real (see Chapter 2). Even if it is logically necessary to *conceive* of a necessary Being as necessarily existing, it does not follow that It necessarily does exist. It might be necessary to *think* that It exists but this does not prove that It really *does exist.* It is necessary to *think* of triangles with three sides on them; there is no other way to think of triangles. However, it is still possible that no triangles exist. All the nontheist must show is that there is a logical possibility that a necessary Being does not exist. This can be readily illustrated from the fact that it is a logical possibility that nothing ever existed including God. For the nonexistence of everything is a logically *conceivable* state of affairs. If a theist objects that the proposition "nothing exists" is unaffirmable without self-destruction, the nontheist may correctly reply that this is true only because one is really beginning with the actual existence of the affirmer. But to argue "something actually exists undeniably so (viz., an affirmer), therefore, it is *unaffirmable* that nothing exists" is not the same as arguing from the mere *inconceivability* of the nonexistence of a necessary Being. The necessity is merely conceptual and not actual. And if there is no actual necessity that God exists, then it is conceivable that he does not exist. But in this case the theistic proof fails. Invoking actually the undeniability that something exists to rescue the argument from collapse really imports a cosmological move from experience and the argument is no longer strictly a priori. It says in effect, I exist, therefore, one cannot deny that something necessarily exists. But this is a move from what does exist to a necessary ground or cause for its existence, which is not an a priori argument but an a posteriori type argument from effect to cause.[16] There is no purely rational a priori way to prove God's existence.

---

15. For a more complete critique of Hume and Kant see my *Philosophy of Religion,* chap. 9, pp. 208-24.

16. See my article "The Missing Premise in the Ontological Argument" in *Religious Studies* IX, No. 3 (September 1973).

*A Posteriori Arguments Are Also Logically Invalid.* Nontheists are correct in observing that there is no way to provide a rationally inescapable argument a posteriori. Experience is never logically necessary. The opposite of any state of affairs in the world is always logically possible. From flux only flux can come. The existence of God cannot be proven without appealing to some principle that is truly independent of experience. But to import an a priori principle is to open the argument to two criticisms. First, no a priori based argument is valid; there are no rationally inescapable arguments about reality, as was just shown. Second, even if one combines a posteriori experience and some a priori based principle, there is still the problem of the justification of that principle.

The principle most often invoked by theists is the Leibnizian principle of sufficient reason. It is argued by theists that this principle is self-evidently true or it is reducible to the law of noncontradiction. But arguments in support of the principle of sufficient reason fail. For it is not contradictory to deny the principle of sufficient reason. The statement *"some* things do not have sufficient reasons" is not contradictory. It would be contradictory to affirm "nothing has a sufficient reason," for that assertion would include itself. And either there is a sufficient reason for affirming there is no sufficient reason for anything (in which case the statement is self-defeating) or else there is not a sufficient reason for saying so (in which case there is no justification or basis for making the statement). But simply to deny the principle of sufficient reason by claiming that *some* things do not have sufficient reasons is not contradictory or self-defeating. Many theists and nontheists believe that something(s) is simply un-caused. Something(s) could simply be "there" or "given" without the need for a cause. Sartre claims that the world is simply there with no explanation or cause needed; Aquinas believed that God was simply there eternally and necessarily as an un-caused Being. It seems both intelligible and defensible to affirm that something is without a cause or sufficient reason. But if it is logically possible that something can exist without a cause, then any theistic argument based on this principle is doomed to demonstrative failure.

Is there any way out for theism? Can the existence of God be proven, if both a posteriori and a priori routes are blocked? We believe the answer is affirmative and that the route is by a combination of the a priori self-evident principle of existential causality combined with the undeniable a posteriori fact that something contingent exists (as was argued above, pp. 239-250). This argument is not subject to many of the traditional antitheistic arguments. First of all, it is not based on logical necessity; it admits that reality cannot be established by logical necessity. It acknowledges that it is logically possible (i.e., conceivable) that nothing ever existed including God. Hence there are no rationally inescapable proofs for the existence of God. The contrary to any state of affairs is always logically possible. Second, not everything from experience lacks certainty. I am certain that I exist; I cannot deny that I exist without affirming that I exist in that very denial. Hence, it is undeniable (though not logically necessary) that something exists. For even though my nonexistence is not inconceivable, it is unaffirmable. Or, positively put, my nonexistence can be conceived but it cannot be affirmed. I undeniably exist. Finally, the principle of existential causality is self-evidently true. It may be stated this way: "everything that has been actualized has an actualizer" or "everything that passes from potentiality to actuality does so under the influence of some actuality." Simply stated it is: "every effect has a cause." Once one understands that an "effect" is something that is caused and a "cause" is that which can produce an effect, then the principle of causality is as self-evident as "all wives are married women." One need do no more than examine the nature of the subject and predicate to see that the predicate is reducible to the subject; they are both saying the same thing. With this in mind the basic theistic argument (pp. 239-250) can be summarized as follows:

> Every effect has a cause;
> The world is an effect;
> Therefore, the world has a cause.

*Unsuccessful Attempts to Invalidate the Argument for Theism.* Most traditional arguments of Hume,[17] Kant,[18] and others do not touch the above argument for theism; and other arguments fail as well. Let us examine some of the more important ones.

a. An Infinite Regress of Causes Is Impossible

An infinite regress of current simultaneous causes of what exists here-and-now is clearly not possible (see p. 245). There may be an infinite series of causes of *becoming* but not an infinite series of causes of here-and-now *being*. As long as there is a dependent being in the universe, there must be something independent on which it depends. If there is an existing effect, something must be effecting or causing it. No effect exists without its cause. If something existed without a cause then it would not be an effect; it would be self-caused or uncaused. But since I am not self-caused or uncaused (p. 243), then my existence must be effected or caused by a cause. Hence, my existence demands a current here-and-now cause of its continuing *be*-ing. But one never reaches the needed cause by adding up effects; even an infinite number of effects never equals a cause. Hence, no infinite series of effects (which is what a serial "cause" is, since every "cause" in an infinite series is being caused by another)

---

17. See David Hume, *Dialogues Concerning Natural Religion.*
18. See Immanuel Kant, *Critique of Pure Reason,* p. 327 f.

can ever replace the need for a cause of that which is being caused right now (viz., my existence).

b. The Principle of Causality Is Justifiable

The principle of existential causality—that every existing effect has a current cause—is justifiable (see p. 244). In fact it is self-evidently true once one understands what is meant by "cause" and "effect." A "cause" is that which is producing an effect and an "effect" is that which is being produced by a cause. The real issue is not seeing the self-evident validity of the principle of causality, but it is with showing that the world is an "effect." The method by which this is accomplished may be described as a metaphysical analysis or unpacking of the nature of a finite, limited, changing being of which I am undeniably one. The argument may be summarized this way: my current existence must be either self-caused (which is impossible), uncaused, or caused by another. But it cannot be uncaused because I am a possible existence, that is, one that exists but might possibly not exist. But whatever is only in potentiality to being must have a cause. For the potential is not the actual; no potential can actualize itself any more than the mere potential for a rock to be a building can form it into a building. Potentialities are actualized only by actualizers; things whose capacity has been actualized are caused by another. Hence, whatever exists but might not exist is caused to exist by another. But the world might not exist. Therefore, the world is caused by another, that is, the world is an "effect."

c. The World as a Whole Needs a Cause

Nontheists sometimes object to the theistic argument on the basis that only parts of the world need a cause but not the world as a whole. They see the theistic argument as the fallacy of composition. Simply because each part of a puzzle is triangular does not mean the whole puzzle is triangularly shaped. But this objection does not apply to the above argument because the *very nature of the parts* demands that the whole world be caused. For example, by the very nature of brown floor tile, a whole floor of them must also be brown.[19] Likewise, by the very nature of a wooden table, if each part is made of wood, then the whole table must be wooden. So it is that by the very nature of effects or caused things that the whole group of them needs a cause just as much as any one of them does. It is possible that the whole world might not exist. The world as a whole is contingent. And whatever is contingent is dependent on a cause beyond it. Hence, there must be a cause beyond the whole world on which it depends.

Sometimes nontheists press this argument a step further. They argue that the whole is more than the parts the way a triangle ($\triangle$) is more

---

19. See Bruce Reichenbach, *The Cosmological Argument,* pp. 100-2.

than a three-sided figure (△). All the parts are there in the latter but it lacks the wholeness of the former. In this sense, they say, the whole universe could be necessary while all of the parts are merely contingent on the whole. This move, however, is insufficient because it proves to be only a back door kind of theism. By admitting that the whole transcends, or is more than the parts, and that the whole is both eternal and necessary, and that all the parts depend on it, they have admitted there is a transcendent, eternal, necessary cause on which everything in the universe depends for its existence. But this is what the theist means by God! The nontheist has simply couched his description of God in the phrase "universe as a whole," by which he means the same thing the theist means by "God." However, if the "universe" is thought of merely as equal to the *sum* total of all the contingent, changing, and finite parts, then there must be a cause beyond it to ground its existence as whole or sum total. If, on the other hand, "universe" means what is eternal, necessary, and *more than* the sum of all the parts, then it is the equivalent of what the theist calls God. But in either case one cannot avoid the conclusion that God exists.

d. There Is No Four-Term Fallacy in the Theistic Argument

Some nontheists have insisted that the argument for theism equivocates on the term *cause*. They insist that the word *cause* in the premises means "finite cause" but in the conclusion it means "infinite cause."[20] But the meaning of the same term may not be broader or different in the conclusion than in the premises. Therefore, the conclusion of an infinite God is invalidly drawn from the premises of the argument. However, this objection misses the meaning of "cause" in the premises. "Cause" in the premise simply means "that actuality (whether finite *or* infinite) which produces an effect." In other words, in the premises it is an open question as to whether it is an infinite or a finite cause. But as it turns out, the conclusion demands a not-finite kind of cause which is causing everything else that exists (see p. 247). For *every* finite thing needs a cause; hence, the first cause must be not-finite. If it were finite, then it too would need a cause. But since it does not have a cause it must be a not-finite (i.e., in-finite) cause of all finite things. Therefore, an infinite cause is possible in the premise but necessitated by the conclusion of the argument. No four-term fallacy has occurred.

e. The Terms *Necessary Being* and *Uncaused Cause* Are Not Meaningless.

Some nontheists insist that the terms *Necessary Being, Uncaused Cause,* or their equivalents have no meaning.[21] Necessity, they claim,

---

20. See Allan P. Wolter, *The Transcendentals and Their Function in the Metaphysics of Duns Scotus,* p. 44.
21. See Kai Nielsen, *Contemporary Critiques of Religion,* chaps. 2 and 3.

cannot be a characteristic of existence; necessity is a logical but not an ontological category. There are several ways to respond to this. First, the theist might claim that God is not a logically necessary Being but the *statement* "God exists" is a logically necessary statement. In this case, either the nontheist's contention is self-defeating or else it does not really succeed in eliminating the possibility that some logically necessary statements about existence are possible. For either his statement is a necessary statement about existence or it is not. If it is a necessary statement about existence to the effect that no necessary statements about existence can be made, then it is self-destructive. On the other hand, if it is not a *necessary* statement about existence, then it leaves open the possibility that there might be some necessary statement(s) about existence. Second, the nontheist's argument confuses two kinds of necessity: logical necessity and ontological necessity. We have already conceded that no reality (God included) is logically necessary. Hence, we are willing to grant the nontheist the point that it is meaningless to speak of God as a *logically* necessary Being. But the nontheist has not proven that any contradiction has been shown regarding the meaningfulness of an *actually* necessary Being. The only way to understand "necessary Being" as contradictory is to view it as self-caused rather than as un-caused. Furthermore, if the above theistic argument is valid, then it is undeniably true that an actually necessary ground of the whole contingent is not only meaningful and possible but it is actually necessary. For an actual effect demands an actual cause, and a contingent being demands a necessary Being to ground it. Therefore, it follows that the actual contingent world demands an actually necessary Being as its cause.

Nontheists sometimes claim that the terms *necessary Being* and *uncaused Cause* are purely negative or vacuous concepts devoid of all positive meaning. This objection is clearly not valid. There is a negative element in the concept but it is not entirely negative. God is *not* finite; this is the negative element. But God is a Cause whose essence is pure actuality, knowing, good, and so on; these are all positive concepts. That is, our positive knowledge of the term *God* is provided by the similarity he bears to all perfections in the created being by way of the causal connection. However, since God is a *not*-finite (i.e., infinite) kind of cause, knower, good, and so on, then these positive attributes must be affirmed of God in an infinite or unlimited manner (see p. 247 above). Thus, there is both positive content in our understanding of God and a negative removal of all limitation in the affirmations about his essense.[22]

Finally, it is self-defeating to deny any meaning to the term *God*. The proposition "God does not exist" is either meaningless (since we do

---

22. For further discussion on the meaningfulness of the positive attributes of God, see chap. 12 of my *Philosophy of Religion*.

not know what "God" means in the statement) or else it is self-defeating, because it supposes that we do know what "God" means in the very statement affirming that we do not know what "God" means.[23] Hence, either the nontheist must show that "God" is a contradictory concept such as "square circles" or else no meaningful statement can be made denying the possibility that the concept "God" can be meaningful. But if God is conceived as an "un-caused" Being there is no contradiction in the concept. For self-caused, caused, and uncaused are logically exclusive categories; there are no other possibilities. But it would be contradictory to view God as "caused by another," since he is the *first* cause and first causes have no causes before or behind them. And it is contradictory to view God as "self-caused," for no being can be ontologically prior to itself. Therefore, the only remaining view (viz., God is "un-caused") must be noncontradictory, since the categories of self-caused, caused, and un-caused are logically exhaustive of reality, and it is impossible for *all* views about reality to be contradictory (see Chapter 1). At least one position about reality must be possible, for the affirmation that no position about reality is possible is self-destructive (since it too is a position about reality). In other words, logic does apply to reality. Any meaningful denial of the law of noncontradiction of reality is itself a noncontradictory statement about reality. But if it is impossible to deny that reality is noncontradictory, then whenever all other logically possible views about reality turn out to be impossible, the only remaining view cannot be logically contradictory. Therefore, God as an uncaused being cannot be a logically contradictory concept.

f. The Contingency-Necessity or Act-Potency Models Are Not Arbitrary

Sometimes nontheists contend that it is arbitrary or a loaded way of speaking of the world that leans in favor of theism.[24] This criticism is clearly unfounded. Reality must be viewed in terms of the possible, the impossible, or the necessary; there are no other logical possibilities. These are logically exhaustive ways to speak of reality and it is far from arbitrary to speak of reality in logically exhaustive categories, especially since logic is applicable to reality. Likewise, to speak of the world and God as either caused, self-caused, or uncaused is not arbitrary; again, there are no other logical possibilities. Therefore, to base a metaphysical view on what includes all the comprehensive possibilities about reality and to eliminate some as actually impossible, and to establish the remaining one as actually necessary, is far from an arbitrary imposition of some so-called loaded model on reality.

---

23. St. Anselm made this point in his reply to Gaunilon. See *St. Anselm: Basic Writings,* "I Reply to Gaunilon," p. 153 f.
24. See Milton K. Munitz, *The Mystery of Existence,* pp. 103-25.

### g. Other Objections to Theism Are Faulty

There are, of course, other objections to theism. But these too are unjustified as applied to the above argument. (1) It is not a God of pure reason who is disassociated from the *God of revelation,* for they are one and the same (as was shown on p. 250). (2) Neither is it *religiously insignificant,* for it is the God who is worthy of worship that is concluded from the argument (see p. 249). (3) Nor is it true that we cannot know anything about reality, for *agnosticism* involves the self-defeating claim that one *knows* enough about reality that he can affirm that one cannot know anything about reality (see Chapter 1). (4) Finally, it is not *irrelevant* if God exists. For if there is a God with whom we have to do, we cannot say in sobriety "so what?" For if God exists, either one must choose to say "Thy will be done" or listen to God say to him, "thy will be done." This will make a real and abiding difference in both the quality and meaning of one's life. Indeed, if Christian theism is correct, it will make an eternal difference.

## Summary and Conclusion

We offer the claim that theism is the only adequate world view. All others are self-defeating or actually unaffirmable. Only theism is actually undeniable. It offers an argument with undeniable premises that leads inescapably to the existence of an infinitely perfect and powerful Being beyond this world who is the current sustaining cause of all finite, changing, and contingent beings.

Most criticisms of theism miss the significance of this argument based on existential causality and are directed toward invalid a priori arguments, such as the ontological argument, or toward insufficient a posteriori arguments that either assume an unjustified causal premise (as the teleological and moral arguments), or else are based on a rationally unjustifiable form of the principle of sufficient reason. In this sense neither a priori nor a posteriori proofs for God's existence are rationally inescapable.

There is however a valid argument that combines both the a priori self-evident principle of existential causality and the undeniable a posteriori fact that something exists (e.g., I exist).[25] The criticisms of this argument are insufficient. Theism has found a firm ground in existence for the conclusion that God exists. This is a theistic universe.

## SELECT READINGS FOR CHAPTER THIRTEEN

**Exposition of Theism**

Clarke, Samuel. *The Works of Samuel Clarke.*

---

25. Some view this kind of argument as a transcendental argument. If so, positing God is more than a rational presupposition; it is an undeniably necessary reality condition for all contingent existence.

Farrer, Austin. *Finite and the Infinite*.
Garrigou-Lagrange, Reginald. *God: His Existence and His Nature*.
Geisler, Norman. *Philosophy of Religion*.
Grisez, Germain. *Beyond the New Theism*.
Hackett, Stuart. *The Resurrection of Theism,* pt. III.
Mascal, Eric. *He Who Is*.
Owen, H. P. *The Christian Knowledge of God*.
Reichenbach, Bruce. *The Cosmological Argument*.
Rowe, William. *The Cosmological Argument*.
Tennant, F. R. *Philosophical Theology*.
Thomas Aquinas. *On Being and Essence*.
————. *Summa Theologica* I, 2, 3; I, 3, 4.

## Evaluation of Theism

Flew, Antony (ed.). *New Essays in Philosophical Theology*.
Hume, David. *Dialogues Concerning Natural Religion*.
Kant, Immanuel. *Critique of Pure Reason*.
Munitz, Milton. *The Mystery of Existence*.
Nielsen, Kai. *Contemporary Critiques of Religion*.
Penelhum, Terence. *Religion and Rationality*.
Russell, Bertrand. *Why I Am Not a Christian*.

# Part
# THREE

## Christian

## Apologetics

Naturalism and the Supernatural
Objectivism and History
The Historical Reliability of the
    New Testament
The Deity and Authority of
    Jesus Christ
The Inspiration and Authority of
    the Bible

# Chapter 14

# Naturalism and the Supernatural

In Part One the various types of apologetic systems were discussed. The conclusion was twofold: first, the only adequate test for the truth of a world view is the principle of actual undeniability. Part Two followed with a survey of the major world views and concluded that only theism is affirmable and is based on undeniable premises; all other positions are self-defeating. Now in this final section we will argue for the truth of Christian theism vis-à-vis the other possibilities within a theistic universe. That is, there are several types of theism (Islam, Christianity, and Judaism, e.g.); and we must now discuss how to choose between these.

The decision *among* the truth claims of various world views (as pantheism, atheism, and theism) could not be to remain agnostic, for this position falsifies itself by claiming that we know we cannot know anything about reality (Chapter 1). Neither can it be based on rationalism, because there were no rationally inescapable arguments and the law of non-contradiction is only a test for falsity but not a test for truth (Chapter 2). Neither could that decision be based simply on fideistic belief nor on a claim to divine revelation, since that simply begs the question and is a claim open equally to all conflicting systems (Chapter 3). Furthermore, the conflicting truth claims among the various world views could not be adjudicated by an appeal to bare facts since all facts gain their meaning in the context of the world view. Hence, it begs the question to use a fact as interpreted by a given world view as an evidence for the truth of that world view. That same fact as interpreted by another world view would be an evidence for the truth of that other world view, and so on (Chapter 5). The same problems are implicit within experientialism

(Chapter 4), and pragmatism is simply an experientialism with reference to future experience (Chapter 6). Finally, no form of combinationalism is a sufficient test for the truth of a world view because opposing views can fare equally well using the combinational method. Simply adding inadequate tests for truth does not equal an adequate one (Chapter 7). The only adequate test for a world view is what is actually undeniable. For what is unaffirmable is false and what is undeniable is true (Chapter 9).

However, once we have decided *among* the conflicting world views, we are faced with a quite different question as to how to decide conflicting truth claims *within* an overall world view. The answer to this latter question will be found in a different test for truth. Within a world view or system, truth must always be decided on the basis of *systematic consistency* (i.e., combinationalism). Whatever explains *most* facts (comprehensiveness), in the *best* fashion (adequacy), in a *noncontradictory* way (consistency), and in a manner that *fits* with the overall system (coherence) will be true.[1]

It is the claim of Part Three in this book that Christianity is the most systematically consistent of the theistic world views; that is, that Christianity is true. Of course, systematic consistency is not a knock-down argument; its conclusions are not incorrigible. The argument for the truth of Christianity, then, will not be based on undeniability as was the argument for theism. Rather, it will be based on a degree of probability. Further, it will be open to both verification and falsification. That is, if it could be shown that another form of theism had a better explanation for more facts, and so on, then this other form of theism should be accepted as true. On the other hand, if the Christian interpretation of the facts of our world is the most systematically consistent, then it ought to be accepted as true. For a further elaboration of what is meant by systematic consistency, a review should be made of the positions of Ferré and Carnell in Chapter 7 above.

The first step in establishing the truth of the Christian interpretation of the facts of history is a discussion of the possibility of supernatural events. Historical Christianity is inseparable from claims of the miraculous. Indeed, the central premise in the Christian apologetic is the miraculous and historical incarnation of God in Jesus of Nazareth. The argument takes on the following form:

(1) Undeniability is the only adequate test for the truth of a world view (Chapters 1-9).

(2) Theism is the only world view that meets the test of undeniability (Chapters 10-13).

(3) Therefore, theism is true.

---

1. In this context the work of Edward J. Carnell is most helpful. See *Introduction to Christian Apologetics,* chaps. 3, 6.

(4)  In a theistic universe miracles are possible (Chapter 14).

(5)  Historical events are knowable in a theistic universe (Chapter 15).

(6)  Systematic consistency is the test for the truth of claims *within* a world view (see Chapter 7).

(7)  The claim that Christ's coming was a miracle is the most systematically consistent position (Chapter 16).

(8)  Therefore, it is true that Christ's coming was a miracle.

(9)  The claim that Christ is God is the most systematically consistent view (Chapter 17).

(10)  Therefore, Christ is God.

(11)  Christ verified that the Bible is the Word of God (Chapter 18).

## An Examination of the Claims of Naturalism Over Against Supernaturalism

If this is a theistic universe, it follows that miracles are possible. For if there is a God who can act in the world, then it is possible that there can be acts of God (i.e., miracles). Since we have already established on reasonable grounds that God exists (Chapter 13), the possibility of miracles follows naturally. In short, the objections to miracles are really at root objections to the existence of a theistic God. This fact notwithstanding, the persistent attacks of naturalism and antisupernaturalism must be answered. The discussion that follows will be an attempt to both understand and refute the claims that miracles are impossible in principle and in practice. This refutation is necessary for two reasons: first, if the Christian view can be shown to be contradictory, then it cannot be held to be true. Second, the Christian must establish the possibility of miracles, or else his case for the truth of Christianity, based on the unique and confirming miracles of Christ, will fail.

### Hume: Miracles Are a Violation of the Laws of Nature

The basic objections to miracles emanate from the pen of David Hume.[2] The first objection of Hume is based on the nature of natural law. According to Hume the laws of nature are based on the highest degree of probability. Even though one cannot be absolutely certain about any matter of fact, nonetheless, if an event occurs over and over again with no known exception, we may have a kind of practical certainty about it. Hume is even willing to use the word "proof" of events in this category. By "proof" he means something known from experience that is so probable that it leaves no room for doubt, although it is always logically possible that one is wrong about it. With this in mind Hume's argument against miracles may be summarized as follows:

2.  David Hume, *Enquiry Concerning Human Understanding*, sec. X, pt. I.

(1) A miracle by definition is a violation of (or exception to) a law of nature;

(2) But the laws of nature are built upon the highest degree of probability;

(3) Hence, a miracle by definition (as an exception) is based on the lowest degree of probability;

(4) Now the wise man should always base his belief on the highest degree of probability;

(5) Therefore, the wise man should never believe in miracles.

Let us examine Hume's argument in more detail. The first premise could be defended as follows: If a miracle is an event within the purview of natural law, then it would not be a miracle but simply an unusual natural happening. Hence, to sustain the claim that miracles are really super-natural, they must be viewed as exceptions to natural law. If this is what Hume means by "violation" then there is no objection to this premise. However, if "violation" means breaking some inviolable law on which the natural order depends, then the theist would object that "violation" begs the question by defining miracles as impossible.

First, a theist would want to examine more carefully what is meant by "natural law." If it is meant in the *prescriptive* sense as a kind of immutable way things *must* operate, then the possibility of miracles is already precluded in the question-begging definition. If, on the other hand, "natural law" is meant only as a *description* of the way things *do* happen, then the theist can readily agree. Second, it does not necessarily follow that an unusual natural event rules out the possibility of the miraculous. The unusual natural process may be the means by which God performs what as a total event is miraculous. Science may be able to describe the process but not able to explain the total meaning of the product of that process in completely naturalistic terms.

Certainly the theist does not want to contest Hume's second and third premises. A miracle would not even be possible unless there was a regular established pattern of events to which it was the exception. Whatever else is meant by natural law, it is minimal to the definition to understand that a miracle is a highly unusual event. If it happened in a regular and predictable way, then it would no longer qualify as a miracle. Hence, the theist must agree with Hume that by their very nature, natural events must be based on high probability and miracles must be highly exceptional.

Hume's fourth premise is the one with which the theist must disagree. Why should a wise (critical, thinking) man always adjust his belief to the highest degree of probability based on *past* experience? Even Hume argued that we cannot be sure the sun will rise tomorrow simply because it has always risen in the past. There is no necessary connection between the past and the present, as Hume would be the first to admit.[3] That being the case, then there is no logical way that Hume can exclude the possibility of a miracle occurring today as an exception to the universally established pattern of the past. In contradistinction to Hume, we would argue that the wise (critical, thinking) man is the one who judges the truth or falsity of a miracle on the basis of the available *evidence* for its happening. However great the odds against something happening, it is always possible that it *will* happen anyway. This is true of both factual and theoretical probability. As nontheists are the first to point out in criticizing the teleological argument, the odds against the universe happening by chance may be great; but it still could have happened by chance. The odds of rolling three dice and getting 3 sixes are $1/216$, but a person could get them on the first toss.

Allowing theoretical mathematical probability to outweigh the actual evidence of the present is a very unwise thing to do. The chances for one person being dealt a perfect hand of bridge are computed at 1 in 635,-013,559,600. Now a wise man ought not allow those mathematical odds against its happening to take precedence over the testimony of four sane, sober, honest, and intelligent eyewitnesses who saw the perfect hand. In like manner the wise man does not allow antecedent regularity in nature to outweigh consequent evidence for an irregular event. The probability based on the past should never take precedence over the evidence of the present.

By defining a wise man as one who would always take past regularity over the evidence for a violation of that pattern in the present, Hume has in effect set up an invincible naturalism. He has said that in practice he would never allow an exception to the laws of nature. Hence, on this account, natural law has become practically inviolable. But this begs the whole question, since it assumes miracles will never happen in order to prove that they never occur. Such is the circular nature of a strict naturalism. Without assuming the practical impossibility of belief in miracles, Hume's argument against the possibility of miracles fails.

## Antony Flew: Unrepeatability of Miracles Shows Their Impossibility

Hume's argument has been updated by Antony Flew.[4] It takes the following form:

(1)  Miracles are by nature particular and unrepeatable events.

(2)  Scientific laws by nature describe general and repeatable events.

(3)  But the evidence for the repeatable and general is always greater than the evidence for particular and unrepeatable events.

---

3. Hume, *Enquiry Concerning Human Understanding.*
4. See Antony Flew, "Miracles," in *Encyclopedia of Philosophy,* Paul Edwards, ed., vol. 5, pp. 346-53.

268 / CHRISTIAN APOLOGETICS

(4) And the scientific or critical man will never base his belief on the lesser or weaker evidence.

(5) Therefore, the critical man will never believe in miracles.

Technically speaking, neither this nor Hume's argument rules out the *possibility* of miracles; they simply argue against their *believability*. Miracles are still possible even *if* the evidence for believing in them is weak. Nonetheless, the Christian theist wishes to challenge Flew's contention that the evidence for miracles will always be the weaker evidence.

First, let us examine the other premises. There is no reason why a theist could not accept the truth of the first two premises. For if miracles were not particular and unrepeatable by natural means, then they would not be miracles. Once one can control or repeat an event over and over it becomes a general event. And once it is repeatable and general it is indistinguishable from a natural event. Hence, in order for miracles to maintain distinguishability from natural events they must be particular and unrepeatable in the natural course of events.

Properly understood, the Christian theist may accept the truth of the fourth premise. Certainly the Christian, too, should always accept the position based on the stronger evidence. This is precisely what systematic consistency means as a test for truth. The view that best explains the most evidence in a consistent and coherent way is held to be true; the opposing views are believed to be false.

Christian theism challenges the third premise of Flew's naturalism, which asserts that the evidence for the repeatable and general is always greater than that for the particular and unrepeatable. We may reply to Flew in two ways: first, by pointing out his unfalsifiable naturalistic assumption. It begs the question to assume in advance of looking at the facts that the evidence will always be greater against miracles than for it. Indeed, Flew of all people should not be making such an unfalsifiable assertion. It was he who put the challenge to theism to allow something that could actually falsify theism as a ground for the meaningfulness of the theistic position. He asked, "What would have to occur or to have occurred to constitute for you a disproof . . . [of] the existence of God?"[5] If the believer will not allow anything to count *against* his belief in God, charged Flew, then neither may he allow anything to count *for* it. Now we would like to ask Mr. Flew the same thing with respect to his unfalsifiable naturalistic presupposition, namely, how can your naturalism be falsified?

Flew has entertained the question and his answer is insufficient. He claims that his position is falsifiable in principle but not in practice. He argues that the possibility of miracles is a matter of evidence and not

5. Flew, "Theology and Falsification," in *New Essays in Philosophical Theology*, Antony Flew, ed., p. 99.

simply of dogmatism, but that the evidence is always against miracles happening since by nature they are particular and unrepeatable, as opposed to a natural event which is general and repeatable. The evidence for the latter is always stronger because, argued Flew, it can be tested any time and any place. A miracle, on the other hand, cannot be tested so easily. Further, even if the evidence for an event contrary to the laws of nature did occur, "that event could now no longer be described as truly miraculous."[6] Now this latter comment, even more so than the former, reveals Flew's invincible naturalistic bias. The argument implied may be put this way:

(1)  Whatever happens in the natural world is a natural event.

(2)  Once an alleged miracle occurs in the natural world it is a natural event.

(3)  Hence, once an alleged miracle occurs it is *ipso facto* a natural event.

In short, this argument reduces to "everything that happens *in* the natural world is caused *by* the natural world." But this clearly begs the question; for if there are some events caused from *beyond* the world, they will nevertheless have to occur *in* the world in order for us to experience them. It means that if one could show convincing evidence that the resurrection of Christ actually occurred in the space-time world, then the naturalist would simply shrug his shoulder and say, "Well, now we know that resurrections are not miraculous!" Whether unfalsifiable in principle or in practice makes no difference, his naturalistic unbelief is invincible. Flew has what Hare called a "blik."[7] No amount of evidence of actual happenings will ever convince him that a miracle has indeed occurred. Whenever what was previously believed to be impossible comes to pass, the naturalist promptly concludes it was not miraculous after all. Why cannot the theist argue similarly that in principle the existence of God can be falsified but in actual practice it cannot? Why cannot the theist insist in like manner that in principle some events may be caused by nature but that in actual practice once an event occurs in the world (God's world) it is *ipso facto* a God-caused event? What right does a naturalist have to claim all events as naturally caused any more than a theist has to claim that all events are divinely caused (some in a *regular* way and some on *special* occasions)? If one position can beg the question, then the other should have the same privilege. At any rate, Flew's argument is an almost classic case of an unfalsifiable position which in the process of justification begs the whole question in favor of naturalism.

---

6. See Flew, "Miracles," *Encyclopedia*, p. 352.
7. See R. M. Hare, "Theology and Falsification," in *New Essays in Philosophical Theology*, Antony Flew, ed., p. 100.

## The Descriptive Nature of Natural Law Eliminates Miracles

Since Hume's time the discussion on miracles has taken on some modern sophistication. The following argument against miracles from the descriptive nature of scientific law is an example of this point.[8] The argument can be summarized like this:

(1) Scientific laws are merely descriptions of events and not prescriptive norms.

(2) But descriptions cannot be violated; they can merely be revised.

(3) However, a miracle by nature must be a violation of a law of nature.

(4) Therefore, miracles by nature cannot occur.

The Christian theist has no need to disagree with the first premise. Indeed, viewing natural laws as descriptive is both an answer to Hume's first objection and the way to show that miracles are possible in an "open universe." For a closed system of prescriptive norms presents a much more formidable obstacle to showing that exceptions occur. But if "natural law" is nothing but an open system of human description, based on statistical probability, then a miraculous exception to this is not really violating any immutable law of the universe.

In support of the second premise the antisupernaturalist urges the following argument. Scientific descriptions are like maps; namely, when they are found to be inaccurate one does not violate the map but simply revises it. If the landscape is found not to conform to a topographical map, what one does is draw a more accurate map. Nothing has been violated; the description is simply changed to conform to reality. In like manner, the naturalist argues, once a new and unusual event is known to have occurred we do not scream "miracle!" The scientific mind simply finds ways to include this event in a broader, more accurate description of the world in which this event is known to have occurred. Hence, the very descriptive nature of scientific law rules out the miraculous; for any exception or inaccuracy in previous laws or "maps" is simply a reason to revise the map to include the so-called miraculous event under the overall natural umbrella.

It is precisely at this point that the theist objects. For this argument, too, is based on the unjustified presupposition that "whatever happens *in* nature is caused *by* nature."[9] It assumes that all events in the world are natural events. Of course if this is so, then miraculous events in the world are impossible.

8. Flew, "Miracles," *Encyclopedia,* p. 349.

9. As a matter of fact, a naturalist would be hard pressed to prove that any event in nature is caused by natural law. If "laws" are merely descriptions then laws can't cause anything any more than arithmetic causes ten pennies in one's pocket because he can add up the number accurately. See C. S. Lewis, *God in the Dock,* p. 77.

Further, there is confusion on the use of the word *violate*. A miracle would "violate" a previous description only in the sense that the law as a general description did not apply in this particular case. For example, if a man were found walking on water this would be a "violation" of the general principle that men cannot walk on water. Perhaps "violation" is too technical a term and we should speak rather of the general rule and the particular exception, of the regular and the irregular, or of the usual and the unusual. At any rate, the naturalist makes an unjustified jump from "violation" to the need for "revision." Why revise the topographical map unless change in the landscape can be repeatedly observed? Would the map need revision if a mountain suddenly appeared, was verified, and then disappeared again? Why revise the belief that one's wife loves him because of a single contrary outburst of anger? Revision is only necessary when there is (or can be) a repetition of the observation. Not all exceptions call for revision. Even scientists do not revise their theories because of unexplainable and unrepeated anomalies. If anomalous situations do not demand a new law then neither do supernatural occurrences. For in neither case does one have a natural law *(nomos)* to explain the event.

## Guy Robinson: Nature of the Scientific Method Eliminates Miracles

The contemporary scientific naturalist sometimes replies to the above solution with the argument that the scientific method as such eliminates belief in the miraculous.[10] The argument runs like this:

(1) Science qua science must assume that all events are naturally explainable.

(2) But if all events are scientifically explainable then no events are supernatural or miraculous.

(3) Therefore, science as science eliminates the supernatural.

The Christian theist may object to both premises of this argument. The naturalist defends the first premise by pointing out that if a scientist gave up looking for an explanation to an event he would be giving up science as such. Science is predicated on the belief that events have natural explanations, and to forfeit this would be to forsake the cause of science. Exceptions never bring science to a screeching halt. On the contrary, exceptions (whether they claim to be miraculous or not) are goads to more research. For an exception is often the tip that the present law is inadequate. The scientist as scientist must assume there are natural explanations. So goes the argument of scientific naturalism.

As sound as this argument may appear, there is within it a subtle but essential naturalistic presupposition. Actually there is no reason why science *must* assume naturalism. It is more scientific to recognize the limits of the scientific domain. Scientific methodology as such should not

10. Guy Robinson, "Miracles," in *Ratio* 9 (December 1967), pp. 155-66.

make metaphysical claims. It may be that there is *not* a naturalistic explanation for every event. In this case it is not wise to seek explanations where none can be found. Simply to *assume,* as the argument does, that there must be a naturalistic explanation for every event begs the whole question in favor of naturalism. Furthermore, the theist may make a distinction between a pragmatic working assumption and a metaphysical or ontological presupposition. Why could not the theist agree as a matter of working procedure to push the scientific method as far as it will go? Why could he not continue to *look* for a natural explanation—not because he believes there is one, but in order to show that it is highly unlikely that one will ever be found? For example, a Christian in science could try to discover how to make living things from nonliving things. This he could do not because he will thereby show that the original formation of life was a natural event, but, on the contrary, that in the process of discovering how life was formed in the beginning he might provide scientific evidence that life did not occur spontaneously or accidentally.

In any event, adopting the working procedure of always looking for a natural explanation need not be extended into a rigid naturalistic metaphysical position that there are no nonnatural explanations. The scientific frame of mind should not *legislate* what kind of explanations there can be. Rather, it should *look* for the best explanation possible. And if the best explanation is a supernatural one, then it would be entirely unreasonable to reject it on the grounds of the practical benefits that come from adopting a scientific working procedure that continues to look for natural explanations. Science can be adopted as a *practical* procedure without buying into naturalism as a *metaphysical* view.

In short, this objection to miracles confuses science and naturalism. It assumes that one cannot be a scientist without being a naturalist. But this begs the question as to the meaning of "science." Science as such is not a metaphysic but a methodology. Science as science should be neutral to metaphysical presuppositions. There is no necessity flowing from the scientific method as such that forces one to adopt a naturalistic world view.

The Christian theist will object to the second premise of Robinson's argument as well. It may be that the same events have both scientific and theological explanations. Even if science could explain *how* an event occurred, it does not follow that it can explain *why* it occurred or even why it occurred *when* it occurred. Showing that there was a strong wind blowing all night on the Red Sea does not thereby explain why this wind blew precisely *when* it did in order to enable Israel to escape from Egypt (see Exod. 12). Even if science can reduplicate in a laboratory the means of producing certain events that have happened only rarely in history (say, a virgin birth), it does not follow that the occurrence of such an event in history was not a miraculous event. There is no reason why God cannot use some natural processes in producing a supernatural event.[11] Indeed, in the case of Biblical miracles there is usually, if not always, a natural process employed as part of the miraculous event. The virgin birth employed the natural process of pregnancy along with the unusual occurrence of having no male sperm implantation. Jesus is not represented as creating the loaves and fishes to feed the multitude; he simply multiplied some natural loaves that already existed.

Further, one has no right to claim that miracles cannot happen unless he can show that the scientific explanation is the *only* explanation of the event. For there may be multileveled explanations of the same event—one in the natural world and another in a spiritual world. The only way one can eliminate the possibility of there being a spiritual world or spiritual explanation is to offer some disproof of God. But such attempted disproofs have already been examined and found self-defeating (see Chapter 12). And apart from disproving God, there is no way to eliminate the possibility that God may be using exceptional natural events in order to perform supernatural acts.

Finally, science has no right to claim an event is natural simply because it can describe the *how*, or the process, by which it occurred. An event does not qualify as "natural" unless it can be repeated, predicted, or controlled by scientific means. Description of a process is not the guarantee that an event is natural. The scientist may be merely describing the supernatural process by which God caused the event. Only if the scientist gains control of the process so that he can repeat it regularly and predictably would he have the right to claim it as a natural event. And even then the theist may claim that in some cases events whose process can be explained naturally are not purely natural events. There may be other aspects of the event such as its timing, purpose, or results that are best explained supernaturally. In any event, the scientific method in no way demands a naturalistic explanation.

## Alastair McKinnon: Miracles Are Impossible in the Natural Course of Events

The extent to which the naturalistic bias has penetrated modern thought is very evident in the following argument against miracles:[12]

(1) A natural happening is what occurs in the actual course of events.

(2) A miracle by definition would be contrary to the actual course of events.

(3) But nothing can be contrary to the actual course of events; what is, is.

11. See C. S. Lewis, *Miracles,* p. 61.
12. Alastair McKinnon, " 'Miracle' and 'Paradox' " in *American Philosophical Quarterly* 4 (October 1967), pp. 308-14.

(4) Therefore, miracles cannot occur.

In support of the first premise the naturalist could argue that all natural events must occur in the actual course of events in the natural world. To this the theist need not object. However, the converse of this is not true, namely, that everything that happens in the natural world is *ipso facto* a natural event. "All events that are natural occur in the natural world" cannot be logically converted into "all events that occur in the natural world are natural events." Again, this would beg the whole question.

Furthermore, the Christian theist would definitely object to the naturalistic understanding of the second premise. A miracle is not "contrary" to the natural course of events in the sense that it cannot happen *within* a natural sequence but simply because it cannot be explained as a *result* of the natural sequence. Not everything that occurs *in* a natural sequence is a necessary part *of* that natural order. Human freedom can occur within a natural order without being a necessary part of that order. For example, I can choose to jump out of the way of a speeding car without acting contrary to (or violating) any physical law. Likewise, in the moral realm I may choose *not* to do what comes naturally. I may, for example, choose not to retaliate against one who injures me—a natural reaction—without acting contrary to anything in the actual course of events. In like manner miracles can happen *within* the natural order without being a necessary part *of* that natural order.

Finally, the Christian theist must scrutinize the use of the third premise as well. Of course, what is, is. This is a tautology. But in the sense in which the naturalist intends this, it is a naturalistic truism that begs the whole question. He must mean it in the sense that whatever happens in the actual course of events is *ipso facto* not a miracle. But if we already know in advance that whenever anything occurs that is proof positive that it is not a miracle, then it follows that we can forever give up looking for any miracle to occur. Here again, the antisupernaturalist prejudice is *legislating* against the possibility of miracles; it is not *looking* at the evidence for or against an actual event being a miracle. "What is, is; nothing happens *contrary* to the actual course of events." In one sense this is true. But it is also true that a miracle could occur *within* the natural course of events. It may be that one or more of the events in the midst of the ongoing process of history have been supernatural events. That is, they may have been events that occurred *in* nature but were neither caused *by* nature nor *contrary* to nature.

The antisupernaturalist must do more than point to the actual happening and claim its occurrence as proof positive that it is not a miracle. The *actual* is not automatically the *natural*. What actually occurs may just as well be a *supernatural* event. What the naturalist must do in order to prove that an actual event is a natural event is to show that the event is naturally connected with antecedent and consequent events. Or, at least he must show that the event is part of a natural chain of events that are *repeatable* and *predictable*. For unless the event fits into a general and regular pattern on which predictions can be made, the naturalist has no right claiming that it is an event explainable by natural law. Naturalism grossly begs the question in its own favor by claiming that everything that does happen is unquestioned proof that it was not miraculous.

## Hume's Other Objections to Miracles

David Hume offered two other objections against miracles.[13] The first is based on the self-canceling nature of conflicting miracle claims, and the second is based on the untrustworthiness of the testimony in favor of a miracle. The first objection may be stated like this:

(1) No truth claim can be supported by miracles if any contrary truth claim is also supported by like miracles; contrary truth claims are mutually self-canceling.

(2) But all religious systems claim miracles in support of their truth claim.

(3) Therefore, no miracles can be used in support of a religious truth claim.

The Christian theist need not object to the first premise. It is not only true, but later it will be helpful to Christianity. In the final analysis it will serve to eliminate all truth claims based on like "miracles." Contraries are indeed mutually self-canceling when they are each supported by the same kind of "evidence." Equipollence of evidence does lead to skepticism. If these claims are all based on the same kind of evidence, no one of these claims has any more right to truth than the others. As a matter of fact, this situation can lead to a strong argument in favor of Christianity as follows:

(1) All theistic truth claims supported by *like* "miracles" are mutually self-canceling; that is, none of them can lay rightful claim to truth.

(2) But Christianity alone is supported by unique miraculous events.

(3) Therefore, Christianity alone can lay rightful claim to truth.

It is not our purpose here to support the minor premise; this will be done later (in Chapters 15-17). It is sufficient to point out here that *if* evidence can be provided that Christianity has unique and supporting miracles the like of which are not found in any other theistic system, then Hume's argument does not apply against the Christian truth claims. At least the question of miracles is open to factual verification. Hume's objection is not only unsuccessful but it can be turned into a proof for the uniqueness of the Christian truth claim. For *if* all other religious claims

13. Hume, *Enquiry*, sec. X, pt. II.

are supported by like "miracles" of a self-canceling nature and if only Christianity has a unique miraculous support, then only Christianity is verified as true. At least at this point we may conclude that it is *possible* that unique miraculous events are supportive of the truth of Christianity vis-à-vis other positions.

Hume's second argument against miracles is based on the untrustworthy nature of eyewitnesses. It runs like this:

(1)   No miracle can be established without sufficient evidence in its favor.

(2)   Sufficient evidence must include a sufficient number of witnesses, with sufficient education and with unquestioned integrity.

(3)   But there never has been sufficient evidence to support the claim that any miraculous event has occurred.

(4)   Therefore, no miracle has ever been established.

The merit of this argument is that it is de facto and not de jure; that is, it is open to factual confirmation or disconfirmation. Again, not only is the major premise true, but it is also to the advantage of Christian theism to acknowledge the truth of that premise. For unless there is sufficient evidence for miraculous truth claims, then many conflicting truth claims could be established. But if sufficient evidence is demanded, then it narrows down considerably the claimants to truth.

Our objection is to the second step in the argument. Hume must go in one of two directions in supporting the claim that there never has been "sufficient" evidence. Either he may make the definition of sufficient evidence so narrow that practically nothing historical could be believed including the existence of Napoleon or maybe even the existence of Hume himself. Or else he may make a sensible definition of what "sufficient" evidence would be and thereby open the door for the substantial historical evidence in favor of the eyewitnesses of the resurrection of Christ (see Chapter 16). In any event, Hume's argument does not eliminate the possibility of miracles, which is all we are concerned with at this point.

## Some Conclusions About the Natural and the Supernatural

With the preceding discussion in mind, we are now in a position to draw certain conclusions regarding the nature of miracles. First, we will consider the difference between what may be two different kinds of miraculous events.

### The Difference Between First and Second Class Miracles

Antony Flew offered an objection to miracles that forces a clarification within the Christian theistic position.[14] His argument may be summarized as follows:

(1) A miracle must be identifiable before it can be used as evidence.

(2) Now there are only two ways to identify (or define) a miracle:
    a. As an unusual event within nature, or—
    b. As an exception to nature.

(3) But an unusual event within nature is not a miracle; it is simply a rare but natural event.

(4) And there is no natural way to know that an exception to nature has occurred.

(5) Therefore, there is no way to identify (or define) a miracle.

(6) But what is unidentifiable has no evidential value.

(7) Therefore, no miracle can have any evidential value.

There are two responses to this from a theistic point of view. First, even as an unusual event within nature a miracle can have evidential value. For simply explaining *how* something occurred does not thereby explain *why* it happened nor why it happened *when* it happened. Even unusual natural events can have evidential value when viewed in their total context. It may be that some things are so highly unusual and co-incidental that, when viewed in connection with the moral or theological context in which they occurred, the label "miracle" is the most appropriate one for the happening. Let us call this kind of supernaturally guided event a *second class miracle,* that is, one whose natural *process* can be described scientifically (and perhaps even reduplicated by humanly controlled natural means) but whose end *product* in the total picture is best explained by invoking the supernatural. Providing that the theist can offer some good reasons (by virtue of the moral or theological context of the event) for not accepting a purely natural explanation, then there is no reason to rule out the evidential value of such unusual natural events.

Second, the theist may argue for the possibility of what may be called *first class miracles* by taking Flew's other definition of a miracle, namely, an exception to the natural process. How would one know an exception to the natural process has occurred? Of course he could not know it on any supernatural grounds (such as that God told him or that the Bible says so, etc.) for this would beg the whole question. But what *natural* grounds could there be for identifying a *super*natural event? This question poses a problem that can only be answered by a defense of the possibility of a supernatural realm (e.g., God). If it is possible to argue *from* the natural world to something *beyond* the natural world (as was done in the case for theism, Chapter 13), then the problem is resolved. That is to say, if by examining nature we find that nature cannot

---

14. Flew, "Miracles," *Encyclopedia*, p. 348 f.

adequately explain its own existence, and if it becomes necessary to conclude that there is something (or, Someone) beyond nature, then the ontological ground is thereby established for making a distinction between the natural and the supernatural without begging the question.

The remaining question is this: What are the epistemological conditions by which one can distinguish a supernatural event *in* the natural world from an event *of* the natural world? The answer to this question emerges from an earlier discussion. We proposed that a natural event is one that occurs generally or regularly and that can be repeated or predicted by natural means. In order to even qualify as a first class supernatural event, on the other hand, an event must be one which does not generally or regularly occur in the natural course of events and which cannot be repeated or predicted by natural means. In addition to these minimal conditions, a miracle also possesses some moral or theological characteristics (see below). It suffices here to note that there are recognizable earmarks for the distinction of the miraculous from the natural.

There remains another problem to be discussed. If a first class miracle is one where the natural process is not known and, hence, cannot be repeated or predicted by natural means, then what if the natural means are subsequently discovered? Does this mean that future scientific research is a threat to the belief that some event is miraculous? How can one claim that there is any such thing as a first class miracle unless he knows for sure the process by which it occurred is not only undiscovered but also undiscoverable? For once the scientific *how* is known, then by definition it ceases to be a first class miracle.

The theist may make two responses to these questions. First, he may admit the possibility that the *modus operandi* of all miracles is discoverable by science. He may admit that science *can* know how virgin births and resurrections occur and that science may even be able to repeat the process. Even so, this admission amounts to no more than the acknowledging that all first class miracles may be reducible to second class miracles. So it would not destroy the miraculous altogether nor eliminate its evidential value to admit that science may one day discover how these miracles took place. Second, the theist may wish to make a distinction between what *can* happen by controlled repeating of scientific process and what *does* happen in the actual course of events without outside interference. The theist may claim that outside interference (by a mind) in the natural process (in order to bring about unusual results) is really an argument in favor of the miraculous. If nature left to itself *did not* (or could not) produce the unusual effect except by controlled interjection from an outside intelligence, then this may be precisely the case with a first class miracle. Perhaps a miracle is the interjection of factors into the natural process by an outside Mind (i.e., God) that produces the highly unusual results that would otherwise not have occurred. If this is so, then a theist may claim that there are first class miracles and that they are known by the fact that nature has not or does not produce them on its own without the intelligent manipulation of factors in the natural world. In this case only what nature can and does do generally or repeatedly without outside intelligent interference is known to be a natural event.[15] Therefore, anything that does not occur generally or repeatedly in the natural course of events *could* be a miraculous event. Whether it is a miracle or an anomaly will depend on the other distinguishable characteristics of a miracle to be discussed later. But even if there were no way to identify first class miracles on the basis of the distinction between what *does* happen in nature without the outside interference of mind and what *can* happen with such interference, nevertheless first class miracles are still possible on another ground. A theist might simply hold that a first class miracle is one where science has *not yet* shown (and may never show) the natural means of repeating it. If this is so, then a Christian might believe that the resurrection of Christ is a first class miracle which science does not as yet know how to repeat. The epistemological status of belief in this kind of first class miracle would be that it is a *thus-far unfalsified* belief. Taken one way, a first class miracle is that which *cannot* be produced by natural processes. Taken the other way, a first class miracle is what nature *does not* produce. In either case, miracles of both classes are possible; naturalism has failed to eliminate them.

## The Possibility of Miracles Follows from Theism

Actually there is a much simpler way to argue for the possibility of miracles than by way of the foregoing discussion. Miracles follow naturally from the nature of the theistic God. The argument takes the following shape:

(1)  An omnipotent, omniscient, and omnibenevolent theistic God exists.

(2)  Now an omnipotent intelligence can do anything that is possible.

(3)  Miracles are not impossibilities.

(4)  Therefore, miracles can occur.

The first premise has already been established (Chapter 13). The second premise follows from the nature of omnipotence. An omnipotent God is one who has enough power to do anything that is not either logically or actually impossible. The only limits on omnipotence are what is either logically or actually impossible. For example, an omni-

---

15.  See Lewis, *Miracles*, p. 58 f.

potent God cannot make square circles; this is *logically* impossible. Nor can an omnipotent God cease to be God; this is *actually* impossible.

The third premise can be established as follows: first, there is no logical contradiction in the concept of a miracle. A miracle is not an *anti*natural event; it is *super*natural. Only an antinatural event would be contradictory to nature. Hence, a miracle is not a logical contradiction. Or, to put it another way, in a theistic universe, where everything is dependent on God's continual sustaining causality, there is no contradiction in affirming that by "natural" we mean the way God operates *generally* and by "miracle" we mean the way he operates on *special* occasions. Conceived this way there is no logical contradiction in the concept of the miraculous. Modern scientific understanding of the universe as an "open system" of which laws are merely descriptions and not a "closed system" of immutable, prescriptive laws is certainly in accord with this conclusion.

Second, there is no *actual* contradiction or impossibility with some miracle(s) occurring. Some miracles may be actually impossible, for example, a miracle performed to counteract a miracle or event which God willed to perform. God cannot actually will to annul what he has willed to do. But there is no more contradiction involved in affirming that some natural events do not actually contradict some other natural events than to say that some miraculous events do not contradict some natural events. All such events are acts of God, and once it is granted that there are acts of God there is no actual contradiction in saying some acts (i.e., miracles) are performed only rarely and others are performed regularly. But if a miracle is neither a logical nor actual impossibility for a theistic God, then it follows that miracles are both logically and actually possible.

## The Distinguishing Earmarks of a Miracle

It is not enough to define a miracle as an exception to the general pattern of events. This characteristic merely indicates that the event is a nonnatural one; that is, it is not known to come under any scientific law. But there are at least two other possibilities within the category of non-natural events: anomalies and satanic signs. It is possible there are evil spirits in the universe and that they perform rare events which are not explainable by known scientific laws.

*Miracles vs. Satanic Signs.* First of all, let us distinguish a divine miracle from a satanic sign.[16] Granting the possibility of evil spiritual powers in the universe working in opposition to God, then whatever intervention they may be able to make in the natural world would be in accord with their purposes. Hence, satanic signs would, by their very

---

16. See Kurt Koch, *Between Christ and Satan,* p. 96 f.

nature, have the following characteristics: (1) They would not be associated with truth about God but with error; they would not be used to confirm truth but to confirm error. (2) Satanic signs would not bring about moral good but evil; they would not stimulate conduct in accord with God's will but in opposition to it. (3) Finally, satanic signs would not help fulfill God's purposes but would work to destroy them; they would not glorify God but would magnify evil men or the evil spirits behind them.

*Miracles vs. Magic.* What is commonly known as "magic," but which is really only trickery, is not miraculous at all. It is simply built on natural laws (such as "the hand is quicker than the eye") which can be repeated and predicted. That is, magic is under the control of man. Then too, magic as such does not bring glory to God nor moral good to man. Neither does magic have theological meaning. A magic trick is amoral and nontheological by nature. Magic does not bring glory to God but to the magician who performs it. It is man-centered not God-centered. There is nothing supernatural or anomalous about magic tricks; all the laws involved are natural and knowable. Of course, what is known as "black magic" is, for the Christian, another matter. It is not trickery by natural physical laws; rather, it involves spiritual forces which go beyond the normal happenings in the physical world. But ordinary magic is simply a natural phenomenon that is explainable or repeatable by natural means.

*Miracles vs. Anomalies.* An anomaly is also a nonnatural event in the sense that there is no *known* natural explanation for it. There is a natural explanation for it, but the explanation is not known. How then does an anomaly differ from a miracle? An anomaly is amoral and atheological. There are no truth claims associated with it nor moral consequences flowing from it. All it shares with a miracle is the fact that it is unusual and unrepeatable, or at least it is unrepeatable at the present by those to whom it is an anomaly. We may differentiate an anomaly from a miracle by the following illustration. If one were to observe a fish rise out of the water, hover for thirty seconds in midair and splash back into the pond, that would be an anomaly. There is no apparent or known scientific explanation as to how a wingless fish should seemingly defy the law of gravity. Furthermore, the event has no theological truth claims connected with it, nor any moral consequences following from it. On the other hand, if a man claiming to be a prophet of God challenges believers in idols to a duel in which, upon his prayer, fire comes from the sky and consumes soaking wet wood, this would be a miracle. This event is not only scientifically unusual but it is accompanied also by truth claims and has definite moral implications and consequences.

We may now summarize the characteristics of a miracle. (1) A miraculous event must be *nonnatural* or scientifically *unusual,* that is, an exception to the normal pattern of events. It may be unusual because natural events *rarely* turn up that way (called a second class miracle) or because they *never* turn out that way (called a first class miracle). They may never turn out in that unusual way either because they *cannot* (because the process cannot be understood or repeated by scientific means) or because they simply *will not* (because it takes outside interference of a mind manipulating natural processes in order to accomplish that kind of event). (2) A miracle entails some theological *truth claim*. Acts of God involve some truth about God. Signs come with sermons and miracles come with messages to interpret them. (3) A miracle must have a good *moral impact*. That is, it must not only help confirm some truth about God, but it must be fitting of the moral nature of God. Acts of God cannot be contrary to the attributes of God. (4) Miracles are not anti-natural. They *fit* into nature. They are exceptions but not contradictions; they suspend normal patterns but do not really violate or break natural processes. Even a miraculous virgin birth will be subject to the normal laws of pregnancy, and water turned to wine can still intoxicate.

In short, miracles get man's *gaze* because they are unusual; they present God's Word; they make some claim for *God;* they bring *glory* to God by manifesting his moral nature. Finally, miracles must bring *good* into the creation of God. Miracles *may* have the first named characteristic in common with satanic signs, magic, or anomalies; but the last named characteristics clearly distinguish miracles. Of all these, only a miracle *befits* God, *benefits* creation, and *fits* into the natural order without being a natural product of it.

## Summary and Conclusion

The arguments against miracles beg the question. They presuppose that miracles are impossible either in principle or in practice. Rather than *looking* at the evidence for or against miracles, they end up *legislating* in advance the impossibility of the miraculous. They say in effect: "whatever happens in the natural world is a natural event." But some things that happen *in* the natural world may have a supernatural origin. In point of fact, if there is a God who can act (viz., a theistic God), then acts of God (i.e., miracles) are automatically possible.

There is, of course, the problem of identifying a miracle. Here the theist may argue that a miracle is a *highly unusual* event within nature, either what rarely (second class miracles) or never (first class miracles) occurs by known natural causes. Further, a miracle is an event that is *morally* and *theologically* compatible with a theistic God. In short, a miracle as an act of God would be performed in confirmation of the truth and will of God. Whether or not a miracle has ever occurred cannot be settled by *philosophy* alone; that is a matter of *history*. It can be shown philosophically that miracles are possible, but whether or not miracles have actually happened can be known only experientially and historically. It is to this experiential and historical point we will turn our attention in the next chapters.

## SELECT READINGS FOR CHAPTER FOURTEEN

**Exposition of Miracles**

Aquinas, Thomas. *Summa Contra Gentiles* III, 98-107.

Augustine. *City of God,* Book X.

Lewis, C. S. *Miracles.*

Swinburne, Richard. *The Concept of Miracles.*

Tennant, F. R. *Miracle and Its Philosophical Presuppositions.*

Warfield, B. B. *Counterfeit Miracles.*

**Evaluation of Miracles**

Diamond, Malcolm. "Miracles," in *Religious Studies* 9 (Sept. 1973).

Flew, Antony. "Miracles," in *Encyclopedia of Philosophy,* vol. 5.

Grant, R. M. *Miracle and Natural Law in Graeco-Roman and Early Christian Thought.*

Hume, David. *Enquiry Concerning Human Understanding,* secs. X and XI.

Robinson, Guy. "Miracles," in *Ratio* 9 (Dec. 1967).

# Chapter 15

## Objectivism and History

Christianity is a historical religion. It makes historical claims about miraculous events that allegedly confirm its truth claims. In order to verify these truth claims one must first establish the objectivity of historical fact. This leads the discussion naturally into the whole question of whether or not there is such a thing as an objective historical fact, that is, whether history is really knowable. First, let us examine the arguments against the objectivity of history. Following this we will discuss whether or not miracles can be part of history.

## An Evaluation of Objections to the Objectivity of History

There are several arguments that have been advanced against the position that history is objectively knowable. We will examine those arguments crucial to the central historical claims of Christianity.

### Several Objections Against the Objectivity of History Considered

Charles Beard has offered at least eight arguments against the objectivity of history.[1] If these arguments are valid, it will make verification of Christianity via a historical method impossible.

*The Subject Matter of History Is Not Directly Observable.* The subjectivists argue that the subject of history, unlike science, is not directly observable. The historian does not deal with past events but with

---

1. See Charles Beard, "That Noble Dream," in *The Varieties of History,* pp. 323-25. The discussion here follows an excellent summary found in an unpublished master's thesis by William L. Craig, "The Nature of History..." (Trinity Evangelical Divinity School, Deerfield, Ill., 1976).

*statements* about past events. It is this fact which enables the historian to deal with facts in an imaginative way. Historical facts, they insist, exist only within the creative mind of the historian. The documents do not contain facts but are, without the historian's understanding, mere ink lines on paper. Further, once the event is gone it can never be fully re-created. Hence, the historian must impose meaning on his fragmentary and secondhand record. "The event itself, the facts, do not say anything, do not impose any meaning. It is the historian who speaks, who imposes a meaning."[2]

There are two reasons offered as to why the historian has only indirect access to the past. First, it is claimed that, unlike a scientist, the historian's world is composed of records and not events. This is why the historian must contribute a "reconstructed picture" of the past. In this sense the past is really a product of the present.

Second, the historical subjectivists assert that the scientist can test his view whereas the historian cannot. Experimentation is not possible with historical events. The scientist has the advantage of repeatability; he may subject his views to falsification. The historian cannot. The un-observable historical event is no longer verifiable; it is part of the forever departed past. Hence, what one believes about the past will be no more than a reflection of his own imagination. It will be a subjective construction in the minds of present historians, but it cannot hope to be an objective representation of what really happened.

*The Fragmentary Nature of Historical Accounts.* The second objection to the objectivity of history relates to its fragmentary nature. At best a historian can hope for completeness of documentation, but completeness of the events themselves is never possible. Documents at best cover only a small fraction of the events themselves.[3] From only fragmentary documents one cannot validly draw full and final conclusions. Furthermore, the documents do not present the events but only an interpretation of the events mediated through the one who recorded them. So at best we have only a fragmentary record of what someone else thought happened. So "what really happened would still have to be reconstructed in the mind of the historian."[4] Because the documents are so fragmentary and the events so distant, objectivity becomes a will-o'-the-wisp for the historian. He not only has too few pieces of the puzzle but the partial pictures on the few pieces he does have are not the original but were painted out of the mind of the one who passed the pieces down to us.

*The Selective Nature of Historical Methodology.* As was suggested,

---

2. Carl L. Becker, "What Are Historical Facts?" in *The Philosophy of History in Our Time*, p. 131.
3. Beard, "That Noble Dream," p. 323.
4. E. H. Carr, *What Is History?*, p. 20.

the historian does not have access to the events of the past but merely to fragmentary interpretations of those events contained in historical documents. Now what makes objectivity even more hopeless is the fact that the historian makes a selection from these fragmentary reports and builds his interpretation of the past events on a select number of partial reports of the past events. There are volumes in archives that most historians do not even touch.[5]

The actual selection among the fragmentary accounts is influenced by many subjective and relative factors including personal prejudice, availability of materials, knowledge of the languages, personal beliefs, social conditions, and so on. Hence, the historian himself is inextricably involved with the history he writes. What is included and what is excluded in his interpretation will always be a matter of subjective choice. No matter how objective a historian may attempt to be, it is practically impossible for him to present what really happened. His "history" is no more than his own interpretation based on his own subjective selection of fragmentary interpretations of past and unrepeatable events.

So it is argued that the facts of history do not speak for themselves. "The facts speak only when the historian calls on them; it is he who decides to which facts to give the floor, and in what order or context."[6] Indeed, when the "facts" speak, it is not the original events that are speaking but later and fragmentary opinions about those events. The original facts or events have long since perished. So, according to historical relativism, by the very nature of the project the historian can never hope for objectivity.

*The Need for Structuring the Facts of History.* Partial knowledge of the past makes it necessary for the historian to "fill in" gaping holes out of his own imagination. As a child draws the lines between the dots on a picture, so the historian supplies all the connections between events. Without the historian the dots are not numbered nor are they arranged in an obvious manner. The historian must use his imagination in order to provide continuity to the disconnected and fragmentary facts provided him.

Furthermore, the historian is not content to tell us simply what happened. He feels compelled to explain *why* it happened.[7] In this way history is made fully coherent and intelligible. Good history has both theme and unity which are provided by the historian. Facts alone do not make history any more than the disconnected dots make a picture. Herein, according to the subjectivist, lies the difference between chronicle and history. The former is merely the raw material used by the historian to construct history. Without the structure provided by the historian, the

5. Beard, "That Noble Dream," p. 324.
6. Carr, *What Is History?*, p. 9.
7. W. H. Walsh, *Philosophy of History*, p. 32.

mere "stuff" of history would be meaningless. The study of history is a study of causes. The historian wants to know *why;* he wishes to weave a web of interconnected events into a unified whole. Because of this he cannot avoid interjecting his own subjectivity into history. Hence, even if there is some semblance of objectivity in chronicle, nonetheless there is no hope for objectivity in history. History is in principle nonobjective because the very thing that makes it history (as vs. mere chronicle) is the interpretive structure or framework given to it from the subjective vantage point of the historian. Hence, it is concluded that the necessity of structure inevitably makes objectivity impossible.

*The Historian Cannot Avoid Value Judgments.* To borrow Dray's words, the very subject matter of history is "value-charged."[8] The facts of history consist of murders, oppression, and so forth, that cannot be described in morally neutral words. By his use of ordinary language the historian is forced to make value judgments. Further, by the very fact that history deals with flesh-and-blood human beings with motives and purposes, an analysis of history must of necessity comment on these. Whether, for instance, one is called a "dictator" or a "benevolent ruler" is a value judgment. How could one describe Hitler without making some value judgments? And if one were to attempt a kind of scientifically neutral description of past events without any stated or implied interpretation of human purposes, it would not be history but mere raw-boned chronicle without historical meaning.

Once the historian admits what he cannot avoid, namely, that he must make some value judgments about past events, then his history has lost objectivity. In short, there is no way for the historian to keep himself out of his history. He cannot be other than he is, and he is a person with perspectives and prejudices expressed in a value language by which and through which he views the world. In this sense objectivity is unattainable. Every writer will inevitably evaluate things from his own subjective perspective and by his own choice of words.

*Historians Cannot Avoid World Views.* Every historian interprets the past in the overall framework of his own Weltanschauung. Basically there are three different philosophies of history within which historians operate. There are the chaotic, the cyclical, and the linear views of history.[9] Which one of these the historian adopts will be a matter of faith or philosophy and not a matter of mere fact. Unless one view or another is presupposed, no interpretation is possible. The Weltanschauungen will determine whether the historian sees the events of the world as a meaningless maze, as a series of endless repetitions, or as moving in a purposeful way toward a goal. These world views are both necessary and inevitably

8. W. H. Dray, *Philosophy of History,* p. 23.
9. Beard, "Written History as an Act of Faith," in *Philosophy,* ed. Meyerhoff, p. 151.

value oriented. So, it is argued, without one of these world views the historian cannot interpret the events of the past; but through a world view objectivity becomes impossible.

A world view is not generated from the facts. Facts do not speak for themselves. The facts gain their meaning only within the overall context of the world view. Without the structure of the world-view framework the "stuff" of history has no meaning. Augustine, for example, viewed history as a great theodicy, but Hegel saw it as an unfolding of the divine. It is not any archaeological or factual find but simply the religious or philosophical presuppositions which prompted each man to develop his view. Eastern philosophies of history are even more diverse; they involve a cyclical rather than a linear pattern. But without some overarching viewpoint there would be no framework in which to interpret specific events. And once one admits the relativity or perspectivity of his world view as opposed to another, the historical relativists insist that he has thereby given up all right to claim objectivity. If there are several different ways to interpret the same facts, depending on the overall perspective one takes, then there is no single objective interpretation of history.

*Every Historian Is a Product of His Time.* Besides the conscious use of philosophical frameworks, the historian is subject to unconscious programming which makes him a product of his time. It is impossible for the historian to stand back and view history objectively because he too is part of the historical process. Hence, historical synthesis depends on the personality of the writer as well as the social and religious milieu in which he lives.[10] In this sense one must study the historian before he can understand his history.

Since the historian is part of the historical process, objectivity can never be attained. The history of one generation will be rewritten by the next, and so on. No historian can transcend his historical relativity and view the world process from the outside.[11] At best there can be successive, less than final historical interpretations, each viewing history from the vantage point of its own generation of historians. Therefore, there is no such person as a neutral historian; each remains a child of his own day.

*The Selection and Arrangement of Materials Is Subjective to the Historian.* Once the historian takes his fragmentary documents (p. 286), which he must view indirectly through the interpretation of the original source (p. 285), and takes his selected amount of material from the available archives (p. 287), and begins to provide an interpretive structure to it (p. 287), by the use of his own value-laden language (p. 288), and within the overall world view that he presupposes (p. 288),

---

10. See Henri Pirenne, "What Are Historians Trying to Do?" in *Philosophy,* ed. Meyerhoff, p. 97.

11. R. G. Collingwood, *The Idea of History,* ed. T. M. Know, p. 248.

then he not only understands it from the relative vantage point of his own generation (p. 289) but he must select and arrange the topic of history in accordance with his own subjective preferences (p. 290). In short, the dice are loaded against objectivity before he picks up his pen. That is, in the actual writing of the fragmentary, secondhand accounts from his own philosophical and personal point of view there is a further subjective choice of arrangement of the material.

The selection and arrangement of material will be determined by personal and social factors already discussed. The final written product will be prejudiced by what is included in and by what is excluded from the material. It will lack objectivity by how it is arranged and by the emphasis given to it in the overall presentation. The selection made in terms of the framework given will either be narrow or broad, clear or confused. Whatever its nature, the framework is necessarily a reflection of the mind of the historian.[12] This moves one still further away from objectively knowing what really happened. It is concluded, then, by the subjectivists that the hopes of objectivity are finally dashed.

### Attempts to Preserve the Objectivity of History

Despite these seemingly formidable objections to the possibility of historical objectivity, there have been some staunch defenders of the objective position. We will at this time consider their counter arguments in an attempt to determine whether or not there is an objective basis for believing in historical miracles that allegedly support Christian truth claims.

*The Problem of Indirect Access.* If by "objective" one means *absolute* knowledge, then of course no human historian can be objective. This we will grant. On the other hand, if "objective" means a *fair but revisable* presentation that reasonable men should accept, then the door is still open to the possibility of objectivity. Assuming this latter sense, it can be argued that history can be just as objective as some sciences.[13] For example, paleontology (historical geology) is considered one of the most objective of all sciences. It deals with physical facts and processes of the past. However, the events represented by the fossil finds are no more directly *accessible* to the scientists or *repeatable* than are historical events to the historian. True, there are some differences. The fossil is a mechanically true imprint of the original event and the eyewitness of history may be less precise in his report. But the historian may rejoin by pointing out that the natural processes that mar the fossil imprint parallel the personal filtering of events through the testimony of the eyewitness. At least it may be argued that if one can determine the integrity and relia-

---

12. Beard, "Written History as an Act of Faith," pp. 150-51.
13. Marc Block, *The Historian's Craft,* p. 50.

bility of the eyewitness, one cannot slam the door on the possibility of objectivity in history any more than on objectivity in geology.

The scientist might contend that he can repeat the processes of the past by present experimentation whereas the historian cannot. But even here the situations are similar, for in this sense history too can be "repeated." Similar patterns of events, by which comparisons can be made, recur today as they occurred in the past. Limited social experiments can be performed to see if human history "repeats," and widespread "experiments" can be observed naturally in the differing conditions in the ongoing history of the world. In short, the historian, no less than the scientist, has the tools for determining what really happened in the past. The lack of direct access to the original facts or events does not hinder the one more than the other.

Likewise, scientific facts do not "speak for themselves" any more than historical facts do.[14] First of all, if "fact" means original event, then neither geology nor history is in possession of any facts. "Fact" must be taken by both to mean information about the original event, and in this latter sense facts do not exist merely subjectively in the mind of the historian. Facts are objective data and data are data whether anyone reads them or not. What one does with data, that is, what meaning or interpretation he gives to them, can in no way eliminate the data. There remains for both science and history a hard core of objective facts. The door is thereby left open for objectivity. In this way one may draw a valid distinction between propaganda and history: the former lacks sufficient basis in objective fact but the latter does not. Indeed, without objective facts no protest can be raised either against poor history or propaganda. If history is entirely in the mind of the beholder, there is no reason one cannot decide to behold it any way he desires.

This brings us to the crucial question as to whether "facts speak for themselves" because they are objective. An argument might be advanced in favor of an affirmative answer as follows: It is self-defeating to affirm that there are any facts without meaning, since the very affirmation about the allegedly meaningless fact is a meaningful statement about the fact. Therefore, all facts are meaningful; there are no so-called bare facts. But this argument does not really prove that facts speak for themselves. It does show that facts can and do bear meaning. But what it must prove (and fails to prove) is that facts bear only *one* meaning and that they bear it evidently. The fact that no meaningful statement about facts can be made without attributing some meaning to the facts does not prove that the meaning emanated from the facts. It is possible that the meaning was assigned to the facts by the one making the meaningful statement

14. See critique of Evidentialism in chap. 5.

292 / CHRISTIAN APOLOGETICS

about them. Indeed, only "mean-ers" (i.e., minds) can emanate meaning. It is not at all clear in what sense an objective fact can mean anything in and of itself. It is a subject (e.g., a mind) that utters meaning about objects (or about other subjects), but objects as such are not subjects that are emitting meaning. This is so, unless we assume that all objective facts are really little minds transmitting meaning or transmitters through which some other minds or Mind is communicating. But to assume this would be to invoke one particular world view over another in order to prove that "facts speak for themselves." And even then it could be argued that the facts are not speaking for themselves but for the Mind (God) who is speaking through them.

It seems best to conclude, then, that objective facts do not speak for themselves. Finite minds may give differing interpretations of them or an infinite Mind may give an absolute interpretation of them, but there is no one objective interpretation a finite mind can give to them. Of course, if there is an absolute Mind from whose vantage point the facts are given absolute or ultimate meaning, then there is an objective interpretation of the facts which all finite minds should concur is the ultimate meaning. If theism is the correct world view (as was argued in Chapter 13), then there is an objective meaning to all facts in the world. All facts are theistic facts, and no nontheistic way of interpreting them is objective or true. Hence, objectivity in history is possible, since in a theistic world history would be His-story. Objectivity, then, is possible within a world view.

*The Problem of Fragmentary Accounts of History.* The fact that accounts of history are fragmentary does not destroy its objectivity any more than fragmentary fossil remains destroy the objectivity of geology. The fossil remains represent only a very tiny percentage of the living beings of the past. This does not hinder scientists from attempting to reconstruct an objective picture of what really happened in geological history. Likewise, the history of man is transmitted to us by only a partial record. Scientists sometimes reconstruct a whole man on the basis of only partial skeletal remains—even single jaw bones. While this procedure is perhaps rightly suspect, nonetheless one does not need every bone in order to fill in the probable picture of the whole animal. Like a puzzle, as long as one has the key pieces he can reconstruct the rest with a measurable degree of probability. Of course, the reconstruction of both science and history is subject to revision. Subsequent finds may provide new facts that call for new interpretations. But at least there is an objective basis in fact for the meaning attributed to the find. Interpretations can neither create the facts nor can they ignore them, if they would approach objectivity. We may conclude, then, that history need be no less objective than geology simply because it depends on fragmentary accounts. Scientific knowledge is also partial and depends on assumptions and an overall framework which may prove to be inadequate upon the discovery of more facts.

Whatever difficulty there may be, from a strictly scientific point of view, in filling in the gaps between the facts, once one has assumed a philosophical stance toward the world, the problem of objectivity in general is resolved. If there is a God, then the overall picture is already drawn; the facts of history will merely fill in the details of its meaning. If this is a theistic universe then the artist's sketch is already known in advance; the detail and coloring will come only as all the facts of history are fit into the overall sketch known to be true from the theistic framework. In this sense, historical objectivity is most certainly possible within a given framework such as a theistic world view. Objectivity resides in the view that best fits the facts into the overall system, that is, in systematic consistency.

*The Problem of the Selection of Material.* The fact that the historian must select his materials does not automatically make history purely subjective. Jurors make judgments "beyond reasonable doubt" without having all the evidence. If the historian has the relevant and crucial evidence, it will be sufficient to attain objectivity. One need not know everything in order to know something. No scientist knows all the facts and yet objectivity is claimed for his discipline. As long as no important fact is overlooked there is no reason to eliminate the possibility of objectivity in history any more than in science.

The selection of facts can be objective to the degree that the facts are selected and reconstructed in the context in which the events represented actually occurred. Since it is impossible for any historian to pack into his account everything available on a subject, it is important for him to select the points representative of the period of which he writes.[15] Condensation does not necessarily imply distortion. The mini can be an objective summary of the maxi.

There remains, however, the whole question as to whether the real context and connections of past events are known (or, are knowable). Unless there is an accepted framework or structure for the facts, there is no way to reconstruct in miniature what really happened. The objective meaning of historical events is dependent on knowing the connections that the events really had when they occurred. But the events are subject to various combinations depending on the structure given to them by the historian, the relative importance placed on them, and whether prior events are considered causal or merely antecedent. Hence, there is really no way to know the original connections without assuming an overall hypothesis or world view by which the events are interpreted. Of course

15. See R. G. Collingwood, "The Limits of Historical Knowledge," in *Essays in the Philosophy of History,* ed. William Debbins, p. 100.

objectivity of bare facts and mere sequence of antecedent and consequent facts are knowable without assuming a world view. But objectivity of the *meaning* of these events is not possible apart from a meaningful structure such as that provided by an overall hypothesis or world view. Hence, the problem of objective meaning of history, like the problem of objective meaning in science, is dependent on one's Weltanschauung. Objective meaning is system-dependent. Only within a given system can the objective meaning of events be understood. Once that system is known, it is possible by fair and representative selection to reconstruct an objective picture of the past.

*The Problem of Structuring the Material of History.* All the historian could possibly know about past events without assuming the truth of one interpretive framework over another is the sheer *facticity* and the *sequence* of the events. When the historian moves beyond bare facts and mere order of events and begins to speak of causal connections and relative importance, he has assumed an interpretive framework through which he is understanding the facts. Whether or not the facts are determined to have originally had the assumed causal connection and the attributed importance will depend on whether or not the assumed world view is correct. To affirm that facts have "internal arrangement" begs the question. The real question is, How does one know the correct arrangement? Since the facts are arrangeable in at least three different ways (chaotic, cyclical, and linear), it begs the question merely to assume that one of these is the way the facts were really arranged. The same set of dots can have the lines drawn in many ways. The assumption that the historian is merely discovering (and not drawing) the lines is gratuitous. The fact is that the lines are not known to be there apart from an interpretive framework through which one views them. Therefore, the problem of the objective meaning of history cannot be resolved apart from appeal to a world view.[16] Once the skeletal sketch is known, then one can know the objective placing (meaning) of the facts. However, apart from a structure the mere "stuff" means nothing.

Apart from an overall structure there is no way to know which events in history are the most significant and, hence, there is no way to know the true significance of these and other events in their overall context. The argument that importance is determined by which events influence the most people is inadequate for several reasons. First, it is a form of historical utilitarianism and as such is subject to the same criticisms as any utilitarian test for truth (see Chapter 6). The most does not determine the best; all that is proved by great influence is great influence, not great importance or value. Even after most people have been influenced, one

16. See Part I, Chapter 5.

can still ask the question as to the truth or value of the event that influenced them. Significance is not determined by ultimate outcome but by overall framework. Of course, if one assumes as an overall framework that the events which influence the most people in the long run are most significant, then that utilitarian framework will indeed determine the significance of an event. But what right does one have to assume a utilitarian framework any more than a nonutilitarian one? Here again, it is a matter of justifying one's overall framework or world view.

The argument advanced by some objectivists that past events must be structured or else they are unknowable is faulty. All this argument proves is that it is necessary to understand facts through *some* structure, otherwise it makes no sense to speak of facts. The question of *which* structure is correct must be determined on some basis other than the mere facts themselves. If there were an objectivity of bare facts, it would provide at best only the mere *what* of history. But objective meaning deals with the *why* of these events; this is impossible apart from a meaning-structure in which the facts may find their placement or significance. Objective meaning apart from a world view is impossible.

However, granted that there is justification for adopting a theistic world view, the objective meaning of history becomes possible. For within the theistic context each fact of history becomes a theistic fact. Granted the factual order of events and the known causal connection of events, the possibility of objective meaning surfaces. The chaotic and the cyclical frameworks are eliminated in favor of the linear. And within the linear view of events causal connections emerge as the result of their context in a theistic universe. Theism provides the sketch on which history paints the complete picture. The pigments of mere fact take on real meaning as they are blended together on the theistic sketch. In this context, objectivity means systematic consistency. That is, the most meaningful way all of the facts of history can be blended together into the whole theistic sketch is what really happened. In this way theism can provide an objective framework for historical facts.

*The Problem of Value-Laden Language.* It may be granted that ordinary language is value laden and that value judgments are inevitable. This by no means makes historical objectivity impossible.[17] Objectivity means to be fair in dealing with the facts. It means to present *what* happened as correctly as possible. Further, objectivity means that when one interprets *why* these events occurred, the language of the historian should ascribe to these events the value which they really had in their original context. Granting within an established world view the fact that certain things have a given value, then an objective account of history must reconstruct

17. See Herbert Butterfield, "Moral Judgments in History," in *Philosophy,* ed. Meyerhoff, p. 244.

and restructure these events with the same relative value. In this way objectivity demands value judgments rather than avoiding them. The question asks not whether value language can be objective, but rather it asks, *Which* value statements objectively portray the events the way they really were? Once the world view has been determined, value judgments are not undesirable or merely subjective; they are in fact essential and objectively demanded. If this is a theistic world, then it would not be objective to place anything but a proper value on the facts of history.

*The Problem of an Overall World View.* Those who argue against the objectivity of history apart from an overall world view must be granted the point. Without a world view it makes no sense to talk about objective meaning.[18] Meaning is system-dependent. Within a given system a given set of facts has a given meaning, but within another system it may have a very different meaning. Without a context meaning cannot be determined, and the context is provided by the world view and not by the bare facts themselves.

But granted that this is a theistic universe for the reasons already given (Chapter 13), then it follows that objectivity is possible. It is possible because in a theistic universe each fact has an objective meaning; each fact is a God-fact. All events in a theistic world bear a divine meaning; they all fit into the overall context of his ultimate purpose. Hence, once one can determine what the facts are and can assign them a meaning in the overall context of the theistic universe by showing that they fit most consistently with a given interpretation, then he may lay claim to having arrived at the objective truth about history. For example, granted that this is a theistic universe and that the corpse of Jesus of Nazareth returned from the grave, then the Christian can argue that this unusual event is a miracle that confirms the associated truth claims of Christ. But apart from this theistic framework it is not even meaningful to make such a claim. Overarching hypotheses are necessary to determine the meaning of events, and a theistic hypothesis is essential to claim that any historical event is a miracle.

*The Problem of Overcoming Historical Conditioning.* It is undoubtedly true that every historian is a product of his time. Each person occupies a relative place in the changing events of the spacio-temporal world. However, it does not follow that because the *historian* is a product of his time that his *history* is also a product of the time. Simply because a *person* cannot avoid a relative place in history does not mean that his *perspective* cannot attain some meaningful degree of objectivity. The criticism confuses the *content* of knowledge and the *process* of attaining it.[19] It confuses

---

18. See Karl Popper, *The Poverty of Historicism,* p. 150 f.
19. See Maurice Mandelbaum, *The Problem of Historical Knowledge,* p. 94.

the *formation* of a view with its *verification*. Where one derives a hypothesis is not essentially related to how he can establish its truth.

Further, if relativity is unavoidable the position of the historical relativists is self-refuting. For either their view is historically conditioned and, therefore, unobjective or else it is not relative but objective. If the latter, then it thereby admits that it is possible to be objective in viewing history. On the contrary, if the position of historical relativism is itself relative, then it cannot be taken as objectively true. It is simply subjective opinion which has no basis to claim to be objectively true about all of history. In short, if it is a subjective opinion it cannot eliminate the possibility that history is objectively knowable; and if it is an objective fact about history then objective facts can be known about history. In the first case objectivity is not eliminated and in the second relativity is self-defeated. Hence, in either case, objectivity is possible.

Finally, the constant rewriting of history is based on the assumption that objectivity is possible. Why strive for accuracy unless it is believed that the revision is more objectively true than the previous view? Why critically analyze unless improvement toward a more accurate view is the assumed goal? Perfect objectivity may be practically unattainable within the limited resources of the historian on most if not all topics. But be this as it may, the inability to attain 100 percent objectivity is a long way from total relativity. Reaching a degree of objectivity which is subject to criticism and revision is a more realistic conclusion than the relativist's arguments. In short, there is no reason to eliminate the possibility of a sufficient degree of historical objectivity.

*The Problem of the Arrangement of Materials.* There is no reason why the historian cannot rearrange without distorting the past.[20] Since the original construction of events is available to neither the historian nor the geologist, it is necessary to reconstruct the past on the basis of the available evidence. But reconstruction does not necessitate revision; selecting material may occur without neglecting significant matters. Every historian must arrange his material. The important thing is whether or not it is arranged or rearranged in accordance with the original arrangement of events as they really occurred. As long as the historian incorporates consistently and comprehensively all the significant events in accordance with his overall and established world view, he has not sacrificed objectivity. Arranging the facts in accordance with the way things really were is being objective. It is neglecting important facts and twisting facts that distorts objectivity.

The historian may desire to be selective in the compass of his study. He may wish to study only the political, economic, or religious dimensions

20. See Ernest Nagel, "The Logic of Historical Analysis," in *Philosophy,* ed. Meyerhoff, p. 208.

of a specific period. But such specialization does not demand total subjectivity. One can focus without losing the overall context in which he operates. It is one thing to focus on specifics within an overall field but quite another to totally ignore or deliberately neglect or distort the overall context in which the intensified interest is occurring. As long as the specialist stays in touch with reality rather than reflecting the pure subjectivity of his own fancy, there is no reason why a measurable degree of objectivity cannot be maintained.

**Conclusions Regarding the Objectivity of History**

There are several general conclusions to be drawn from the foregoing analysis of the subjectivity-objectivity controversy. (1) Absolute objectivity is possible only for an infinite Mind. Finite minds must be content with systematic consistency, that is, fair but revisable attempts to reconstruct the past based on an established framework of reference which comprehensively and consistently incorporates all the facts into the overall sketch provided by the frame of reference. (2) In this acceptable sense of objectivity the historian can be as objective as the scientist. Neither geologists nor historians have direct access to nor complete data on repeatable events. Further, both must use value judgments in selecting and structuring the partial material available to them. (3) In reality, neither the scientist nor the historian can attain objective meaning without the use of some world view by which he understands the facts. Bare facts cannot even be known apart from some interpretive framework. Hence, the need for structure or a meaning-framework is crucial to the question of objectivity. Unless one can settle the question as to whether this is a theistic or nontheistic world on grounds independent of the mere facts themselves, there is no way to determine the objective meaning of history. If, on the other hand, there are good reasons to believe that this is a theistic universe (as we argued in Part II), then objectivity in history is a possibility. For once the overall viewpoint is established, it is simply a matter of finding the view of history that is most consistent with that overall system. That is, systematic consistency is the test for objectivity in historical matters as well as in scientific matters.

# Some Objections Against the Objectivity of Miraculous History

We have already argued for the philosophical possibility of miracles (in Chapter 14). Further, we have just offered reasons for holding that historical events can be known objectively within a theistic framework. There remain, however, some further problems before we may claim that any miracle has actually happened. The first problem is whether or not the *miraculous* is knowable in a historical way.

### Theological Objection: Miracles Are Suprahistorical

Granting that secular history can be known objectively, there still remains the problem of the subjectivity of religious history. Some writers make a strong distinction between *Historie* and *Geschichte*.[21] The former is empirical and objectively knowable to some degree, but the latter is spiritual and unknowable in a historical or objective way. As spiritual or superhistory there is no objective way to verify it. Spiritual history has no necessary connection with the spacio-temporal continuum of empirical events. It is a "myth" with subjective religious significance to the believer but with no objective grounding. Like the story of George Washington and the cherry tree, *Geschichte* is a story made up of events which probably never happened but which inspire men to some moral or religious good.

If this distinction is applied to the New Testament, then even granted that the life and central teachings of Jesus of Nazareth can be objectively established, there is no historical way to confirm the miraculous dimensions of the New Testament. Miracles do not happen as part of *Historie* and therefore are not subject to objective analysis; they are *Geschichte* events and as such cannot be analyzed by historical methodology. Many contemporary theologians have accepted this distinction. Paul Tillich claimed that it is "a disastrous distortion of the meaning of faith to identify it with the belief in the historical validity of the Biblical stories."[22] He believed with Sören Kierkegaard that whether all the events surrounding Jesus of Nazareth really occurred is irrelevant to faith. The important thing about a "myth" or "miracle" is not whether it happened in history but whether or not it evokes an appropriate religious response. With this Rudolf Bultmann and Shubert Ogden would also concur, along with much of contemporary theological thought.

Even those like Karl Jaspers—who oppose Bultmann's more radical demythologization view—accepted, nevertheless, the distinction between the spiritual and empirical dimensions of miracles.[23] On the more conservative end of those maintaining this distinction is Ian Ramsey. According to Ramsey even C. H. Dodd (*The Interpretation of the Fourth Gospel*, C.U.P., 1953) must admit that "it is not enough to think of the facts of the Bible as 'brute historical facts' to which the Evangelists give distinctive 'interpretation.' " For Ramsey the Bible is historical only if " 'history' refers to situations as odd as those which are referred to by that paradigm of the Fourth Gospel: 'the Word became flesh.' " Ramsey concludes: "No attempt to make the language of the Bible conform to a precise

---

21. See Martin Kahler, *The So-Called Historical Jesus*, p. 63.
22. Paul Tillich, *Dynamics of Faith*, p. 87.
23. See Karl Jaspers and Rudolf Bultmann, *Myth and Christianity*, pp. 16-17.

straight-forward public language—whether that language be scientific or historical—has ever succeeded." More positively, the Bible is about situations "to which existentialists refer when they speak of something being 'authentic' or 'existential-historical.' "[24] There is always something "more" than the empirical in every religious or miraculous situation. The purely empirical situation is "odd" and thereby evocative of a discernment that calls for a commitment of religious significance.[25]

In response to these analyses of the historical objectivity of miracles it is important to make several observations. (1) Surely the Christian apologist does not want to contend that miracles are a mere product of the historical process. The supernatural occurs *in* the historical but it is not a product *of* the natural process. What makes it miraculous is the fact that the natural process alone does not account for it; there must be an injection from the realm of the supernatural into the natural or else there is no miracle. This is specially true of what was called a first class miracle (see Chapter 14), where the process by which God performed the miracle is unknown. It is also true to some degree of a second class miracle, where we can describe *how* the miracle occurred by scientific means but not *why* it occurred when it did. Even in a second class miracle, *why* the unusual event occurred when it did cannot be explained as part *of* the natural process. So in either case it seems best to admit that the miraculous dimensions of a historical event are *in* but not *of* the natural process. (2) In accordance with the objectivity of history just discussed, there is no good reason why the Christian should yield to the radical existential theologians on the question of the objective and historical dimensions of miracles. Miracles may not be of the natural historical process but they do occur *in* it. Even Karl Barth made a similar distinction when he wrote, "The resurrection of Christ, or his second coming . . . is not a historical event; the historians may reassure themselves . . . that our concern *here* is with the event which, though it is the only real happening *in* is not a real happening *of* history."[26]

But unlike many existential theologians we must also preserve the historical context in which a miracle occurs, for without it there is no way to verify the objectivity of the miraculous. Miracles do have a historical dimension without which no objectivity of religious history is possible. And as was argued above, historical methodology can identify this objectivity (just as surely as scientific objectivity can be established) within an accepted framework of a theistic world. In short, miracles may be *more* than historical but they cannot be *less* than historical. It is only if miracles do have historical dimensions that they are both objectively

---

24. Ian Ramsey, *Religious Language*, pp. 118, 119, 122.
25. Ramsey, chap. 1.
26. Karl Barth, *The Word of God and the Word of Man*, p. 90.

meaningful and apologetically valuable. (3) A miracle can be identified within an empirical or historical context both directly and indirectly, both objectively and subjectively. A miracle possesses several characteristics. It is an event that is both scientifically unusual and theologically and morally relevant. The first characteristic is knowable in a directly empirical way; the latter are knowable only indirectly through the empirical in that it is "odd" and "evocative" of something "more" than the mere empirical data of the event. For example, a virgin birth is scientifically "odd" but in the case of Christ it is represented as a "sign" that was used to draw attention to him as something "more" than human. The theological and moral characteristics of a miracle are not empirically objective. In this sense they are experienced subjectively. This does not mean, however, that there is no objective basis for the moral dimensions of a miracle. If this is a theistic universe, then morality is objectively grounded in God. Hence, the nature and will of God are the objective grounds by which one can test whether or not the event is subjectively evocative of what is objectively in accord with the nature and will of God. The same thing applies to the truth dimensions of a miracle. They are subjectively evocative of a response to an associated truth claim. However, the truth claim must be in accord with what is already known of God; otherwise one should not believe the event is a miracle. It is axiomatic that acts of a theistic God would not be used to confirm what is not the truth of God.

To sum up, miracles happen *in* history but are not completely *of* history. Miracles, nonetheless, are historically grounded. They are *more* than historical but are not *less* than historical. There are both empirical and superempirical dimensions to supernatural events. The former are knowable in an objective way and the latter have a subjective appeal to the believer. But even here there is an objective ground in the known truth and goodness of God by which the believer can judge whether or not the empirically odd situations which appeal to him for a response are really acts of this true and good God.

## Philosophical Objection: Miracles Are Historically Unknowable

On the basis of Troeltsch's principle of analogy, some historians have come to object to the possibility of ever establishing a miracle based on testimony about the past. Troeltsch stated the problem this way:

> On the analogy of the events known to us we seek by conjecture and sympathetic understanding to explain and reconstruct the past. . . . Since we discern the same process of phenomena in operation in the past as in the present, and see, there as here, the various historical cycles of human life influencing and intersecting one another. . . .

Without uniformity we could know nothing about the past, for without an analogy from the present we could know nothing about the past.[27] In accord with this principle some have argued that "no amount of testimony is ever permitted to establish as past reality a thing that cannot be found in present reality. . . . In every other case the witness may have a perfect character—all that goes for nothing. . . ."[28] In other words, unless one can identify miracles in the present he has no experience on which to base his understanding of alleged miracles in the past. The historian, like the scientist, must adopt a methodological skepticism toward alleged events in the past for which he has no parallel in the present. The present is the foundation of our knowledge of the past. As F. H. Bradley put it:

> We have seen that history rests in the last resort upon an inference from our experience, a judgment based upon our own present state of things . . . ; when we are asked to affirm the existence in past time of events, the effects of causes which confessedly are without analogy in the world in which we live, and which we know—we are at a loss for any answer but this, that . . . we are asked to build a house without a foundation. . . . And how can we attempt this without contradicting ourselves?[29]

Upon examination, Troeltsch's principle of analogy turns out to be similar to Hume's objection to miracles built on the uniformity of nature. No testimony about alleged miracles should be accepted if it contradicts the uniform testimony of nature. In like manner Troeltsch would reject any particular event in the past for which there is no analogue in the uniform experience of the present. Now there are at least two reasons for rejecting Troeltsch's argument from analogy. First, it begs the question in favor of a naturalistic interpretation of *all* historical events. It is a methodological exclusion of the possibility of accepting the miraculous in history. The testimony for regularity in *general* is in no way a testimony against an unusual event in *particular*. The cases are different and should not be evaluated in the same way. Empirical generalizations (e.g., "men do not rise from the dead") should not be used as countertestimony to good eyewitness accounts that in a particular case someone did rise from the dead. The historical evidence for any particular historical event must be assessed on its own merits completely aside from the generalizations about other events.

There is a second objection to the Troeltsch analogy type argument, namely, it proves too much. As Richard Whately convincingly argued, on this uniformitarian assumption not only miracles would be excluded but

27. E. Troeltsch, "Historiography," in *Encyclopedia of Religion and Ethics,* ed. James Hastings.
28. Carl Becker, "Detachment and the Writing of History," in *Detachment and the Writing of History,* ed. Phil L. Synder, pp. 12-13.
29. F. H. Bradley, *The Presuppositions of Critical History,* p. 100.

so would many unusual events of the past including those surrounding Napoleon Bonaparte.[30] No one can deny that the probability against Napoleon's successes was great. His prodigious army was destroyed in Russia; yet in a few months he led another great army in Germany which likewise was ruined at Leipzig. However, the French supplied him with yet another army sufficient to make a formidable stand in France. This was repeated five times until at last he was confined to an island. There is no doubt that the particular events of his career were highly improbable. But there is no reason on these grounds that we should doubt the historicity of the Napoleonic adventures. History, contrary to scientific hypothesis, does not depend on the universal and repeatable. Rather, it stands on the sufficiency of good testimony for particular and unrepeatable events. Were this not so, then nothing could be learned from history.

It is clearly a mistake to import uniformitarian methods from scientific experimentation into historical research. Repeatability and generality are needed to establish a scientific law or general patterns (of which miracles would be particular exceptions). But this method does not work at all in history. What is needed to establish historical events is credible testimony that these particular events did indeed occur. So it is with miracles. It is an unjustifiable mistake in historical methodology to assume that no unusual and particular event can be believed no matter how great the evidence for it. Troeltsch's principle of analogy would destroy genuine historical thinking. The honest historian must be open to the possibility of unique and particular events of the past whether they are miraculous or not. He must not exclude a priori the possibility of establishing events like the resurrection of Christ without a careful examination of the testimony and evidence concerning them.

## Summary and Conclusion

Christianity makes miraculous claims about historical events. Some historians complain, however, that there is no objective basis for determining the past. And even if there were an objective basis, miracles are not part of objective history. In support of this contention it is argued that the historian has only fragmentary, secondhand material from which he selects but a portion for which he provides his own interpretive value structure and by which he constructs the past for his own generation in terms of his own overall world view. The net result is that objectivity is impossible. It is further argued by subjectivists that miracle-history is not empirical nor observable; it is superhistory or myth used to evoke a subjective religious response but is not reliably descriptive of the past.

These objections, however, fail. History can be as objective as science. The geologist too has only secondhand, fragmentary, and unrepeatable

30. Richard Whately, *Historical Doubts Relative to Napoleon Bonaparte.*

evidence viewed from his own vantage point and in terms of his own values and interpretive framework. In this regard history can be as objective as geology. Although it is true that interpretive frameworks are necessary for objectivity, it is not true that every world view must be totally relative and subjective. Indeed this argument is self-defeating, for it assumes that it is an objective statement about history that all statements about history are necessarily not objective.

As to the objection that miracle-history is not objectively verifiable, two points are important. First, miracles can occur *in* the historical process without being *of* that natural process. Surely there is "more" to a miracle than the purely empirical. Christian miracles claim to be more than empirical but they are not less than historical. This is important because at least the historically and scientifically unusual dimensions of miracles are subject to objective and historical verification. Further, the moral and theological dimensions of miracles are not totally subjective. They call for a subjective response but there are objective standards of truth and goodness (in accordance with the theistic God) by which the miracle can be objectively assessed. It is concluded, then, that the door for the objectivity of history and thus the objective historicity for miracles is open. No mere question-begging uniformitarian principle of analogy can slam the door a priori. Evidence that supports the *general* nature of scientific law may not be legitimately used to rule out good historical evidence for unusual but *particular* events of history. This kind of argument is not only invincibly naturalistic in its bias but if applied consistently it would rule out much of known and accepted secular history. The only truly honest approach is to examine carefully the evidence for an alleged miracle in order to determine its authenticity. This will be done in the next chapter.

## SELECT READINGS FOR CHAPTER FIFTEEN

Clark, Gordon. *Historiography: Secular and Religious.*
Collingwood, R. G. *The Idea of History.*
————. *Essays in the Philosophy of History.*
Dray, W. H. (ed.). *Philosophy of History.*
Harvey, Van A. *The Historian and the Believer.*
Meyerhoff, Hans (ed.). *The Philosophy of History.*
Montgomery, John W. *The Shape of the Past.*
Popper, Karl. *The Poverty of Historicism.*
Stern, Fritz (ed.). *The Varieties of History.*
Whately, Richard. *Historical Doubts Relative to Napoleon Bonaparte.*

# Chapter 16 | The Historical Reliability of the New Testament

In the previous chapter it was shown that history is objectively knowable. In the present chapter we will discuss whether or not the reports of the life, teachings, death, and resurrection of Christ as presented in the New Testament documents are historically reliable. This chapter is an important step in the overall apologetic for historical Christianity. It will serve not only as a basis for the historicity of Christ's claims to be the Incarnate Son of God but also for the historicity of the confirming miracle of the resurrection of Christ from the grave.

There are two important steps in establishing the historical reliability of the New Testament. First, there is the matter of the *authenticity* of the New Testament documents. Second, there is the question of the *reliability* of the New Testament writers.

## The Authenticity of the New Testament Documents

The direction of the argument in these chapters is as follows: (1) the New Testament documents are historically reliable (Chapter 16); (2) these documents accurately present Christ as claiming to be God Incarnate and confirm his claim by showing that he fulfilled prophecy, that he lived a sinless and miraculous life, and that he predicted and accomplished his resurrection from the dead (Chapter 17); (3) therefore, the deity of Christ is historically and miraculously confirmed.

There are three elements in establishing the authority of the New Testament documents: first, an examination of the extant manuscript copies; second, a comparison of New Testament manuscripts with those of ancient secular history; third, the dating of the original sources of these manuscripts.

## The Extant Manuscript Evidence for the New Testament

There is more abundant and accurate manuscript evidence for the New Testament than for any other book from the ancient world. There are more manuscripts copied with greater accuracy and earlier dating than for any secular classic from antiquity. First, let us examine the number and nature of the New Testament manuscripts themselves.[1]

*The John Rylands Fragment* (P52). This papyrus contains five verses from John 18:31-33, 37-38. It is dated between A.D. 117-138. The great philologist Adolf Deissmann argued that it may be even earlier. The manuscript is housed in the John Rylands Library in Manchester, England.

*The Bodmer Papyri* (P66, P72, P75). These papyri date from around A.D. 200. They contain most of the Gospels of John and Luke along with the books of Jude, I Peter, and II Peter. These manuscripts contain the earliest complete copies of New Testament books.

*Codex Vaticanus* (B). This manuscript dates from between A.D. 325-350. It is a vellum manuscript containing the whole New Testament as well as the Greek (LXX) Old Testament. It was discovered by modern textual scholars in 1475 when it was catalogued in the Vatican Library where it still remains.

*Codex Sinaiticus (Aleph).* This manuscript dates from around A.D. 340. It too is vellum and contains the whole New Testament and half of the Old Testament. Count Tischendorf discovered it in a monastery on Mount Sinai in 1844. It is contained in the collection at the University Library in Leipzig, Germany.

*Codex Ephraemi Rescriptus* (C). This manuscript dates from around A.D. 350. It contains only part of the Old Testament but most of the New Testament. This early manuscript was written over but retrieved by chemical reactivation. The National Library in Paris possesses it.

*Codex Alexandrinus* (A). Dating from about A.D. 450, this too is a complete vellum manuscript of the Bible with only minor mutilations. It is housed in the National Library of the British Museum.

It should be kept in mind that although the foregoing great vellum manuscripts date from the fourth and fifth centuries, they represent in whole or in part an "Alexandrian" (mode Alexandria, Egypt) type text that dates from A.D. 100-150.

*Codex Bezae* (D). Dating from A.D. 450 or 550, this manuscript is written in both Greek and Latin. It was discovered in 1562 by the French theologian Theodore de Beza, who gave it to Cambridge University. This manuscript contains the four Gospels, Acts, and part of III John.

---

1. For further information see N. L. Geisler and William Nix, *A General Introduction to the Bible,* Chapters 20-27.

*Other Early Greek Manuscripts.* There are numerous early Greek manuscripts. *Codex Claromontanus* (D2) dates from A.D. 550 and contains much of the New Testament. *Codex Basiliensis* (E) has the four Gospels from the eighth century. *Codex Laudianus* (E2) contains Acts from the sixth or seventh century. These are followed by numerous other manuscripts with everything from parts to the whole New Testament dating from the ninth century on.

The total count of Greek manuscripts of the New Testament is now around 5,000.

The New Testament scholar Bruce Metzger counts 76 papyri, 250 uncials, 2,646 minuscules, and 1,997 lectionary manuscripts. This would total 4,969.[2] No other book from antiquity possesses anything like this abundance in manuscripts.

### Comparison of the New Testament with Ancient Secular Writings

From the standpoint of a documentary historian the New Testament has vastly superior evidence to that of any other book from the ancient world. The following chart will reveal the superior number, dating, and degree of accuracy of the New Testament over other books.[3]

## COMPARISON OF ANCIENT TEXTS

| Author | Date Written | Earliest Copy | Number of Copies | Accuracy of Copy |
|---|---|---|---|---|
| Caesar | 1st Cent. B.C. | 900 A.D. | 10 | —— |
| Livy | 1st Cent. B.C. | —— | 20 | —— |
| Tacitus | c. 100 A.D. | 1100 A.D. | 20 | —— |
| Thucydides | 5th Cent. B.C. | 900 A.D. | 8 | —— |
| Herodotus | 5th Cent. B.C. | 900 A.D. | 8 | —— |
| Demosthenes | 4th Cent. B.C. | 1100 A.D. | 200 | —— |
| *Mahabharata* | —— | —— | —— | 90% |
| Homer | 9th Cent. B.C. | —— | 643 | 95% |
| New Testament | 1st Cent. A.D. (50-100 A.D.) | 2nd Cent. A.D. (c. 130 A.D. f.) | 5,000 | 99 + % |

2. Bruce Metzger, *The Text of the New Testament,* pp. 31-33.
3. See F. W. Hall, "Manuscript Authorities for the Text of the Chief Classical Writers," in *Companion to Classical Text,* and Bruce Metzger, *Chapters in the History of New Testament Textual Criticism.*

Several observations are pertinent to the above chart. (1) No other book is even a close second to the Bible on either the *number* or early dating of the copies. The average secular work from antiquity survives on only a handful of manuscripts; the New Testament boasts thousands. (2) The average *gap* between the original composition and the earliest copy is over 1,000 years for other books. The New Testament, however, has a fragment within one generation from its original composition, whole books within about 100 years from the time of the autograph, most of the New Testament in less than 200 years, and the entire New Testament within 250 years from the date of its completion. (3) The degree of *accuracy* of the copies is greater for the New Testament than for other books that can be compared. Most books do not survive with enough manuscripts that make comparison possible. A handful of copies that are 1,000 years after the fact do not provide enough links in the missing chain nor enough variant readings in the manuscript to enable textual scholars to reconstruct the original. Bruce Metzger does provide an interesting comparison of the New Testament with the Indian *Mahabharata* and Homer's *Iliad*. The New Testament has about 20,000 lines. Of these only 40 are in doubt (i.e., about 400 words). The *Iliad* possesses about 15,600 lines with 764 of them in question. This would mean that Homer's text is only 95 percent pure or accurate compared to over 99.5 percent accuracy for the New Testament manuscript copies. The national epic of India has suffered even more textual corruption than the *Iliad*. The *Mahabharata* is some eight times the size of the *Iliad,* of which some 26,000 lines are in doubt. This would be roughly 10 percent textual corruption or a 90 percent accuracy copy of the original.[4] From this documentary standpoint the New Testament writings are superior to comparable ancient writings. The records for the New Testament are vastly more abundant, clearly more ancient, and considerably more accurate in their text.

### The Dating of the Original New Testament Sources

The manuscript evidence takes us to within a generation of the completion of the original New Testament documents. But the death of Christ is computed to have occurred somewhere between A.D. 29 and 33. The next link in the argument for the historical reliability of the Gospel records deals with the date of the original composition of the Gospel records.

The German posthegelian Tübingen school of F. C. Baur once dated the completion of the New Testament into the second century. Using a dialectical presupposition, they argued that the thesis of Paul's Gentile Christianity was opposed by the antithesis of Peter's and James's Jewish Christianity that was not synthesized until the second century by Johannine

---

4. Bruce Metzger, *Chapters in New Testament Textual Criticism.*

Christianity. However, this opinion is no longer reasonable in view of the evidence for the Gospel of John being a first century composition. The dating for all the New Testament books falls well within the first century. No less authority than Biblical archaeologist William F. Albright said that "every book of the New Testament was written by a baptized Jew between the forties and the eighties of the first century A.D. (very probably sometime between A.D. 50 and 75)."[5] Let us examine the evidence for the dating of the documents of the New Testament.

*Paul's Writings.* The apostle Paul was martyred under Nero in A.D. 67. His earliest epistles were written before his imprisonment in Rome between A.D. 60-62 (Acts 28). Of the thirteen epistles attributed to Paul, I Corinthians, II Corinthians, Romans, and Galatians are conceded even by ardent critics of the Tübingen school to be genuine. The only substantial debate on the thirteen epistles is over the pastoral epistles (I and II Timothy, Titus). In the remaining ten authentic epistles there are found all the essential points of the life, teachings, death, and resurrection of Christ written by a contemporary of the eyewitnesses (see I Cor. 15:5 f.). Paul taught that Jesus was virgin born (Gal. 4:4) and that he was the preexistent Creator of the universe (Col. 1:15-16) who existed both in the "form of man" and in the "form of God" (Phil. 2:5, 8). Jesus was a descendant of Abraham and David (Rom. 9:5; 1:3) who lived under the Jewish law (Gal. 4:4), who was betrayed the night he instituted a memorial meal of bread and wine (I Cor. 11:23 f.), was crucified under the Romans (I Cor. 1:23; Phil. 2:8) although the responsibility lay with the Jewish authorities (I Thess. 2:15). This same Jesus is said by Paul to have been buried for three days, to have risen from the dead, and to have been seen by over five hundred eyewitnesses, the majority of whom were still alive when Paul wrote (I Cor. 15:4).

Paul knew the Lord's apostles personally (Gal. 1:17 f.). Peter, James, and John are mentioned as "pillars" of the Jerusalem community (Gal. 2:9). Paul knew that the Lord's brothers and Peter were married (I Cor. 9:5). On occasions Paul quoted sayings of Jesus (I Cor. 7:10; 9:14; 11:23). Elsewhere Paul summarized the Sermon on the Mount (Rom. 12:14-21) and insisted on following the example of Christ (Rom. 13:14). In short, to use the words of F. F. Bruce, "The outline of the Gospel story as we can trace it in the writings of Paul agrees with the outline which we find elsewhere in the New Testament, and in the four Gospels in particular."[6]

Several observations about Paul's testimony are pertinent to the question of the authenticity of the New Testament documents. First, although Paul was not personally an eyewitness of Jesus' life, death, and resurrec-

---

5. Taken from an interview in *Christianity Today*, January 18, 1963.
6. F. F. Bruce, *The New Testament Documents: Are They Reliable?*, p. 79.

tion, he was a contemporary of many who were. Second, Paul wrote within thirty years of the actual events themselves, far too short a time for the alleged distortions and dialectical development claimed by the Tübingen school. Third, Paul challenged his readers to check with the eyewitnesses—most of the five hundred were still alive—if they wanted to verify the truth of his message (I Cor. 15:5). There is no indication from history that Paul's challenge was ever taken or his claims falsified. On the contrary, these writings of Paul—particularly Romans, Corinthians, and Galatians—bear every indication of authenticity.

*The Writings of John the Apostle.* The Gospel of John claims to be written by "the Disciple whom Jesus loved, who had lain close to his breast at the supper . . ." (John 21:20). By the process of elimination this disciple must have been John. Other disciples as Peter, Philip, Thomas, and Andrew are named in the third person (1:41; 6:9; 14:5, 8). Furthermore, the writer was one of the inner circle of James, Peter, and John, as is evidenced by the fact that he leaned on Jesus' bosom (John 13:23-25), that he had eyewitness and inside information (John 18:15), and that Jesus on his death committed his mother to John's care (John 18:26, 27). But James died very early (c. A.D. 44) in the persecution of Herod (Acts 12:2) and Peter is named in the third person (John 21:21). Hence, by elimination, the author of the fourth Gospel must have been John.

There is ample external and internal evidence to confirm that this eyewitness Gospel was written by the young disciple of Christ. Externally we have both the John Rylands Fragment and the testimony of the early Church Fathers. The Rylands Fragment argues strongly for a first century origin of the Gospel, since an early second century copy (c. A.D. 117 f.) was found in Egypt. E. F. Harrison summarized the evidence well: "Among the earliest witnesses to Johannine authorship are the *Anti-Marcionite Prologue to John* and the Muratorian Canon, both in the second half of the second century. Irenaeus, Tertullian, and Clement of Alexandria from approximately the same period, agree on John the Apostle." The testimony of Irenaeus is crucial because only one generation stood between him and John. John's disciple, Polycarp, was among Irenaeus' teachers (Eusebius, V, xx.6).[7] The statement of Papias (Eusebius III, xxxix.4) alleging two Johns, one an apostle and the other an elder, even if true, in no way affects the evidence that John the apostle was the author of the fourth Gospel. And the Alogoi sect (A.D. 170), who denied John's authorship, seems to have been a fabrication to deny John's authority in teaching about the Logos (John 1:1, 14). In short, the external evidence for John the apostle is strong.

Internal evidence for the Johannine authorship of the fourth Gospel

7. Eusebius, *Church History.* See *A Select Library of Nicene and Post-Nicene Fathers,* ed. Philip Schaff, second series, vol. I.

is even stronger than the external. (1) There is the identification with John by the process of elimination discussed above. (2) The Gospel was written by an eyewitness, as is indicated by the many first person references (cf. 20:2; 21:4). (3) The author was a Jew who was thoroughly acquainted with Jewish customs of purification (2:6), burial (19:40), feasts (5:1), and even Jewish attitudes (7:49). (4) The author was a Palestinian Jew who was familiar with the geography and topography of the land (cf. 2:12; 4:11; 5:2; 18:11; 19:17). All of this evidence points collectively in the single direction of John the apostle of Christ.

The Johannine authorship of the fourth Gospel is important whatever date is assigned to the book, whether the late date of A.D. 80-100 traditionally given to it by scholars or the earlier date argued more recently on the basis of comparison with Qumran literature. George Ladd summed up the early view as follows: "Many contemporary scholars now recognize a solid Johannine tradition, independent of the Synoptics, stemming from Palestine and dating from A.D. 30-66."[8] If the early date can be established, then so much the better. But even with the late date we have in our possession a historian's treasure—a firsthand, eyewitness account of the life, teachings, death, and resurrection of Christ!

*The Synoptic Gospels.* The Gospels of Matthew, Mark, and Luke pose an interdependent question with respect to the time of their composition. As early as A.D. 130 Papias wrote, "Matthew compiled the Logia in the 'Hebrew' speech [i.e., Aramaic], and every one translated them as best he could."[9] Traditionally scholars have taken this to indicate the chronological priority of the Gospel of Matthew, but more recently New Testament source critics have argued for the priority of Mark.

F. F. Bruce provides a good summary for the evidence that Mark's Gospel was written first:

> We find, for example, that the substance of 606 out of the 661 verses of Mark appear in Matthew, and that some 380 of Mark's verses reappear with little material change in Luke. Or, to put it another way, out of 1,068 verses in Matthew, about 500 contain material also found in Mark; of the 1,149 verses of Luke, about 380 are parallel in Mark. Altogether, there are only 31 verses in Mark which have no parallel in Matthew or Luke.[10]

With this kind of literary dependence of Matthew and Luke on Mark it seems reasonable to posit Mark as the earliest Gospel. There is, of course, the remaining problem of the 250 verses common to Matthew and Luke (called Q from *Quelle,* or source) not found in Mark. There

8. George E. Ladd, *A Theology of the New Testament,* pp. 219-20.
9. Bruce, *N.T. Documents,* p. 38.
10. Bruce, p. 31.

are also 300 verses peculiar to Matthew (M) and about 520 verses in Luke (L) not found in the other Gospels. There are a number of possible explanations of these other sources. Some posit an early edition of Mark which did not have the 31 verses not used by Matthew and Luke. As to the verses peculiar to Matthew and Luke respectively, they may have had independent sources. If Matthew was written by the tax-collector disciple of Christ, he may have taken notes of his own on Jesus' ministry which he incorporated into Mark's accepted framework. Luke states in the prologue of his Gospel that he had many eyewitness and written accounts from which he worked.

Whatever the status of the sources and material, the key to dating the Gospels is the Book of Luke. If Luke was dependent on Mark, then the dating of Luke will demand a prior dating of Mark, and Matthew by implication can be fitted into the same pattern. Let us examine the probable date of the Gospel of Luke. The key to dating Luke is the dating of the sequel of Luke, namely, the Book of Acts. (1) Acts was written by a companion of Paul as is indicated by the "we" sections written in the first person (Acts 16:10-17; 20:5-21; 27:1 f.). The rest of the book is in the same style. (2) By the process of elimination, the only close companion of Paul not mentioned in the third person is Luke the beloved physician. Timothy, Silas, Mark, Barnabas, and so on, are all named (see 15:39; 16:1, 25). Only Luke remains. The high quality of the Greek, the use of medical terminology, and the obvious knowledge-ability of the author all fit the character of Luke the physician. (3) The narration of Acts ends with Paul's detention in a Roman prison (A.D. 60-62). Since Paul is presented as still alive when Luke wrote and since he stopped his story at this point in history, we must assume that A.D. 60-62 is the time of composition. Surely the death of Paul (c. A.D. 67) would have been included had Luke written after that time. (4) Now the Gospel of Luke is Part I of the two-part Luke-Acts history. Acts refers to the "first book" written to the same person, Theophilus (1:1; cf. Luke 1:3). The interests, writing style, and Gentile emphases of both books support a common author as well. It is reasonable to conclude, then, that Luke, the companion of the apostle Paul, wrote the Gospel of Luke sometime around A.D. 60. If Mark is prior to Luke, then this would place Mark between A.D. 50 and 60. Since Papias said Mark was the secretary of Peter, the external evidence would support this early dating of Mark. Matthew, likewise, can be assumed to date from about the same time.

There are of course some internal problems with this dating of Matthew and Luke at approximately A.D. 60. Some critics argue that: (1) Matthew 22:7 refers to the destruction of Jerusalem (A.D. 70) as already past (cf. Luke 14); (2) that Matthew 18:15 f. depicts an already organized Christian church; (3) that Matthew 28:18-20 reflects an advanced ecclesiology. Upon examination none of these arguments is decisive or even substantial. The references in Matthew to the "church" could be either retrospective to the Jewish synagogue or anticipatory of the New Testament church which Jesus said was yet future (see Matthew 16:16 f.). The baptismal formula in "the name of the Father and of the Son and of the Holy Spirit" (Matt. 28:19) need be no later than the belief that Jesus was God's Son—which is taught in both Matthew (16:16 f.) and Mark (14:61-65). The only argument of significance is the possible reference to the destruction of Jerusalem and this could be an implied prediction given before the fact (see Matt. 22:7). Indeed, the real basis of the whole objection to the early date for the synoptics seems to be an antisupernatural bias. It is assumed that a description of the destruction of Jerusalem (Matt. 24–25) in A.D. 70 would not be possible before the fact. But if there is a theistic God who knows all, including the future, then there is no problem believing that both Matthew 22 and Matthew 24 could be predictive. And since there is good reason to believe that Matthew and Luke are dependent on Mark and that Luke was written by A.D. 60, it is reasonable to conclude that Mark and Matthew were written before A.D. 60. It is the testimony of the earliest Church Fathers that Matthew the disciple wrote the Gospel and that Mark, Peter's secretary, wrote the Gospel of Mark. This being the case, we have another Gospel by an eyewitness, contemporary, and disciple of Christ (Matthew) and a third by a secretary to the apostle Peter (Mark).

To summarize, we have five different authentic sources for the life of Christ. Paul, the contemporary of the eyewitnesses, wrote some ten epistles between A.D. 50 and 60 which contain the essential teachings about Christ. Luke, the companion of Paul, using *written documents* and eyewitness accounts, wrote a complete life of Christ and history of the early Christian Church up to A.D. 60-62. Mark is believed on literary grounds to be prior to Luke and Matthew and, hence, must be dated between A.D. 50 and 60. Mark was a secretary and an associate of the apostle Peter who was an eyewitness disciple of Christ. John uses independent sources of his own that can be traced on linguistic grounds to between A.D. 30 and 66, though many place his composition between A.D. 80 and 100. All in all we possess eyewitness testimony in documents that were recorded between twenty to fifty or so years after the actual events themselves. This means that the New Testament records are authentic first century and firsthand information about the life, teachings, death, and resurrection of Christ. The only remaining link in establishing their historical reliability is the examination of the trustworthiness of the writers of the documents.

# The Reliability of the New Testament Writers

There are several divergent lines of testimony that support the reliability of the New Testament writers. Despite criticisms like those of David Hume that impugn the ability or integrity of any eyewitnesses to miracles, there is overwhelming evidence to the contrary. First, there is the unquestioned integrity of the witnesses in both number and nature. Second, there is the evident sanity of the writers. Third, there is the verified accuracy of their testimony through the collaborative testimony of external sources.

## The Integrity of the New Testament Witnesses

*The Number of New Testament Eyewitnesses to the Events.* The number of eyewitnesses supporting or writing the New Testament accounts is large. (a) The direct eyewitnesses who either wrote or superintended what was written of Christ's miraculous *life* and teachings are Matthew, Peter (through Mark), and John. Add to this the numerous eyewitness and written accounts used by Luke and Paul, and the resultant testimony is more than substantial. (b) The *death* of Christ was actually witnessed by the apostle John (John 19:26, 27), by Jesus' mother, as well as by the soldiers, the crowd, and many other women standing nearby (v. 25; cf. Mark 15:40, 41). John wrote about what he had seen himself, and the other writers used the testimony of those present. (c) On the crucial doctrine of the resurrection of Christ there were over five hundred persons to whom Christ appeared bodily. He appeared to Mary Magdalene (John 20:1), to Mary the mother of James (Matt. 28:2), to Salome and Joanna (Luke 24:10), and to several other women from Galilee (see Luke 23:55). Christ appeared to Peter (Luke 24:34) and later to Cleopas and the other disciple on the road to Emmaus (Luke 24:13-32). Later Christ revealed himself to the ten apostles in Jerusalem (John 20:24) and then to the eleven when Thomas was present a week later (John 20:26-29). The next Sunday Jesus appeared to seven disciples on the Sea of Galilee (John 21:1-24). Further, Jesus appeared to the eleven disciples on a mountain in Galilee (Matt. 28:16-20) and to more than five hundred brethren at one time (I Cor. 15:6). Finally, Jesus appeared to his brother James (I Cor. 15:7a) and to the disciples on the Mount of Olives just before he ascended to heaven (Acts 1:4-12). The number of individual appearances is more than sufficient to determine the validity of their testimony. No like testimony is possessed for any event from ancient times.

*The Nature of the New Testament Eyewitnesses to Christ.* Not only was there an overwhelming number of witnesses to the life, death, and resurrection of Christ, but the nature of their testimony places it way beyond reasonable doubt. Several factors support this contention. (a) The witnesses were in most cases independent of one another. There were at least ten different appearances spaced over forty days (Acts 1:3). (b) There was an initial disinclination to believe what they saw, which would eliminate the possibility of hallucination (cf. John 20:25 f.; Luke 24:15 f.; Matt. 28:17). (c) Physical and tangible evidence was presented that he was indeed the bodily resurrected Christ. He ate fish, showed his hands and feet, asked them to handle his flesh and bones (Luke 24:39-43), and even challenged Thomas to put fingers and hands into his wounds (John 20:27). Furthermore, Christ spent much time with them doing "many other signs" (John 20:31), "speaking of the kingdom of God," and showing "many proofs" of his resurrection (Acts 1:3). He even ate breakfast with seven of them and had a prolonged discussion with Peter (John 20:15 f.). He also ate with two other disciples in Emmaus (Luke 24:28 f.).

(d) Furthermore, the accounts of the resurrection appearances are divergent enough to draw the allegation of contradiction. Although it is possible to reconcile the accounts, the divergence of perspective argues strongly for the independence and integrity of the witnesses. There is certainly no collusion among them for all to tell the same story. If there were collusion, they could have easily ironed out some problems, such as the report in Luke that there were two men (angels) by the tomb whereas Matthew speaks of only one. The same independence of testimony holds true for other things in the Gospels. For example, Matthew speaks of both thieves railing on Christ (27:44), but Luke speaks of one rebuking the other and asking Christ for a place in his kingdom (Luke 13:39 f.). It is possible that one repented, but the recorded divergence speaks for the integrity of the witnesses. (e) All that is known about the apostles testifies to their honesty and integrity. That they taught honesty, sincerity, and truthfulness is abundantly clear from their writings. What is recorded of their lives clearly supports their teachings. They did not fear men, even under the threat of imprisonment or death (see Acts 4:18 f.; 5:27 f.). They did not tolerate lying (Acts 5:1 f.); they refused to be bought with money (Acts 8:18). And on top of it all, they remained steadfast in their testimony under extreme persecution (see II Cor. 11:23 f.) and even to the point of martyrdom, which almost all the apostles underwent. As has been pointed out before, men will sometimes die for what they believe to be true but never for what they know to be false. A man becomes extremely honest and truthful under the threat of death.

In summary, both the vast number of the independent eyewitness accounts of Jesus' death and resurrection as well as the nature and integrity of the witnesses themselves leave beyond reasonable doubt the reliability of the apostolic testimony about Christ. There seems to be no way to deny the historicity of Christ's life, death, and resurrection without impugning the integrity of the apostolic eyewitnesses. And there are ample reasons (without any significant evidence to the contrary) that Christ's disciples were at least honest and truthful men.

## The Sanity of the New Testament Eyewitnesses and Writers

A man can be honest but yet be psychologically unbalanced. Perhaps the apostles were under some psychological delusion or hallucination. These charges have been made but must be ruled out by the known facts of the case. Mass hallucination or delusion is eliminated by several factors. First, there was the inclination to disbelieve the reports of the resurrection. Hallucination is a phenomenon which occurs when people are already inclined to believe in something. Second, the apostles and eyewitnesses were persons who had known Jesus intimately for years. Recognition was no real problem. Third, there were numerous and independent occasions of long duration, involving conversation and verification by various groups of people, that rule out any possibility of psychological deception. Fourth, mass delusion is ruled out by the numerous independent occasions when one, two, seven, ten, eleven persons had the same experience that the five hundred had. Some of the individuals saw Christ on at least four or five different occasions. Peter saw Christ alone, with the seven, with the ten, with the eleven, and at the ascension. John saw Christ on at least the last four of these occasions as well. Fifth, the resurrected Christ did what was familiar to them to convince them of his reality; for example, he showed the fishermen how to catch fish (John 21:4 f.). A man can be fooled on things with which he is not familiar but the staunch fishermen could not be tricked at their own trade. Sixth, Jesus performed "many proofs" and "signs" after his resurrection to convince the disciples of his reality (John 20:30; Acts 1:3). The number and repetition of these miracles rule out any reasonable possibility of delusion.

Since, then, there is no evidence for either individual or collective delusion or hallucination of the eyewitnesses it is necessary to conclude that they were not only honest but also sane witnesses of the events of which they spoke. This leaves us with but one obstacle between their witness and the truth of the events of which they spoke, and that concerns the accuracy of their testimony.

## The Accuracy of the New Testament Eyewitnesses

Two theories stand in the way of accepting the accuracy of the New Testament records: Form Criticism and the "faulty memory" hypothesis.

*An Evaluation of the Form Criticism Hypothesis.* Form criticism holds that the life and teachings of Christ have been historically obscured by the religious needs and interests of the early church. These critics believe that the oral traditions were formed into various "stories" and woven into continuous narratives by means of editorial summaries devoid of historical value in accordance with the life-setting of the early church. Because it is impossible to know what really happened, the "sayings" of Jesus are strung together like pearls on the thread of religious interest without regard for historical accuracy. According to the more radical critics, when the records are demythologized, all that remains is at best the mere fact that an unusual man, Jesus of Nazareth, lived in the early first century. Even the original words of Jesus are for the most part lost within the re-forming and reshaping process.

There were no doubt many needs and interests of the early church that revealed themselves in the way the Gospel writers put together their material on the life of Christ. Each writer clearly manifests motifs and interests which are characteristic of his work. It has been long observed that Matthew presents Christ as King, Mark presents him as a Servant, Luke as a perfect Man, and John as God Incarnate. Each writer worked his material around his particular motif. Each writer, too, had a particular audience in mind in the early church of a generation or so after Christ's death. The needs of that particular audience no doubt influenced the way the writer put his material together. Furthermore, each writer had to be selective of the vast material, both oral and written (cf. Luke 1:1-3; John 21:25) available to him. However, having admitted all this, we are a long way from the charge that the Gospel records are not a reliable historical summary of the major events and teachings of Christ. There are several definitive reasons for rejecting the Form Criticism hypothesis in favor of the historical reliability of the Gospels.[11]

a. It Minimizes or Neglects the Role of the Apostles and Eyewitnesses

If the Form critics are correct then we must assume that the eye-witnesses allowed distortions of the life of Christ to occur in the documents during their lifetime. A number of apostles outlived the first Christian writings about Jesus' life, death, and resurrection. The writings began around A.D. 50 and most apostles lived until the Neronian persecutions (around A.D. 67) and John probably lived on to near the end of the century. Even granting for the sake of argument the assumption that their interests were not primarily historical but religious, it is inconceivable that they would allow gross misrepresentations regarding central teachings and events in Christ's life.

b. It Is Highly Improbable That the Early Church Had No Biographical Interests

The assumption that the early church had only a religious interest is gratuitous and contrary to fact. Each of the Gospels has the same overall

---

11. These criticisms are an expansion on criticisms made by Everett F. Harrison, *Introduction to the New Testament*, pp. 149-51.

outline or history of events. The synoptic Gospels reveal an even closer parallel. Matthew and Luke apparently follow the basic outline of Mark who reflects the elements in the early *kerygma* (proclamation) of Peter in Acts 10:37-42.

Luke shows a special interest in history, taking pains to point out political personages and events that paralleled the life of Christ. Luke mentions three emperors in his writings (Augustus, Tiberius, and Claudius; see Luke 2:1; 3:1 and Acts 11:28). Luke fixes the time of Jesus' birth during Caesar Augustus and Herod the Great (1:5; 2:1). Numerous Roman governors appear in Luke's writings including Pilate, Sergius Paulus, Gallio, Felix, and Festus. The descendants of Herod the Great— Herod Antipas, the vassal kings Herod Agrippa I and II, Bernice, and Drusilla—are also mentioned by Luke. Leading members of the Jewish priestly caste are also recorded, including Annas, Caiaphas, Ananias, and the famous Rabbi Gamaliel. Luke mentions the proconsul of Achaia, Gallio (Acts 18:12), who came to prominence, according to the Delphi Inscription, in July of A.D. 51. There are numerous other references of historical interest in Luke's works which leave no doubt as to his historical interest.[12]

The other Gospels are not without historical, chronological, and biographical interests. Matthew records Jesus' family lineage (chap. 1). He mentions the visit of the Magi from the East, the decree of Herod to slaughter the babies around Bethlehem (chap. 2), the imprisonment and beheading of John the Baptist by Herod Tetrarch (chap. 14), and the leaders associated with the trial and crucifixion of Christ such as Pilate and Caiaphas (chaps. 26–27). John is replete with chronological references such as to the "first" miracle of Jesus (John 2:11), numerous references to the time of day (John 4:6; 19:14), and other references to the time of the year (John 2:23; 6:4; 7:2). Mark too reflects both a general chronological interest in the order of events in Christ's life and specific interest in times and places. Mark alone records all three times of day that relate to Jesus' crucifixion (see 15:25, 33). In the face of these and many more facts it is simply untrue to claim that the Gospel writers had no historical interests.

    c. Form Criticism Neglects the Testimony of Luke in the Prologue of His Gospel

Luke not only reflects a historical interest but he openly claims to have one and reveals that many others in the early church reflected the same interest in their written accounts. Luke wrote, "Inasmuch as many have undertaken to compile a narrative of the things which have been accomplished among us, . . . it seemed good to me also having

---

12. See Bruce, *N.T. Documents,* pp. 80-92.

followed all things closely for some time past, to write an orderly account
. . . that you may know the truth concerning the things of which you
have been informed" (Luke 1:1-3). Several things are apparent from
Luke's comments. First, there were in his day (by A.D. 60) already
"many" written accounts of Jesus' life. Second, Luke was definitely
interested in the historical "truth," in an "orderly account." Third, the
sources of these written accounts were "eyewitnesses." On the supposition
of Form Criticism this testimony would be false, since the critics depend
on oral tradition being re-formed over a prolonged period of time in
order to fit the religious needs of the early church. Hence, the hypotheses
of Form Criticism fly in the face of the clear testimony of Luke. Since
the evidence for the date and authorship of Luke is good, it is best to
reject the unjustified assumption of the Form critics.

    d.  There Is No Explanation as to Why Details Are Remembered
        and the General Outline Is Forgotten

On the presupposition of the Form critics many of the details of
Jesus' sayings were remembered but the general outline of the events was
forgotten. This seems highly implausible on the face of it. Why should
the early church forget the overall order of events? One must assume
either a terrible lapse of memory on the part of the first generation of
believers or else that the Gospels were not put together until much later
than the times already established above. Neither supposition fits the
facts well. Their memories were very good on many little details including
the exact Aramaic words Jesus used on occasions (see Mark 5:41; 15:34),
and the first Gospel (perhaps Mark) was composed only twenty or so
years after Jesus died.

    e.  Necessary Time for Classification and Formation of Material Is
      Not Available

As has already been stated, the time lapse between Jesus' death
(A.D. 29-33)[13] and the first Gospel record (A.D. 50-60) is too short to
fit the Form Criticism theory. According to this view the early church
would need enough time to disseminate, collect, classify, and form the
"stories" and "sayings" of Jesus out of their original context into the
"life-setting" of the early church. One generation is not enough time to
accomplish this for several reasons. First, some of the eyewitnesses would
still be alive to correct any distortions. Second, it would take more than a
generation to accomplish all the steps in the process. As long as the
generation of people following the apostles was alive (say, A.D. 60-90)
it would be exceedingly difficult to conceive of how they would be
unable to detect major divergence from the truth taught them by the
apostles. In order to make the theory work for this short a time period

---

13. See Harold W. Hoehner, "Chronological Aspects of the Life of Christ," in
*Bibliotheca Sacra,* October 1973, pp. 338-51.

one would have to assume several things contrary to fact: (1) that there was no historical interest on the part of the apostles; (2) that there were no written accounts during the first generation after Christ (say c. A.D. 30-60); and (3) that memories of even the general outline of events were so diminished in one generation that nothing significant of historical value can be retrieved. It is easier to believe the testimony of Luke and the early Church Fathers who claimed that Matthew, Mark, and John wrote Gospels.

f. The Gospels Are Vastly Different from Folklore and Myth

According to Form Criticism the Gospels are more like folklore and myth than historical fact.[14] They were passed on and preserved like a tale because of their religious value and not because of their historical value. But even a quick comparison of the New Testament first century Gospels with the apocryphal Gospels of the second and third centuries will reveal the difference. The fanciful tales of Jesus' alleged childhood miracles, the heretical admixture of gnosticism, and the unrealistic portrayal of the apostles marks off the apocryphal from the authentic Gospels as clear as night from day. The truth of Form Criticism is appropriately applied to these apocryphal writings of the second and third centuries. But by clear contrast the New Testament documents have the ring of authenticity.

g. Form Criticism Wrongly Assumes That the Early Church Did Not Distinguish Between Jesus' Statements and Their Own Words

Form Criticism is contradicted by the facts of the early church's usage of Jesus' words. Contrary to the Form theory, the early church did make a clear distinction between their own words and those of Jesus. For the most part it is not difficult to make a red-letter edition of the Bible. Paul clearly differentiated between Jesus' words and his own on the question of marriage (I Cor. 7:10, 12, 25). Likewise, Paul delineated the words of Jesus on paying ministers (I Tim. 5:18) and on the Lord's Supper (I Cor. 11:24, 25). Again, when preaching to the Ephesian elders Paul quoted a saying of Jesus that is not even found in the four Gospels (Acts 20:35). In view of New Testament practice it is a gratuitous assumption to argue that the early church indistinguishably blurred the sayings of Jesus with their own.

h. Form Criticism Neglects the Individuality and Creativity of New Testament Writers

Why should we assume that the Gospels were put together by the early church over a period of years? Were the apostles incapable of composing them? Luke was an educated man. Mark probably came from a cultured family. John wrote in very simple language. Matthew was used

---

14. For a critical introduction to these books see Edgar Hennecke, *New Testament Apocrypha*.

to keeping records as a tax collector. There is no apparent reason why the Gospels in their present form could not have been the works of these men. Further, why not assume the differences in the Gospels are due to the separate sources, individual interests, and creativity of the different authors? Luke tells where he got his information (Luke 1:1-3), namely, from extant written accounts. Matthew could have obtained his unique material from his own notes on Jesus' life and teaching. Mark appears to follow the outline of Peter's *kerygma* (Acts 10) and was no doubt privy to Peter's firsthand information. John was probably confidant of many private conversations by virtue of his youth and by his family's entrance into the upper circles in Jerusalem. In view of these situations, there is no reason why the facts cannot be easily explained via the separate sources, styles, and interests of the individual writers.

i. Gospel Stories Do Not Grow by Accretion over the Years

The evolutionary theory of the Gospel material is contrary to several other facts. Not every story grew in detail over the years. Some material not found in later accounts is found in earlier ones. For example Mark's Gospel is considered earlier than the others and yet Mark alone names the blind man Bartimaeus (10:46). Further, Mark names the disciples who came to Jesus on the Mt. of Olives (13:3), whereas Matthew does not (24:3). Mark alone records that Jesus was himself a "carpenter" (Mark 6:3) and not merely the "son of a carpenter" as Matthew 13:35. Mark alone gives the details of the young man who streaked out of the Garden (Mark 14:51), a reference which many believe refers to Mark himself. In any event, there is no evidence that the later versions of the stories were more detailed than the earlier ones, as Form critics would have us believe.

In summation, Form Criticism fails to controvert the most substantial evidence that the first-century eyewitness reports recorded in the Gospels provide valid historical material concerning the life of Christ. There is no reason why the Gospel accounts should not be accepted as reliable versions of what Jesus really did and said.

*The "Faulty Memory" Hypothesis Evaluated.* Some scholars are willing to grant an early date for some written accounts of Jesus' life but are unwilling to grant their accuracy. They would argue that after thirty years the disciples had "misty memories." How, for example, could the Watergate hearings have been held thirty years after the fact? Even within months after the Watergate event many of the witnesses had difficulty recalling precisely what was said and done!

This "Faulty Memory" hypothesis is itself based on a faulty memory. It forgets several important facts about the New Testament situation that make it quite different from Watergate. First, memory was much more developed in ancient times than it is for literate peoples today. Before the ready availability of written and printed documents, life depended much more heavily on memory. Like a muscle, the brain works better with usage. The need to use it in ancient time was more acute and, hence, the memory more developed. Second, the miraculous events of the incarnation covering several years of Jesus' adult life left a far more vivid impression than the surreptitious events of Watergate covering only a few months. Third, there were numerous eyewitnesses to all the major events and teachings of Jesus. One could serve as a cross-check on the memory of the other. Fourth, the critics forget that there were many early written notes and records on Jesus' life (Luke 1:1-3). Fifth, the critics forget that Jesus promised that he would not let his disciples forget what he had taught them. He promised to "bring to their remembrance all that he had said to them" (John 14:26). If men by the natural powers of hypnotism can bring up forgotten detail, it should be no problem for a supernatural power to do so.

Were this all the evidence we possessed about the honesty and accuracy of the apostolic writings it would be more than sufficient to conclude they are both authentic and accurate. There is, however, an important source by which we can cross-check the accuracy of the apostles' testimony about Christ. There are the supportive services of secular history and archaeology that can be called on for testimony.

**Archaeological and Secular Testimony to the Accuracy of the New Testament**

The archaeological evidence in support of the Bible in general is overwhelming. Donald J. Wiseman summed it up well when he wrote, "The geography of Bible lands and visible remains of antiquity were gradually recorded until today more than 25,000 sites within this region and dating to Old Testament times, in their broadest sense, have been located...."[15] Whole books are written on the subject, which we will not try to summarize here. We wish to focus attention briefly on two points: the secular confirmation of the historicity of early Christianity in general and verification of specific persons and events in the New Testament in particular. And besides the thousands of archaeological confirmations of the Bible, it is noteworthy to read an eminent archaeologist's writing that no archaeological find has ever been made that contradicts the history of the Bible.[16]

*Secular History's Confirmation of the Reliability of the New Testa-*

15. Donald J. Wiseman, "Archaeological Confirmation of the Old Testament," in C. F. Henry, *Revelation and the Bible*, pp. 301-2.
16. Quoted by R. K. Harrison, *Introduction to the Old Testament*, p. 94.

*ment.*[17] First century historians confirm the general historical outline of the New Testament.

a. Jewish Historian, Josephus (A.D. 37-100)

The Jewish historian Josephus, contemporary of Christ, abounds with references to figures familiar to New Testament readers. F. F. Bruce summarized the evidence:

> Here, in the pages of Josephus, we meet many figures who are well-known to us from the New Testament; the colourful family of the Herods; the Roman emperors Augustus, Tiberius, Claudius, and the procurators of Judea; the high priestly families—Annas, Caiaphas, Ananias, and the rest; the Pharisees and the Sadducees; and so on.[18]

Moreover Josephus wrote of "the brother of Jesus, the so-called Christ, whose name was James . . ." (*Antiquities* XX 9:1). And in a more explicit but disputed passage the *Antiquities* says:

> At this time there was a wise man who was called Jesus. . . . Pilate condemned Him to be condemned and to die. And those who had become His disciples did not abandon His discipleship. They reported that He had appeared to them three days after His crucifixion and that He was alive; accordingly, He was perhaps the Messiah concerning whom the prophets have recounted wonders (xviii.33, Arabic text).

b. Roman Historian, Cornelius Tacitus (A.D. 55?-after 117)

He wrote of Nero's attempt to relieve himself of the guilt of burning Rome:

> Hence to suppress the rumor, he falsely charged with the guilt, and punished with the most exquisite tortures, the persons commonly called Christians, who were hated for their enormities. Christus, the founder of the name, was put to death by Pontius Pilate, procurator of Judea in the reign of Tiberius: but the pernicious superstition, repressed for a time broke out again, not only through Judea, where the mischief originated, but through the city of Rome also (Annals XV.44).

c. Greek Satirist, Lucian (second century)
Lucian alludes to Christ in these words:

> . . . the man who was crucified in Palestine because he introduced this new cult into the world. . . . Furthermore, their first lawgiver persuaded them that they were all brothers one of another after they have transgressed once for all by denying the Greek gods and by worshipping that crucified sophist himself and living under his laws (*On the Death of Peregrine*).

---

17. For a critical and scholarly presentation of secular sources of early Christianity, see F. F. Bruce, *Non-Christian Origins.*
18. Bruce, *N.T. Documents,* p. 104.

d. Roman Historian, Suetonius (c. A.D. 120)

Suetonius, court official under Hadrian, made two references to Christ: in the *Life of Claudius* (25.4) he wrote, "As the Jews were making constant disturbances at the instigation of Chestus [another spelling of *Christus* or *Christ*], he expelled them from Rome." Elsewhere in the *Lives of the Caesars* (26.2) he wrote: "Punishment by Nero was inflicted on the Christians, a class of men given to a new and mischievous superstition."

e. Pliny the Younger (c. A.D. 112)

Writing to the emperor of his achievements as governor of Bithynia, Pliny the Younger gave information on how he had killed multitudes of Christians—men, women, and children. He said he attempted to "make them curse Christ, which a genuine Christian cannot be induced to do." In the same letter (*Epistles* X.96) he wrote of Christians:

> They were in the habit of meeting on a certain fixed day before it was light, when they sang in alternate verse a hymn to Christ as to a god, and bound themselves to a solemn oath, not to do any wicked deeds, and never to deny a truth when they should be called upon to deliver it up.

f. Samaritan-born historian, Thallus (c. A.D. 52)

According to Julius Africanus (c. A.D. 221), "Thallus, in the third book of his histories, explains away this darkness [at the time of the crucifixion] as an eclipse of the sun—unreasonably, as it seems to me." It was unreasonable, of course, because a solar eclipse could not take place at the time of the full moon, and it was the time of the paschal full moon when Christ died.

g. Letter of Mara Bar-Serapion (after A.D. 73)

According to F. F. Bruce this letter residing in the British Museum is by a father to his son in prison. In it he compares the deaths of Socrates, Pythagoras, and Jesus as follows:

> What advantage did the Jews gain from executing their wise King? It was just after that that their kingdom was abolished.... But Socrates did not die for good; he lived on in the teaching of Plato. Pythagoras did not die for good; he lived on in the statue of Hera. Nor did the wise King die for good; he lived on in the teaching which he had given.[19]

h. The Jewish Talmud (completed by A.D. 500)

The Babylonian Talmud (Sanhedrin 43a, "Eve of Passover") contains the following explicit reference to Jesus:

> On the eve of Passover they hanged Yeshu (of Nazareth) and the

---

19. Bruce, *N.T. Documents,* p. 14.

herald went before him for forty days saying (Yeshu of Nazareth) is going to be stoned in that he hath practiced sorcery and beguiled and led astray Israel. Let everyone knowing aught in his defense come and plead for him. But they found naught in his defense and hanged him on the eve of Passover.

Another Talmudic section says R. Shimeon ben' Azzai wrote concerning Jesus, "I found a genealogical roll in Jerusalem wherein was recorded, Such-an-one is a bastard of an adulteress" (Yeb. IV 3; 49 a). It should be noted that the Jewish belief that Jesus was an illegitimate son and demon-possessed is the same as that presented in the New Testament (cf. Mark 3:22; John 8:41).

Combining the above secular testimony to Christ, we get the following picture: (1) Jesus was crucified under Pontius Pilate at Passover time. (2) He was believed by his disciples to have risen from the dead three days later. (3) Jewish leaders charged Christ with sorcery and believed he was born of adultery. (4) The Judean sect of Christianity could not be contained but spread even to Rome. (5) Nero and other Roman rulers bitterly persecuted and martyred early Christians. (6) These early Christians denied polytheism, lived dedicated lives according to Christ's teachings, and worshiped Christ. This picture is perfectly congruent with that of the New Testament.

*Archaeological Confirmation of New Testament History.* Besides the general outline of New Testament history confirmed by secular sources close to Christ, there is specific confirmation of specific facts of New Testament history from archaeology. We will center brief attention on the history given by Luke. There are literally hundreds of archaeological finds that support specific persons, events, and facts presented in Luke-Acts, including many which were once thought to be incorrect. Especially noteworthy is Luke's correct usages of official titles. He calls the rulers of Thessalonica "politarchs," Gallio the "Proconsul of Achaea," the one in Ephesus a "temple warden," the governor of Cyprus a "proconsul" and the chief official in Malta "the first man of the island," a title confirmed in Greek and Latin inscriptions.[20]

Likewise, Luke is known to be correct in chronological references. His reference to "Lysanias the tetrarch of Abilene" at the time John the Baptist began his ministry (A.D. 27), once thought to be incorrect, is now known by Greek inscriptions to be correct. Lysanias was tetrarch between A.D. 14 and 29. Other chronological references are known to be correct including those to Caesar, Herod, and even Gallio (Acts 18:12-17).[21]

20. Edwin Yamauchi, *The Stones and the Scriptures,* pp. 115-19.
21. Yamauchi, pp. 99, 116.

Numerous places named in the Gospels including the Pool of Siloam (John 9:7-11) and the "judgment seat" near Corinth (II Cor. 5:10) have been verified by archaeology.[22] Further, names of persons mentioned in the New Testament appear in the finds of archaeology. Near the theater at Corinth was found an inscription: "Erastus in return for his aedileship laid the pavement at his own expense." It is possible that this was the same Erastus who became a coworker of Paul (Acts 19:22).

These illustrations are only a few of the countless finds that confirm the New Testament presentation in its every detail. We may summarize the situation in the words of the distinguished Roman historian A. N. Sherwin-White about the writings of Luke: "For Acts the confirmation of historicity is overwhelming. . . . Any attempt to reject its basic historicity even in matters of detail must now appear absurd. Roman historians have long taken it for granted."[23]

In like manner Luke is commended by the classical historian, G. D. Williamson for showing "complete familiarity with the thought, expression, and habitual terminology of the speakers, and . . . what memories the people of that time possessed!—if not on written notes, which we have reason to believe were commonly made."[24]

It has been largely due to the archaeological efforts of the late great Sir William Ramsay that the critical views of New Testament history have been overthrown and its historicity established. Ramsay was himself converted from the critical view by his own research into the evidence. He wrote:

> I began with a mind unfavorable to it [Acts], for the ingenuity and apparent completeness of the Tübingen theory had at one time quite convinced me. It did not lie then in my line of life to investigate the subject minutely; but more recently I found myself often brought into contact with the book of Acts as an authority for the topography, antiquities, and society of Asia Minor. It was gradually borne in upon me that in various details the narrative showed marvelous truth.[25]

The irony of the situation is that today the professional historians accept the historicity of the New Testament. It is the critics who use pre-archaeological and philosophical presuppositions that reject the historicity of the New Testament. As the renowned archaeologist and paleographer, William F. Albright, notes, "All radical schools in New Testament criticism which have existed in the past or which exist today are pre-archaeological, and

---

22. Yamauchi, pp. 100, 116.
23. A. N. Sherwin-White, *Roman Society and Roman Law in the New Testament,* p. 189.
24. G. A. Williamson, *The World of Josephus,* p. 290.
25. William M. Ramsay, *St. Paul the Traveller and the Roman Citizen,* p. 8.

are, therefore, since they were built *in der Luft* [in the air], quite anti-quated today."[26]

## Summary and Conclusion

Both the *authenticity* and the historicity of the New Testament documents are firmly established today. The authentic nature and vast amount of the manuscript evidence is overwhelming compared to the classical texts from antiquity. Furthermore, many of the original manuscripts date from within twenty to thirty years of the events in Jesus' life, that is, from contemporaries and eyewitnesses.

The *historicity* of these contemporary accounts of Christ's life, teachings, death, and resurrection is also established on firm historical grounds. The integrity of the New Testament writers is established by the character of the witnesses as well as by the quantity and independent nature of their witness. As to the accuracy of their reports there is support in general from the secular history of the first century and in particular from numerous archaeological discoveries supporting specific details of the New Testament account.

The words of the great classical scholar Sir Fredric Kenyon serve well to summarize the question of reliability of the New Testament documents:

> The interval then between the dates of original composition and the earliest extant evidence becomes so small as to be in fact negligible, and the last foundation for any doubt that the Scriptures have come down to us substantially as they were written has now been removed. Both the *authenticity* and the general *integrity* of the books of the New Testament may be regarded as finally established.[27]

## SELECT READINGS FOR CHAPTER SIXTEEN

Bruce, F. F. *Jesus and Christian Origins Outside the New Testament.*
———. *The New Testament Documents: Are They Reliable?*
Geisler, Norman L. *General Introduction to the Bible.* Chapters 16-27.
Guthrie, Donald. *New Testament Introduction.*
Harrison, Everett F. *Introduction to the New Testament.*
Kenyon, Sir Frederic. *The Bible and Archaeology.*
———. *Our Bible and the Ancient Manuscripts.*
Metzger, Bruce. *The Text of the New Testament.*
Montgomery, John W. *Christianity and History.*
Ramsay, Sir William. *St. Paul the Traveller and the Roman Citizen.*

---

26. William F. Albright, "Retrospect and Prospect in New Testament Archaeology," in *The Teacher's Yoke,* ed. E. Jerry Vardaman, p. 29.
27. Sir Frederic Kenyon, *The Bible and Archaeology,* pp. 288 f.

# Chapter 17

## The Deity and Authority of Jesus Christ

Orthodox Christianity claims that Jesus of Nazareth was God in human flesh. This doctrine is absolutely essential to true Christianity. If it is true, then Christianity is unique and authoritative. If not, then Christianity does not differ in kind from other religions. This chapter will move from the historical to the theological, from Jesus of Nazareth to Jesus the Son of God.

The basic logic of this apologetic for Christianity is: (1) The New Testament is a historically reliable record of the life, teachings, death, and resurrection of Jesus Christ (see Chapter 16); (2) Jesus taught that he was God Incarnate (Chapter 17a); (3) Jesus proved to be God Incarnate by fulfilling Old Testament prophecy, by a miraculous life, and by rising from the grave (Chapter 17b). Therefore, Jesus of Nazareth is Deity.

### An Examination of the Claims for the Deity of Jesus Christ

We have already shown that the New Testament documents are historically reliable. The New Testament has been confirmed to be accurate not only in its general outline of history but in its specific detail as well. We have noted also that the ear- and eyewitnesses of Christ passed down contemporary accounts of Christ's words and deeds (Chapter 16). These words of Jesus were not only memorized but were written down by qualified witnesses (Luke 1:1-3). Furthermore, the New Testament writers made a clear distinction between their words and the words of Jesus (Acts 20:28; I Cor. 7:10, 12; 11:24, 25). Hence, a red-letter edition of the Bible which distinguishes the words of Jesus from those of the authors of the Gospels is a realistic possibility. That is, since there is both proven integrity and accuracy of the New Testament writers, there is consequent historical reliability in their quotations of Jesus. It is not necessary to assume that the New Testament relates always a word-for-word record of Jesus' teachings. It will be sufficient to hold that it presents the essence of his teaching on the subject at hand. Building on this basis, we will now examine precisely what it was that Jesus claimed with respect to his own origin and nature. Following this we will examine what his most immediate followers taught about his deity.

### An Examination of Jesus' Claims to Be Deity

There are several lines of evidence that prove (whether or not the claim is true) that Jesus did claim to be God. This can be seen from his claims to be the Jehovah of the Old Testament, from his acceptance of the titles of deity, from his messianic claims, from his acceptance of worship, from the implications of many of his actions, from the authority of his commands, and from the reaction of the first century monotheistic Jews to his claims and actions.

*Jesus' Claim to Be Jehovah.* The most forthright claims of Christ to be God are revealed in his identification with the Jehovah of the Old Testament. "Jehovah" (or Yawey) is the spelling given to the tetragrammaton or designation for God (i.e., JHWH, or YHWH) in the Old Testament. This word for God is spelled with all capital letters in the English Old Testament of the King James (1611) and Revised Standard versions (1952), namely, L-O-R-D. The American Standard Version (1901) transliterated it as "Jehovah." In every case these terms refer to deity. Unlike the word *adonai* (usually translated "lord") which sometimes refers to men (cf. Gen. 18:12) and other times to God, the word LORD (Jehovah) always refers to God. To avoid confusion we will quote here from the ASV Old Testament which uses the term "Jehovah." For example, "I am Jehovah and I appeared unto Abraham, unto Isaac, and unto Jacob, as God Almighty; but by my name Jehovah I was not known to them" (Exod. 6:2, 3). So sacred was this name, JHWH, that devout Jews would not even pronounce it. Many take the word to mean "underived existence" or "He who is" from the "I AM" of Exodus 3:14, but the meaning of the term is not certain. It is known for sure that Jehovah is the I AM of Exodus 3:14 and that for the Jews he alone is God. Everything else is an idol or false god. Nothing else was to be worshiped or served, nor were sacrifices to be made to them (Exod. 20:5). Jehovah was a "jealous God" and would not share either his name or his glory with another. Isaiah wrote, "Thus saith Jehovah . . . I am the first, and I am the last; and besides me there is no God" (44:6). Again, "I am

Jehovah, that is my name; and my glory will I not give to another, neither my praise unto graven images" (Isa. 42:8; cf. 48:11).

In view of the fact that the Jehovah of the Jewish Old Testament would not give his name, honor, or glory to another, it is little wonder that the words and deeds of Jesus of Nazareth drew stones and cries of "blasphemy" from first-century Jews. The very things that the Jehovah of the Old Testament claimed for himself Jesus of Nazareth also claimed, as the following verses reveal: Jesus said "I am the good shepherd" (John 10:11), but the Old Testament declared "Jehovah is my shepherd" (Ps. 23:1). Jesus claimed to be judge of all men and nations (John 5:27 f. and Matt. 25:31 f.) but Joel, quoting Jehovah, wrote: "for there I will sit to judge all the nations round about" (Joel 3:12). Jesus said, "I am the light of the world" (John 8:12) whereas Isaiah says, "Jehovah will be unto thee an everlasting light, and thy God thy glory" (60:19). Jesus claimed in prayer before the Father to share his eternal glory, saying, "Father, glorify thou me in thy own presence with the glory which I had with thee before the world was made." But Isaiah quoted Jehovah vowing, "my glory will I not give to another" (42:8). Jesus spoke of himself as the coming "bridegroom" (Matt. 25:1), which is exactly how Jehovah is depicted in the Old Testament (cf. Isa. 62:5; Hos. 2:16). In the Book of Revelation Jesus is quoted by John as saying, "I am the first and the last" (1:17), which are precisely the words Jehovah used to declare that there was no other God besides himself (Isa. 42:8). The Old Testament declares that "Jehovah is our light" (Ps. 27:1), but Jesus said "I am the light of the world" (John 8:12).

Perhaps the strongest and most direct claim of Jesus to be Jehovah occurs in John 8:58 where he said to the Jews, "Truly, truly, I say to you, before Abraham was, I am." The Jews' reaction left no doubt as to how they understood his claim. They knew he had claimed not only preexistence before Abraham but also equality with God. They promptly picked up stones to stone him (cf. John 8:58 and 10:31-33). Jesus had clearly claimed to be the "I AM" of Exodus 3:14 that refers to Jehovah alone. The claim was either blasphemy or else an indication of deity. Jesus left no doubt as to which interpretation he wished them to take. This claim to be "I am" is repeated in Mark 14:62 and in John 18:5, 6. In the latter case the effect on those around Christ was dramatic: "they drew back and fell to the ground."

*Jesus' Claim to Be Equal with God.* On numerous occasions Jesus claimed to be equal with God in other ways than assuming the titles of deity. Jesus said to the scribes, "That you may know that the son of man has authority on earth to forgive sins . . . I say to you [the paralytic], rise, take up your pallet and go home" (Mark 2:10, 11). Jesus had just said to the paralytic, "My son, your sins are forgiven" (v. 5), to which the outraged scribes retorted, "Why does this man speak thus? It is blasphemy! Who can forgive sins but God alone?" (v. 7). Jesus' claim to be able to forgive sins, the scribes' understanding of that claim, and Jesus' healing of the man are all evidence of his authority, and make it clear that Jesus was claiming a power that God alone possessed (cf. Jer. 31:34).

Jesus solemnly claimed another power that God alone possessed, namely, the power to raise and judge the dead: "Truly, truly, I say to you, the hour is coming, and now is, when the dead will hear the voice of the Son of God, and those who hear will live . . . and come forth, those who have done good, to the resurrection of life, and those who have done evil, to the resurrection of judgment" (John 5:25, 29). Jesus removed all doubt of the intentions of his claim when he added, "For as the Father raised the dead and gives them life, so also the Son gives life to whom he will" (v. 21). According to the Old Testament, however, God alone is the giver of life (I Sam. 2:6; Deut. 32:39) and can raise men from the dead (Ps. 2:7). Hence, in the face of orthodox Jewish belief that God alone could resurrect the dead, Jesus not only boldly proclaimed his ability to bring the dead back but also his right to judge them. The Scriptures, however, reserved for Jehovah the right to judge men (Joel 3:12; Deut. 32:35).

Another way that Jesus made claim to be God was by his statement that all men should "honor the Son, even as they honor the Father," adding, "he who does not honor the Son does not honor the Father" (John 5:23). In this same category, Jesus exhorted his disciples, "believe in God, believe also in me" (John 14:1). The pretensions of this claim to a monotheistic people were evident. The Jews knew well that no man should claim honor and belief with God. They reacted with stones (John 5:18).

*Jesus' Claim to Be the Messiah-God.* The Old Testament foreshadowings of the Messiah also pointed to his deity. Hence, when Jesus claimed to fulfill the Old Testament messianic predictions he thereby also claimed the deity attributed to the Messiah in those passages. For example, the famous Christmas text from Isaiah speaks of the Messiah as the "Mighty God" (9:6). The psalmist wrote of the Messiah, "Thy throne, O God, is for ever and ever" (from 45:6 A.V., quoted in Heb. 1:8). Psalm 110:1 relates a conversation between the Father and the Son: "Jehovah saith unto my Lord (Adonai), sit thou at my right hand." Jesus applied this passage to himself in Matthew 22:43-44. Isaiah the prophet, in a great messianic prophecy, exhorted Israel, "Behold your God" (40:9). Indeed the great messianic passage from Daniel 7:13, quoted by Jesus at his trial before the high priest, is a text implying the deity of the Messiah. In Daniel's vision, the Son of man (Messiah) is also called the "ancient of days" (7:22), a phrase that is used twice in the same passage to describe God the Father (vv. 9, 13). When Jesus quoted this passage to the high priest who demanded that Jesus declare whether or not he was Deity, the high priest left no doubt as to how he interpreted Jesus' claim. "Are you the Christ [Messiah], the Son of the Blessed?" the high priest asked. "And Jesus said, 'I am; and you will see the Son of man sitting at the right hand of Power, and coming with the clouds of heaven.' " At this the high priest tore his garment and said, "Why do we still need witnesses? You have heard his blasphemy!" (Mark 14:61-64).

In short, the Old Testament not only predicted the Messiah but also proclaimed him to be God. And when Jesus claimed to be a fulfillment of the Old Testament messianic passages (cf. Luke 24:27, 44; Matt. 26:54), he laid claim to possessing the deity these passages ascribed to the Messiah. Jesus removed all doubts of his intentions by his answer before the high priest at his trial.

*Jesus' Acceptance of Worship.* The Old Testament forbids worship of anyone but God (Exod. 20:1-4; Deut. 5:6-9). In the Bible men were not to accept worship (see Acts 14:15) and even angels refused to be worshiped (Rev. 22:8, 9). And yet Jesus received worship on at least nine occasions without rebuking his worshipers. The healed leper worshiped him (Matt. 8:2) and the ruler knelt before him with his petition (Matt. 9:18). After Jesus had stilled the storm, "those in the boat worshipped him, saying, 'Truly you are the Son of God' " (Matt. 14:33). The Canaanite women bowed before Christ in prayer (Matt. 15:25), as did the mother of the sons of Zebedee (Matt. 20:20). Just before Jesus commissioned his followers to disciple all nations, "they worshipped him" (Matt. 28:17). Earlier in the same chapter the women who had just been at the tomb met Jesus "and they came up and took hold of his feet and worshipped him" (v. 9). Mark writes of the demoniac of the Gerasenes that "when he saw Jesus from afar, he ran and worshipped him" (Mark 5:6) and the blind man said, " 'Lord, I believe;' and he worshipped him" (John 9:38). Not to rebuke these people who knelt before him, prayed to him, and worshiped him was not only utterly pretentious but it was blasphemous, unless Jesus considered himself to be God. The repetition and the context necessitate the conclusion that Jesus not only accepted but sometimes even elicited worship from the disciples, as he did from Thomas who cried out, "My Lord and my God" (John 20:28).

*The Authority of Jesus' Commands.* Jesus not only accepted the titles and worship due Deity alone but he often placed his words on a par with God's. "You have heard that it was said to men of old, . . . But I say unto you . . ." (Matt. 5:21, 22) is repeated over and over again. "All authority on heaven and on earth has been given to me. Go therefore and make disciples of all nations . . ." (Matt. 28:18, 19). God had given the Ten Commandments through Moses, but Jesus added, "A new commandment I give to you, that you love one another" (John 13:34). Jesus once taught that "till heaven and earth pass away, not an iota, not a dot, will pass from the Law" (Matt. 5:18). Later Jesus put his own words on the same level as the Old Testament Law of God, saying, "Heaven and earth will pass away, but my words will not pass away" (Matt. 24:35). Speaking of those who reject him, Jesus declared, "The word that I have spoken will be his judge on the last day" (John 12:48). In view of his categorical and authoritative pronouncements we are left with but one conclusion: Jesus intended his commands to be on the level with those of God. His words were equally authoritative with God's words.

*Jesus Requested That Men Pray in His Name.* Jesus not only asked men to believe in him (John 14:1) and to obey his commandments (John 14:15), but he asked men to pray in his name. "Whatever you ask in my name, I will do it," he said (John 14:13). Again, "if you ask anything in my name, I will do it" (John 14:14). Later, Jesus added, "If you abide in me, and my words abide in you, ask whatever you will, and it shall be done for you" (John 15:7). Indeed, Jesus insisted that "no man comes to the Father, but by me" (John 14:6). It is interesting to note in this regard that not only did the disciples of Christ pray in Christ's name (I Cor. 5:4) but they also prayed to Christ (Acts 7:59). There is no doubt that both Jesus intended and his disciples understood it was Jesus' name that was to be invoked both before God and as God's in prayer.

Throughout Jesus' claims several important points emerge. First, there is no question that Jesus often accepted and sometimes even encouraged the appellations and attitudes appropriate only for God. Second, Jesus himself unquestionably affirmed by words and actions these characteristics and prerogatives appropriate only to deity. Third, the reaction of those around him manifests that they too understood him to be claiming deity. The disciples responded with "you are the Christ, the Son of the living God" (Matt. 16:16) or "my Lord and my God" (John 20:28). Unbelievers exclaimed, "Why does this man speak thus? It is blasphemy!" (Mark 2:7). When Jesus claimed to be one with the Father, the Jews wanted to stone him, as they said, "for blasphemy; because you, being a man, make yourself God" (John 10:33). This they repeated on several occasions (cf. John 5:18; 8:59). The high priest reacted similarly when he heard Christ solemnly swear to his divine origin (Mark 14:62-64). Whatever one may think about the truth or falsity of Christ's claims, it should be clear to the unbiased observer of the New Testament record that Jesus claimed to be equal to and identical with the Jehovah of the Old Testament.

*Some Alleged Counterclaims of Christ.* It is sometimes alleged that

Jesus denied his equality with God on the basis of the following data: (1) Jesus said, "My Father is greater than I" (John 14:28); (2) Jesus claimed ignorance of the time of his second coming (Mark 13:32); (3) Jesus said that neither he nor anyone else is "good" except God (Mark 10:18); (4) Jesus prayed on the cross, "My God, my God, why hast thou forsaken me?" (Mark 15:34).

On closer examination none of these passages is contradictory with Jesus' evident claims to deity just discussed. (1) The Father was greater than Jesus in *office* but not in *nature.* Jesus claimed equality with God in *essence* (John 5:18; 10:30); it was only in his *function* as Son that he was less than the Father. (2) Jesus was ignorant of the time of his coming again *as man,* just as he was ignorant of whether the fig tree had fruit (Matt. 21:19). As man Jesus tired, hungered, and thirsted; but *as God* he never slumbered nor slept (Ps. 121:4). Jesus the person possessed two distinct natures: one divine nature by which he knew all things and one human nature which was finite in knowledge and grew in wisdom (Luke 2:52). (3) Upon careful examination Jesus did not deny that he was good or that he was God to the rich young ruler. Rather, Jesus said to him in essence, "Do you realize what you are saying? Are you calling me God?" Jesus' reply left only two alternatives: either he was good and God or else he was bad and merely human. (4) Jesus' prayer on the cross does not imply he is not God. There are other examples of God talking to God (or, better, one person of the Godhead speaking to another person of the Godhead). Psalm 110:1 says, "The LORD said unto my Lord, sit thou at my right hand." Likewise, in the Old Testament the LORD sometimes speaks to the Angel of the LORD (cf. Zech. 1:12) who also is deity (cf. Exod. 3:2 f.; Judg. 13:15 f.). These so-called counterclaims for deity turn out to be not only completely congruous with the uniform claim of Christ to be equal with God, but in at least one case a closer examination of them evidences a covert claim to deity.

### The Claim of Jesus' Disciples That He Was God

It is one thing for a first century Jew to claim to be God, but it is quite another to get other monotheistic Jews to believe it. Both Jesus and the disciples knew the Jewish Shema very well: "Hear, O Israel: The Lord our God, the Lord is one" (Mark 12:29). Paul stated the Jewish belief well when he wrote, "For although there may be so-called gods in heaven or on earth . . . yet for us there is one God" (I Cor. 8:5, 6). Both polytheism and idolatry were abhorrent to a Jew, and yet these first century Jewish disciples of Jesus found it necessary to attribute deity to Jesus of Nazareth in many ways.

*Jesus Was Given the Names of Deity.* John called Jesus the "first and the last" (Rev. 1:17; 2:8; 22:13), a title which Jehovah had taken to himself in the Old Testament (Isa. 41:4; 44:6; 48:12). Both Jesus and Jehovah are viewed as the author of eternal words (cf. Matt. 24:35 and Isa. 40:8). The psalmist wrote, "Jehovah is my light" (27:1) but John claimed Jesus was "the true light" (John 1:9). Likewise, "Jehovah is our rock" is a common appellation of God in the Old Testament (see Ps. 18:2; 95:1), but the disciples call Jesus their "rock" (I Cor. 10:4) or "stone" (I Peter 2:6-8). Jehovah was also a husband or "bride-groom" to Israel (Hos. 2:16; Isa. 62:5), which is how the New Testament relates Christ to his church (Eph. 5:28-33; Rev. 21:2). "Jehovah is my shepherd," David wrote (Ps. 23:1), Peter called Christ "the chief Shep-herd" (I Peter 5:4), and the writer of the Hebrews spoke of Christ as "the great shepherd" (13:20). Whereas the Old Testament speaks of Jehovah as the forgiver of sins (Jer. 31:34; Ps. 130:4), the apostles boldly proclaim that only in Jesus' name are sins forgiven (Acts 5:31; Col. 3:13). The Old Testament function of "redeemer" (cf. Hos. 13:14; Ps. 130:7) is in the New Testament given over to Christ (Titus 2:13; Rev. 5:9). The same is true of the title "savior" (Isa. 43:3); Jesus is called "the savior of the world" (John 4:42). The Old Testament Jehovah jealously guarded his glory, declaring, "I am Jehovah, that is my name; my glory I give to no other" (Isa. 42:8), and yet Paul speaks of Jesus as "the Lord of glory" (I Cor. 2:8). The title of "judge" of mankind was reserved for Jehovah in the Old Testament, but the disciples taught that "Jesus Christ . . . is to judge the living and the dead" (II Tim. 4:1).

*Jesus Was Considered to Be the Messiah-God.* Many Old Testament messianic passages make it clear that it is Jehovah who is to be the Messiah. Jehovah is called "king" (Zech. 14:9) and it is the "angel of Jehovah" who will redeem them (Isa. 63:9). Jehovah is the "stone" and yet the Messiah is to be the rejected "stone" (Ps. 118:22). The Messiah is spoken of in the Old Testament as "Lord" when it is written, "Jehovah saith unto my Lord" (Ps. 110:1), a passage which the New Testament writers apply to Christ (Acts 2:34, 35). Isaiah provided a messianic challenge to the Jews, saying, "Behold your God!" (40:9). Indeed, there is no clearer messianic passage on the deity of Christ than Isaiah 9:6: "For unto us a child is born . . . and his name will be called 'Wonderful, counsellor, Mighty God, Everlasting Father, Prince of Peace.'" With these predictions the New Testament writers concur, declaring Jesus to be "Emmanuel" (which means, God with us) (Matt. 1:23, from Isa. 7:14). In brief, the Old Testament Messiah was Jehovah and the New Testament writers identify Jesus with the Old Testament Messiah.

One often overlooked passage in Zechariah says literally in the Hebrew text, "When they look on *me* [Jehovah speaking] whom they have pierced" (12:10). The New Testament writers do not hesitate to apply this twice to Jesus, thereby affirming the identity of the Jehovah pierced and the Jesus crucified (cf. John 19:37; Rev. 1:7). In his role as Messiah one day "every knee should bow . . . and every tongue confess that Jesus Christ is Lord, to the glory of God the Father" (Phil. 2:11). But the passage from which Paul takes this citation declares: "For I am God, and there is no other. . . . To me every knee shall bow, and every tongue swear" (Isa. 45:22, 23). The implications of this are strong: Jehovah alone is God and to him every knee shall one day bow. But Paul declares that it is Jesus-Jehovah before whom one day all will bow; they will all confess that "Jesus is Lord (Jehovah) to the glory of God."

*Jesus Was Given Powers Possessed Only by God.* The disciples of Christ not only gave him the titles of Jehovah or deity but they also attributed to him powers that only God possesses. The New Testament writers declare that Jesus raised the dead (John 5, 11), and yet the Old Testament declares, "Jehovah killeth, and maketh alive" (I Sam. 2:6; cf. Deut. 32:39). Isaiah pronounced Jehovah as "the everlasting God . . . the Creator of the ends of the earth" (4:9) and Jeremiah called him the "former of all things" (10:16); the New Testament writers speak of all things being created through Christ (John 1:2; Col. 1:16). Likewise, for the Jews "who can forgive sins but God alone?" (Mark 2:7; cf. Jer. 31:34); and yet without hesitation the New Testament writers attribute this same power to Jesus (Acts 5:31; 13:38). Such an attribution should remove all reasonable doubt as to whether they believed in the deity of Christ.

*The Association of Jesus' Name with God.* The Jehovah of the Old Testament jealously guarded his name and glory; it was utter blasphemy to associate any other name with God's. And yet without hesitation the disciples used the name of Jesus in prayer (I Cor. 5:4). On occasion they even prayed directly to Jesus (Acts 7:59). Often in prayers or benedictions Jesus' name is used alongside of God the Father's in such phrases as "grace to you and peace from God the Father and our Lord Jesus Christ" (Gal. 1:3; cf. Eph. 1:2). At other times three names are associated in a "trinitarian" formula, such as the command to baptize "in the *name* of the Father and of the Son and of the Holy Spirit" (Matt. 28:19). The same association is made in the apostolic benediction, "The grace of the Lord Jesus Christ and the love of God and the fellowship of the Holy Spirit be with you all" (II Cor. 13:14). Such association in a monotheistic context is tantamount to claiming deity for the person so associated with God.

*Direct Declarations of Jesus' Deity.* Thomas's pronouncement "My Lord and my God!" (John 20:28) is more than an exclamation; properly understood in the context of the fourth Gospel it is the climax of the disciple's progressive understanding of who Jesus really is. In

Colossians Paul forthrightly declares Christ to be the one in whom "the whole fulness of deity dwells bodily" (2:9). In Titus Jesus is called "our great God and Savior" (2:13) and the writer of Hebrews addresses Christ thus: "Thy throne, O God, is for ever and ever" (1:8). Paul elsewhere speaks of Christ as the "form of God," a phrase that obviously means of the essence of God, paralleling the phrase "form of man," which means the essence of man (Phil. 2:5, 8). A similar phrase "the image of God" is used to portray Christ's deity in the New Testament (Col. 1:15), meaning in this context not only the representation (as it means elsewhere, cf. Gen. 1:26) but the manifestation of God himself. Hebrews strengthens this description of Christ's deity, saying that "he reflects the glory of God and bears the very stamp of his nature, upholding the universe by his word of power" (1:3).

The prologue of John is unequivocal on the subject of Christ's deity: "In the beginning was the Word, and the Word was with God, and the Word was God" (John 1:1). The absence of the definite article "the" does not indicate that this verse should be translated "the Word was a god." The grammatical construction without the definite article means "the Word was of the essence of God," which is a strong way to describe his deity. The New Testament contains many other intimations of Christ's deity, the strongest of which are those that relate to his being Creator of all things.

*Jesus Was Considered the Creator of the Universe.* There is no doubt that the Old Testament presents God alone as Creator of the universe (Gen. 1, Isa. 40, Ps. 8). And when the disciples of Christ declare Jesus to be the One through whom all things were created, the conclusion that they were thereby attributing deity to him is unavoidable. John wrote, "All things were made through him, and without him was not anything made that was made" (1:2). Paul said, "All things were created through him and for him" (Col. 1:16) and then added, "and in him all things hold together" (v. 17). The context of this passage makes it clear that there are no exceptions; Christ is the Creator of all things including all angels and everything visible or invisible (v. 15). Nowhere is it made more clear that Christ is not a creature—angelic or otherwise—than in the relation of angels to him. Since Christ could not be both the Creator of everything and at the same time a creature himself, it is necessary to conclude that he is himself the uncreated Creator of all creation.[1]

---

1. In view of the clear teaching that Christ is Creator and not creature, the Arian misinterpretations of phrases like Christ is "firstborn" (Col. 1:15) or "beginning" of creation (Rev. 3:14) are wrong. Christ is "firstborn" in the sense of being the unique (not created) Son of God. Christ is first *over* creation, not first *in* it. Likewise, Christ is subordinate to God the Father (I Cor. 15:28) as his "head" (I Cor. 11:3) not in *nature* but in *office* or function as Son.

*Jesus Was Obeyed and Worshiped by Angels.* Jesus received worship from men on at least nine occasions (cf. Matt. 28:17; John 9:38). This he did without ever rebuking the worshiper, and sometimes he seems to have encouraged it (see p. 333). But what removes any lingering doubt that the disciples of Christ believed that he should be worshiped as God is the fact of angelic worship. Jesus is portrayed as "being far above all rule and authority and power and dominion, and above every name that is named, not only in this age but also in that which is to come" (Eph. 1:21). Even the demons submitted to his commands (Matt. 8:32). What is more, angels who themselves refused to be worshiped in the Bible (see Rev. 22:8, 9) are presented as worshiping Christ. In an unmistakably lucid affirmation the Book of Hebrews says, "For to what angel did God ever say, 'Thou art my Son, today I have begotten thee'?" And yet "when he brings the firstborn into the world, he says, 'Let *all* God's angels worship him' " (1:5, 6). What could be more emphatic; Christ is not an angel but the unique Son of God, and *all* the angels must worship him.

Whether this view of Christ is correct or not, there should be no doubt that it is what the disciples of Christ taught. Indeed, as was already shown, it is what Jesus thought of himself. He claimed to be all that God is, and his disciples believed it. As C. S. Lewis pointedly observed, in the context of Christ's claims we are faced with marked alternatives.

> I am trying here to prevent anyone saying the really foolish things that people often say about Him: "I'm ready to accept Jesus as a great moral teacher, but I don't accept His claim to be God." That is the one thing we must not say. A man who was merely a man and said the sort of things Jesus said would not be a great moral teacher. He would either be a lunatic—on a level with the man who says he is a poached egg—or else he would be the Devil of Hell.[2]

## The Substantiation of Christ's Claims to Be God

It is one thing to claim deity and quite another to have the credentials to support that claim. Christ did both. He offered three unique and miraculous facts as evidence of his claim: the fulfillment of prophecy, a uniquely miraculous life, and the resurrection from the dead. All of these are historically provable and unique to Jesus of Nazareth. We will argue, therefore, that Jesus alone claims to be and proves to be God incarnate.

### Jesus' Unique Fulfillment of Prophecy Is Evidence of His Deity

The logic of the argument here is this: a miracle is an act of God that confirms the truth of God associated with it. The miracles associated with Christ's claim to be God are acts of God that confirm him to be the Son of God. And in Jesus' case there is a convergence of three great

---

2. C. S. Lewis, *Mere Christianity*, pp. 55, 56.

miraculous happenings—prophecy, his sinless life and miraculous deeds, and his resurrection—that lead forthrightly to the conclusion that he alone is the unique Son of God.

*There Were Dozens of Predictive Prophecies About Christ in the Old Testament.* It should be obvious to any serious student of the New Testament that not every Old Testament Scripture applied to Christ in the New Testament was necessarily understood in its Old Testament context as a prediction. Prophecies such as those that Jesus would be a "Nazarene" (see Matt. 2:23) or that he would flee to Egypt (Matt. 2:15) undoubtedly fall into this category. On the other hand, there are many Old Testament prophecies that are best understood as applying to the Messiah; and many of these do not make good sense in any other way. In this latter category we will single out the most significant predictive prophecies which Christ fulfilled.

(1) The Messiah will be born of a woman (Gen. 3:15; cf. Gal. 4:4).
(2) He would be born of a virgin (Isa. 7:14; cf. Matt. 1:21 f.).
(3) He would come some 483 years after 444 B.C. (see Dan. 9:24 f.).[3]
(4) He will be of the seed of Abraham (Gen. 12:1-3 and 22:18; cf. Matt. 1:1 and Gal. 3:16).
(5) He will be of the tribe of Judah (Gen. 49:10; cf. Luke 3:23, 33; Heb. 7:14).
(6) He will be of the House of David (II Sam. 7:12 f.; cf. Matt 1:1).
(7) His birthplace will be Bethlehem (Mic. 5:2; cf. Matt. 2:1; Luke 2:4-7).
(8) He will be anointed by the Holy Spirit (Isa. 11:2; cf. Matt. 3:16, 17).
(9) He will be heralded by a messenger of the Lord (Isa. 40:3 and Mal. 3:1; cf. Matt. 3:1, 2).
(10) He will have a ministry of miracles (Isa. 35:5, 6; cf. Matt. 9:35).
(11) He will cleanse the temple (Mal. 3:1; cf. Matt. 21:12).
(12) He will be rejected by his Jewish people (Ps. 118:22; cf. I Peter 2:7).
(13) He will die a humiliating death (Ps. 22 and Isa. 53; cf. Matt. 27) involving:
(a) rejection by his own people (Isa. 53:3; cf. John 1:10, 11; 7:5, 48)
(b) silence before his accusers (Isa. 53:7; cf. Matt. 27:12-19)
(c) being mocked (Ps. 22:7, 8; cf. Matt. 27:31)

---

3. See Harold Hoehner, "Chronological Aspects of the Life of Christ: Part II," in *Bibliotheca Sacra,* vol. 131 (Jan.-March 1974), no. 521, pp. 41-54.

(d) piercing his hands and feet (Ps. 22:16; cf. Luke 23:33)

(e) being crucified with thieves (Isa. 53:12; cf. Matt. 17:38)

(f) praying for his persecutors (Isa. 53:12; cf. Luke 23:34)

(g) piercing of his side (Zech. 12:10; cf. John 19:34)

(h) buried in a rich man's tomb (Isa. 53:9; cf. Matt. 27:57-60)

(i) casting lots for his garments (Ps. 22:18; cf. John 19:23, 24).

(14) He will rise from the dead (Ps. 2:7; 16:10; cf. Acts 2:31 and Mark 16:6).

(15) He will ascend into heaven (Ps. 68:18; cf. Acts 1:9 f.).

(16) He will sit at the right hand of God (Ps. 110:1; cf. Heb. 1:3). There are numerous other prophecies about the Messiah that were fulfilled by Jesus but not all of them are clearly predictive. Such include his teaching in parables (Ps. 78:2 and Matt. 13:34), the slaughter of the babies by Herod (Jer. 31:15; cf. Matt. 2:16), his betrayal by Judas (Ps. 41:9; cf. Matt. 10:4), being sold for thirty pieces of silver (Zech. 11:12; cf. Matt. 26:15), being beaten (Isa. 50:6; cf. Matt. 26:67), suffering thirst on the cross (Ps. 69:21; cf. John 19:28), and others. Because these are not clearly predictive in their Old Testament context, we will not use them as part of our argument.

*These Old Testament Predictions About Christ Were Made Hundreds of Years in Advance.* What is truly amazing about these Old Testament predictions is that there is no way they could be made by "intelligent guesses" or by reading the "trend of the times" or even by "reading minds," methods used by some present-day forecasters. Even the most liberal critic of the Old Testament admits to the completion of the prophetic books by some four hundred years before Christ and the Book of Daniel by about 167 B.C.[4] Although there is good evidence for accepting a more conservative dating view of the eighth century for the earlier prophets and the ninth century for some psalms, let us accept for the sake of argument that these prophecies about Christ came from only the second to the fifth or sixth centuries B.C. What difference does it make if a prophecy is given only two hundred years in advance rather than six hundred years? Can one with less than divine power make predictions like these four hundred years in advance but not six hundred years ahead? And when there are dozens of these prophecies converging in the lifetime of one man, it becomes nothing less than miraculous.

*These Prophecies Were Actually Fulfilled in Jesus of Nazareth.* This conclusion follows from the facts already established, namely, (1) the Old Testament statements about Christ were made hundreds of years before he was born; (2) the New Testament is a historically reliable

---

4. See S. R. Driver, *An Introduction to the Literature of the Old Testament*, p. 497.

account of Jesus' life (see Chapter 16); (3) the New Testament records these predictions as being fulfilled in Jesus' life, death, resurrection, and so forth. Since the New Testament is historically reliable, we must conclude that all of these things did indeed happen in his life, just as the above quoted verses indicate they did.

However, the fact that events in the life of Jesus of Nazareth correspond to these predictions does not automatically prove he is the fulfillment of them. There are at least two other possibilities that must be considered: (1) they may be merely an accidental concurrence of events in Jesus' life, or (2) Jesus may have deliberately attempted to fake "fulfillment" of them.

    a. Jesus Was Not a Messianic Pretender Deliberately Attempting to "Fulfill" Prophecy

The hypothesis that Jesus was an innocent messianic pretender who deliberately connived to "fulfill" prophecy in his own life has been made popular by Schonfield's *The Passover Plot*.[5] In the face of the facts, however, this view is nothing but a speculative thesis which knits together the most circumstantial evidence on the loom of the author's own imagination. There are several factual reasons this hypothesis must be rejected. First, it does not fit the known character of Christ. He was anything but cunning and deceptive; he was open and honest. Further, such a plot to prove that he was the Messiah would have been anything but "innocent."[6] It would have been a deliberate deception of world-wide messianic importance. The thesis, if proven true, would make Christ out to be a major liar and not even a good man. Second, the alleged plot to prove Christ was the Messiah does not fit with the facts known about Jesus' closest disciples. How was it that Jesus could hide from his most intimate friends this intricate plot while allegedly confiding only in the young man, Lazarus, and Joseph of Arimathea? It is implausible that Jesus would pick these men for such a plot to feign death by drugs and pretend to rise again. And the honest character of his disciples is incongruous with the inclusion of them in the alleged plot. Third, even assuming that Jesus could have cleverly connived this plan concealed from his closest disciples, how then can we explain his sinless and miraculous life (discussed below)? As the Jews said in John 9:16, "How can a man who is a sinner do such signs [as opening the eyes of the blind]?" Finally, the messianic-pretender hypothesis is rendered implausible by the nature of many of the prophecies themselves. There are many prophecies over which Jesus had absolutely no control, including when (Dan. 9), where (Mic. 5:2), how (Isa. 7:14),

---

5. H. J. Schonfield, *The Passover Plot*.

6. For a definitive critique of Schonfield's *The Passover Plot* see Edwin M. Yamauchi's "Passover Plot or Easter Triumph?" in John W. Montgomery, *Christianity for the Tough-Minded*, pp. 261-71.

THE DEITY AND AUTHORITY OF JESUS CHRIST / 343

and from what tribe (Gen. 49:10) or dynasty (II Sam. 7) he would be born. Nor is it plausible to suppose that Jesus could have staged or manipulated the reactions of others to himself, including John's heralding (Matt. 3), his accuser's reactions (Matt. 27:12), how the soldiers would cast lots for his garments (John 19:23, 24), and how they would pierce his side with a spear (John 19:34). Indeed, even Schonfield admits that Jesus' plot failed when the Romans actually pierced him on the cross. The facts of the matter are that there are many prophecies that Jesus fulfilled over which he had no control and others over which he had virtually no influence. It takes an even bigger miracle to believe that Jesus possessed superhuman manipulative powers to bring about the apparent fulfillment of the Old Testament predictions about the Messiah in his life.

b. These Prophecies Were Not Accidentally "Fulfilled" in Christ

God makes no mistakes. In a theistic universe where God is in control of the course of events and where God makes predictions hundreds of years in advance about his plan of salvation for the world, an accidental "fulfillment" will not happen. It is virtually inconceivable that God would allow either a total deception in his name or an accidental "fulfillment" in the life of the wrong person. Hence, on the already established grounds that God exists, the chance fulfillment hypothesis is ruled out. Of course chance is not ruled out on a strictly logical level but only on moral and theological grounds. It is logically or mathematically possible that all of these prophecies could have converged in the fortuitous events of the life of Jesus of Nazareth. But even here the mathematical odds are staggering. It has been computed by mathematicians that the chances for only 16 prophecies about Christ to come true in Jesus' life are 1 in $10^{45}$.[7] For 48 prophecies the chances are an even more amazing 1 in $10^{157}$. It is almost impossible to conceive how large a figure this really is. But it is not the logical improbability but the moral impossibility that rules out chance as an explanation. An all-powerful, all-knowing, and all-perfect God will not allow anything to thwart his plans. Predictions made hundreds of years in advance in the name of the true and living theistic God cannot fail. This God cannot lie and he cannot break a promise (Heb. 6:18), nor is it in accord with his nature that those desiring the truth can be totally deceived (Heb. 11:6; John 7:17).

The Word of God will be fulfilled by an act of God. As the writer of the Hebrews states it, "God also bore witness by signs and wonders and various miracles and by gifts of the Holy Spirit . . ." (2:4). If in the life of Jesus of Nazareth, who claimed fulfillment of these predictions about the Messiah made hundreds of years before, there came to pass all that had been prophesied of him, then we must conclude that he indeed is the

---

7. See Peter W. Stoner, *Science Speaks,* p. 108.

Messiah. In short, if Jesus fulfilled the prophecies about the coming Messiah, this fulfillment must be an act of God showing him to be the Son of God.

All of the earmarks of a miracle surround Jesus' fulfillment of Old Testament prophecy.[8] (1) It was an *unusual* event; the chances were highly improbable; (2) it was accompanied by *theological* truth claims to be the Son of God and the fulfillment of messianic prophecy; (3) the event of Christ's coming brought with it *moral* good through his teaching, life, and influence; (4) the incarnation was not a scientific misfit; it was supernatural but *not unnatural*. His miracles not only fit the natural order but they helped the natural order fulfill itself by way of the resurrection. In all these ways the first coming of Christ does indeed qualify as a miracle, that is, as an act of God that confirms the message of God and brings glory to God. And in the case of this particular miracle of the incarnation, it is an act of God that proves Christ to be the unique Son of God. In short, Christ's claims to be God are confirmed by the miracle of the fulfillment of messianic prophecy in his life and death.

### Jesus' Sinless and Miraculous Life Is Evidence of His Deity

Simply living a sinless life, as difficult as that would be, would not necessarily prove someone is God. However, if someone both claims to be God and offers a sinless life as evidence, that is an entirely different matter. All men are sinners; God knows it and so do we. If a man lives an impeccable life and offers as the truth about himself that he is God incarnated we must at least take his claim seriously. There are some who dare to claim perfection, but few take these claimants seriously, least of all those who know them best. With Jesus it is quite different; those who knew him best thought the most highly of him. Outsiders cast unsubstantiated allegations at him. "We are not born of fornication [as you were]" (John 8:41), or "he is leading the people astray" (John 7:12). Some even dared to say, "He has a demon, and is mad" (John 10:19). At his "trial" a false accusation brought forth that Jesus had said he would destroy the temple (Mark 14:58), "yet not even so did their testimony agree" (v. 59). Pilate's verdict as to Jesus' alleged crime has been the verdict of history as to his character: "I find no crime in this man" (Luke 23:4). The soldier at the cross exclaimed, "Certainly this man was innocent!" (Luke 23:47) and the dying thief, having earlier derided Christ (Matt. 27:39), came to see that "this man has done nothing wrong" and asked for a place in Jesus' kingdom (Luke 23:41, 42).

The most significant testimony as to any man's character comes from those closest to him. From the lips of Jesus' most intimate friends and

---

8. See Chapter 14 for further definition of a miracle.

disciples who had lived with him for several years at close range came glowing testimonies. Peter called Christ "a lamb without blemish or spot" (I Peter 1:19) and added, "no guile was found on his lips" (2:22). John called him "Jesus Christ the righteous" (I John 2:1; cf. 3:7). The apostle Paul adds to this testimony the unanimously expressed belief of the first Christians that Jesus "knew no sin" (II Cor. 5:21). And the writer of the Hebrews clearly affirmed that Jesus was tempted like a man "yet without sinning" (4:15). Jesus himself challenged his accusers, saying, "Which of you convicts me of sin?" (John 8:46). Neither they nor anyone else has successfully pinned a sin on the remarkable and impeccable character of Jesus. This being the case, it is reasonable to conclude that Jesus really was who he claimed to be. For his sinlessness would both testify to the truthfulness of his self-testimony and serve as supporting evidence for it. What mere man can live a consistently sinless life when viewed at such close range?

Jesus' life was not only sinless but it was miraculous from the beginning. He was born of a virgin (Matt. 1:21 f.; cf. Luke 2:26 f.), he turned water into wine (John 2:7 f.), walked on water (Matt. 14:25), multiplied bread (John 6:11 f.), opened the eyes of the blind (John 9:7 f.), made the lame to walk (Mark 2:3 f.), cast out demons (Mark 3:11 f.), healed the multitudes of all kinds of sicknesses (Matt. 9:35), and even raised the dead to life again on several occasions (see John 4:11). When asked whether he was the Messiah, he offered his miracles as evidence, saying, "Go and tell John what you hear and see: the blind receive their sight and the lame walk, lepers are cleansed and the deaf hear, and the dead are raised up . . ." (Matt. 11:4, 5). Miracles of these kinds were accepted by the Jews of Jesus' day as an evident sign of divine favor on the person performing them. And the special outpouring of messianic miracles was proof that the performer was the Messiah (see Isa. 35:5, 6). Even the Jews who knew Jesus had healed the blind man asked, "How can a man who is a sinner do such signs?" (John 9:12). The ruler Nicodemus stated the Jewish position well when he acknowledged to Jesus, "Rabbi, we know that you are a teacher come from God; for no one can do these signs that you do, unless God is with him" (John 3:2). To a first-century monotheistic Jew, miracles such as Christ performed were an obvious indication of divine approval. But in Christ's case divine approval is an evidence of Christ's deity. Just as the voice from heaven at Jesus' baptism pronounced him to be God's unique Son (Matt. 3:16, 17), so the outpouring of messianic miracles coupled with the claims of Christ to be Jehovah-Messiah is unmistakable evidence of his true deity. An act of God verifies the message of God given through the one performing the act. And in Christ's case the message was "I am God; here are the acts of God to prove it."

### Jesus' Resurrection Is Evidence of His Deity

There is a third miracle or act of God confirming Christ's claim to deity; it is his resurrection from the dead. This is truly the grand miracle and the greatest of them all. The fact that both the Old Testament and Jesus predicted in advance that he would rise from the dead makes the miracle even that much stronger. Since we have already given the evidence for the reliability of the New Testament eyewitnesses to the events recorded therein (see Chapter 16), it will be necessary here to examine only the testimony itself.

*Both Old Testament Prophets and Jesus Predicted the Resurrection.* A Jewish monotheist believed that only God can give life (Deut. 32:39; I Sam. 2:6). The Egyptian magicians reduplicated Moses' wonders until Moses was used of God to turn dust into living gnats, at which miracle they exclaimed, "This is the finger of God" (Exod. 8:19). Only God can create life and only God can bring men back to life, they believed. Hence, in this monotheistic context the most convincing evidence of God is a resurrection from the dead.

What makes Jesus' resurrection even more amazing is that it was predicted in advance both in the Old Testament and by Jesus. There are two lines of Old Testament argument for the resurrection. First, there are the passages, such as Psalms 2 and 16, that are cited by the New Testament as applying to the resurrection of Christ (cf. Acts 2:27 f. and Heb. 1:5). It was no doubt passages such as these that Paul used in Jewish synagogues as "he argued with them from the scriptures, explaining and proving that it was necessary for Christ to suffer and to rise from the dead" (Acts 17:2, 3). Second, the resurrection of Christ is taught by logical deduction from two Old Testament teachings: (1) the Messiah will come and *die* (cf. Isa. 53; Ps. 22) and (2) the Messiah will have an enduring political *reign* from Jerusalem (Isa. 9:6; Dan. 2:44; Zech. 13:1 f.). The only way one and the same Messiah can accomplish the actual fulfillment of these two lines of prophecy is by a resurrection from the dead. Jesus died before he could ever begin a reign. Only a resurrection could make the royal prophecies realizable.

On top of these Old Testament predictions of Christ's resurrection are those he made on several occasions himself. According to John, Jesus predicted his resurrection from his earliest ministry, saying, "Destroy this temple [of my body], and in three days I will raise it up again" (John 2:19, 21). Even in the synoptics Jesus said as early as Matthew 12:40 that "as Jonah was three days and three nights in the belly of the whale, so will the Son of man be three days and three nights in the heart of the earth." After Peter's confession Jesus "began to teach them [his disciples] that the Son of man must suffer many things . . . and be killed, and after three days rise again" (Mark 8:31). Jesus repeated this same prediction again on the way to Jerusalem and the cross (cf. Mark 14:59; Matt. 27:63). Further, Jesus said he would raise himself from the dead. "I have power to lay it down and I have power to take it again" (John 10:18).

Now in view of the prediction of the resurrection, the event is given special confirming significance. Karl Popper argued that whenever a "risky prediction" is fulfilled, it counts as confirmation of the hypothesis which comes with it.[9] If so, what could be a riskier prediction than a resurrection; and hence, what could have greater confirmational force than the resurrection of Christ? If a man would not accept a predicted resurrection as evidence of a truth claim, then he has an unfalsifiable bias against the truth (cf. Luke 16:31).

*Jesus Actually Died on the Cross and Was Buried in Joseph's Tomb.* Before it can be established that Jesus really rose from the grave it must be established that he actually died. The Koran declares that Jesus did not die on the cross but that he feigned death (Surah IV:157). Some skeptics have adopted a "swoon theory" wherein Jesus appeared dead but was revived later in the tomb. Along with this can be categorized the "drug" hypothesis that Jesus was only doped and appeared dead but that he recovered later.

Against any such view that Christ did not really die the following evidence can be offered. (1) Jesus refused to take the common pain-killing drug offered crucifixion victims (Mark 15:23). He was later given only a small nonintoxicating amount of some cheap wine to quench his thirst (Mark 15:36). There is no evidence that Jesus was drugged; both the obvious agony and death cry do not befit a man who is drugged. (2) The heavy loss of blood indicates Jesus was dead. He had five wounds and was on the cross from nine in the morning (cf. Mark 15:25) until just before sunset (Mark 15:42). (3) Jesus was heard to have uttered a death cry by those standing by (John 19:30). (4) When pierced in the side by the soldiers "blood and water" flowed out (John 19:34); and this is an indisputable medical sign of death, indicating that the red and white blood corpuscles had separated.[10] (5) The experienced Roman soldiers examined Jesus and pronounced him dead without even breaking his legs to hasten death as was their usual practice (John 19:33). (6) Jesus was hurriedly embalmed in about one hundred pounds of spices and bandages and laid in a guarded tomb (John 19:39-40). Even if he had resuscitated, he could not have rolled back the heavy stone, overcome the guards, and escaped (Matt. 27:60). (7) Further, Pilate inquired to make sure that Jesus was dead before he gave the body to Joseph of

9. See Karl Popper, *Conjectures and Refutations,* p. 36.
10. The medical evidence of Christ's death has been substantiated by the work of physicians. Compare Dr. Stroud, *On the Physiological Cause of Christ's Death.*

348 / CHRISTIAN APOLOGETICS

Arimathea for burial. (8) After all this, if Jesus were somehow miraculously still alive, his appearances would have been more those of a resuscitated wretch than of a resurrected and triumphant Savior. It would scarcely have transformed the disciples, led to the conversion of thousands a few weeks later, or ultimately turned the world upside down. (9) The undisturbed appearance of the grave clothes—apparently like an empty cocoon (John 20:7)—is further indication that he was dead. Otherwise, why were the grave clothes undisturbed if there had not been a miraculous rising through them? If it was a mere physical resuscitation or revival of a swooned or drugged body, then Christ would have had to break out of the grave clothes. But since he simply rose through them, it would indicate that he was really dead and rose to a glorified body that could move through grave clothes as it could walk through closed doors (John 20:19 f.). The cumulative weight of the above evidence, particularly the firm medical evidence of "blood and water," places the evidence for Christ's death beyond the shadow of doubt. In fact, there is more evidence that Jesus died than there is that most important people from the ancient world ever lived.

*Jesus Bodily Rose from the Dead.* There are many alternate explanations for the resurrection of Christ, but none of them satisfy the facts of the case.[11] The only reasonable explanation for the missing body, the many appearances, the transformed disciples, and the amazing origin and spread of Christianity is the bodily resurrection of Jesus of Nazareth from Joseph's tomb.

    a. Joseph Did Not Remove the Body

It is unreasonable to suppose that Joseph removed the body of Jesus. When could he have done it? If in the dark with torches, he could have been seen. If in the morning at dawn, the women were already there (Luke 24:1). Further, what motive would Joseph have to remove the body? Certainly this was not to keep the disciples from stealing it, since Luke claims that he himself was a disciple of Christ (Luke 23:50-51). And if he were not a disciple, then he could have produced the body and squelched the false story of the resurrection. Furthermore, Joseph was a pious man and would not have removed the body on the sabbath (see Luke 23:50-56). And by the next day the guard was placed at the tomb (Matt. 27:62-66). What is more, where could Joseph have taken the body? It was never found despite the fact that almost two months elapsed before the disciples began preaching the resurrection. This was plenty of time to expose the fraud, if it were one. The truth of the matter is that the character of Joseph, the anxiety of the Jewish leaders, and the

11. Many skeptics have become Christians after examining the evidence for the resurrection of Christ. One of the most convincing books by a converted skeptic is that of Frank Morison, *Who Moved the Stone?*

inability of anyone to find any corpse of Jesus are strong negative arguments against this hypothesis. On top of this, there is the overwhelming positive evidence of the many resurrection appearances of Christ. If Joseph stole the body, how can some ten different appearances to a total of over five hundred people be explained?

b. Roman or Jewish Authorities Did Not Remove the Body of Jesus

The hypothesis that the authorities took the body is completely untenable. If the authorities had the body, they could have easily produced it and disproven the Christian claims. This they would have been more than happy to do, as is evidenced by the manner in which Christians were challenged and persecuted from the very beginning (see Acts 4, 5, 7). Furthermore, it is ridiculous to suppose that the authorities took the body and then turned around and blamed the disciples for stealing it (Matt. 28:11-15). The fact that the consistent attitude of authorities toward the disciples was one of *resistance* not refutation is a strong indication of the reality of the resurrection of Christ. Finally, neither does the view that the authorities took the body explain the many unquestioned appearances of Christ to hundreds of disciples.

c. The Disciples Did Not Steal the Body of Jesus

The allegation that the disciples stole the body of Christ is a derogation of their character as honest men. It is also inconsistent with their unimaginative minds; they were not clever plotters. Even Schonfield looks to someone else to fit his clever plot thesis. The disciples were fearful men who had fled the scene for fear of being caught (Mark 14:50). Furthermore, the tomb was heavily guarded (Matt. 27:64). And the story of the guards that the body was stolen is highly implausible, since they were not reprimanded for falling asleep on duty. This hypothesis, if true, would make out the disciples to be the most pious frauds that ever lived. We would have to believe, contrary to psychological fact, that they died for what they knew to be false, and that they were transformed from cowards to courageous men in a few weeks by a deceptive plot that enabled them to turn the known world upside down. It is hardly more miraculous to believe in the resurrection itself than to believe this highly unlikely hypothesis.

d. The Women Did Not Make a Mistake at the Tomb

Some have suggested that the women went to the wrong tomb while it was yet dark and that, seeing it empty, they reported that Jesus had risen. This position, too, is untenable. If it was so dark, why was the gardener already working (John 20:15)? If they went to the wrong tomb, why did not the authorities go to the right tomb, produce the body of Jesus, and disprove the disciples' claim? Further, why is it that Peter later made the same "mistake" in broad daylight (John 20:6)? How is it that both the women and Peter saw the empty grave clothes, if they were at the wrong tomb? Finally, how can we account for the numerous subsequent appearances of Christ to others in broad daylight over a forty-day period (Acts 1:3)?

e. It Is Not True That the Tomb Was Never Visited

It has been suggested that almost two months went by before the disciples proclaimed the resurrection and that their belief was based on spiritual appearances to them, but that no one ever really visited the tomb to verify a bodily resurrection. This hypothesis is contradicted by a host of facts, most of which have already been discussed. First of all, the Gospels clearly indicate that several people did visit the tomb at different times (Matt. 28; Mark 16; Luke 24; John 20). Furthermore, the repeated bodily appearances of Christ belie this theory. In addition, if the disciples had not visited the tomb the authorities could have done so and refuted the claim of the resurrection. But instead of refuting it, the authorities resisted it. Likewise, this theory would not account for the miraculous transformation of the disciples, nor for the conversion of thousands of people in the very city in which it occurred only a few weeks after it occurred (Acts 2:41).

f. The Bodily Resurrection of Christ Is Confirmed by Many Proofs

The only plausible explanation of the data available is that Jesus of Nazareth, who was crucified under Pontius Pilate, really died and was buried for three days in Joseph's tomb, and miraculously came back to life again, permanently and bodily vacating the tomb.

The physical or bodily nature of the resurrection is proven by the fact that Jesus was "seen" by over five hundred people (I Cor. 15:1 f.), that he claimed to "have flesh and bones" (Luke 24:39), that he ate fish to prove he was physical (Luke 24:42, 43), and that he challenged the doubters to look at his wounds—"handle me, and see" (Luke 24:39). Doubting Thomas was challenged thus: "Put your finger here, and see my hands; and put your hand, and place it in my side" (John 20:27). John, who recorded this event, wrote later of Christ: "That which was from the beginning, which we have heard, which we have seen with our eyes, which we have looked upon and touched with our hands, . . . this life was made manifest . . ." (I John 1:1, 2). The repeated contact with the bodily Christ after the resurrection by ear, eye, and touch leaves only one conclusion—they were in physical contact with a bodily resurrected Jesus of Nazareth.

We have already discussed elsewhere the nature and number of the eyewitnesses of the resurrected Christ (see Chapter 16). We will simply summarize the evidence here that places the experiences beyond illusion, delusion, and reasonable doubt. (1) Jesus was seen by a sufficient number of people—over five hundred (I Cor. 15:5)—to verify the reality of the event; (2) this was spread over a sufficiently long period of time—

forty days (Acts 1:3)—to prove that it was not an anomalous single occurrence; (3) he was seen on a sufficiently large number of different occasions—about ten—to provide ample independent testimony as to his reality; (4) Jesus appeared for a sufficiently long enough duration each time to make the identity unquestionable. For instance, he walked and talked with some, eating in their home with them (Luke 24:28 f.); he fished and ate breakfast with others (John 21:1 f.); and he stayed long enough on occasions to teach them concerning the kingdom of God (Acts 1:3), and to perform more indisputable miracles for them (Acts 1:3; cf. John 20:30). (5) Finally, the witnesses were sufficiently skeptical of his appearances to eliminate the possibility of hallucination (John 20:25; cf. Matt. 28:17). The nature of such testimony places the reality of Christ's resurrection beyond reasonable doubt.

## Summary and Conclusion

On the basis of the historical reliability of the New Testament we can be sure that we possess the essence of the teachings of Christ about himself. In view of the messianic prophecies Jesus fulfilled, the titles of deity he applied to himself, and the worship he accepted, as well as the other claims to deity Christ made, we must conclude that Jesus thought of himself as God Incarnate in human form. An examination of his disciples' beliefs about him reveals that they too taught that he was equal with and identical to God.

Jesus not only claimed deity but he provided a unique and threefold proof that he was truly the person he claimed to be. He miraculously fulfilled dozens of prophecies made hundreds of years before his birth; he lived a sinless and miracle-filled life, and he died and rose triumphantly and bodily out of the grave. This convergence of three lines of the miraculous in one man—Jesus of Nazareth—confirms his claims to be the unique Son of God. Jesus alone claimed and proved to be deity.

We are now in a position to answer another of David Hume's objections to miracles. Hume argued that all religions present miracles in support of their truth claims; hence, no religion can appeal to miracles since their claims are mutually self-canceling. Now we can see this is not true. Only Christianity has a triune concurrence of unique miracles in the person and claims of Christ. Hence, we may argue two things: first, only Christianity is true; and second, all other religions (based as they are on similar sub-Christian evidence) are false, since they *are* mutually self-canceling. This argument for the truth of Christianity will stand unless a similar or unique miraculous concurrence can be historically verified for another religion.

One very important consequence follows from the conclusion that Christ is God, namely, his divine authority. As we will see in the next chapter, whatever Christ taught comes to us as the word of God. And since God cannot lie or teach what is false (Heb. 6:18; John 17:17), it will follow that whatever Jesus taught is true. It is from this point that we will be able to leave the Bible as a historical document which verifies who Jesus claimed and proved to be and show that the Bible is more than a historical document. The Bible is what Jesus taught it to be, namely, the authoritative Word of God.

## SELECT READINGS FOR CHAPTER SEVENTEEN

Anderson, J. N. D. *Christianity: The Witness of History.*

Bushnell, Horace. *The Supernaturalness of Christ.*

Montgomery, John W. *History and Christianity.*

Morison, Frank. *Who Moved the Stone?*

Payne, J. Barton. *An Encyclopedia of Biblical Prophecy.*

Stoner, Peter. *Science Speaks.*

Tenney, Merrill C. *The Reality of the Resurrection.*

Warfield, B. B. *The Lord of Glory.*

Yamauchi, Edwin. "Passover Plot or Easter Triumph?", in *Christianity for the Tough-Minded,* John W. Montgomery, ed.

# Chapter 18 | The Inspiration and Authority of the Bible

Two great revelations stand at the center of historic Christianity: the personal revelation of God in Christ and the propositional revelation of God in Scriptures. The Christian claims that God has disclosed himself in the Scriptures and in the Savior, in the written Word and in the living Word of God. The evidence that the Bible is the written Word of God is anchored in the authority of Jesus Christ. The basic argument in support of this runs as follows: (1) the New Testament documents are historically reliable (Chapter 16); (2) these documents accurately present Christ as claiming to be God Incarnate and proving it by fulfilled messianic prophecy, by a sinless and miraculous life, and by predicting and accomplishing his resurrection from the dead (Chapter 17); (3) whatever Christ (who is God) teaches is true; (4) Christ taught that the Old Testament is the written Word of God and promised that his disciples would write the New Testament (Chapter 18); (5) therefore, it is true on the confirmed divine authority of Jesus Christ that the Bible is the written Word of God.

## The Teaching of Christ and the Apostles About the Old Testament

Christ and the apostles did much of their teaching *from* the Old Testament, but what is sometimes overlooked is that they also taught a great deal *about* the Old Testament. Both direct and indirect references unmistakably manifest their affirmation that the Old Testament writings are the inscripturated Word of God.[1] If Jesus did indeed teach that the Jewish

---

1. For a more complete discussion on the Bible's claim for its own inspiration see N. L. Geisler, *A General Introduction to the Bible,* Chapters 1-9, or my *From God to Us,* Chapters 1-5.

Scriptures were the inspired Word of God, then on his confirmed divine authority it can be established that the Old Testament is the written revelation of God.

Since we have already argued for both the reliability of the New Testament and the integrity of Christ's apostles as eyewitness reporters of what Jesus taught (Chapter 16), we need not separate here the words of Jesus from those of the apostles for two reasons. First, the testimony of the apostles about the Old Testament does not differ from Christ's nor does it add in kind to Jesus' view. Second, according to the confirmed integrity of the apostolic witness, they were not giving merely their own personal views but were expressing what Jesus himself taught (cf. John 14:26; 16:13; Acts 1:1).

*The Old Testament Teaching About Its Own Authority.* From the very beginning, the Old Testament writings of Moses were held to be sacred and were stored in the ark of God (Deut. 10:2) and later in the tabernacle (Deut. 6:2). Prophetic writings were added to this collection as they were written (Josh. 24:26; I Sam. 10:25; etc.). Moses claimed that his writings were from God (cf. Exod. 20:1; Lev. 1:1; Num. 1:1; Deut. 1:3), and the remainder of the Old Testament recognizes the divine authority of Moses' writings (Josh. 1:8; I Sam. 12:6; Dan. 9:12; Neh. 13:1). After Moses came a succession of prophets who claimed "thus saith the Lord." Near the end of Old Testament history there were collections of "Moses and the prophets" held as divinely authoritative (Dan. 9:2; Zech. 7:12). The acknowledgment of the divine authority of Moses and the prophets' writings continued through the period between the Testaments (cf. 2 Macc. 15:9) and into the Qumran literature (*Manual of Discipline* 1:3; 8:15).

*The New Testament Teaching About the Divine Authority of the Old Testament.* There are numerous ways that Jesus and the New Testament writers indicated their belief that the Old Testament was God's Word. Sometimes they referred to the Old Testament as a whole; other times they mentioned specific sections or books, and sometimes even words, tenses, or parts of words as possessing the authority of God.

    a.  New Testament Teaching About the Inspiration of the Old Testament as a Whole

II Timothy 3:16 declares *"all* scripture is inspired of God," which in context refers to the *"sacred writings"* of the Jewish faith in which young Timothy was taught (v. 15). The comprehensive use of these writings for all "faith and practice" indicates the belief that these writings included the entire canon of Jewish sacred Scripture (v. 17). The New Testament often refers to the authoritative writings of the Jews as *"the scriptures."* Jesus said, "The scriptures cannot be broken" (John 10:35). Or, "You are wrong, because you know neither the scriptures, or the power of God"

(Matt. 22:29). The less common but more powerful designation "the Word of God" is used interchangeably with the "scriptures" (John 1:35). Paul employs the same phrase (Rom. 9:6; II Cor. 4:2). A similar phrase, "the oracles of God," is used by Paul in reference to the whole Old Testament (Rom. 3:2). Sometimes the word "Law" (of God) is used to denote the authority of the Old Testament (John 10:34; cf. John 12:34). But probably the most common way of referring to the whole Old Testament is the phrase "law and prophets." This is used a dozen times in the New Testament and it depicts all the Old Testament writings as the authoritative voice of God. Jesus claimed that the law and prophets will never pass away (Matt. 5:17). Jesus said that the law and the prophets included all the divine revelation up to John the Baptist (Luke 16:16), and Paul claimed that it was the "whole counsel of God" (Acts 24:14). The phrase "it is written" is used more than nineteen times in the New Testament; some have application to the Old Testament in general (Mark 9:12; Luke 21:22) and indicate the divine authority of what is written. Likewise the phrase "that it might be fulfilled" is sometimes used in connection with references to the divine authority of the whole Old Testament (cf. Matt. 5:17; Luke 24:44).

b. New Testament Teaching About Sections of the Old Testament

The usual way of referring to the Old Testament indicates two divisions, the law and the prophets. The former was Moses' writings, believed by the Jews to include the first five books of the Old Testament. "Moses" (II Cor. 3:15), the "law of Moses" (Acts 13:39), or the "books of Moses" (Mark 12:26) are often alluded to by the New Testament as the Word of God. The word *prophets* identifies the second part of the Old Testament (John 1:45; Luke 18:31). II Peter makes it very clear that all prophetic writings come from God "because no prophecy ever came by the impulse of man, but men moved by the Holy Spirit spoke from God" (1:21).

c. New Testament Teaching About the Divine Authority of Specific Books of the Old Testament

Jesus and the New Testament writers did not have specific occasion to quote every book in the Old Testament, but when they did cite a specific book it was often with introductory phrases that indicated their belief in the divine authority of that specific book. Of the twenty-two (twenty-four)[2] books numbered in the Jewish Old Testament some eighteen are cited by the New Testament. There is no explicit citation of Judges, Chronicles, Esther, or the Song of Solomon, although Hebrews 11:32 refers to events in Judges, II Chronicles 24:20 may be alluded to in Matthew 23:35,

---

2. The Talmud and Jewish Bibles today number them as 24 but Josephus and others combine Ruth with Judges and Lamentations with Jeremiah making the number 22. See Josephus, *Against Apion* I, 8.

Song of Solomon 4:15 may be reflected in John 4:15, and the feast of Purim established in Esther was accepted by the New Testament Jews.

Virtually all of the remaining books of the Old Testament are cited with divine authority by the New Testament. Jesus himself cited Genesis (Matt. 19:4-5), Exodus (John 6:31), Leviticus (Matt. 8:4), Numbers (John 3:14), Deuteronomy (Matt. 4:4), and I Samuel (Matt. 12:3-4). He also referred to Kings (Luke 4:25) and II Chronicles (Matt. 23:35), as well as Ezra-Nehemiah (John 6:31). Psalms is frequently quoted by Jesus (see Matt. 21:42; 22:44), Proverbs is quoted by Jesus in Luke 14:8-10 (see Prov. 25:6-7), and Song of Solomon may be alluded to in John 4:10. Isaiah is often quoted by Christ (see Luke 4:18-19). Likewise, Jesus alludes to Jeremiah's Book of Lamentations (Matt. 27:30) and perhaps to Ezekiel (John 3:10). Jesus specifically quoted Daniel by name (Matt. 24:21). He also quoted passages from the twelve (minor) prophets (Matt. 26:31). Other books, such as Joshua (Heb. 13:5), Ruth (Heb. 11:32), and Jeremiah (Heb. 8:8-12), are quoted by New Testament writers. The teachings of Ecclesiastes are clearly reflected in the New Testament (cf. Gal. 6:7 and Eccles. 11:1 or Heb. 9:27 and Eccles. 3:2).

More than the number of individual books cited, the authoritative manner in which they are often cited indicates that Jesus taught the full divine authority of these books. Quotations are prefaced with "it is written," "that it might be fulfilled," "till heaven and earth pass away" (Matt. 5:18), "you are wrong" if you do not believe (Matt. 22:29), and even "God commanded" (Matt. 15:4). In short, the written words of these books were considered to be God's words.

d. New Testament Teaching About the Historicity of Specific Events in the Old Testament

Jesus and the New Testament writers not only cited sections and books of the Old Testament as inspired but they often taught the truth of specific Old Testament events recorded in these books. Jesus himself taught the creation of Adam and Eve (Matt. 19), Noah's flood (Luke 17:27), Jonah and the Great Fish (Matt. 12:40), Elijah's miracles (Luke 4:25), and Moses' miracles in the wilderness (John 3:14; 6:32), plus many other persons and events. Taking the total testimony of Jesus and the New Testament writers who related his teaching one can virtually reconstruct the main events of the Old Testament including creation (John 1:3), the fall of man (Rom. 5:12), the murder of Abel (I John 3:12), the flood of Noah's day (Luke 17:27), Abraham and the patriarchs (Heb. 11:8 f.), the destruction of Sodom and Gomorrah (Luke 17:29), the offering of Isaac (Heb. 11:17), Moses and the burning bush (Luke 20:32), the exodus from Egypt (I Cor. 10:1-2), miraculous provision of the manna (I Cor. 10:3-5), lifting up of the brazen serpent (John 3:14), the fall of Jericho (Heb. 11:30), the miracles of Elijah (James 5:17), the famous judges (Heb. 11:32) and kings (Matt. 12:41-42), Daniel in the lions' den (Heb. 11:33), and the rejection of the Old Testament prophets (Matt. 23:35).

In this sample listing several things should be noted. First, most of the major Old Testament events are taught to be historically true by Jesus or the New Testament writers. Second, often the passages are cited with emphatic parallel to events which Christ claimed to be historical facts (see Matt. 12:40). Third, sometimes Jesus clearly affirmed the plain historical truth of his teachings on the authenticity of those Old Testament persons or events (Matt. 22:32). Jesus once challenged a Jewish leader by saying, "If I tell you earthly things and you do not believe, how can you believe if I tell you heavenly things?" (John 3:12).

e. New Testament Teaching About Words and Parts of Words as Authoritative

Sometimes the New Testament hinges the authority of its teaching on the very tense of a verb or a single letter of a word. Jesus taught the doctrine of the resurrection on the present tense of the Old Testament phrase "I *am* the God of Abraham and the God of Isaac, and the God of Jacob" (Matt. 22:32). Paul contended that the singular form of the "offspring of Abraham" gave it messianic significance (Gal. 3:16). Even granting hyperbole for the sake of emphasis, it is significant to the complete authority of every part of the Old Testament that Jesus proclaimed that "not the smallest letter or the smallest part of a letter of the law would pass away until all is fulfilled," literally, "not an iota, not a dot" (Matt. 5:18).

## Affirmation or Accommodation?

The objection is sometimes raised that Christ did not affirm the inspiration and authority of the Old Testament; he merely accommodated himself to the accepted but false Jewish belief about the Old Testament. According to this accommodation theory, Christ affirmed neither the authority of the Scriptures nor the authenticity of the events recorded therein; he simply appealed to the accepted Jewish beliefs about the Old Testament and used them as a starting point in his discourses. If this is so, then Jesus did not really teach Jonah was in the great fish but simply used the story like a parable or illustration of his own resurrection.

Jesus, as it were, adapted his message to the Jewish tradition and culture in which he found himself. Accordingly, he never really affirmed or taught anything about the Old Testament; he simply taught from it as an accepted religious model or myth structure.

In response to this theory we should observe first that it is a confusion of divine adaptation and human accommodation. Certainly an infinite

God must *adapt* his revelation to the finite human understanding of the people to whom he communicates. However, it is quite another thing for God to *accommodate* his revelation to the error of sinful minds. Adaptation to finitude is necessary but accommodation to error is neither necessary nor is it morally possible for a God of absolute truthfulness (Heb. 6:18).[3]

Furthermore, there are numerous facts known from the life and activity of Christ that render the accommodation theory untrue.[4] The combined testimony against the accommodation theory makes it so highly implausible that no sensible reader of the New Testament ought embrace it.

*The Emphatic Manner of Citation of the Old Testament by Jesus.* Oftentimes Jesus cited the Old Testament with such emphasis that it eliminates the possibility of accommodation. "Truly, truly, I say unto you . . ." or "you have heard that it was said . . . but I say unto you" (John 3:11; Matt. 5:38-39). Elsewhere Jesus said that "heaven and earth will pass away but my words will not pass away" (Matt. 24:35). Jesus' teaching that the "scriptures cannot be broken" (John 10:35) and that "not an iota, not a dot will pass away from the law until all is accomplished" flatly contradicts the accommodation hypothesis.

*The Direct Comparison of Old Testament Events with Historical Happenings.* Often Jesus compares Old Testament events with historical occurrences in a strong manner. When responding to an evil generation's demand for a sign from heaven Jesus replied, "No sign shall be given to it except the sign of the prophet Jonah. For as Jonah was three days and three nights in the belly of the whale, so will the Son of man be three days and three nights in the heart of the earth" (Matt. 12:39-40). It seems highly improbable that Jesus would contrast something so essential as the historicity of his own death and resurrection with a mythology of Jewish belief. It is much more reasonable to conclude that Jesus is affirming the historicity of Jonah, as indeed the Old Testament itself does (see II Kings 14:25). In like manner, the teachings of Christ about the destruction of Sodom and the flood of Noah are used in strong contrast with historical teachings about his own ministry and coming again (see Luke 17:26-30).

*Historicity of Old Testament Events Is Sometimes Crucial to the Doctrine Taught.* Often it is impossible to separate the doctrine being taught by Jesus from the historicity of the event to which he refers. The point Jesus is making about marriage and divorce—an obviously physical union of two bodies into "one flesh"—is void unless the Old Testament

---

3. For support of the belief in absolute moral norms see my *Ethics: Alternatives and Issues,* Chapters 1-7.

4. An excellent exposition of Christ's verification of the Old Testament is found in John W. Wenham, *Christ and the Bible.*

quotation about Adam and Eve refers to actual and historical persons of flesh and bone. "Have you not read that he who made them in the beginning made them male and female.... What therefore God joined together, let no man put asunder" (Matt. 19:4, 6). Here the very validity of Jesus' answer to the question about marriage and divorce depends on the reliability of there being a literal creation in the beginning of a male and a female whom God had joined together as "one flesh." Hence, there is no way here to completely separate the doctrinal or spiritual from the physical and historical in Jesus' teaching.

*Jesus Often Rebuked False Jewish Tradition and Error.* The evidence of the Gospel record is that Jesus is anything but an accommodator. He did not hesitate to make forthright pronouncements. Jesus rebuked the Jewish ruler Nicodemus saying, "Are you a teacher of Israel, and yet *you do not understand* this?" (John 3:10). To the Sadducees Jesus said plainly, *"You are wrong,* because you know neither the scriptures nor the power of God" (Matt. 22:29). In the Sermon on the Mount Jesus repeatedly debunked false Jewish belief with the emphatic phrase, "you have heard that it was said ... but *I say unto you"* (Matt. 5:38, 39). On another occasion Jesus deliberately decried Jewish teaching that went contrary to God's truth with the challenge, "Why do you transgress the commandment of God for the sake of *your tradition?"* (Matt. 15:3). It seems plain from these events that Jesus did not hesitate to refute error whether it was accepted Jewish belief or not. The same consistent picture of Jesus' rejection of false Jewish tradition and teaching is evident in his relation to the belief about keeping the sabbath (see Matt. 12:12).

*Jesus Was Forthright in His Condemnation of False Prophets.* The portrait of a young revolutionary attacking the inflexible religious establishment of the day fits Christ much better than that of an accommodator to accepted traditions and teachings. The severe denunciations of Matthew 23 have led some unbelievers even to charge that Jesus was unkind.[5] Yet the fact that other unbelievers consider Jesus so soft that he capitulated truth to his hearers' fancy indicates the extreme dilemma of unbelief. The Jesus that gave his life for this sinful world and that forgave his enemies for crucifying him (Luke 23:34) was not unkind or unloving (John 10:11; 15:13). However, Jesus' love for men and for truth did prompt him to take a firm stand against error and false teachers. "Woe to you, blind guides. . . . Woe to you, scribes and Pharisees, hypocrites! for you build the tombs of the prophets. . . . You serpents, you brood of vipers, how are you to escape being sentenced to hell?" (Matt. 23:16, 29, 33). Even in what is universally acknowledged to be Jesus' greatest moral discourse and what some interpret in a very pacifistic manner, Jesus had

5. Bertrand Russell, "Why I Am Not a Christian," in *The Basic Writings of Bertrand Russell,* p. 594.

strong words of warning about avoiding error: "Beware of false prophets, who come to you in sheep's clothing but inwardly are ravenous wolves" (Matt. 7:15). And in the great Mount Olivet discourse near the end of his life Jesus was still warning against "false Christs and false prophets" (Matt. 24:24). The Gospel picture of Christ is consistent; he is a debunker of error and a rebuker of false teachers but definitely not an accommodator to either.

In summary, neither the activity, attitudes, nor affirmations of Jesus were accommodations to error. When Jesus affirmed something as true it was because he believed it to be so. And as the Son of God his affirmations carry divine authority. Hence, when Jesus taught the divine origin and authority of the Old Testament, he was not mouthing false Jewish beliefs; rather, he was teaching divine truth.

### Limitation or Authorization?

It has been hypothesized that Jesus' human knowledge did not extend to matters such as the authority and authenticity of the Old Testament. His teaching was purely doctrinal and spiritual but not historical and critical. Some critics have argued that in the incarnation Jesus "emptied himself" of omniscience. He was ignorant of the time of his second coming (Mark 13:32), of whether there were figs on the tree (Mark 11:13). Jesus "increased in wisdom" as other humans do (Luke 2:52), and asked many questions that revealed his ignorance of the answers (Mark 5:9, 30; 6:38; John 14:9). This being the case, perhaps Jesus was ignorant of the origin of the Old Testament and of the historical truth of the events in it.

This "Limitation Theory" is much more plausible and potentially damaging to the case for the authority of the Old Testament than is the "Accommodation Theory." Let us examine the evidence carefully.

First, it seems necessary to grant that Jesus was indeed ignorant of many things *as a man. As God,* of course, Jesus was infinite in knowledge and knew all things (Ps. 147:5).[6] But Christ has two natures: one infinite or unlimited in knowledge, and the other finite or limited in knowledge. Could it be that Jesus did not really err in what he taught about the Old Testament but that he simply was so limited as a human being that his knowledge and authority did not extend into those areas? The evidence in the New Testament records demands an emphatically negative answer to this question for many reasons.

*Jesus Had a Supernormal Knowledge Even as a Human Being.* Even in his human state Christ possessed supernormal if not supernatural knowledge of many things. He saw Nathanael under the fig tree, although he was not within normal visual distance (John 1:48). Jesus amazed the

---

6. See also chap. 13 above on why God must be infinite.

woman of Samaria with the information he knew about her private life (John 4:18-19). Jesus knew who would betray him in advance (John 6:64) and "all that would befall him" in Jerusalem (John 18:4). He knew about Larazus's death before he was told (John 11:14) and of his crucifixion and resurrection before it occurred (Mark 8:31; 9:31). Jesus had superhuman knowledge of the location of fish (Luke 5:4). There is no indication from the Gospel record that Jesus' finitude deterred his ministry or teaching. Whatever the limitations to his knowledge, it was vastly beyond normal men and completely adequate for his mission and doctrinal teaching.

*Christ Possessed Complete and Final Authority for Whatever He Taught.* One thing is crystal clear: Christ claimed that whatever he taught came from God with absolute and final authority. He claimed "Heaven and earth will pass away but my word will not pass away" (Matt. 24:35). Jesus believed and proclaimed that "all things have been delivered to me by my Father" (Matt. 11:27). When Jesus commissioned his disciples he claimed "all authority in heaven and on earth has been given me. Go therefore and make disciples . . . teaching them to observe all that I have commanded you" (Matt. 28:18-19). Elsewhere Jesus claimed that the very destiny of men hinged on his words (Matt. 7:24-26) and that his words would judge men in the last day (John 12:48). The emphatic "truly, truly" is found some twenty-five times in John alone, and in Matthew he declared, "Not an iota, not a dot, will pass from the law" which he came to fulfill. Jesus then placed his own words on a par with it (Matt. 5:18, 21 f.). Jesus claimed that his words bring eternal life (John 5:24) and vowed that all his teaching came from the Father (John 8:26-28). Furthermore, despite the fact that he was a man on earth, Christ accepted the acclaims of deity and allowed men to worship him on many occasions (cf. Matt. 28:18; John 9:38).

In view of the foregoing evidence, the only reasonable conclusion is that Jesus' teachings are possessed of divine authority. Despite the necessary limitations involved in a human incarnation, there is no error or misunderstanding in whatever Christ taught. Whatever limits there were in the extent of Jesus' knowledge, there were no limits to the truthfulness of his teachings. Just as Jesus was fully human and yet his *moral* character was without flaw (Heb. 4:15), likewise he was finite in human knowledge and yet without *factual* error in his teaching (John 8:40, 46). In summation, whatever Jesus taught came from God. Hence, if Jesus taught the divine authority and historical authenticity of the Old Testament, then this teaching is the truth of God.

## The Nature of the Inspiration of the Old Testament

Granted that Jesus affirmed the inspiration of the Old Testament, just what does it mean when we speak of "inspiration"? The answer to this question has several aspects. For Jesus, as for the Jews, an inspired writing meant that it was sacred (cf. John 10:35 and II Tim. 3:15) and that it was "from God." "Inspired" means "God-breathed" (II Tim. 3:16) and "Spirit-moved" (II Peter 1:20-21).

*Inspiration Is Verbal.* It was not merely the thoughts or the oral pronouncements of the prophets that were inspired but the very "words." Moses "wrote all the *words* of the Lord" (Exod. 24:4) and David confessed, "His *word* is upon my tongue" (II Sam. 23:2). Jeremiah was told to "diminish not a *word*" (Jer. 26:2 KJV). Jesus repeated over and over that the authority was found in what "is *written*" (see Matt. 4:4, 7). Paul testified that he spoke in *"words* . . . taught by the Spirit"* (I Cor. 2:13). And the classic text in II Timothy 3:16 declares that it is the *"writings,"* the *graphē,* that are inspired of God.

*Inspiration Is Plenary.* Jesus not only affirmed the written revelation of God but he taught that the *whole* (complete, entire) Old Testament was inspired of God. Everything including Moses and the prophets is from God (Matt. 5:17, 18) and must be fulfilled (Luke 24:44). Paul added that *"whatever* was written in former days [in the Old Testament] was written for our instruction" (Rom. 15:4) and that *"all scripture* is inspired of God" and therefore "profitable for teaching, for reproof, for correction, and for training in righteousness" (II Tim. 3:16, 17). That is to say, the inspiration of the Bible extends to everything it *teaches* whether spiritual or factual. Of course, not everything *contained* in the Bible is *taught* by the Bible. The Bible contains a true record of Satan's lies (see Gen. 3:4), but the Bible is not thereby teaching that these lies are true. Plenary inspiration means only that whatever the Bible teaches is true, is actually true.

*Inspiration Conveys Authority.* Further, the authority of the Bible's teaching flows from its divine origin as the oracles or Word of God (see Rom. 3:2). Jesus said of the Old Testament, "The scriptures cannot be broken" for they are the "word of God" (John 10:35). Jesus claimed the authority of "it is written" for his teaching over and over again (cf. Matt. 22:29; Mark 9:12). He resisted the devil by the same written authority (see Matt. 4:4, 7, 10). The written Word, then, is the authority of God for settling all disputes of doctrine or practice. It is God's Word in man's words; it is divine truth in human terms.[7]

*Inspiration Implies the* Inerrancy *of the Teaching.* Jesus believed that God's Word is true (John 17:17) and the apostles taught that God cannot

---

7. This does not mean that the Bible was verbally dictated as some have mistakenly taught (cf. John R. Rice, *Our God-Breathed Book,* pp. 265-67, 281-91). There are stylistic differences easily recognizable in Scripture which indicate that God used the various personalities of the different authors in a dynamic way.

lie (Heb. 6:18). Furthermore, Jesus affirmed that every "iota and dot" of the Old Testament was from God. This, of course, is a claim only for the writings as they were given by God, namely, the *autographs,* and not for the copies which have been in minor detail subjected to scribal errors. The net result, however, is the necessary conclusion that the Old Testament is without error (i.e., inerrant) in whatever it teaches. Simply put: whatever God utters is true and without error. The original writings of the Old Testament are the utterance of God through men. Therefore, the writings of the Old Testament are the inerrant Word of God. This is what both Jesus and the apostles taught with divine authority, an authority confirmed by the unique concurrence of three miracles in the life, death, and resurrection of Christ (see Chapter 17).

### The Extent of the Old Testament Scriptures

There is some dispute as to which books are to be included in the Old Testament canon of Scripture. Some claim that the so-called apocryphal books written between 250 B.C. and the time of Christ are also part of the Old Testament canon. Hence, we must turn our attention from the nature of the Old Testament as the inspired Word of God to the *extent* of those inspired writings.[8]

*Arguments Advanced in Support of the Apocrypha Examined.* The basic debate is between the Roman Catholic position that the books of the so-called Alexandrian Canon should be included in the Old Testament and the Protestant position that only the books of the so-called Jewish Palestinian Canon are inspired. The books involved in the dispute are named as follows by Protestants (and Catholics):

1. Esdras (III Esdras)
2. II Esdras (IV Esdras)
3. Tobit
4. Judith
5. Addition to Esther (Esther 10:4—16:24)
6. The Wisdom of Solomon
7. Ecclesiasticus or Sirach
8. Baruch and the Letter of Jeremiah (Baruch)
9. The Prayer of Azariah and the Song of the Three Young Men (Dan. 3:24-90)
10. Susanna (Dan. 13)
11. Bel and the Dragon (Dan. 14)
12. The Prayer of Manasseh
13. I Maccabees
14. II Maccabees

8. For a fuller treatment of the canonicity of Scripture see my *A General Introduction to the Bible,* Chapters 10-15, or my *From God to Us,* Chapters 6-10.

In favor of the acceptance of the Apocrypha the following arguments have been advanced:[9] (1) The New Testament makes direct quotes from the book of Enoch (Jude 14) and alludes to II Maccabees (Heb. 11:35); (2) Some apocryphal books were found in the first century Jewish community at Qumran; (3) Many early Christian Fathers including Origen (A.D. 185-253), Athanasius (A.D. 293-373), and Cyril of Jerusalem (A.D. 315-386) quoted some apocryphal books; (4) Many early Greek manuscripts of the Old Testament such as Codex Vaticanus (A.D. 325) and Codex Sinaiticus (A.D. 350) contained the Apocrypha; (5) Augustine accepted all the apocryphal books later proclaimed canonical by Trent (in 1546); (6) Many early church synods, such as the Synod by Pope Damasus (A.D. 382), Synod of Hippo (A.D. 393), and three synods at Carthage (A.D. 393, 397, 419), accepted the Apocrypha; (7) Some later bishops and councils between the ninth and fifteenth centuries listed the apocryphal books as inspired; (8) This long line of Christian usage culminated in the official pronouncement of the Council of Trent (A.D. 1546) that the Apocrypha (or "deutero-canonical" books, as Roman Catholics call them) is part of canonical Scripture.

Despite the long list of names and churches associated with the apocryphal books, these arguments must be rejected in view of the following considerations: (1) No apocryphal book is quoted as Scripture in the New Testament. The New Testament writers allude to and even cite pagan poets whose books were not considered inspired Scripture (see Acts 17:28). (2) The Qumran community was not an orthodox Jewish community and, hence, is not an official voice of Judaism. (3) Many of the early Christian Fathers including Origen, Cyril of Jerusalem, Athanasius, and all important Fathers before Augustine clearly rejected the Apocrypha. Some of these men made presumable or occasional reference to one or more apocryphal books in a homiletical way but none of the major early Fathers accepted the apocryphal books into the Christian canon. (4) Augustine's acceptance of the Apocrypha is refuted by his contemporary Jerome who was the greatest Biblical scholar of his day. (5) No local synod or canonical listing included these apocryphal books for almost the first four hundred years of the church's existence. Neither early church synods nor Augustine listed the apocryphal books as inspired until after the appearance of the Greek translations of the Old Testament containing these books (i.e., after A.D. 325). These local listings are based on a Greek Alexandrian tradition where the Hebrew Old Testament was translated (250 B.C. following) and not a Jewish Palestinian tradition where the Old Testament was actually written and accepted by Jewish

---

9. For a fuller discussion of this point see my article "The Extent of the Old Testament Canon," in *Current Issues in Biblical and Patristic Studies,* ed. Gerald F. Hawthorne, pp. 31-46.

people. (6) Even up to and through the time of the Reformation (A.D. 1517) some Roman Catholic scholars, including Cardinal Cajetan who opposed Luther, did not accept the Apocrypha as authentic Old Testament books. (7) Furthermore, Christian usage of the Apocrypha has varied greatly down through the years. Fathers before Augustine accepted only a fraction of the Apocrypha, sometimes only one or two books. Many Fathers would "quote" and even "read" some apocryphal books in church but excluded them from their canonical lists. The best explanation seems to be that they had two groupings: one a doctrinal canon which determined matters of faith and the other a broader homiletical collection which they used to illustrate and expand on their beliefs. (8) Trent was inconsistent in accepting only eleven of the fourteen apocryphal books. They rejected the Prayer of Manesseh, I Esdras (III Esdras), and II Esdras (IV Esdras) which contains a strong verse against praying for the dead (viz., 7:105) and accepted a book with a verse supporting prayer for the dead (viz., II Macc. 12:45 [46]). Proclaiming this book canonical some twenty-nine years after Luther lashed out against prayers for the dead is highly suspect, especially since the book disclaiming the efficacy of such prayers was rejected.

*The Extent of the Jewish Canon of Jesus' Day.* The mistake in the broader canon theory is that it employs Christian usage as the determinative factor in deciding the Jewish canon. This is wrong for two reasons: first, these were Jewish books written by Jewish writers for Jewish people and rejected by the Old Testament Jewish community. It is presumptuous for Christians hundreds of years after the fact to inform Jews which books belong in their sacred writings. Second, the New Testament clearly informs Christians that the Old Testament was given into the custodianship of the Jews. Paul wrote, "The Jews are entrusted with the oracles of God" (Rom. 3:2). In view of this it behooves us to ask, What is the extent of the Old Testament canon according to the Jews? To this question there is only one answer, as even Roman Catholic scholars readily admit, namely, the twenty-four (thirty-nine) books of the Jewish and Protestant Bibles of today comprise the Jewish Old Testament canon.

There is an even more decisive argument than Jewish custodianship against the Apocrypha, namely, the authoritative testimony of Christ. Which books were included in the Old Testament of which Jesus spoke when he proclaimed it the unbreakable and authoritative Word of God? The answer to this question seems clear: there were no more (and no less) than twenty-four (thirty-nine) books of the Jewish Old Testament to which Christ attested.

a. The Jewish Scriptures of the Time of Christ

The best authority for the Jewish canon of the time of Christ is the Jewish historian Josephus. Josephus lists twenty-two books, "five belonging to Moses . . . the prophets, who were after Moses . . . in thirteen books. The remaining four books containing hymns to God and precepts for the conduct of human life."[10] Ruth was no doubt appended to Judges and Lamentations to Jeremiah, thus accounting for the difference between the numbering of twenty-four and twenty-two. Job was probably listed among the historical books, since Josephus cites it in his writings and since there would be only twelve historical books without it. This would leave Psalms, Proverbs, Ecclesiastes, and Song of Solomon in the last category. With this arrangement we have the identical books of the thirty-nine now in the Protestant Old Testament, since by counting I and II Samuel as one book, I and II Kings as one book, I and II Chronicles as one book, Ezra-Nehemiah as one book, and the twelve (minor) prophets as one book, the difference between the numbering of thirty-nine and twenty-four is accounted for. That Josephus considered this to be the complete and final Jewish canon is made clear by his declaration that the succession of Jewish prophets ended in the fourth century B.C. Likewise the Talmud teaches that "after the latter prophets Haggai, Zechariah . . . and Malachi, the Holy Spirit departed from Israel."[11] Since all the apocryphal books were written after the fourth century (viz., from 250 B.C. to the time of Christ), it is clear that they were not in the Jewish Old Testament. This fact is supported by the apocryphal books themselves, for not only do they lack the claim to any divine inspiration, but they are devoid of any predictive or messianic prophecy, and do in fact disclaim inspiration. I Maccabees says that in those days "there was great distress in Israel, such as has not been since the time the prophets ceased to appear among them" (9:27).

b. The Old Testament Canon of Jesus and the Apostles

The best evidence for the extent of the Jewish canon of the time of Christ is found in the New Testament. Both Jesus and the apostles affirm only the canon containing the thirty-nine (twenty-four) books of the Protestant Old Testament. This is supported by several lines of evidence. First, no apocryphal book is ever cited as Scripture by either Jesus or the New Testament writers, despite the fact that they obviously possessed them and even made allusions to them. Coupled with the fact that Jesus and the apostles did have occasion to quote from some eighteen of the twenty-two (twenty-four) books in the Jewish Old Testament, the omission of any quotations from the Apocrypha actually entails a rejection of these books. Second, the New Testament makes at least a dozen references to the whole Old Testament under the phrase "law and prophets" (cf. Matt. 5:17; Luke 24:27); and yet the apocryphal books are admitted by

10. Josephus, *Against Apion* I, 83.
11. *Babylonian Talmud*, "Sanhedrin," VII-VIII, 24.

both friend and foe to have never been in the section of the canon known as "the prophets." Their late date would automatically have placed them in the "writings" or so-called third section of the Old Testament. Even during the intertestamental period (see II Macc. 15:9) and in the Qumran literature (*Manual of Discipline,* I, 3; VIII, 15), the Old Testament is referred to under the standard phrase "the law and the prophets." The threefold division that emerged by the time of Christ and is reflected in Philo, Josephus, and possibly in the introduction to Sirach was apparently an alternate way of subdividing "the prophets" into "prophets" and "writings" for festal or literary reasons. Jesus' possible allusion to a threefold division that emerged by the time of Christ and is reflected in prophets and the psalms" (Luke 24:44) is used in direct parallel with the phrase "Moses and all the prophets" earlier in the same chapter (v. 27).

According to New Testament usage the phrase "law and the prophets" includes "all the scripture" (Luke 24:27) and "all the prophets [who] prophesied until John [the Baptist]" (Mark 13:31). Paul the apostle staked his complete orthodoxy on the grounds that he believed "everything laid down in the law or written in the prophets" (Acts 24:14). Jesus said he had come to fulfill "all" according to what was predicted in the "law and prophets" (Matt. 5:17).

We cannot avoid the conclusion that the phrase "law and prophets" referred to all divine written revelation from Moses to Jesus.[12] This being the case, the fact that neither the first century Jews, Jesus himself, nor the apostles accepted or quoted the apocryphal books as inspired is sufficient evidence that these books were not part of their canon of Scripture. This conclusion has been the uniform testimony of Judaism throughout the centuries. The extent of the Old Testament canon is limited, by both the Jews who wrote it and by Jesus about whom it is written, to the thirty-nine (twenty-four) books listed in Protestant Old Testament Bibles today.

## Conclusion

Jesus taught emphatically that the Jewish Old Testament was the very inspired and written revelation of God. In this teaching he neither accommodated himself to false tradition nor was limited in his knowledge of the matters of which he spoke. His teaching was with all authority in heaven and on earth. And since Christ has been verified to be the unique Son of God, whatever he teaches is the very truth of God. Hence, on the testimony and authority of Christ it is established as true that the Old

---

12. For further support of this point see Laird Harris, *Inspiration and Canonicity of the Bible.*

Testament, with all of its historical and miraculous events, is an in-scripturated revelation of God.

There are many other evidences that the Bible is the Word of God—for example, its supernatural predictive prophecy, its amazing unity, its superior moral quality, its world-wide publicity, and its dynamic power.[13] It is sufficient evidence, however, that Jesus verified the Old Testament to be God's Word. Since Jesus is confirmed to be the Son of God, his testimony that the Bible is the Word of God is more than adequate. Either a person accepts the authority of Scripture or he must impugn the integrity of the Son of God; they stand together.

## Christ Promised the Inspiration of the New Testament

Jesus not only confirmed the divine authority of the Old Testament but he also guaranteed the inspiration of the New Testament. He promised to lead his disciples into "all truth" by the Holy Spirit. This promise was not only claimed by the apostles but was fulfilled in the apostolic writings of the New Testament. With these twenty-seven books God completed the fulfillment of all things that had been promised and closed the canon of revelation.

### The Life and Ministry of Christ Is the Fulfillment of All Things

The New Testament teaches that Christ is the full and final fulfillment of *"all* things" (see Luke 21:22). Jesus claimed that he was the fulfillment of the *whole* Old Testament on many occasions (cf. Matt. 5:17; Luke 24:27, 44). The Jews knew only two days, "the former days" and "the latter days." Jesus brought in the fulfillment of all the prophecies of the latter days so that the apostles announced that they were in the *"latter* times" (I Tim. 4:1) or the *"last* hour" (I John 2:18). The Book of Hebrews declares that God spoke in many ways through the Old Testament prophets in times past "but in these *last* days he has spoken to us by a Son" (1:3) who is the full and final revelation of God, "the very stamp of his nature" (1:3) who brings both *eternal* (5:9) and *final* salvation (10:10-12). Daniel was told, "Shut up the words, and seal the book, until the time of the end" (12:4); but in the last apocalypse (unveiling) John is told, "Do not seal up the words of the prophecy of this book, for *the time is near"* (Rev. 22:10). All of God's revelation comes to a culmination in Christ. In him are "hid *all* the treasures of wisdom and knowledge" (Col. 2:3). The very theme of Colossians is *completion* of perfection in Christ (1:28). Christ is not only the completion of God's revelation but the complete revelation of God is about him. On at least five occasions Christ declared himself to be the theme of the Scriptures

---

13. See Bernard Ramm's *Protestant Christian Evidences* for an elaboration of some of these arguments.

(Matt. 5:17; Luke 24:27, 44; John 5:39; Heb. 10:7). John said that "the testimony of Jesus is the spirit of prophecy" (Rev. 19:10) and it was by "the Spirit of Christ" that the prophets spoke (I Peter 1:11).

## Jesus Promised to Guide His Disciples into All Truth

Jesus promised his disciples that he would send them the Holy Spirit who "will teach you *all things,* and bring to your remembrance *all things* that I have said to you" (John 14:26). Jesus added, "When he the Spirit of truth comes, he will guide you into *all the truth"* (John 16:13). The phrase "all truth" obviously does not refer to all scientific or all historical truth, and so on, but to "all truth" necessary for faith and practice (see II Tim, 3:16, 17). After Jesus died he continued "to do and teach" through the apostles (Acts 1:1). Even so, the promise is doctrinally all-inclusive and very important, since it ties in with the claim that Jesus is the fulfillment of all prophecy and that all truth resides in him. The important question is not *whether* Jesus is the final and complete revelation of God—that is repeatedly declared in Scripture—but rather *where* that full and final revelation can be found and *who* are its authorized agents.

## The Twelve Apostles Are the Only Authorized Agents of Christ

Jesus chose twelve apostles and commissioned them with divine authority. He gave them power to forgive sins (John 20:23). Through the apostles' hands the early believers received the Holy Spirit (Acts 8:14, 15) and to the apostles were committed the "keys to the kingdom" (Matt. 16:19; cf. 18:18). The early church was built on the "foundation of the apostles . . ." (Eph. 2:20), it continued the "apostles' teaching . . ." (Acts 2:42), and it was bound by apostolic decision (see Acts 15). Even Paul, whose apostleship and revelation came from God (Gal. 1), had his credentials confirmed by the Jerusalem Twelve (see Gal. 2:2, 9). The writer of the Hebrews acknowledged that the message of Christ "was attested to us by those who heard him" (2:4). This latter phrase is important; there were prophets and writers of New Testament books other than the twelve apostles (Mark, Luke, Paul, James, Jude, and the writer of the Hebrews), but each of these had his message confirmed by the twelve apostles. Mark was an associate of Peter; James and Jude were associates of the apostles and were probably brothers of Jesus. Luke was a companion of Paul whose message was confirmed by the apostles (Acts 15; Gal. 2) and also by Peter (II Peter 3:15, 16). The writer of Hebrews acknowledges his debt to the twelve apostles (2:3) who "heard" Christ. In fact, when Judas died two qualifications for being one of the Twelve were set forth: a potential candidate had to be (1) a member of the eyewitness circle of disciples from the beginning of Jesus' ministry, and (2) an eyewitness of the resurrected Christ (Acts 1:21, 22). Only two men qualified, and Matthias was elected and then "enrolled with the eleven apostles" (v. 26).

The implications of these facts have a most significant bearing on the limits of the New Testament canon of Scripture, namely, no writing after the death of the Twelve can be canonical. Only the Twelve can attest to the truth of a writing about Christ. When all the eyewitnesses had died, the canon of revelation about Christ ceased. And since Christ is the full and final revelation of God, we must conclude that the collection of books authorized by the twelve apostles is the full and final revelation of God to men.

### The Twenty-seven Books of the New Testament Are the Only Authentic Apostolic Writings Extant

Once the facts were generally known, the Christian church has been unanimous down through the years as to the authenticity of the twenty-seven books of the New Testament. It is true that some second century Christians had doubt about various New Testament books such as Hebrews, James, II Peter, II and III John, Jude, and Revelation (called "antilegomena" or "spoken against").[14] But once the authorship and message were attested, there was universal acceptance of their divine authority. And despite the prearchaeological higher criticism of some of these books in modern times, there is ample evidence to support the traditional first century authorship of all of these books.[15] In this regard it is important to observe that the often challenged epistle of II Peter has much more evidence for its authenticity than do the works of Tacitus.

Even within the New Testament there is ample evidence of a developing canon of apostolic literature as it was written. First, there was a deliberate effort made to *select* only the authentic writings about the life of Christ (Luke 1:1-4) and only the authentic epistles of apostles (II Thess. 2:2). The apostles were a kind of "living canon" of eyewitnesses for the teachings about Christ that were circulating (cf. II Peter 1:16; I John 1:3; 4:1, 6). Second, those books that were authorized by the apostles were recommended for *reading* in the churches (Col. 4:16; Rev. 1:3). Third, these books were both circulated in other churches (Col. 4:16; Rev. 1:11) and collected along with the Old Testament Scriptures (II Peter 3:15, 16). There is even evidence within the New Testament that later books quoted earlier ones as Scripture. Paul quoted Luke (I Tim. 5:18; cf. Luke 10:7) and Jude quoted Peter (cf. Jude 17 and II Peter 3:2). Likewise, Luke assumed Theophilus possessed his "first

14. See Geisler, *A General Introduction to the Bible,* chap. 15, or *From God to Us,* chap. 10.
15. See Everett F. Harrison, *Introduction to the New Testament,* or Donald Guthrie, *New Testament Introduction,* vol. 4.

book" (Acts 1:1). Many of the books were probably intended for a wide group of churches. The Book of James is addressed to the "twelve tribes in the dispersion" (1:1); Peter is written to "the exiles of the dispersion" (1:1) and Revelation was sent to "the seven churches" of Asia Minor (1:11). So from the very earliest of times there was a selected group of apostolically approved writings circulating and being read in the churches.

Only twenty-seven such authentic books have been passed down to us from the apostles. Inasmuch as Jesus promised to lead the apostles into "all truth" we may assume that these twenty-seven books fulfill that promise. Even if there were other books by an apostolically authorized New Testament writer, such as the epistle to which Paul referred in I Corinthians 5:9, we may assume that it contained no truth about Christ not found in these twenty-seven extant books. The so-called Letter of the Laodoceans (Col. 4:16) may refer to what we know as the Book of Ephesians.[16] If not, then it would fall into the same classification as Paul's so-called "lost" letter to the Corinthians. What we do know is that there are twenty-seven authentic books from the apostolic period which provide a fulfillment of the "all truth" Jesus promises. In addition we know that this revelation about Christ is the complete and final wisdom of God for men (Col. 2:3; Heb. 1:1 f.). We may conclude, then, that with the apostolic writings of the New Testament the canon of Scripture is complete. John, the last of the apostles to die, seemed to recognize that he was completing the canon of Scripture when he signed off his Apocalypse. He not only wrote of the final revelation of Jesus Christ, which was to be unsealed, for the time of final fulfillment was at hand (22:10), but he recorded an anathema for anyone who added to or took away from his book (vv. 18-19). Since John was allegedly the last living apostle writing his last book, and since there could be no apostolic book after he died, and since "all truth" was committed to the apostles, this concluding statement about not adding to "the words of the prophecy of this book" has at least an indirect bearing on the whole canon of Scripture. Christ fulfilled all, his apostles told all, and his last apostle completed the canon.

## The Test of a False Prophet or False Writing

The Old and New Testaments are not the only writings that claim divine origin. The Koran claims to be inspired as do the Book of Mormon and the writings of the Bahai prophet, Bahá'U'lláh. There are also many contemporaries who are acclaimed as prophets, the most famous of whom are the late Edgar Cayce and Jeane Dixon. Space does not permit a systematic analysis of the claims and credentials of all the writings of these persons. It will be sufficient for our purposes here to lay down the

---

16. See Harrison, *Introduction to N.T.*, p. 311.

tests for a false prophet or writing and illustrate the same by examples drawn from these alleged prophets.

*Do They Claim to Have a New Revelation from God for Mankind?* Properly speaking, most of the forecasts of Edgar Cayce and Jeane Dixon are not religious; they do not come as a revelation of God for mankind. Mohammed, Joseph Smith, and Bahá'U'lláh are different. They each claim divine inspiration. The same is true of David Berg of the Children of God cult.

When any alleged prophet comes with a new revelation of God for mankind, then we know he is not a prophet of God. According to the New Testament he may appear to be a "minister of righteousness" but he is really an emissary of the devil or the satanic "angel of light" himself (II Cor. 11:14, 15). We have already seen that Christ is the full and final revelation of God and that his apostles were commissioned to speak "all truth" about him. When the last of the twelve apostles died, the revelation was completed. Anyone who adds to it is under the anathema of God. Hence, all these modern "prophets" who claim they are adding some new and additional revelation to that of the Bible must be classed as false prophets.

*Do They Have a Different Revelation for Mankind?* Not all who have a different revelation from that of Scripture claim to be saying something different. Here the believer must be careful; he must "not believe every spirit, but test the spirits to see whether they are of God; for many false prophets have gone out into the world" (I John 4:1). In like manner, Paul warned the Corinthians "not to be quickly shaken in mind or excited, either by spirit or by word, or by letter purporting to be from us. . ." (II Thess. 2:2). Jesus warned his disciples on several occasions to "beware of false prophets" (Matt. 7:15) and that "false Christs and false prophets will arise and show great signs and wonders, so as to lead astray. . ." (Matt. 24:24).

How will one know if these "prophets" are false? Moses laid down the conditions in Deuteronomy 13 and 18. "If he says, 'Let us go after other gods,' which you have not known, 'and let us serve them,' you shall not listen to the words of that prophet or to that dreamer of dreams" (13:2). Moses adds, "You shall walk after the Lord your God and fear him, and keep his commandments and obey his voice. . ." (13:4). Likewise Moses warned that the prophet "who speaks in the name of other gods, that same prophet shall die" (18:20). In short, any prophet speaking in the name of a different god or giving a different revelation from that of the God of the Bible is a false prophet. The apostle Paul summed it up well for the Christian when he charged: "Even if we, or an angel from heaven, should preach to you a gospel contrary to that which we preached to you let him be accursed" (Gal. 1:8). There is only one gospel; it is the gospel of salvation by the grace of God apart from any human works (Gal. 2:21; 3:11; cf. Rom. 4:5; Titus 3:5-7; Eph. 2:8-9).

Another essential doctrinal test for truth is the confession of Jesus Christ as God Incarnate in human flesh (I John 4:1; cf. John 1:1, 14). Those who deny the apostolic confession of Christ are of the "spirit of antichrist" (I John 4:3). The apostle John added, "Whoever knows God listens to us, and he who is not of God does not listen to us. By this we know the spirit of truth and the spirit of error" (v. 6).

On these two doctrinal criteria alone—the deity and humanity of Christ and justification by faith alone—we know that the writings of the Mormons, Jehovah's Witnesses, Bahá'U'lláh, Mohammed, and many other modern cults are not of God. Mormons deny both the deity of Christ and salvation by faith alone.[17] Mohammed and Bahá'U'lláh believed Christ was only a prophet who did not die for our sins and who was superseded by prophet(s) after him.[18] Jehovah's Witnesses deny the deity of Christ, claiming that he was the created angel Michael.[19] Christ proclaimed that he is the only way to God (John 10:1, 9; 14:6) and the apostles emphasized the same (Acts 4:12; I Tim. 2:5; Heb. 10:10-12). On this ground the writings of Bahá'U'lláh must be rejected since they relegate Christ to the status of a mere prophet whose claims were only for his people and his day but have been superseded by Bahá'U'lláh.[20]

*Do They Obtain Their Revelations from Angels or Spirits?* God spoke to men of old through dreams (Gen. 28; Dan. 2), visions (Dan. 7; Zech. 1), angels (Gen. 18; Dan. 9), and in "various ways" (Heb. 1:1). But we are emphatically informed that "in these last days he has spoken to us by a Son, whom he appointed heir of all things, through whom also he created the world" (Heb. 1:2). Paul warned about revelations from an "angel from heaven" (Gal. 1:8) or from a "spirit" (II Thess. 2:2). In these last days God has given a full and final revelation in his Son and through his authorized apostles. Any other alleged revelation must be in strict accord with what they have said.

The Scriptures also make it plain that any attempt on our part to contact or communicate with spirits from other worlds is forbidden and is not of God. Attempting to communicate with the dead is called "necromancy" and it is explicitly forbidden in Scripture. "There shall not be

---

17. James E. Talmage, *Articles of Faith,* p. 479, calls "justification by faith" a "pernicious doctrine." Jesus is a god for Mormons only in the same sense we are gods (*Journal of Discourses,* I, 51).

18. See Koran, Surah IV, 157, 171.

19. *Let God Be True,* Watchtower Bible and Tract Society, p. 101; and *What Has Religion Done for Mankind?*

20. See J. E. Esslemont, *Bahá'U'lláh and the New Era,* pp. 102, 127, 135-36.

found among you . . . a necromancer. For whoever does these things is an abomination to the Lord" (Deut. 18:11, 12). In view of this warning it is not difficult to determine whether or not David Berg is of God when he confesses to receiving his "revelations" from his dead mother and from an angel named "Abraham."[21] The same is true of Bahá'U'lláh who not only permits but, through his "infallible" interpreter Abdul-Baha, encourages contact with departed spirits:

> The unity of humanity as taught by Bahá'U'lláh refers not only to men still in the flesh, but to all human beings, whether embodied or disembodied. . . . Spiritual communion one with another, far from being impossible or unnatural, is constant and inevitable. . . . To the Prophets and saints this spiritual communion is as familiar and real as are ordinary vision and conversation to the rest of mankind.[22]

This confession leaves no alternative for the Christian but to pronounce Bahá'U'lláh a false prophet in contact with evil spirits.

*Do They Use Any Objects of Divination to Make Their Prophecy?* Another test for a true prophet given by Moses and repeated by the prophets involved the use of physical objects with which one would "divine" results. "There shall not be found among you . . . any one who practices divination. . . . For whoever does these things is an abomination to the Lord" (Deut. 18:10, 12). Isaiah spoke against "diviners" (44:25) and Jeremiah added, "do not listen to your prophets, your diviners. . ." (27:9). According to Zechariah, "the teraphim utter nonsense, and the diviners see lies" (10:2).

On this criterion both Jeane Dixon and Joseph Smith come up wanting. Jeane Dixon confesses to the use of a crystal ball. Joseph Smith is known to have used a stone in a hat over his face when translating the Book of Mormon.[23] It has been established as well that Smith used a divining stone and that he carried an occult Jupiter Talisman around his neck.[24] Such objects of divination are forbidden by God and are signs of a false prophet.

*Does the Prophecy Center in Jesus Christ?* Jesus himself claimed to be the theme of prophetic Scripture on at least five occasions (Matt. 5:17; Luke 24:27, 44; John 5:39; Heb. 10:7). The apostles repeated this claim (Acts 10:43). John wrote, "The testimony of Jesus is the spirit of

---

21. See Letters of Moses David ("MO"), London: Children of God Trust.

22. Esslemont, *Bahá'U'lláh*, p. 197.

23. This is documented in *Mormonism: Shadow or Reality?* by Jerald and Sandra Tanner, p. 32 f.

24. The discovery of Joseph Smith's occult Jupiter Talisman has come to light recently in a revealing, unpublished historical paper given at Navoo, Ill., April 20, 1974 by a Mormon historian Reed Durham entitled "Is There No Help for the Widow's Son?"

prophecy" (Rev. 19:10). Those prophets, then, who testify not of Jesus are not of God. In his epistle John added, "Every spirit which does not confess Jesus is not of God" (I John 4:3).

Even a casual examination of the writings of Jeane Dixon reveal that Jesus is not the center of her writings. The writings of Bahá'U'lláh are clearly not centered in Christ, and it is questionable whether Joseph Smith's works are really Christ-centered. Of course, the Koran is not a testimony to Jesus. We conclude that only those Scriptures which point to Jesus Christ are of God. The Old and New Testaments are the only Scriptures that unmistakably provide a divinely confirmed and unfolding messianic revelation centered in Jesus.

*Do They Ever Utter False Prophecies?* It is a mistake to believe that the coming to pass of a prediction is an unmistakable sign of its divine origin. But the opposite is clearly a negative test for a false prophet, namely, "if the word *does not come to pass* or come true, that is a word which the Lord has not spoken" (Deut. 18:22).

It is this negative test for the truth or falsity of a prophecy that renders Edgar Cayce, Jeane Dixon, and their like false prophets. It is questionable whether they hit on over 60 percent of their predictions, but even 80 per-cent or more would show them wrong 20 percent of the time and thus make them false prophets. Jeane Dixon is known to have been wrong about many predictions and Joseph Smith gave a false prediction about the city of Zion.[25] Bahá 'U'lláh predicted just before the turn of the century that an age of peace was dawning on the world. His prediction has been followed by the worst time of war the world has ever known, including the First and Second World Wars, the Asian wars, the Near Eastern wars, and the many African wars even in this very day some one hundred years later.[26]

*Are They Official or Confirmed Prophets of God?* There is evidence within the Old Testament that there was an official line of prophets beginning with Moses. Each wrote and his book was laid up before the Lord (Deut. 31:24-26; Josh, 24:26). Later Samuel started a school of the prophets (I Sam. 19:20) and Ezekiel speaks of an official "register" of prophets (Ezek. 13:9 ASV margin). If challenged as to his prophetic credentials, a man of God could depend on miraculous confirmation from God. Moses was given the miraculous rod with which he divided the waters of the sea and performed numerous miracles (Exod. 4). Once

25. See *Doctrines and the Covenants,* sec. 97, a prophecy given August 2, 1833. It said: "Zion /Missouri/ cannot fall or be moved out of her place." But two weeks earlier (July 20, 1833) Zion was moved, the Mormon presses were destroyed, and the leading Mormon officials were run out of town. Smith was in Kirtland, Ohio, and unaware of the fall of Zion when he gave his "revelation."

26. Esslemont, *Bahá'U'lláh,* p. 144.

when Moses' prophetic office was challenged the earth opened up and swallowed Korah and his followers (Num. 26:10). Elijah and Elisha performed many miracles to authenticate their prophetic credentials including calling down fire from heaven (I Kings 18:38).

The New Testament prophets confirmed their divine credentials in the same miraculous way. Jesus gave power to his disciples to heal the sick, open the eyes of the blind, cast out demons, and even raise the dead (Matt. 10:1 f.). The writer of the Hebrews summarized well the credentials of true apostles, saying they were those through whom "God also bore witness by signs and wonders and various miracles and by gifts of the Holy Spirit . . ." (Heb. 2:4). If a man claims to be a prophet of God, he must be able to have the confirmation of God by a notable act of God. Paul defended his divine authority to the Corinthians by saying to them, "The signs of a true apostle were performed among you in all patience, with signs and wonders and mighty works" (II Cor. 12:12). There were, of course, some false prophets and apostles. Moses was confronted by the magicians of Egypt who performed some parallel and amazing feats. But when God through the hand of Moses turned the dust into lice, the magicians gave up crying, "This is the finger of God" (Exod. 8:19). Likewise, the power to raise the dead singled out the true New Testament prophets from the false. None of the modern day "prophets" stand in the official line of confirmed prophets of God nor do they possess these unique prophetic powers. They are, then, not prophets of God.

## Summary and Conclusion

Jesus is God incarnate. As God, whatever he teaches is true. Jesus taught that the thirty-nine books of the Old Testament are the authoritative, written Word of God. Likewise, Jesus, who is God's full and final revelation, promised that his twelve apostles would be guided by the Holy Spirit into "all truth." The only authentic and confirmed record of apostolic teaching extant is the twenty-seven books of the New Testament. Hence, the canon of God's revelation to man is closed. With these sixty-six books we have the complete and final revelation of God for the faith and practice of believers. Every spirit or prophet who claims to give a new or different revelation is not of God.

This does not mean that there is no truth in other religious writings or holy books. There is truth in Greek poetry (Acts 17:28), in the Apocrypha (Heb. 11:35), and even some truth in pseudepigraphical writings (Jude 14), as is manifest from the New Testament usage of these books. The point is that the Bible and the Bible alone contains all doctrinal and ethical truth God has revealed to mankind. And the Bible alone is the canon or norm for all truth. All other alleged truth must be brought to the bar of Holy Scripture to be tested. The Bible and the

Bible alone, all sixty-six books, has been confirmed by God through Christ to be his infallible Word.

## SELECT READINGS FOR CHAPTER EIGHTEEN

Archer, Gleason. *Survey of Old Testament Introduction.*
Geisler, Norman. *General Introduction to the Bible.*
Green, William H. *General Introduction to the Old Testament.*
Harris, Laird. *The Inspiration and Canonicity of the Bible.*
Harrison, Everett. *Introduction to the New Testament.*
Ramm, Bernard. *Protestant Christian Evidences.*
Warfield, B. B. *The Inspiration and Authority of the Bible.*
Wenham, John. *Christ and the Bible.*
Westcott, Brooke F. *A General Survey of the History of the Canon of the New Testament.*

# Bibliography

Alexander, Samuel. *Space, Time, and Deity*. London: Macmillan, 1920.

Altizer, Thomas. *The Gospel of Christian Atheism*. Philadelphia: Westminster Press, 1966.

Anderson, J. N. D. *Christianity: The Witness of History*. London: Tyndale Press, 1969.

Anselm. *St. Anselm: Basic Writings*. Translated by S. W. Deane. La Salle, Ill.: Open Court, 1962.

Aquinas, Thomas. *De Ente*. Translated by Joseph Bobik. Notre Dame, Ind.: University of Notre Dame Press, 1965.

―――. *On Truth*. Translated by J. V. McGlynn. Chicago: Henry Regnery, 1952-54.

―――. *Summa Contra Gentiles*. Book One: *God* in *On the Truth of the Catholic Faith*. New York: Doubleday, 1955.

―――. *Summa Theologica*. Translated by the Fathers of the English Dominican Province. New York: Benziger Bros., 1947-48.

Archer, Gleason. *A Survey of Old Testament Introduction*. Chicago: Moody Press, 1964.

Augustine, St. *City of God*. Translated by Marcus Dods. New York: Modern Library, 1950.

Ayer, A. J. *Language, Truth and Logic*. New York: Dover Publications, 1952.

―――. *The Origins of Pragmatism*. San Francisco: Freeman, Cooper, 1968.

―――. *The Problems of Knowledge*. London: Macmillan, 1956.

Barbour, Ian. *Myth, Model and Paradigms*. New York: Harper & Row, 1974.

Barth, Karl. *Anselm*. Translated by Ian W. Robertson. Richmond: John Knox Press, 1960.

————. *Church Dogmatics*. Translated by G. T. Thomson, *et al*. Edinburgh: T. & T. Clark, 1936.

————. *The Epistle to the Romans*. Translated by Edwyn C. Hoskyns. London: Oxford University Press, 1933.

————. "Nein!" in *Natural Theology*. London: The Centenary Press, 1946.

————. *The Word of God and the Word of Man*. Translated by Douglas Horton. London: Hodder & Stoughton, 1928.

Bartley, William. *Retreat to Commitment*. London: Chatto & Windus, 1964.

Bayle, Pierre. *Selections from Bayle's Dictionary*. Translated by R. H. Popkin. Indianapolis: Bobbs-Merrill, 1965.

Bendall, Kent, and Ferré, Frederick. *Exploring the Logic of Faith*. New York: Association Press, 1962.

Bentley, Richard. *Remarks upon Late Discourses of Free-Thinking*. London: 1737.

Bergson, Henri. *Creative Evolution*. Translated by Arthur Mitchell. New York: H. Holt & Co., 1911.

————. *Two Sources of Morality and Religion*. Translated by R. A. Audra, *et al*. New York: H. Holt & Co., 1935.

Blanshard, Brand. *Nature of Thought*. 2 vols. London: Allen & Unwin, 1939.

Bloch, Marc. *The Historian's Craft*. Translated by Peter Putnam. New York: Random House, Vintage Books, 1953.

Bonaventura, St. *The Mind's Road to God*. Translated by George Boas. New York: Liberal Arts Press, 1953.

Boyle, Joseph, *et al*. "Determinism, Freedom, and Self-Referential Arguments." *Review of Metaphysics* 26 (September 1972): 3-37.

Bradley, F. H. *The Presuppositions of Critical History*. Chicago: Quadrangle Books, 1968.

Brown, Delwin, *et al.*, eds. *Process Philosophy and Christian Thought*. Indianapolis: Bobbs-Merrill, 1971.

Bruce, F. F. *Jesus and Christian Origins Outside the New Testament*. Grand Rapids: Eerdmans, 1974.

————. *The New Testament Documents: Are They Reliable?* Grand Rapids: Eerdmans, 1960.

Bultmann, Rudolf, and Jaspers, Karl. *Myth and Christianity*. New York: Noonday Press, 1958.

Burrill, Donald R., ed. *The Cosmological Arguments*. Garden City, N.Y.: Anchor Books, 1967.

Bushnell, Horace. *The Character of Jesus*. New York: Charles Scribner's Sons, 1861.

Butler, Bishop. *The Analogy of Religion*. Translated by Howard Malcom. Philadelphia: Lippincott, 1872.

Camus, Albert. *The Plague*. Translated by Stuart Gilbert. New York: Modern Library, 1948.

Carnell, E. J. *Christian Commitment*. New York: Macmillan, 1957.

—————. *Introduction to Christian Apologetics*. Grand Rapids: Eerdmans, 1948.

Carr, E. H. *What Is History?* New York: Knopf, 1961.

Castell, Alburey, ed. *Essays in Pragmatism*. New York: Hafner, 1968.

Chalmers, Thomas. *On Natural Theology*. New York: Carter, 1840.

Clark, Gordon H. *A Christian View of Men and Things*. Grand Rapids: Eerdmans, 1952.

—————. *Historiography: Secular and Religious*. Grand Rapids: Baker, 1971.

—————. *Religion, Reason and Revelation*. Philadelphia: Presbyterian and Reformed, 1961.

Cobb, John. *A Christian Natural Theology*. Philadelphia: Westminster Press, 1965.

Collingwood, R. G. *Essays in the Philosophy of History*. Edited by William Debbins. Austin, Tex.: University of Texas Press, 1965.

—————. *The Idea of History*. Oxford: Clarendon Press, 1946.

Collins, James. *The Existentialists*. Chicago: Henry Regnery, 1968.

—————. *God in Modern Philosophy*. Chicago: Henry Regnery, 1967.

Cousins, Ewert, ed. *Process Theology*. Glen Rock, N.J.: Newman Press, 1971.

Descartes, René. *A Discourse on Method*. Translated by John Veitch. New York: E. P. Dutton, 1912.

—————. *Meditations*. Translated by Laurence J. Lafleur. New York: Liberal Arts Press, 1951.

Dewey, John. *Reconstruction in Philosophy*. Boston: Beacon Press, 1948.

Diamond, Malcolm, and Litzenburg, Thomas, eds. *The Logic of God*. Indianapolis: Bobbs-Merrill, 1975.

Diamond, Malcolm. "Miracles." *Religious Studies* 9 (September 1973): 307-24.

Dodd, Charles H. *History and the Gospel*. London: Hodder & Stoughton, 1938.

Dray, W. H. *Philosophy of History*. Englewood Cliffs, N.J.: Prentice-Hall, 1964.

Driscoll, John T. *Pragmatism and the Problem of the Idea*. New York: Longmans, Green, 1915.

Driver, S. R. *An Introduction to the Literature of the Old Testament.* Edinburgh: T. & T. Clark, 1913.

Duns Scotus. *Philosophical Writings.* Translated and edited by Allan Wolter. Edinburgh: Nelson, 1962.

*Encyclopedia of Philosophy.* S.v. "Miracles," by Antony Flew.

*Encyclopedia of Religion and Ethics.* S.v. "Historiography," by Ernst Troeltsch.

Esslemont. *Bahá'U'lláh and the New Era.* Wilmette, Ill.: Baha'i Public Trust, 1970.

Eusebius. *Ecclesiastical History.* Translated by Roy Deferrari. Washington: Catholic University of America Press, 1965.

Farrer, Austin. *Finite and the Infinite.* Philadelphia: Westminster Press, 1959.

Ferré, Frederick. *Basic Modern Philosophy of Religion.* New York: Scribner, 1967.

————. *Exploring the Logic of Faith.* New York: Association Press, 1962.

————. *Language, Logic and God.* New York: Harper, 1961.

————. "Mapping the Logic of Models in Science and Theology." *The Christian Scholar* 46 (Spring 1963): 9-39.

————. "Science and the Death of 'God.' " In *Science and Religion,* pp. 134-56. Edited by Ian G. Barbour. New York: Harper & Row, 1968.

————. *Shaping the Future: Resources for the Post-Modern World.* New York: Harper & Row, 1976.

Feuerbach, Ludwig. *The Essence of Christianity.* Translated by George Eliot. New York: Harper Torchbooks, 1957.

Findlay, J. N. "Can God's Existence Be Disproved?" In *The Ontological Argument,* pp. 111-22. Edited by Alvin Plantinga. Garden City, N.Y.: Doubleday, 1965.

Flew, Antony, and MacIntyre, Alasdair. *New Essays in Philosophical Theology.* London: S. C. M. Press, 1955.

Flint, Robert. *Agnosticism.* New York: Charles Scribner's Sons, 1903.

————. *Anti-Theistic Theories.* London: William Blackwood & Sons, 1899.

Freud, Sigmund. *The Future of an Illusion.* Translated by W. D. Robson-Scott. New York: Liveright, 1955.

Garrigou-Lagrange, Reginald. *God: His Existence and Essence.* Translated by Dom. Bede Rose. St. Louis: B. Herder Book Co., 1934.

Geisler, Norman L. *Christ: The Key to Interpreting the Bible.* Chicago: Moody Press, 1975.

————. *Ethics: Alternatives and Issues.* Grand Rapids: Zondervan, 1971.

————. "The Extent of the Old Testament Canon." In *Current Issues in Biblical and Patristic Interpretation,* pp. 31-46. Edited by Gerald F. Hawthorne. Grand Rapids: Eerdmans, 1975.

———— and Nix, William E. *From God to Us.* Chicago: Moody Press, 1974.

———— and Nix, William E. *A General Introduction to the Bible.* Chicago: Moody Press, 1968.

————. "The Missing Premise in the Ontological Argument." *Religious Studies* 9 (September 1973): 289-96.

————. *Philosophy of Religion.* Grand Rapids: Zondervan, 1974.

————. "Process Theology." *Tensions in Contemporary Theology.* Edited by Alan F. Johnson and Stanley N. Gundry. Chicago: Moody Press, 1976.

Gerstner, John. *Reasons for Faith.* New York: Harper, 1960.

Grant, R. M. *Miracle and Natural Law in Graeco-Roman and Early Christian Thought.* Amsterdam: North-Holland, 1952.

Green, William H. *General Introduction to the Old Testament Canon.* New York: Charles Scribner's Sons, 1899.

Grisez, Germain. *Beyond the New Theism.* Notre Dame, Ind.: University of Notre Dame Press, 1975.

Gurr, John E. *The Principle of Sufficient Reason in Some Scholastic Systems, 1750-1900.* Milwaukee: Marquette University Press, 1957.

Guthrie, Donald. *New Testament Introduction.* Chicago: Inter-Varsity Press, 1965.

Hackett, Stuart. *The Resurrection of Theism.* Chicago: Moody Press, 1957.

Hall, Everett. *Philosophical Systems.* Chicago: University of Chicago Press, 1960.

Harris, Laird. *Inspiration and Canonicity of the Bible.* Grand Rapids: Eerdmans, 1964.

Harrison, Everett F. *Introduction to the New Testament.* Grand Rapids: Eerdmans, 1964.

Harrison, R. K. *Introduction to the Old Testament.* Grand Rapids: Eerdmans, 1969.

Hartshorne, Charles. *The Logic of Perfection.* LaSalle, Ill.: Open Court, 1962.

————. *Man's Vision of God.* Chicago: Willett, Clark, 1941.

————. *A Natural Theology for Our Time.* LaSalle, Ill.: Open Court, 1967.

Harvey, Van A. *The Historian and the Believer.* New York: Macmillan, 1965.

Hegel, G. W. F. *The Phenomenology of Mind.* Translated by J. B. Baillie. New York: Macmillan, 1931.

Hennecke, Edgar. *Handbuch zu den Neutestamentlichen Apokryphen.* Tübingen: J. C. B. Mohr, 1914.

Henry, C. F. H. *Revelation and the Bible.* Grand Rapids: Baker, 1958.

Herbert of Cherbury, Edward. *De Veritate.* n.p.: 1639.

Hick, John, ed. *The Existence of God.* New York: Macmillan, 1964.

Hiriyanna, Mysore. *The Essentials of Indian Philosophy.* London: Allen & Unwin, 1949.

Hobbes, Thomas. *Leviathan.* New York: E. P. Dutton, 1914.

Hodge, Charles. *Systematic Theology.* Vol. 1. Grand Rapids: Eerdmans, 1952.

Hoehner, Harold W. "Chronological Aspects of the Life of Christ." *Bibliotheca Sacra* 130 (October 1973): 338-51.

Holmes, Arthur. *Faith Seeks Understanding.* Grand Rapids: Eerdmans, 1971.

Hume, David. *Dialogues Concerning Natural Religion.* Edited by Henry D. Aiken. New York: Hafner, 1948.

————. *An Inquiry Concerning Human Understanding.* Edited by Chas. W. Hendel. New York: Liberal Arts Press, 1955.

————. *A Letter from a Gentleman to His Friend in Edinburgh.* Edited by E. C. Mossner and J. V. Price. Edinburgh: University Press, 1967.

Hunt, John. *Pantheism and Christianity.* Port Washington, N.Y.: Kennikat Press, 1970.

Huxley, Julian. *Evolution in Action.* London: D. D. Harper, 1953.

Huxley, T. H. *Collected Essays.* Edited by Frederick Barry. New York: Macmillan, 1929.

*Infidelity.* New York: American Tract Society, n.d.

James, William. *The Meaning of Truth.* New York: Greenwood Press, 1909.

————. *Pragmatism and Other Essays.* New York: Washington Square Press, 1963.

————. *The Varieties of Religious Experience.* New York: The Modern Library, 1929.

————. "The Will to Believe." In *Essays in Pragmatism.* Edited by Alburey Castell. New York: Hafner, 1968.

Jefferson, Thomas. *The Jefferson Bible.* Edited by Douglas Lurton. New York: Wilfred Funck, 1943.

Kahler, Martin. *The So-Called Historical Jesus and the Historic, Biblical Christ.* Translated by Carl E. Braaten. Philadelphia: Fortress Press, 1964.

Kant, Immanuel. *Critique of Pure Reason.* Translated by Norman Kemp Smith. New York: St. Martin's Press, 1965.

————. *Religion Within the Limits of Reason Alone.* Translated by T. M. Greene and H. H. Hudson. LaSalle, Ill.: Open Court, 1960.

Kenyon, Sir Frederic. *The Bible and Archaeology*. New York: Harper, 1940.

———. *Our Bible and the Ancient Manuscripts*. New York: Harper, 1958.

Kierkegaard, Sören. *Concluding Unscientific Postscript*. Translated by David F. Swenson and Walter Lowrie. Princeton, N.J.: Princeton University Press, 1941.

———. *Either/Or*. Translated by David F. Swenson and Lillian Swenson. Garden City, N.Y.: Doubleday, 1959.

———. *Fear and Trembling*. Translated by Walter Lowrie. Garden City, N.Y.: Doubleday, 1954.

———. *Philosophical Fragments*. Translated by David F. Swenson. Princeton, N.J.: Princeton University Press, 1962.

Koch, Kurt. *Between Christ and Satan*. Berghausen, Germany: Evangelization Press, 1961.

Ladd, George E. *A Theology of the New Testament*. Grand Rapids: Eerdmans, 1974.

Leibniz, G. W. *Discourse on Metaphysics*. Translated by George R. Montgomery. Chicago: Open Court, 1902.

———. *The Monadology*. Translated by Robert Latta. London: Oxford University Press, 1925.

Leland, John. *A View of the Principle Deistic Writers. . . .* London: B. Dod, 1754.

Lepp, Ignace. *Atheism in Our Time*. Translated by Bernard Murchland. New York: Macmillan, 1963.

*Let God Be True*. New York: Watchtower Bible and Tract Society, 1946 (revised 1952).

Lewis, C. S. *The Four Loves*. London: G. Bles, 1960.

———. *God in the Dock*. Grand Rapids: Eerdmans, 1970.

———. *The Great Divorce*. London: G. Bles, 1945.

———. *Mere Christianity*. London: G. Bles, 1961.

———. *Miracles*. New York: Macmillan, 1947.

———. *The Problem of Pain*. London: G. Bles, 1942.

Locke, John. *An Essay Concerning Human Understanding*. Edited by A. D. Woozley. London: Collins, 1964.

———. *The Works of John Locke*. Vol. 9. *A Discourse on Miracles*. London: W. Olridge & Son, 1812.

Luijpen, W. A. *Phenomenology and Atheism*. Translated by Walter van de Putte. Pittsburgh: Duquesne University Press, 1964.

McCloskey, H. J. "God and Evil." *The Philosophical Quarterly* 10 (April 1960): 97-114.

McKinnon, Alastair. " 'Miracle' and 'Paradox.' " *American Philosophical Reviews,* 4 (October 1967): 308-14.

McPherson, Thomas. "Religion as the Inexpressible." In *New Essays in Philosophical Theology,* pp. 131-43. Edited by Antony Flew and Alasdair MacIntyre. London: S. C. M. Press, 1963.

Mandelbaum, Maurice. *The Problem of Historical Knowledge.* New York: Harper & Row, 1967.

Marx, Karl, and Engels, Friedrich. *On Religion.* New York: Schocken Books, 1964.

Mascall, Eric. *He Who Is.* New York: Longmans, Green, 1943.

————. *The Openness of Being.* Philadelphia: Westminster, 1971.

Metzger, Bruce. *Chapters in the History of New Testament Textual Criticism.* Grand Rapids: Eerdmans, 1963.

————. *The Text of the New Testament.* New York: Oxford University Press, 1964.

Meyerhoff, Hans, ed. *The Philosophy of History in Our Time.* Garden City, N.Y.: Doubleday, 1959.

Mill, John Stuart. *Three Essays on Religion.* London: Longmans, Green, Reader, and Dyer, 1874.

*Monist* 54 (July 1970) (entire issue).

Montague, W. P. *The Ways of Knowing.* London: Allen & Unwin, 1925.

Montgomery, John W. *Christianity and History.* Downer's Grove, Ill.: Inter-Varsity Press, 1964.

————. *Christianity for the Tough-Minded.* Minneapolis: Bethany, 1973.

Morison, Frank. *Who Moved the Stone?* London: Faber & Faber, 1958.

Munitz, Milton K. *The Mystery of Existence.* New York: Appleton-Century-Crofts, 1965.

Nash, Ronald H., ed. *The Philosophy of Gordon Clark.* Philadelphia: Presbyterian and Reformed, 1968.

Nielson, Kai. *Contemporary Critiques of Religion.* New York: Herder & Herder, 1971.

Nietzsche, Friedrich. *The Antichrist.* Translated by H. L. Mencken. New York: Knopf, 1920.

Ogden, Shubert. "God and Philosophy: A Discussion with Antony Flew." *Journal of Religion* 48 (April 1968): 161-81.

————. "How Does God Function in Human Life?" *Christianity and Crisis* 27 (May 15, 1967): 105-8.

————. *The Reality of God.* New York: Harper & Row, 1966.

————. "Theology and Philosophy." *Journal of Religion* 44 (January 1964): 1-15.

Orr, John. *English Deism.* Grand Rapids: Eerdmans, 1934.

Otto, Rudolph. *The Idea of the Holy.* Translated by John W. Harvey. London: Oxford University Press, 1967.

Owen, H. P. *Concepts of Deity.* New York: Herder & Herder, 1971.

————. *The Moral Argument for Christian Theism.* London: Allen & Unwin, 1965.

Paine, Thomas. *The Age of Reason.* New York: G. P. Putnam's Sons, 1907.

Paley, William. *Natural Theology.* London: J. Faulder, 1805.

Pascal, Blaise. *Pensées.* Translated by A. J. Krailsheimer. New York: Penguin Books, 1966.

Passmore, John A. *Philosophical Reasoning.* New York: Charles Scribner's Sons, 1961.

Payne, J. Barton. *An Encyclopedia of Biblical Prophecy.* New York: Harper & Row, 1973.

Peirce, Charles S. *The Essential Writings.* Edited by Edward C. Moore. New York: Harper & Row, 1972.

————. *Philosophical Writings of Peirce.* Edited by Justus Buchler. New York: Dover Publications, 1955.

Penelhum, Terence. *Religion and Rationality.* New York: Random House, 1971.

Pike, Nelson, ed. *God and Evil.* Englewood Cliffs, N.J.: Prentice-Hall, 1964.

————. *God and Timelessness.* New York: Schocken Books, 1970.

Plotinus. *The Enneads.* Translated by Stephen MacKenna. New York: Pantheon Books, 1957.

Popper, Karl. *Conjectures and Refutations.* New York: Harper & Row, 1963.

————. *The Poverty of Historicism.* London: Routledge & Kegan Paul, 1957.

Puccetti, Roland. "The Loving God. . . ." *Religious Studies* 2 (April 1967): 255-68.

Radhakrishnan, Sarvepali. *The Hindu View of Life.* London: Allen & Unwin, 1927.

————. *The Principle Upanishads.* London: Allen & Unwin, 1958.

Ramm, Bernard. *Protestant Christian Evidences.* Chicago: Moody Press, 1953.

Ramsay, William M. *St. Paul the Traveller and the Roman Citizen.* New York: G. P. Putnam's Sons, 1896.

Ramsey, Ian. *Models and Mystery.* London: Oxford University Press, 1964.

————, ed. *Prospect for Metaphysics.* New York: Greenwood Press, 1961.

————. *Religious Language.* London: S. C. M. Press, 1957.

Reese, William, ed. *Process and Divinity.* LaSalle, Ill.: Open Court, 1964.

Reichenbach, Bruce. *The Cosmological Argument*. Springfield, Ill.: Chas. C. Thomas, 1972.

Rice, John R. *Our God-Breathed Book—the Bible*. Murfreesboro, Tenn.: Sword of the Lord Publishers, 1969.

Robertson, J. M. *A Short History of Free Thought*. New York: Russell & Russell, 1957.

Robinson, Guy. "Miracles." *Ratio* 9 (December 1967): 155-66.

Robinson, Richard. *An Atheist's Values*. Oxford: Clarendon, 1964.

Russell, Bertrand. *The Basic Writings of Bertrand Russell*. New York: Simon and Schuster, 1961.

————. *Why I Am Not a Christian*. New York: Simon and Schuster, 1957.

Sargant, William. *Battle for the Mind*. London: William Heinemann, 1957.

Sartre, Jean-Paul. *Being and Nothingness*. Translated by Hazel E. Barnes. New York: Washington Square Press, 1966.

————. *Existentialism and Humanism*. Translated by Philip Mairet. London: Methuen, 1948.

Sauvage, G. M. "Fideism." *Catholic Encyclopedia* V. New York: Robert Appleton, 1909.

Schaeffer, Francis. *The God Who Is There*. Chicago: Inter-Varsity Press, 1968.

Schleiermacher, Friedrich. *On Religion: Speeches to Its Cultural Despisers*. Translated by John Oman. New York: Harper Torchbooks, 1958.

Schonfield, H. J. *The Passover Plot*. New York: Bantam Books, 1967.

Schopenhauer, Arthur. *Complete Essays of Schopenhauer*. Translated by T. Bailey Saunders. New York: Wiley, 1942.

Sherwin-White, A. N. *Roman Society and Roman Law in the New Testament*. Oxford: Clarendon Press, 1963.

Smith, Joseph. *Doctrines and the Covenants*. Westport, Conn.: Greenwood Press, 1971.

Smith, Wilder. *Man's Origin, Man's Destiny*. Wheaton, Ill.: Harold Shaw Publishers, 1968.

Spinoza, Benedictus. *Ethics*. Translated by A. Boyle. New York: E. P. Dutton, 1910.

Stace, W. T. *Mysticism and Philosophy*. Philadelphia: Lippincott, 1960.

Stein, Fritz, ed. *The Varieties of History*. Cleveland: World, 1956.

Stephen, Leslie. *An Agnostic's Apology*. New York: G. P. Putnam's Sons, 1893.

Stoner, Peter. *Science Speaks*. Wheaton, Ill.: Van Kampen Press, 1952.

Swinburne, Richard. *The Concept of Miracles*. New York: Macmillan, 1970.

Synder, Phil L. *Detachment and the Writing of History.* Westport, Conn.: Greenwood Press, 1972.

Tanner, Jerald and Sandra. *Mormonism: Shadow or Reality?* Salt Lake City: Modern Microfilm, 1972.

Taylor, A. E. *Does God Exist?* London: Macmillan, 1948.

Tennant, F. R. *Miracle and Its Philosophical Presuppositions.* Cambridge: Cambridge University Press, 1925.

—————. *Philosophical Theology.* 2 vols. Cambridge: The University Press, 1956.

Tenney, Merrill C. *The Reality of the Resurrection.* Chicago: Moody Press, 1972.

Tertullian. "The Prescription Against Heretics." *The Ante-Nicene Fathers.* Edited by A. Roberts and J. Donaldson. Vol. 3. *Latin Christianity: Its Founder, Tertullian.* Grand Rapids: Eerdmans, 1957.

Tillich, Paul. *Dynamics of Faith.* New York: Harper, 1957.

—————. *Ultimate Concern.* New York: Harper & Row, 1965.

Tindal, Matthew. *Christianity as Old as Creation.* London: n.p., 1730.

Toland, John. *Christianity Not Mysterious.* London: n.p., 1702.

Van Buren, Paul. *The Secular Meaning of the Gospel.* New York: Macmillan, 1963.

Van Til, Cornelius. *Common Grace.* Philadelphia: Presbyterian and Reformed, 1947.

—————. *The Defense of the Faith.* Philadelphia: Presbyterian and Reformed, 1967.

—————. *Jerusalem and Athens.* Edited by E. R. Geehan. Grand Rapids: Baker, 1971.

Vardaman, E. Jerry, ed. *The Teacher's Yoke.* Waco, Tex.: Baylor University, 1964.

Walsh, W. H. *Philosophy of History.* New York: Harper & Row, 1960.

Ward, James. *Naturalism and Agnosticism.* New York: Charles Scribner's Sons, 1903.

Warfield, B. B. *Counterfeit Miracles.* London: Banner of Truth Trust, 1972.

—————. *The Inspiration and Authority of the Bible.* Philadelphia: Presbyterian and Reformed, 1948.

—————. *The Lord of Glory.* Grand Rapids: Zondervan, 1907.

Watts, Alan. *Behold the Spirit.* London: J. John Murray, 1947.

—————. *Beyond Theology.* New York: Pantheon Books, 1964.

—————. *The Supreme Identity.* New York: Vintage Books, 1972.

Wenham, John W. *Christ and the Bible.* Downer's Grove, Ill.: Inter-Varsity Press, 1972.

Westcott, B. F. *A General Survey of the History of the Canon of the New Testament.* New York: Macmillan, 1896.

Whately, Richard. *Historical Doubts Relative to Napoleon Bonaparte.* New York: Robert Caster & Bros., 1849.

Whitehead, Alfred North. *Adventure of Ideas.* New York: Macmillan, 1933.

———. *Modes of Thought.* New York: Macmillan, 1938.

———. *Process and Reality.* New York: Macmillan, 1929.

———. *Science and the Modern World.* Paterson, N.J.: Littlefield, Adams, 1948.

Williams, Daniel. *What Present-Day Theologians Are Thinking.* New York: Harper & Row, 1959.

Williamson, G. A. *The World of Josephus.* London: Secker & Warburg, 1964.

Wittgenstein, Ludwig. *Philosophical Investigations.* Translated by G. E. M. Anscombe. New York: Macmillan, 1953.

———. *Tractatus Logico-Philosophicus.* Translated by D. F. Pears and B. F. McGuinness. London: Routledge & Kegan Paul, 1961.

Wollaston, William. *Religion of Nature Delineated.* Glasgow: Une, 1746.

Woolston, Thomas. *Discources on Miracles.* London: J. Roberts, 1733.

Yamauchi, Edwin. *The Stones and the Scriptures.* Philadelphia: Lippincott, 1972.

Yandell, Keith. *Basic Issues in the Philosophy of Religion.* Boston: Allyn and Bacon, 1971.

———. "Metaphysical Systems and Decision Procedures." (Unpublished Doctoral Dissertation, Ohio State University, 1966.)

Zaehner, Robert C. *Mysticism, Sacred and Profane.* Oxford: Clarendon Press, Oxford Paperbacks, 1961.

# Index

Absolute dependence, feeling of, 68 f.
Accommodation theory, 357 f.
Acognosticism, exposition of, 17
    evaluation of, 23
Act-potency, 257
Actual entities, 194 f.
Agnosticism, exposition of, 13 f.
    evaluation of 21 f., 36
Albright, William F., 309, 327
Alexander, Samuel, 194
Analogy, 15, 25, 248
Anomaly, 281
Antinomy, 16, 25, 205 f., 220
Apocrypha, 363 f.
A posteriori proofs for God, 252
A priori proofs for God, 251
Atheism, dialectical, 216
    exposition of, 215 f.
    evaluation of, 223 f.
Augustine, St., 124
Ayer, A. J., 17

Bahá'U'lláh, 372
Barth, Karl, 53
Baur, F. C., 308
Bergson, Henri, 194
Bible, historicity of, 358 f.
    inspiration of, 353 f.
Bolingbroke, Henry, 161
Bayle, Pierre, 218, 226
Brahman, 181
Bruce, F. F., 311
Brunner, Emil, 55

Bultmann, Rudolf, 299
Butler, Bishop, 91

Camus, Albert, 219
Carnell, E. J., 121
Categories of thought, 21
Causality, principle of, 14, 22-24, 242, 254
Christ, death of, 347 f.
    deity of, 329 f.
    prophecies about, 346 f.
    sinlessness of, 344
Chubb, Thomas, 161
Clark, Gordon, 37 f.
Cobb, John, 202 f.
Cogito ergo sum, 30
Collingwood, R. G., 289, 293
Collins, Anthony, 158
Combinationalism, exposition of, 117 f.
    evaluation of, 127 f., 139
    tenets of, 126
Conyers, Middleton, 162
Cooper, Anthony, 157
Cosmological Argument, 238 f.
Creativity, 198-199

Deism, rise of, 151 f.
    principles of, 153, 166
    evaluation of, 168 f.
Descartes, René, 30 f.
Dipolar theism, 201 f.
Dodd, C. H., 83, 299
Dodwell, Henry, 162
Doubt, 30 f.

Empiricism, 22
Epistemology, 61
Eschatological verification, 92-93, 98
Eternal objects, 194 f.
Eusebius, 310
Evidentialism, exposition of, 83 f.
        evaluation of, 94 f., 138
        tenets of, 93
Evolution, 90, 232-233
Experientialism, exposition of, 65 f.
        evaluation of, 76, 138
Ex Deo creation, 176, 190
Ex nihilo creation, 169, 242

Fact, meaning of, 84, 291
Faith and reason, 48, 52
False prophets, test of, 371 f.
Falsifiability principle, 19, 24
Ferré, Frederick, 117 f.
Feuerbach, Ludwig, 222
Fideism, exposition of, 47 f.
        evaluation of, 59 f., 137 f.
Finite godism, 193 f.
Flew, Antony, 19, 267
Form Criticism, 316 f.
Free will, 231

Geschichte, 299
God, attributes of, 210-211
        consequent nature of, 197 f.
        disproofs of, 216 f.
        perfections of, 229
        personality of, 189
        primordial nature of, 197
        proofs of, 237 f.
        superject nature of, 198

Hackett, Stuart, 35 f.
Hare, R. M., 19, 269
Hartshorne, Charles, 200 f.
Hegel, G. W. F., 194
Heilsgeschichte, 86
Hick, John, 92-93
Hinduism, 181
Historical evidence, 58
History, objectivity of, 285 f.
        sacred, 85
Hobbes, Thomas, 154
Hume, David, 13 f., 163, 265, 275, 351
Huxley, Julian, 90, 232

Inerrancy of Bible, 362 f.
Infinite regress, 245, 253
Inspiration of Bible, 353 f., 361 f.
Interprafact, 96, 130 f.
I-thou relation, 187
Intuition, religious, 70

James, William, 105 f.
Josephus, 323

Kant, Immanuel, 13 f., 164
Karma, 183
Kenyon, Sir Frederic, 327
Kierkegaard, Sören, 50
Koch, Kurt, 280

Leibniz, Gottfried, 33 f.
Lewis, C. S., 231, 270, 339
Limitation theory, 360 f.
Locke, John, 155
Lucian, 323

Magic, 281
Mc Closkey, Albert, 219 f.
Mc Kinnon, Alastair, 273 f.
Mc Pherson, Thomas, 75
Metzger, Bruce, 307
Miracles, first class, 276 f.
        second class, 277 f.
        objections to, 265 f.
Models, disclosure, 118
        metaphysical, 119 f.
Monism, 173 f., 185 f.
Montgomery, John W., 88
Moral argument, 248
Morison, Frank, 348
Mysterium tremendum, 73
Mystical experience, 18 f., 23 f., 66
Mysticism, 23
Myth, 320

Nagel, Ernest, 297
Naturalism, 263 f.
Natural law, 266
Necessary being, 240, 256
New Testament, accuracy of, 322 f.
        authenticity of, 305 f.
        dates of, 308 f.
        integrity of writers, 314 f.
        manuscripts of, 306 f.
Nielsen, Kai, 255
Nietzsche, Friedrich, 215 f.
Non-contradiction, law of, 38
Noumena, 16

Objectivity of history, 298 f.
Ogden, Shubert, 203 f.
Omniscience of God, 247
Ontological argument, 31, 43, 201 f.
Ontology, 61
Otto, Rudolf, 72
Owen, H. P., 187

Paley, William, 88
Panentheism, exposition of, 193
    evaluation of, 207 f.
    tenets of, 206 f.
Pantheism, absolute, 173 f.
    emanational, 174 f.
    modal, 177 f.
    tenets of, 184
    evaluation of, 186 f.
Parmenides, 173 f.
Pascal, Blaise, 47
Phenomena, 16
Pierce, Charles S., 101
Pliny the Younger, 324
Plotinus, 66, 174 f.
Popper, Karl, 296
Pragmatic, test for truth, 105 f., 109
    theory of meaning, 101 f.
Pragmatism, exposition of, 101 f.
    evaluation of, 112 f., 140 f.
    tenets of, 11 f.
Prehension, 195
Presuppositionalism, rational, 125 f.
    revelational, 37, 56, 62

Radhakrishnan, S., 181 f.
Ramsay, Ian, 117 f.
Ramsay, Sir William, 326
Rationalism, exposition of, 29 f.
    evaluation of, 41 f., 136 f.
    tenets of, 40
Religious experience, 105
Resurrection of Christ, 346 f.
Robinson, Guy, 271
Russell, Bertrand, 218

Sartre, Jean Paul, 215 f.
Schaeffer, Francis, 110
Schleiermacher, Friedrich, 68 f.
Schonfield, H. L. J., 342 f.
Self-caused being, 223 f.
Self-defeating arguments, 20 f.
Self-stultification as a test for truth, 133 f.
Sin, noetic effects of, 57 f.
Skepticism, critique of, 22 f., 134
Smith, Joseph, 374

Spencer, Herbert, 194
Spinoza, Benedict, 32-33, 177 f.
Suetonius, 324
Suffering, 219 f.
Sufficient reason, principle of, 34, 238
Systematic consistency as test for truth, 122 f., 145 f.

Tacitus, Cornelius, 323
Talmud, Jewish, 324
Taylor, A. E., 89
Teleological argument, 89
Tennant, F. R., 232
Thallus, 324
Thomas Aquinas, 225, 244
Tindal, Matthew, 159
Time, 221
Theism, exposition of, 237 f.
    evaluation of, 250 f.
    monopolar, 201 f.
    bipolar, 193 f.
Tillich, Paul, 249
Toland, John, 156
Troeltsch, E., 301 f.
Truth, perspectivity of, 135 f.
    test for, 133 f., 141 f.
Tübingen school, 308

Uncaused being, 241
Undeniability as test for truth, 141 f.

Value-laden language, 295
Van Til, Cornelius, 56 f.
Verifiability, principle of, 17 f.

Wager, Pascal's, 49
Whately, Richard, 303
Whitehead, Alfred N., 194 f.
Will to believe, 106 f.
Wittgenstein, Ludwig, 18, 23
Wollaston, William, 158
Woolston, Thomas, 159
World view, test for truth of, 145 f.
    unavoidability of, 288, 296

Yamauchi, Edwin, 325
Yandell, Keith, 244